LETTERS
OF
SWAMI VIVEKANANDA

Owing to the antiquity and rarity of this book, certain pages are regrettably absent, and readability is compromised due to the blurring of the original text. If you possess any insights regarding the availability of these missing sections, kindly inform us. Your assistance is crucial in ensuring the completion of this significant work for the benefit of future generations.

LETTERS
OF
SWAMI VIVEKANANDA

SWAMI VIVEKANANDA

GYAN

Published by

Gyan Publishing House
5, Ansari Road
Daryaganj, New Delhi-110002
Phone: 011-47034999, 9811692060
E-mail: books@gyanbooks.com

Distribution Network
gyanbooks.com
India, USA, Canada, UK, Australia

ISBN: 978-93-6780-025-6 (HB)

First Published, 1940

2nd Impression 2024

Printed at: Gyan Press, Delhi.

LETTERS OF SWAMI VIVEKANANDA
Author: SWAMI VIVEKANANDA

LETTERS OF SWAMI VIVEKANANDA

LETTERS
OF
SWAMI VIVEKANANDA

SWAMI VIVEKANANDA

PREFACE

Letters are the reflections of one's mind. From private letters, where thoughts flow freely, we can study the growth and development of a person's mind and the inner history of his being. It is for this reason that the private letters of many public men are so much in demand. From their letters many aspects of the personality of those persons are known to the public, which would otherwise have been a sealed book to all.

The history of Swami Vivekananda's life is co-related with the awakening of India and the resuscitation of Indian religion. But how much agony and suffering that mighty soul had to undergo before he was able to set in motion a machinery which was to bring about an all-round awakening in Indian national life! A nation that seemed to have lost all self-respect and self-confidence, and was apparently dead, had to be roused. That was a tremendous task. Swami Vivekananda felt that this task was his. Very often, he would say he was born with that mission. But he had to accomplish in a short span of life (his real activities covered a period of not more than eight years) a work whose influence would last for many centuries. He wrote to some of his followers in India from across the sea: "Fifty centuries are looking on you, the future of India depends on you." Perhaps the disciples were amazed at such bold words. But the Seer with his prophetic vision saw across the corridor of time what was coming ahead.

The following letters show the plan of his work and the means he wanted to adopt for the fulfilment of his mission. Swami Vivekananda was impatient of the delay and the slow progress the country was making. People listened to him with rapt attention, admired him with almost fanatical zeal, but their actual works were not commensurate with their enthusiasm for hero-worship. Therefore they called for a sharp rebuke from the great Swami who wanted not worship but action.

With the passing of time, however, we find that more and more of Swami Vivekananda's ideas are being fulfilled. But still many things remain unaccomplished. These letters contain hints for the present and future workers for the cause of India as to how the nation should be guided. "What is the secret of a successful organisation?" "Why do Indians lack the power of collective action?" "How India's future is doomed if those defects in national character are not remedied"—these vital questions are answered in these letters, sometimes in very strong language by one whose sharpness of expression was only the outer garb of his great love for his people.

But Swami Vivekananda was not a patriot only. He was a Seer first and a patriot next. As Guru, as a Teacher, as a spiritual leader, he had to solve the deeper problems of the life of many. Every man is a hidden Brahman, but in life almost all act like miserable wretches. What is the cause of this disastrous anomaly? How to remove it? How can a man rise to the full stature of his Divinity?—by answering these questions one who had known his own Divinity was anxious to make others Divine. This is what we find in many of Swami Vivekananda's letters.

Swami Vivekananda was a militant monk, a dynamic personality, and a fiery soul. We can imagine what magnetic effects his letters had upon the life of those to whom they were addressed. His letters contain many passages—a single one of which is sufficient to bring about a great revolution—a complete transformation in one's life. The same fire is hidden in them even now, though they were written many years ago. We have no doubt that this smouldering fire may be ablaze at any time and illumine any life in any clime. So they are presented to the general readers. "The Epistles of Swami Vivekananda" were formerly published in six parts. In the present edition we have brought them out in one handy volume, with some additional matter that has recently reached our hands. The letters are now arranged chronologically as far as possible. We hope that this improved edition will be more useful.

THE EDITOR

ADVAITA ASHRAMA
MAYAVATI, HIMALAYAS
The 1st January, 1940

PREFACE TO THE SECOND EDITION

In the present edition the book has been slightly revised and some more new letters added. The chronological order of a few letters in the previous edition has been altered in the light of some facts that have been discovered. The enthusiasm with which the first edition was received indicates what a great demand existed for this collection of letters. We hope that the book in this edition will be more useful.

February, 1942

PREFACE TO THE FOURTH EDITION

In this edition the book has come under a slight revision and some fifteen more letters have been added. The names of many persons omitted till now from various considerations have been inserted, and short notes on the persons addressed to or mentioned in the letters have been given as far as they could be traced. We hope these features will prove very valuable to the reading public.

May, 1948

CONTENTS

LETTERS OF
SWAMI VIVEKANANDA

(*1*)

To " Master Mahashay "

AUNTPUR,
February, 1888.

DEAR M.—I thank you a hundred thousand times, Master ! You have hit Ramakrishna in the right point.

Few, alas, few understand him !—Yours, VIVEKANANDA.

P.S. My heart leaps with joy—and it is a wonder that I do not go mad when I find anybody thoroughly launched into the midst of the doctrine which is to shower peace on earth hereafter.

(*2*)

To Sj. Pramada Das Mitra

BRINDABAN,*
12th Aug., 1888.

DEAR SIR—Leaving Ayodhya I have reached the holy Brindaban, and am putting up at Kala Babu's Kunja. In the town the mind feels contracted. Places like Radhakunda, I have heard, are delightful; but they are at some distance from the town. I have a mind to proceed very shortly to Hardwar. In case you have any acquaintance there, you would be doing me a great favour if you kindly write to him an introduction for me. What about your visiting this place? Please reply early and oblige.—Yours etc., VIVEKANANDA.

* Letters marked with an asterisk are translated from Bengali.

(3)

To The Same

BRINDABAN,*
20th Aug., 1888.

DEAR SIR—An aged brother-disciple of mine who has just come back to Brindaban after visiting Kedarnath and Badrinath, met Gangadhar. Twice did Gangadhar ascend up to Thibet and Bhotan. He is in great happiness, and felt overwhelmed and wept at the meeting. He spent the winter at Kankhal. The *Karoa* (water-pot) you gave him he still keeps with him. He is coming back and is expected at Brindaban this very month. So in the hope of meeting him, I postpone my going to Hardwar for some days. Please convey my deepest respects to the Brahmin devotee of Shiva who keeps you company and accept the same yourself.—Yours etc., VIVEKANANDA.

(4)

To The Same

THE BARANAGORE MATH,*
19th Nov., 1888.

RESPECTED SIR—I have received the two books sent by you and am filled with joy to read your wonderfully affectionate letter which betokens your broad, generous heart. No doubt, it is due to good merit of my previous births that you show, sir, so much kindness to a mendicant like me who lives on begging. By sending your gift of the "Vedanta", you have laid under lifelong obligation not only myself but the whole group of Sri Ramakrishna's Sannyasins. They all bow down to you in respect. It is not for my own sake alone that I asked of you the copy of Panini's grammar; a good deal of study, in fact, is given to Sanskrit scriptures in this Math. The Vedas may well be said to have fallen quite out of vogue in Bengal. Many here in this Math are conversant with Sanskrit and they have a mind to master the Samhitâ portions of the Vedas. They are of opinion that what has to be done must be done to a finish. So believing that a full measure of proficiency in the Vedic language is impossible without first mastering Panini's grammar, which is the best available for the purpose, a copy of the latter was felt to be a necessity. The grammatical work, Mugdhabodha, we studied in our boyhood, is superior in many respects to Laghukaumudi. You are yourself, however, a deeply learned man and, therefore, the best judge we can have in this matter. So if you consider the Ashtadhyayi (Panini's) to be the most suitable in our case, you will lay us under a debt of lifelong gratitude by sending the same (provided you find it convenient and feel so inclined). This Math is not wanting in men of perseverance, talent and penetrative intellect. I may hope that by the grace of our Master, they will acquire in a short time Panini's system and then succeed in restoring the Vedas to Bengal. I beg to send you two photographs of my revered Master and two parts of some of his teachings as given in his homely style, compiled and published by a certain gentleman—hoping you will give us the pleasure of your acceptance. My health is now much improved and I expect the blessings of meeting you within two or three months. . . . —Yours etc., VIVEKANANDA.

(5)

To The Same

BARANAGORE,*
4th Feb., 1889.

DEAR SIR—For some reasons, I had been feeling to-day agitated and cramped in my mind, when your letter of invitation to the heavenly city of Benares reached me. I accept it as the call of Vishweshwara.[1] I am going now on a pilgrimage to the place of my Master's nativity, and after sojourn of a few days there, I shall present myself to you. He must be made of stone whose mind does not melt at the sight of Kashi and its Lord! I feel now much improved in health. My regards to Jnanananda. I am reaching over there as soon as I can. It all depends ultimately on Vishweshwara's will. . . . . . More when we meet.—Yours etc., VIVEKANANDA.

(6)

To The Same

BARANAGORE,*
26th June, 1889.

DEAR SIR—For sundry reasons I have been unable to write to you for long, for which please excuse me. I have now obtained news of Gangadhar. He met one of my brother-disciples and both are now staying in the Uttarakhanda (the sacred Himalayas). Four of us from here are in the Himalayas now, and with Gangadhar they are five. One brother-disciple named Shivananda came across Gangadhar at Srinagar on the way to holy Kedarnath, and Gangadhar has addressed here two letters. During his first year on the Himalayas, he could not secure permission to enter Thibet, but he got it the next year. The Lamas love him much, and he has picked up the Thibetan language. He says, the Lamas form ninety per cent of the population, but they mostly practise Tântrika forms of worship. The country is intensely cold, eatables there are scarcely any—only dried meat; and Gangadhar had to travel and live on that food. My health is so so, but the state of mind is terrible!—Yours etc., VIVEKANANDA.

[1] i.e. the Lord of the Universe, or Shiva, as installed in the leading temple of Benares.

(7)

To The Same

BAGHBAZAR, CALCUTTA,*
4th July, 1889.

DEAR SIR—It pleased me highly to know all that your letter yesterday informed me of. You have asked me to request Gangadhar* to write to you, but I see no chance thereof, for though they are sending us letters, they do not stop anywhere for more than two or three days and therefore do not receive any of ours.

Some relative of my former life[1] had purchased a bungalow at Simultala (near Baidyanath). The place being credited with a healthy climate, I stayed there for some time. But the summer heat growing excessive, I had an attack of acute diarrhœa and I have just fled off from the place.

Words fail to describe how strong is the desire in my mind to go to Benares and have my soul blessed by meeting you and sojourning with you in good converse, but everything rests on His will! I wonder what linking of heart existed between us, sir, from some previous incarnation that, receiving as I do the love and affection of not a few men of wealth and position in this city of Calcutta, I am apt to feel so much bored by their society, while only through one day's interview my heart felt charmed enough to accept you as a near relative and friend in spiritual life! One reason is that you are a favoured servant of God; another perhaps is:

तच्चेतसा स्मरति नूनमबोधपूर्वं
भावस्थिरानि जननान्तरसौहृदानि ।[2]

[1] i.e. the life he has renounced.

[2] Kalidasa's Shakuntala, Act V : "It must be the memories, unwittingly recalled of affinities firmly established in previous incarnations through depths of heart."

I am indebted to you for the advice which comes from you as the outcome of your experience and spiritual practice. It is very true, and I have also found it so very often, that one has to suffer at times for holding in one's brain novel views of all sorts.

But with me it is a different malady this time. I have not lost faith in a benign Providence—nor am I going ever to lose it,. my faith in the scriptures is unshaken. But by the will of God, the last six or seven years of my life have been full of constant struggles with hindrances and obstacles of all sorts. I have been vouchsafed the ideal Shastra; I have seen the ideal man; and yet fail myself to get on with anything to the end—this is my profound misery.

And particularly, I see no chance of success while remaining near Calcutta. In Calcutta live my mother and two brothers. I am the eldest, the second is preparing for the First Arts Examination and the third is young.

They were quite well off before, but since my father's death, it is going very hard with them—even having to go fasting at times! To crown all, some relatives, taking advantage of their helplessness, drove them away from the ancestral residence. Though a part of it is recovered through suing at the High Court, destitution is now upon them—a matter of course in litigation.

Living near Calcutta I have to witness their adversity, and the quality of Rajas prevailing, my egotism sometimes develops into the form of a desire that rises to plunge me into action; in such moments, a fierce fighting ensues in my mind, and so I wrote that the state of my mind was terrible. Now their lawsuit has come to an end. So bless me that after a stay here in Calcutta for a few days more to settle matters, I may bid adieu to this place for ever.

आपूर्यमाणमचलप्रतिष्ठं
समुद्रमापः प्रविशन्ति यद्वत्।
तद्वत् कामा यं प्रविशन्ति सर्वे
स शान्तिमाप्नोति न कामकामी ॥[1]

Bless me that my heart may wax strong with supreme strength Divine and all forms of Maya may be foiled off from me far away: For "We have taken up the Cross, Thou hast laid it upon us and grant us strength that we bear it unto death. Amen."—Imitation of Christ.

I am now staying in Calcutta. My address is: C/o Balaram Babu, 57, Ramkanta Bose's Street, Baghbazar, Calcutta.—Yours etc., VIVEKANANDA.

(8)

To The Same

BARANAGORE, CALCUTTA,*
7th Aug., 1889.

DEAR SIR—It is more than a week since I received your letter, but being again attacked with fever at that time, I could not send a reply so long, for which please excuse me. For an interval of a month and a half I kept wel, but suffered again for the last ten days; now I am doing well. I have certain questions to put, and you, sir. have a wide knowledge of Sanskrit; so please favour me highly with answers to the following:

1. Does any narrative occur about Satyakâma, son of Jabâlâ, and Jânashruti, anywhere else in the Vedas excepting the Upanishads?[2]

[1] The Gita, II. 70: "Not he that lusteth after objects of desire, but he alone obtaineth peace in whom desires lose themselves like river-water flowing into the ocean but leaving it unaffected and unmodified in spite of constant accession."

[2] The real import of this question lies in the fact that Shankaracharya in his commentary on the Vedanta-Sutras, I. iii. 3-37, interprets the aphorisms to prove that Upanishadic wisdom was imparted to Jânashruti and Satyakâma, only because they were not Shudras, as borne out by actual texts. But as these texts are doubtful even after Shankaracharya's explana-

2. In most cases where Shankaracharya quotes Smriti in his commentary on the Vedanta-Sutras, he cites the authority of the Mahabharata. But seeing that we find clear proofs about caste being based on qualification both in the Bhishma-parva of the Mahabharata and in the stories there of the Ajagara and of Uma and Maheshwara, has he made any mention in his writings of this fact?

3. The doctrine of caste in the Purushasukta of the Vedas does not make it hereditary—so what are those instances in the Vedas where caste has been made a matter of hereditary transmission?

4. The Acharya could not adduce any proof from the Vedas to the effect that a Shudra should not study the Vedas. He only quotes "यज्ञेऽनवक्लृप्त"[1] to maintain that when he is not entitled to perform Yajnas, he has neither any right to study the Upanishads and the like. But the same Acharya contends with reference to 'अथातो ब्रह्मजिज्ञासा'[2] that the अथ here does not mean "subsequent to the study of the Vedas," because it is contrary to proof that the study of the Upanishad is not permissible without the previous study of the Vedic Mantras and Brâhmanas and because there is no intrinsic sequence between the Vedic Karmakânda and Vedic Jnânakânda. It is evident, therefore, that one may attain to the knowledge of Brahman without having studied the ceremonial parts of the Vedas. So if there is no sequence between the sacrificial practices and Jnana, why does the Acharya contradict his own statement when it is a case of the Shudras, by inserting the clause "by force of the same logic"? Why should the Shudra not study the Upanishad?

tion, Swamiji wants to be referred to other Vedic texts where mention has been made of these persons.

[1] "The Shudra is not conceived of as a performer of Yajna or Vedic sacrifices."—Taittiriya Samhitâ, VII. i. 1. 6.

[2] "This is the first aphorism in the Vedanta-Sutras of Vyasa, It means, 'Now then commences hence the enquiry about Brahman."

I mail you, sir, a book named "Imitation of Christ" written by a Christian Sannyasin. It is a wonderful book. One is astonished to find such renunciation, Vairâgya and Dâsyabhakti having existed even among the Christians. Probably you may have read this book before; if not, it will give me the greatest pleasure if you kindly read it.—Yours etc., VIVEKANANDA.

(9)

To The Same

BARANAGORE,*
17th Aug., 1889.

DEAR SIR—You have expressed embarrassment in your last favour for being addressed reverentially. But the blame attaches not to me but to your own excellent qualities. I wrote in one letter before that from the way I feel attracted by your lofty virtues it seems we had some affinity from previous births. I make no distinction as to householder or Sannyasin in this that for all time my head shall bend low in reverence wherever I see greatness, broadness of heart and holiness—Shantih, Shantih, Shantih! My prayer is that among all the many people embracing Sannyasa nowadays, greedy of honour, posing renunciation for the sake of a living, and fallen off from the ideal on both sides, one in a lakh at least may become high-souled like you! To you my Brahmin fellow-disciples who have heard of your noble virtues tender their best prostrations.

About one amongst my several questions to which you sent your replies, my wrong idea is corrected. For this I shall remain indebted to you for ever. Another of these questions was: Whether Acharya Shankara gives any conclusion regarding caste based on Gunas as mentioned in Puranas like the Mahabharata. If he does, where is it to be found? I have no doubt that according to the ancient view in this country, caste was hereditary and it cannot also be doubted that sometimes the Shudras used to be oppressed more than the helots among the Spartans and the Negroes among the Americans! As for myself, I have no partiality for any party in this caste question; because I know it is a social law and is based on diversity of Guna and Karma. It also means grave harm if one bent on going beyond Guna and Karma cherishes in mind any caste distinctions. In these matters, I have got some settled ideas through the grace of my Guru, but if I come to know of your views, I may just confirm some points or rectify others in them. One doesn't have honey dripping unless one pokes at the hive—so I shall put you some more questions. Looking upon me as ignorant and as a boy, please give proper replies without taking any offence.

1. Is the Mukti which the Vedanta-Sutras speak of, one and the same with the Nirvana of the Avadhuta-Gita and other texts?

2. What is really meant by Nirvana, if according to the aphorism "Without the function of creating etc.,"[1] none can attain to the fullest Godhood?

[1] This aphorism is: जगद्व्यापारवर्जं प्रकरणादसंनिहितत्वाच्च IV. iv. 17, Vedanta-Sutras.—"Having regard to the context which ascribes the threefold function relating to the universe only to God, and because the fact of their conscious mental distinction comes between that function and their liberated state, we have to conclude that the state of final liberation or Mukti in the case of men is devoid of the capacity to create, preserve and dissolve the universe." So if this capacity is reserved only for God, what is meant, Swamiji asks, by saying that in Nirvana the human merges completely in the Divine?

We must remember that many of the questions here reflect only the intellectual stages through which Swamiji was reaching out in those days towards that plenitude of Vedantic wisdom, which was his in future years. We also find a glimpse of those processes through which his intellect was growing towards a fuller understanding of our ancient scriptures and customs.

3. Chaitanya-deva is said to have told Sârvabhauma at Puri, "I understand the Sutras of Vyasa, they are dualistic, but the commentator makes them monistic, which I don't understand." Is this true? Tradition says, Chaitanya-deva had a dispute with Prakâshânanda Saraswati on the point and Chaitanya-deva won. One commentary by Chaitanya-deva was rumoured to have been existing in Prakashananda's Math.

4. In the Tantra, Acharya Shankara has been called a crypto-Buddhist; views expressed in Prajnâpâramitâ, the Buddhist Mahâyâna book, perfectly tally with the Vedantic views propounded by the Acharya. The author of Panchadashi also says, "What we call Brahman is the same truth as the Shunya of the Buddhists." What does all this mean?

5. Why have no reasons for the authority of the Vedas been adduced in the Vedanta-Sutras? First, it has been said that the Vedas are the authority for the existence of God and then it has been argued that the authority for the Vedas is the text: "It is the breath of God." Now, is this statement not vitiated by what in Western logic is called an argument in a circle?

6. The Vedanta requires of us faith, for conclusiveness cannot be reached by mere argumentation. Then, why has the slightest flaw, detected in the position of the schools of Sankhya and Nyaya, been overwhelmed with a fusillade of dialectics? Whom, moreover, are we to put our faith on? Everybody seems to be mad over establishing his own view; if, according to Vyasa, even the great Muni Kapila, "the greatest among perfected souls"[1] is himself deeply involved in error, then who would say that Vyasa may not be so involved in a greater measure? Did Kapila fail to understand the Vedas?

[1] Kapila is so spoken of in the Gita, X 26. In his commentary on the Vedanta-Sutras, II. i. 1, Shankara doubts the identity of the Vedic Kapila with the Sankhyan Kapila.

7. According to the Nyaya, "Shabda or Veda, (the criterion of truth), is the word of those who have realised the highest"; so the Rishis as such are omniscient. Then how are they proved, according to the Surya-siddhanta, to be ignorant of such simple astronomical truths? How can we accept their intelligence as the refuge to ferry us across the ocean of transmigratory existence, seeing that they speak of the earth as triangular, of the serpent Vasuki as the support of the earth and so on?

8. If in His acts of creation God is dependent on good and evil Karmas, then what does it avail us to worship Him? There is a fine song of Nareshchandra, where occurs the following: "If what lies in one's destiny is to happen anyhow, O Mother, then what good all this invoking by the holy name of Durga?"

9. True, it is improper to hold many texts on the same subject to be contradicted by one or two. But why then are the long-continued customs of Madhuparka and the like repealed by one or two such texts as, "The horse sacrifice, the cow sacrifice, Sannyasa, meat-offerings in Shrâddha" etc?[1] If the Vedas are eternal, then what are the meaning and justification of such specifications as "this rule of Dharma is for the age of Dwapara," "this for the age of Kali" and so forth?

10. The same God who gives out the Vedas became Buddha again to annul them; which of these dispensations is to be obeyed? Which of these remains authoritative, the earlier or the later one?

11. The Tantra says, in the Kali-yuga the Veda-

[1] Madhuparka was a Vedic ceremony usually in honour of a guest in which a respectful offering was to be made consisting among other dainties, of beef. The text which Swamiji partially quotes forbids such food. For the full text means that in the Kali-yuga the following five customs are to be forsaken: The horse sacrifice, cow-killing ceremonies, meat-offerings in Shrâddha, Sannyasa, and maintaining the line of progeny through the husband's younger brother in case of failure through the husband.

mantras are futile. So which behest of God, the Shiva, is to be followed?

12. Vyasa makes it out in the Vedanta-Sutras that it is wrong to worship the tetrad of divine manifestation, Vâsudeva, Sankarshana, etc., and again that very Vyasa expatiates on the great merits of that worship in the Bhagavata! Is this Vyasa a madman?

I have many such doubts besides these, and hoping to have them dispelled from my mind through your kindness, I shall lay them before you in future. Such questions can't be all set forth except in a personal interview; neither can satisfaction be obtained as much as one expects to. So I have a mind to lay before you all these facts when presenting myself to you, which I expect will be very soon, by the grace of the Guru.

I have heard it said that without inner progress in the practice of religion, no true conclusion can be reached concerning these matters simply by means of reasoning; but satisfaction, at least to some extent, seems to be necessary at the outset.—Yours etc., VIVEKANANDA.

(10)

To The Same

BAGHBAZAR, CALCUTTA,*
2nd Sept., 1889.

DEAR SIR—Some days ago I received your two kind letters. I am very much pleased to find in you a wonderful harmony of Jnana and Bhakti. Your advice to me to give up arguing and disputing is very true indeed, and that is really the goal of life for the individual—"Sundered are the knots of the heart, torn off are all his doubts, and the seeds of his Karma wear off, when the sight of the Transcendent One is gained."[1] But then,

[1] Mundakopanishad, II. ii. 8.

as my Master used to say, when a pitcher is being filled (by immersion), it gurgles, but when full, it is noiseless; know my condition to be the same. Within two or three weeks perhaps, I shall be able to meet you—may God fulfil that wish!—Yours etc., VIVEKANANDA.

(11)

To The Same

BAGHBAZAR,*
3rd Dec., 1889.

DEAR SIR—I have not long heard from you. Hope you are doing well in body and mind. Two of my brother-disciples are shortly leaving for Benares. One is Rakhal by name, the other is Subodh. The first-named was beloved of my Master and used to stay with him much. Please recommend them to some Satra (house of alms) during their stay in the city, if you find it convenient. You will hear from them all my news. With my best regards and greetings.—Yours etc., VIVEKANANDA.

P.S. Gangadhar is now proceeding to Kailas. The Thibetans wanted to slash him up on the way, taking him to be a spy of the foreigners. Eventually some Lamas kindly set him free. We obtain this news from a Thibet-going trader. Gangadhar's blood won't cool down before seeing Lhassa. The gain is that his physical endurance has grown immensely—one night he passed uncovered on a bed of snow, and that without much hardship.—V.

(12)

To The Same

BARANAGORE, CALCUTTA,*
13th Dec., 1889.

DEAR SIR—I have all particulars from your letter, and from Rakhal's which followed I came to know of your meeting. I have received the pamphlet written by you. A kind of scientific Advaitism is spreading in Europe ever since the theory of the conservation of energy was discovered, but all that is Parinâmavâda (evolution by real modification). It is good you have shown the difference between this and Shankara's Vivartavada (progressive manifestation by unreal superimposition). I can't appreciate your citing Spencer's parody on the German Transcendentalists; he himself is fed much on their doles. It is doubtful whether your opponent Gough understands his Hegel sufficiently. Anyway, your rejoinder is very pointed and thrashing.—Yours etc., VIVEKANANDA.

(13)

To Sj. Balaram Bose

BAIDYANATH,*
24th Dec., 1889.

DEAR SIR—I have been staying for the last few days at Baidyanath in Purna Babu's Lodge. It is not so cold, and my health, too, is indifferent. I am suffering from indigestion, probably due to excess of iron in the water. I found nothing agreeable—neither the place, nor the season, nor the company. I leave for Benares to-morrow. At Deoghar Achyutananda stopped at———'s place, and the latter, as soon as he got news of us, earnestly insisted on our becoming his guests. Finally, he met us once again and prevailed on us to accede to his request. The man is a great worker, but has a number of women with him—old women most of them, of the ordinary Vaishnava type. . . . His clerks too revere us much; some of them are very much ill-disposed towards him, and they spoke of his misdeeds. Incidentally, I raised the topic of——. You have many wrong ideas or doubts about her, hence I write all this after particular investigation. Even the aged clerks of this establishment highly respect and revere her. She came to stop with—while she was a mere child, and ever lived as his wife. . . . Everyone admits in one voice that her character is spotless. She was all along a perfectly chaste woman and never behaved with—in any relation but that of wife to husband, and she was absolutely faithful. She came at too early an age to have incurred any moral taint. After she had separated from——, she wrote to him to say that she had never treated him as anything but her husband, but that it was impossible for her to live with a man with a loose character. His old office-bearers, too, believe him to be satanic in character but they consider——a Devi (angel), and remark that it was following her departure that——lost all sense of shame.

My object in writing all this is that formerly I was not a believer in the tale of the lady's early life. The idea that there might be such purity in the midst of a relation which society does not recognise, I used to consider as romance. But after thorough investigation I have come to know that it is all right. She is very pure, pure from her infancy—I have not the least doubt about it. For entertaining those doubts, you and I and everyone are guilty to her; I make repeated salutations to her, and ask her pardon for my guilt. She is not a liar.

I take this opportunity to record that such courage is impossible in a lying and unchaste woman. I have also been told that she had a lifelong ardent faith in religion also.

Well, your disease is not leaving off yet! I don't think this is a place for patients unless one is ready to spend a good deal of money. Please think out some judicious course. Here every article will have to be procured from elsewhere.—Yours sincerely, VIVEKANANDA.

(14)

To Sj. Pramada Das Mitra

BAIDYANATH,*
26th Dec., 1889.

DEAR SIR—After a long attempt I am now in a position to present myself before you. In a day or two I take myself to your feet at holy Kashi.

I have been putting up here for some days with a gentleman of Calcutta, but my mind is much longing for Benares.

My idea is to remain there for some time, and to watch how Vishwanatha and Annapurna[1] deal it out to my lot. And my resolve is something like "either to lay down my life or realise my ideal,"[2]—so help me, the Lord of Kashi.—Yours etc., VIVEKANANDA.

(15)

To The Same

ALLAHABAD,*
30th Dec., 1889.

DEAR SIR—I wrote in a letter to you that I was to go to Benares in a day or two, but who can nullify the decree of Providence? News reached me that a brother-disciple, Jogen by name, had been attacked with smallpox after reaching here from a pilgrimage to Chitrakuta, Omkarnath, etc., and so I come to this place to nurse him. He has now completely recovered. Some Bengalee gentlemen here are of a greatly pious and loving disposition. They are very lovingly taking care of me, and their importunate desire is that I stay here during the month of Magh in the

[1] Shiva and His Divine Spouse as installed in Benares.

[2] शरीरं वा पातयामि मन्त्रं वा साधयामि ।

keeping of the Kalpa vow.[1] But my mind is very keenly harping on the name of Benares and is quite set agog to see you. Yes, I am going to try my best to slip away and avoid their keen importunities in a day or two and betake myself to the holy realm of the Lord of Benares. If one of my monastic brother-disciples, Achyutananda Saraswati by name, calls on you to enquire of me, please tell him, I am soon coming to Benares. He is indeed a very good man and learned. I was obliged to leave him behind at Bankipore. Are Rakhal and Subodh still there in Benares? Please make it out and inform me whether the Kumbha fair this year is going to be held at Hardwar or not.

Many a man of wisdom, of piety, many a Sadhu and Pandit have I met in so many places, and I have been very much favoured by them, but भिन्नरुचिर्हि लोकः "Men are of varying tastes;"[2] I know not what sort of soul-affinity there is between us, for nowhere else it seems so pleasing and agreeable. Let me see how the Lord of Kashi disposes. —Yours etc., VIVEKANANDA.

My address is—C/o Govinda Chandra Basu, Chauk, Allahabad.

(*16*)

To Sj. Balaram Bose

ALLAHABAD,*
5th January, 1890.

MY DEAR SIR—I am very sorry to hear of your illness from your kind note. The gist of the letter I wrote to you about your change to Baidyanath was that it would be impossible for a man of weak and extremely delicate

[1] i.e. special ablutions and worship regularly performed in that holy confluence—a very solemn and sacred practice.

[2] Kalidasa, Raghuvamsha.

physique like you to live in that place unless you spend a good deal of money. If change be really advisable for you, and if you have deferred it so long simply to select a cheaper place and that sort of thing, it is certainly a matter of regret. . . . Baidyanath is excellent so far as the air is concerned, but the water is not good, it upsets the stomach. I used to suffer from acidity every day. I have already written you a letter; have you got it, or finding it a bearing letter, have left it to its fate? In my opinion, if you *have* to go out on a change, the sooner the better. But, pardon me, you have a tendency to expect that everything should fit in exactly with your requirements, but unfortunately, such a state of things is very rare in this world. आत्मानं सततं रक्षेत्—"One must save oneself under any circumstances." "Lord have mercy," is all right, but He helps him who helps himself. If you simply try to save your purse, will the Lord arrange the change for you by drawing on His ancestral capital? If you think you have so much reliance on the Lord, don't call in the doctor, please. . . . If that does not suit you, you should go to Benares. I would have already left this place, but the local gentlemen would not give me leave to depart! . . . . . But let me repeat once more, if change is actually decided upon, please do not hesitate out of miserliness. That would be suicide. And not even God can save a suicide. Please convey my compliments to Tulsi Babu and the rest. With best regards,—Yours affectionately, VIVEKANANDA.

(17)

To Sj. Jajneshwar Bhattacharya

ALLAHABAD,*
5th January, 1890.

MY DEAR Fakir . . . . A word for you. Remember always I may not see you again. Be moral. Be brave.

Be a heart-whole man. Strictly moral, brave unto desperation. Don't bother your head with religious theories. Cowards only sin, brave men never, no, not even in mind. Try to love anybody and everybody. Be a *man* and try to make those immediately under your care, namely Ram, Krishnamayi and Indu, brave, moral and sympathising. No religion for you, my children, but morality and bravery. No cowardice, no sin, no crime, no weakness—the rest will come of itself. . . . And don't take Ram with you ever or ever allow him to visit a theatre or any enervating entertainment whatever.—Yours affectionately, VIVEKANANDA.

(*18*)

Ram, Krishnamayi and Indu

ALLAHABAD,
5th January, 1890.

MY DEAR Ram, Krishnamayi and Indu—Bear in mind, my children, the cowards and those who are weak only, commit sin and go to tell lies. The brave are always moral. Try to be moral, try to be brave, try to be sympathising.—Yours, VIVEKANANDA.

(*19*)

To Sj. Pramada Das Mitra

C/O BABU SATISHCHANDRA MUKHERJI,*
GORABAZAR, GHAZIPUR,
24th Jan., 1890.

DEAR SIR—I reached Ghazipur three days ago. Here I am putting up in the house of Babu Satishchandra Mukherji, a friend of my early age. The place is very pleasant. Close by flows the Ganges, but bathing there is troublesome, for there is no regular path and it is hard work wading through sands. Babu Ishanchandra Mukherji, my friend's father, that noble-hearted man of whom I spoke to you, is here. To-day he is leaving for Benares whence he will proceed to Calcutta. I had a great mind again to go over to Kashi, but the object of my coming here, namely an interview with Babaji,[1] has not yet been realised, and hence the delay of a few days becomes necessary. Everything here appears good, the people are all gentlemen, but very much Westernised; and it is a pity I am so thoroughly against every affectation of the Western idea. Only my friend is very little inclined to such ideas. What a frippery civilisation is it indeed that the foreigners have brought over here! What a materialistic illusion have they created! May Vishwanatha save these weak-hearted! After seeing Babaji, I shall send you a detailed account.—Yours etc., VIVEKANANDA.

P.S. Alas for the irony of our fate, that in this land of Bhagavan Shuka's birth renunciation is looked down upon as madness and sin!

(20)

To Sj. Balaram Bose

GHAZIPUR,*
30th Jan., 1890.

REVERED SIR—I am now stopping with Satish Babu at Ghazipur. Of the few places I have recently visited, this is the healthiest. The water of Baidyanath is very bad—it leads to indigestion. Allahabad is very congested. The few days I passed at Benares, I suffered from fever day and night—the place is so malarious! Ghazipur has

[1] Pavhari Baba, the great saint.

a very salubrious climate—specially the quarter I am living in. I have visited Pavhari Baba's house—there are high walls all round, and it is fashioned like an English bungalow. There is a garden inside and big rooms and chimneys, etc. He allows nobody to enter. If he is so inclined, he comes up to the door and speaks from inside—that is all. One day I went and waited and waited in the cold and had to return. I shall go to Benares on Sunday next. If the meeting with the Babaji takes place in the meantime, all right, otherwise I bid him good-bye. About Pramada Babu's place I shall write definitely from Benares. If Kali Bhattacharya is determined to come, let him do so after I leave for Benares on Sunday, but he should rather not. After a few days' stay at Benares, I shall start for Hrishikesh. Pramada Babu may accompany me. Please accept all of you my cordial greetings,—and blessings to Father, Ram, Krishnamayi etc.—Yours affectionately, VIVEKANANDA.

P.S. In my opinion, it will do you much good if you come and stay for some time at Ghazipur. Here Satish will be able to secure a bungalow for you, and there is a gentleman, Gagan Chandra Ray by name, who is the Head of the Opium Office, and is exceedingly courteous, philanthropic and social—they will arrange for everything. The house-rent is fifteen to twenty rupees; rice is dear, and milk sells at sixteen to twenty seers a rupee; all other things are very cheap. Besides, under the care of these gentlemen, there is no chance of any difficulty. But it is slightly expensive—it will cost over forty to fifty rupees. Benares is horribly malarious. I have never lived in Pramada Babu's garden, he likes to have me always in his company. The garden is indeed very beautiful, richly furnished, spacious and open. This time when I go, I shall live there and report to you.—V.

(21)

To Sj. Pramada Das Mitra

GHAZIPUR,*
31st Jan., 1890.

DEAR SIR—It is so very difficult to meet the Babaji. He does not step out of his home, and when willing to speak at all, he just comes near the door to speak from inside. I have come away with having just a view of his garden-house with chimneys tapering above and encircled by high walls—no means of admittance within! People say, there are cave-like rooms within, where he dwells, and he only knows what he does there, for nobody has had a peep. I had to come away one day sorely used up with waiting and waiting, but shall take my chance again. On Sunday, I leave for holy Benares—only the Babus here won't let me off, otherwise all my fancy to see the Babaji has flattened down. I am prepared to be off to-day; but anyhow, I am leaving on Sunday. What of your plan of going to Hrishikesh?—Yours etc., VIVEKANANDA.

P.S. The redeeming feature is that the place seems healthy.

(22)

To The Same

GHAZIPUR,*
4th Feb., 1890.

DEAR SIR—Received your kind note, and through supreme good fortune, I have obtained an interview with Babaji. A great sage indeed! It is all very wonderful, and in this atheistic age, a towering representation of marvellous power born of Bhakti and Yoga! I have sought refuge in his grace, and he has given me hope—

a thing very few may be fortunate enough for. It is Babaji's wish that I stay on for some days here and he would do me some good. So following this saint's bidding I shall remain here for some time. No doubt, this will also give you much pleasure. I don't mention them in a letter, but the facts are very strange indeed—to be disclosed when we meet. Unless one is face to face with the life of such men, faith in the scriptures does not grow in all its real integrity.—Yours etc., VIVEKANANDA.

(23)

To The Same

GHAZIPUR,*
7th Feb., 1890.

DEAR SIR—I feel very happy to hear from you just now. Apparently in his features, the Babaji is a Vaishnava, the embodiment, so to speak, of Yoga, Bhakti and humility. His dwelling has walls on all sides with a few doors in them. Inside these walls, there is a long underground burrow wherein he remains immersed in Samadhi. He talks to others only when he comes out of the hole. Nobody knows what he eats, and so they call him Pavhari[1] Baba. Once he did not come out of the hole for five years, and people thought he had given up the body. But now again he is out. But this time he does not show himself to people, and talks from behind the door. Such sweetness in speech I have never come across! He does not give a direct reply to questions but says, " What does this servant know?" But then fire comes out as the talking goes on. On my pressing him very much he said, "Favour me highly by staying here some days." But he never speaks in this way; so from this I understood he

[1] i.e. one living on air.

meant to reassure me; and whenever I am importunate, he asks me to stay on. So I wait in hope. He is a learned man no doubt, but nothing in that line betrays itself. He performs scriptural ceremonials; for from the full-moon day to the last day of the month, sacrificial oblations go on. So it is sure he is not retiring into the hole during this period. How can I ask his permission,[1] for he never gives a direct reply; he goes on multiplying such expressions as "this servant," "my fortune," and so on. If you yourself have a mind, then please come sharp on receipt of this note. Or after his passing away, the keenest regret would be left in your mind; in two days you may return after an interview, I mean, a talk with him from outside. My friend Satish Babu will receive you most warmly. So, do please come up directly you receive this; I shall meanwhile let Babaji know of you.—Yours etc., VIVEKANANDA.

P.S. Even though one can't have his company, no trouble taken for the sake of such a great soul can ever go unrewarded.

(24)

To The Same

GHAZIPUR,*
13th Feb., 1890.

DEAR SIR—I am in anxiety to hear of your illness. I am also having some sort of a pain in the loins which being aggravated of late gives much trouble. For two days I could not go out to meet Babaji, and so a man came from him to enquire about me. For this reason, I go to-day. I shall convey your countless compliments. "Fire comes out," that is, a wonderful devotion to Guru and resignation are revealed; and such amazing endurance

[1] Evidently for a proposed visit to the saint by the Benares correspondent.

and humility I have never seen. Whatever good things I may come by, be sure, you have your share in them.—Yours etc., VIVEKANANDA.

(25)

To The Same

GHAZIPUR,
14th Feb., 1890.

DEAR SIR—In my note of yesterday I perhaps forgot to ask you to return brother Sarat's letter. Please send it. I have heard from brother Gangadhar. He is now in Rambag Samadhi, Srinagar, Kashmir. I am greatly suffering from lumbago.—Yours etc., VIVEKANANDA.

P. S. Rakhal and Subodh have come to Brindaban after visiting Omkar, Girnar, Abu, Bombay and Dwarka.

(26)

To Sj. Balaram Bose

C/O SATISH MUKHERJI,*
GORABAZAR, GHAZIPUR,
14th Feb., 1890.

REVERED SIR—I am in receipt of your letter of contrition. I am not leaving this place soon—it is impossible to avoid the Babaji's request. You have expressed remorse at not having reaped any appreciable results by serving the Sadhus. It is true, and yet not true; it is true if you look towards ideal bliss, but if you look behind to the place from which you started you will find that before you were an animal, now you are a man, and will be a god or God Himself in future. Moreover, that sort of regret and dissatisfaction is very good, it is the prelude to improvement. Without this none can rise. He who puts on a turban and immediately sees the Lord, progresses thus far and no farther. You are blessed indeed to have that constant dissatisfaction preying on your mind—rest assured that there is no danger for you. . . . You are a keenly intelligent man, and know full well that patience is the best means of success. In this respect I have no doubt that we light-headed boys have much to learn from you. . . . You are a considerate man, and I need not add anything. Man has two ears but one mouth. You specially are given to plain-speaking, and are chary of making large promises—things that sometimes make me cross with you, but upon reflection I find that it is you who have acted with discretion. " Slow but sure." "What is lost in power is gained in speed." However, in this world everything depends upon one's words. To get an insight behind the words (specially, with your economical spirit masking all) is not given to all, and one must associate long with a man to be able to understand him. . . . Religion is not in sects, nor in making a fuss—why do you forget these teachings of our revered Master? Please help as far as it lies in you, but to judge what came of it, whether it was turned to good or evil account, is perhaps beyond our jurisdiction. . . . Considering the great shock which Girish Babu has received, it will give him immense peace to serve Mother at this moment. He is a very keen-witted person. And our beloved Master had perfect confidence in you, used to dine nowhere else except at your place, and I have heard, Mother too has the fullest confidence in you. In view of these you will please bear and forbear all shortcomings of us fickle boys, treating them as if they were done by your own boy. This is all I have got to say. Please let me know by return of post when the Anniversary is to take place. A pain in the loins is giving me much trouble. In a few days the place will look exceedingly beautiful, with miles and miles of rose-banks all in flower. Satish says he will then send some fresh roses and cuttings for the Festival. . . . May the Lord ordain that your son becomes a man, and never a coward!—Yours affectionately, VIVEKANANDA.

P.S. If Mother has come, please convey to her my countless salutations, and ask her to bless me that I may have unflinching perseverance. Or, if that be impossible in this body, may it fall off soon!—V.

(27)

To Swami Sadananda

GHAZIPUR,*
14th Feb., 1890.

MY DEAR GUPTA—I hope you are doing well. Do your own spiritual exercises, and knowing yourself to be the humblest servant of all, serve them. Those with whom you are staying are such that even I am not worthy to call myself their humblest servant and take the dust of their feet.—Knowing this serve them and have devotion for them. Don't be angry even if they abuse or even hurt you desperately. Never mix with women. Try to be hardy little by little, and gradually accustom yourself to maintain the body out of the proceeds of begging. Whoever takes the name of Ramakrishna, know him to be your Guru. Everyone can play the role of a master, but it is very difficult to be a servant. Specially you should follow S——. Know it for certain that without steady devotion for the Guru, and unflinching patience and perseverance, nothing is to be achieved. You must have strict morality. Deviate an inch from this and you are gone for ever.—Yours affectionately, VIVEKANANDA.

(28)

To Sj. Pramada Das Mitra

GHAZIPUR,*
Feb., 1890.

DEAR SIR—I wrote a letter to brother Gangadhar asking him to stop his wanderings and settle down somewhere and to send me an account of the various Sadhus he had come across in Thibet and their ways and customs. I enclose the reply that came from him. Brother Kali is having repeated attacks of fever at Hrishikesh. I have sent him a wire from this place. So if from the reply I find I am wanted by him, I shall be obliged to start direct for Hrishikesh from this place, otherwise I am coming to you in a day or two. Well, you may smile, sir, to see me weaving all this web of Maya—and that is no doubt the fact. But then there is the chain of iron and there is the chain of gold. Much good comes of the latter, and it drops off by itself when all the good is reaped. The sons of my Master are indeed the great objects of my service, and here alone I feel I have some duty left for me. Perhaps I shall send brother Kali down to Allahabad or somewhere else as convenient. At your feet are laid a hundred and one faults of mine—"I am as thy son, so regulate me who have taken refuge in thee."[1]—Yours etc., VIVEKANANDA.

(29)

To Swami Akhandananda

GHAZIPUR,*
February, 1890.

BELOVED AKHANDANANDA—Very glad to receive your letter. What you have written about Thibet is very

[1] An adaptation from the Gita, II. 7.

promising, and I shall try to go there once. In Sanskrit Thibet is called the Uttarakuruvarsha, and is not a land of Mlechchhas. Being the highest tableland in the world it is extremely cold, but by degrees one may become accustomed to it. Of the manners and customs of the Thibetans you have written nothing; why, if they are so hospitable, did they not allow you to go on? Please write everything in detail, in a long letter. I am sorry to learn that you will not be able to come, for I had a great longing to see you. It seems that I love you more than all others. However, I shall try to get rid of this Maya too.

The Tântric rites among the Thibetans that you have spoken of arose in India itself during the decline of Buddhism. It is my belief that the Tantras in vogue amongst us, were the creation of the Buddhists themselves Those Tantric rites are even more dreadful than our doctrine of Vâmâchâra; for in them adultery had got a free rein, and it was only when the Buddhists became demoralised through immorality, that they were driven away by Kumarila Bhatta. As some Sannyasins speak of Shankara, or the Bâuls of Sri Chaitanya, that he was in secret an epicure, a drunkard and one addicted to all sorts of abominable practices—so the modern Tantric Buddhists speak of the Lord Buddha as a dire Vâmâchârin, and give an obscene interpretation to the many beautiful precepts of the Prajnâpâramitâ, such as the Tattvagatha and the like. The result of all this has been that the Buddhists are divided into two sects nowadays; the Burmese and the Sinhalese have generally set the Tantras at naught, have likewise banished the Hindu gods and goddesses, and at the same time have thrown overboard the Amitâbha Buddha held in regard among the Northern School of Buddhists. The long and short of it is that the Amitabha Buddha and the other gods whom the Northern School worship, are not mentioned in books like the Prajnaparamita, but a lot of gods and goddesses are recommended for worship. And the Southern people have wilfully transgressed the Shastras and eschewed the gods and goddesses. The phase of Buddhism which declares "Everything for others," and which you find spread throughout Thibet, has greatly struck modern Europe. Concerning that phase, however, I have a good deal to say—which it is impossible to do in this letter. What Buddha did was to break wide open the gates of that very religion which was confined in the Upanishads to a particular caste. What special greatness does his theory of Nirvana confer on him? His greatness lies in his unrivalled sympathy. The high orders of Samadhi etc., that lend gravity to his religion, are almost all there in the Vedas; what are absent there are his intellect and heart, which have never since been paralleled throughout the history of the world.

The Vedic doctrine of Karma is the same as in Judaism and all other religions, that is to say, the purification of the mind through sacrifices and such other external means—and Buddha was the first man who stood against it. But the inner essence of the ideas remained as of old—look at that doctrine of mental exercises which he preached, and that mandate of his to believe in the Suttas instead of the Vedas. Caste also remained as of old, (caste was not wholly obsolete at the time of Buddha) but it was now determined by personal qualifications, and those that were not believers in his religion were declared as heretics, all in the old style. "Heretic" was a very ancient word with the Buddhists, but then they never had recourse to the sword (good souls!) and had great toleration. Argument blew up the Vedas, but what is the proof of your religion?—Well, put faith in it!—the same procedure as in all religions. It was however an imperative necessity of the times and that was the reason of his having incarnated himself. His doctrine is like that of Kapila.

But that of Shankara, how far more grand and rational! Buddha and Kapila are always saying—the world is full of grief and nothing but that—flee from it—aye, for your life, do! Is happiness altogether absent here? It is a statement of the nature of what the Brahmos say—the world is full of happiness! There is grief, forsooth, but what can be done? Perchance some will suggest that grief itself will appear as happiness when you become used to it by constant sufferance. Shankara does not take this line of argument—he says this world *is and is not—manifold* yet *one*, I shall unravel its mystery—I shall know whether grief be there, or anything else; I do not flee from it as from a bugbear. I will know all about it—as to the infinite pain that attends its search, well, I am embracing it in its fullest measure .Am I a beast that you frighten me with happiness and misery, decay and death, which are but the outcome of the senses? I will know about it—will give up my life for it. There is nothing to know about in this world—therefore, if there be anything beyond this relative existence—what the Lord Buddha has designated as Prajnâpâram—the transcendental—if such there be, I want that alone. Whether happiness attends it or grief, I do not care. What a lofty idea! How grand! The religion of Buddha has reared itself on the Upanishads, and upon that also the philosophy of Shankara. Only, Shankara had not the slightest bit of Buddha's wonderful heart, dry intellect merely—for fear of the Tantras, for fear of the mob, in his attempt to cure a boil he amputated the very arm itself![1] One has to write a big volume if one

[1] In his anxiety to defend the purity of the Vedic religion against the excesses of Tantrikism, which was capturing the rank and file of his countrymen, Shankara neglected the problem of the latter, stigmatised as Shudras by the Vedicists. This is perhaps the meaning of Swamiji. It seems he could never forgive Shankara for applying in his commentary on the Brahma-Sutras the old logic of forbidding Vedic rituals to the Shudras to the

has to write about them at all—but I have neither the learning nor the leisure for it.

Lord Buddha is my Ishtam—my God. He preached no theory about Godhead—he was himself God, I fully believe it. But no one has the power to put a limit to God's infinite glory. No, not even God Himself has the power to make Himself limited. The translation of the Gandâra-Sutta that you have made from the Suttanipâta, is excellent. In that book there is another Sutta—the Dhaniya-Sutta—which has got a similar idea. There are many passages in the Dhammapadam too, with similar ideas. But that is at the last stage, when one has got perfectly satisfied with Knowledge and Realisation, is the same under all circumstances, and has gained mastery over his senses—

ज्ञानविज्ञानतृप्तात्मा कूटस्थो विजितेन्द्रियः ।

He who has not the least regard for his body as something to be taken care of—it is he who may roam about at pleasure like the mad elephant caring for naught. Whereas a puny creature like myself should practise devotion, sitting at one spot, till he attains Realisation—and then only should he behave like that—but it is a far-off question—very far indeed.

विन्ताशून्यमदैन्यभक्ष्यमशनं पानं सरिद्वारिषु
स्वातन्त्र्येण निरङ्कुशा स्थितिरभीर्निद्रा स्मशाने वने ।
वस्त्रं क्षालनशोषणादिरहितं दिग्वास्तु शय्या मही
सञ्चारो निगमान्तवीथीषु विदां क्रीडा परे ब्रह्मणि ॥

more modern question of their right to higher modes of worship (Upâsanâ) and knowledge (Jnâna) of the Jnânakanda.

विमानमालम्ब्य शरीरमेतद्-
भुनक्त्यशेषान् विषयानुपस्थितान् ।
परेच्छया बालवदात्मवेत्ता ।
योऽव्यक्तलिङ्गोऽतनुषक्तबाह्यः ॥
दिगम्बरो वापि च साम्बरो वा
त्वगम्बरो वापि चिदम्बरस्थः ।
उन्मत्तवद्वापि च बालवद्वा
पिशाचवद्वापि चरत्यवन्याम् ॥[1]

—To a knower of Brahman food comes of itself, without effort—he drinks water wherever he gets it. He roams at pleasure everywhere—he is fearless, sleeps sometimes in the forest, sometimes in a crematorium, and treads the Path which the Vedas have taken but whose end they have not seen. His body is like the sky, and he is guided, like a child, by others' wishes; he is sometimes naked, sometimes in gorgeous clothes, and at times has only Jnanam as his clothing; he behaves sometimes like a child, sometimes like a madman, and at other times again like a ghoul, indifferent to cleanliness.

I pray to the holy feet of our Guru that you may have that state, and you may wander like the rhinoceros.
—Yours affectionately, VIVEKANANDA.

(30)

To Sj. Pramada Das Mitra

GHAZIPUR,*
25th Feb., 1890.

DEAR SIR—The lumbago is giving a good deal of trouble, or else I would have already sought to come to you. The mind does not find rest here any longer. It is

[1] Vivekachudâmani.

three days since I came away from Babaji's place, but he enquires of me kindly almost every day. As soon as the lumbago is a little better, I bid good-bye to Babaji. Countless greetings to you.—Yours etc. VIVEKANANDA.

(31)

To Swami Akhandananda

GHAZIPUR,*
March, 1890.

BELOVED AKHANDANANDA—Very glad to receive your letter yesterday. I am at present staying with the wonderful Yogi and devotee of this place, called Pavhariji. He never comes out of his room—and holds conversations with people from behind the door. Inside the room there is a pit in which he lives. It is rumoured that he remains in a state of Samadhi for months together. His fortitude is most wonderful. Our Bengal is the land of Bhakti and of Jnana, where Yoga is scarcely so much as talked of even. What little there is, is but the queer breathing exercises, of the Hatha-yoga—which is nothing but a kind of gymnastics. Therefore I am staying with this wonderful Raja-yogin—and he has given me some hopes, too. There is a beautiful bungalow in a small garden belonging to a gentleman here; I mean to stay there. The garden is quite close to Babaji's cottage. A brother of the Babaji stays there to look after the comforts of the Sadhus, and I shall have my Bhikshâ at his place. Hence, with a view to see to the end of this fun I give up for the present my plan of going to the hills. For the last two months I have got an attack of lumbago in the waist, which also makes it impossible to climb the hills now. Therefore let me wait and see what Babaji would give me.

My motto is to learn whatever good things I may come across anywhere. This leads many friends to think that it will take away from my devotion to the Guru. These ideas I count as those of lunatics and bigots. For all Gurus are one, and are fragments and radiations of God, the Universal Guru.

If you come to Ghazipur you have but to enquire at Satish Babu's or Gagan Babu's at Gorabazar, and you will know my whereabouts. Or, Pavhari Baba is so well-known a person here that everyone will inform you about his Ashrama at the very mention of his name, and you have only to go there and enquire about the Paramahamsa, and they will tell you of me. Near Moghul Sarai there is a station named Dildarnagar, where you have to change to a short Branch Railway and get down at Tarighat, opposite Ghazipur; then you have to cross the Ganges to reach Ghazipur.

For the present, I stay at Ghazipur for some days and wait and see what the Babaji does. If you come, we shall stay together at the said bungalow for some time, and then start for the hills, or for any other place we may decide upon. Don't, please, write to anyone at Baranagore that I am staying at Ghazipur.

With blessings and best wishes,—Ever yours, VIVEKANANDA.

(32)

To Sj. Pramada Das Mitra

GHAZIPUR,*
3rd March, 1890.

DEAR SIR—Your kind letter comes to hand just now. You know not, sir—I am a very soft-natured man in spite of the stern Vedantic views I hold. And this proves to be my undoing. At the slightest touch I give way; for howsoever I may try to think only of my own good, I slip off in spite of myself to think of other people's interests. This time it was with a very stern resolve that I set out to pursue my own good, but I had to run off at the news of the illness of a brother at Allahabad! And now comes this news from Hrishikesh, and my mind has run off with me there. I have wired to Sarat, but no reply yet—a nice place indeed to delay even telegrams so much! The lumbago obstinately refuses to leave me, and the pain is very great. For the last few days, I haven't been able to go to see Pavhariji, but out of his kindness, he sends every day for my report. But now I see the whole matter is inverted in its bearings! While I myself have come a beggar at his door, he turns round and wants to learn of me! This saint perhaps is not yet perfected—too much of works, vows, observances, and too much of self-concealment. The ocean in its fulness cannot be contained within its shores, I am sure. So it is not good, I have decided, to disturb this Sadhu for nothing and very soon I shall take leave of him. No help you see; Providence has dealt me my death to make me so tender! Babaji does not let me go and Gagan Babu (whom probably you know—an upright, pious and kind-hearted man) does not give me leave. If the wire in reply requires my leaving this place, I go; if not, I am coming to you at Benares in a few days. I am not going to let you off—I must take you to Hrishikesh—no excuses or objections will do. What are you saying about difficulties there of keeping clean? Lack of water in the hills, or lack of room!! Tirthas places of pilgrimage) and Sannyasins of the Kali-yuga—you know what they are. Spend money and the owners of temples will fling away the installed god to give you room; so no anxiety about a resting place! No trouble to face there, I say; the summer heat has set in there now, I believe, though not that degree of it as you find at Benares—so much the better. Always the nights are quite cool there, from which good sleep is almost a certainty.

Why do you get frightened so much? I stand guarantee that you shall return home safe and that you shall have no trouble anywhere. It is my experience that in this British realm no Fakir or householder gets into any trouble.

Is it a mere idle fancy of mine that between us there is some connection from previous birth? Just see how one letter from you sweeps away all my resolution, and I bend my steps towards Benares leaving all matters behind!. . .

I have written again to brother Gangadhar and have asked him this time to return to the Math. If he comes, he will meet you. How is the climate at Benares now? By my stay here I have been cured of all other symptoms of malaria, only the pain in the loins makes me frantic; day and night it is aching and chafes me very much. I know not how I shall climb up the hills. I find wonderful endurance in Babaji and that's why I am begging something of him, but no inkling of the mood to give, only receiving and receiving! So I also fly off.—Yours etc., VIVEKANANDA.

P.S. To no big person am I going any longer,—

"Remain, O mind, within yourself, go not to anybody else's door; whatever you seek, you shall obtain sitting at your ease, only seek for it in the privacy of your heart. There is the supreme Treasure, the philosopher's stone, and He can give whatever you ask for; for countless gems, O mind, lie strewn about the portals of His abode. He is the wishing-stone that confers boons at the mere thought." Thus says the poet Kamalakanta.

So now the great conclusion is that Ramakrishna has no peer; nowhere else in this world exists that unprecedented perfection, that wonderful kindness for all that does not stop to justify itself, that intense sympathy for man in bondage. Either he must be the Avatara as he himself used to say, or else the ever-perfected divine man, whom the Vedanta speaks of as the free one, who assumes a body for the good of humanity. This is my conviction sure and certain—and the worship of such a divine man has been referred to by Patanjali in the aphorism, "Or the goal may be attained by meditating on a saint."[1]

Never during his life did he refuse a single prayer of mine. Millions of offences has he forgiven me. Such great love even my parents never had for me. There is no poetry, no exaggeration in all this. It is the bare truth and every disciple of his knows it. In times of great danger, great temptation, I have wept in extreme agony with the prayer, "O God, do save me," and no response has come from anybody, but this wonderful saint, or Avatara, or anything else he may be, has come to know of all my affliction through his powers of insight into human hearts and has lifted it off—in spite of my desire to the contrary—after getting me brought to his presence. If the soul be deathless and so if he still lives, I pray to him again and again, "O Bhagavân Ramakrishna, thou infinite ocean of mercy and my only refuge, do graciously fulfil the desires of my esteemed friend, who is every inch a great man." May he impart to you all good, he whom alone I have found in this world to be like an ocean of unconditioned mercy! Shantih, Shantih, Shantih.

Please send a prompt reply—Yours etc., VIVEKANANDA.

[1] Patanjali's aphorism has "Ishvara" in place of "saint." Narada has an aphorism which runs thus : Bhakti (Supreme Love) is attainable chiefly through the grace of a saint or by a bit of Divine Grace. The passage at any rate gives Swamiji's views on the question, which are borne out by the purport of Narada and Patanjali.

(33)

To The Same

GHAZIPUR,*
8th March, 1890.

DEAR SIR—Your note duly reached me, and so I too shall be off to Prayâg. Please write to inform where you mean to put up while there.—Yours, VIVEKANANDA.

P.S. In case Abhedananda reaches your place in a day or two, I shall be much obliged if you help him to start for Calcutta.—V.

(34)

To Sj. Balaram Bose

GHAZIPUR,*
15th March, 1890.

REVERED SIR—Received your kind note yesterday. I am very sorry to learn that Suresh Babu's illness is extremely serious. What is destined to come will transpire. It is a matter of great regret that you too have fallen ill. So long as egoism lasts, any shortcoming in adopting remedial measures is to be considered as idleness—it is a fault and a guilt. For one who has not that egoistic idea, the best course is to forbear. The dwelling-place of the Jivatman, this body, is a veritable means of work, and he who converts this into an infernal den is guilty, and he who neglects it is also to blame. Please act according to circumstances as they present themselves, without the least hesitation.

नाभिनन्देत मरणं नाभिनन्देत जीवितम्।
कालमेव प्रतीक्षेत नियमं भृतको यथा॥

—"The highest duty consists in doing the little that lies in one's power, seeking neither death nor life, and biding one's time like a servant ready to do any behest."

There is a dreadful outbreak of influenza at Benares and Pramada Babu has gone to Allahabad. Baburam has suddenly come here. He has got fever; he was wrong to start under such circumstances. . . . I am leaving this place to-morrow. . . . My countless salutations to Mother. You all bless me that I may have sameness of vision, that avoiding the bondages which one is heir to by one's very birth, I may not again get stuck in self-imposed bondages. If there be any Doer of good and if He have the power and the opportunity, may He vouchsafe the highest blessings unto you all—this is my constant prayer.—Yours affectionately, VIVEKANANDA.

(35)

To Sj. Atul Chandra Ghose

GHAZIPUR,*
15th March, 1890.

DEAR Atul Babu—I am extremely sorry to hear that you are passing through mental afflictions. Please do only what is agreeable to you.

यावज्जननं तावन्मरणं
तावज्जननीजठरे शयनम् ।
इति संसारे स्फुटतरदोषः
कथमिह मानव तव सन्तोषः ॥

—"While there is birth there is death, and again entering the mother's womb. This is the manifest evil of transmigration. How, O man, dost thou want satisfaction in such a world?"—Yours affectionately, VIVEKANANDA.

P.S. I am leaving this place to-morrow. Let me see which way destiny leads!

(36)

To Swami Akhandananda

GHAZIPUR,*
March, 1890.

BELOVED AKHANDANANDA—Received another letter of yours just now and with great difficulty deciphered the scribblings. I have written everything in detail in my last letter. You start immediately on receipt of this. I know the route to Thibet via Nepal that you have spoken of. As they don't allow anyone to enter Thibet easily, so they don't allow anybody to go anywhere in Nepal, except Katmandu, its capital, and one or two places of pilgrimage. But a friend of mine is now a tutor to His Highness the Maharaja of Nepal, and a teacher in his school, from whom I have it that when the Nepal Government send their subsidy to China, they send it via Lhassa. A Sadhu contrived in that way to go to Lhassa, China, Manchuria, and even to the *Pitha* (holy seat) of Târâ Devi, in North China. We, too, can visit with dignity and respect Thibet, China, Lhassa, and all, if that friend of mine tries to arrange it. You therefore start immediately for Ghazipur. After a few days' stay here with the Babaji, I shall correspond with my friend, and everything arranged, I shall certainly go to Thibet via Nepal.

You have to get down at Dildarnagar to come to Ghazipur. It is three or four stations from Moghul Sarai. I would have sent you the passage if I could collect it here; so you get it together and come. Gagan Babu—with whom I am putting up—is an exceedingly courteous, noble and generous-minded man. No sooner did he come to know of Kali's illness than he sent him the passage at Hrishikesh; he has besides spent much on my account. Under the circumstances it would be violating a Sannyasin's duty to tax him for the passage to Kashmir, and I desist from it.

You collect the fare and start as soon as you receive this letter. Let the craze for visiting Amarnath be put back for the present.—Yours affectionately, VIVEKANANDA.

(37)

To Sj. Pramada Das Mitra

GHAZIPUR,*
31st March, 1890.

DEAR SIR—I haven't been here for the last few days and am again going away to-day. I have asked brother Gangadhar to come here, and if he comes, we go over to you together. For some special reasons, I shall continue to stay in secret in a village some distance off this place, and there's no facility for writing any letter from that place, owing to which I could not reply to your letter so long. Brother Gangadhar is very likely to come, otherwise the reply to my note would have reached me. Brother Abhedananda is putting up with Doctor Priya at Benares. Another brother of mine was with me, but has left for Abhedananda's place. The news of his arrival is not yet received and his health being bad, I am very anxious for his sake. I have behaved very cruelly towards him—that is, I have harassed him much to make him leave my company. There's no help, you see; I am so very weak-hearted, so much overmastered by the distractions of love! Bless me that I may harden. What shall I say to you about the condition of my mind! Oh, it is as if the hell-fire was burning there day and night! Nothing, nothing could I do yet! And this life seems muddled away in vain; I feel quite helpless as to what to do! The Babaji throws out honeyed words and keeps me from leaving. Ah, what shall I say? I am committing hundreds of offences against you—please excuse them as so many mis-doings of a man driven mad with mental agonies.

Abhedananda is suffering from dysentery. I shall be very much obliged if you kindly enquire of his condition and send him down to our Math in case he wants to go there with our brother who has reached from here. My Gurubhais must be thinking me very cruel and selfish. Oh, what can I do? Who will see deep down into my mind? Who will know how much I am suffering day and night? Bless me that I may have the most unflinching patience and perseverance. With countless greetings,—Yours etc., VIVEKANANDA.

P.S. Abhedananda is staying in Doctor Priya's house at Sonarpura. My lumbago is as before.—V.

(38)

To Swami Abhedananda

GHAZIPUR,*
2nd April, 1890.

MY DEAR Kali—Glad to receive your letter as well as Pramada Babu's and Baburam's. I am doing pretty well here. You have expressed a desire to see me. I too have a similar longing, and it is this that makes me afraid of going. Moreover, the Babaji forbids me to do so. I shall try to go on a few days' leave from him. But there is this fear that by so doing I shall be drawn up to the hills by the attraction I have for Hrishikesh, and it will be very difficult to shake it off, specially for one weak-minded, you see, like myself. The attack of lumbago, too, will not leave me on any account—a botheration! But then I am getting used to it. Please convey my countless salutations to Pramada Babu; his is a friendship which greatly benefits both my mind and body. And I am particularly indebted to him. Things will turn up some way, anyhow. With best wishes.—Yours affectionately. VIVEKANANDA.

(39)

To Sj. Pramada Das Mitra

GHAZIPUR
April, 1890.

DEAR SIR—Where shall I get that renunciation you speak of in your advice to me? It's for the sake of that very thing that I am out a tramp through the earth. If ever I get this true renunciation, I shall let you know; and if you get anything of the kind, please remember me as a partner thereof.—Yours, VIVEKANANDA.

(40)

To The Same

BARANAGORE,*
10th May, 1890.

DEAR SIR—I could not write to you because of various distractions and a relapse into fever. Glad to learn from Abhedananda's letter that you are doing well. Gangadhar has probably arrived at Benares by this time. Death happens here to be casting into his jaws these days many of our friends and own people, hence I am very much taken up. Perhaps no letter for me has come there from Nepal I know not how and when Vishwanatha (the Lord of Kashi) would choose to vouchsafe some rest to me. Directly the hot weather relaxes a little I am off from this place, but I am still at a loss where to go. Do please pray for me to Vishwanatha that He may grant me strength. You are a devotee, and I beseech you with the Lord's words coming to my mind, "Those who are the devoted ones to My devotees, they are indeed considered the best of My devotees.' --Yours etc., VIVEKANANDA.

(41)

To The Same

57, Ramkanta Bose's Street,*
Baghbazar, Calcutta,
26th May, 1890.

Dear Sir—I write this to you while caught in a vortex of many untoward circumstances and great agitatione of mind; with a prayer to Vishwanatha, please think of the propriety and possibility, or otherwise, of all that I set forth below and then oblige me greatly by a reply.

1. I have already told you at the outset that I am Ramakrishna's slave, having laid my body at his feet "with *til* and *tulsi* leaves." I cannot disregard his behest. If it is in failure that that great sage laid down his life after having attained to superhuman heights of Jnana, Bhakti. Love and powers and after having practised for forty years stern renunciation, non-attachment, holiness and great austerities, then where is there anything for us to count on? So I am obliged to trust his words as the words of one identified with Truth.

2. Now his behest to me was that I should devote myself to the service of the order of all-renouncing devotees founded by him, and in this I have to persevere, come what may, being ready to take heaven, hell, salvation or anything that may happen to me.

3. His command was that his all-renouncing devotees should group themselves together and I am entrusted with seeing to this. Of course, it matters not if any one of us goes out on visits to this place or that, but these shall be but visit, while his own opinion was that absolute homeless wandering, suited him alone who was perfected to the highest point. Before that state, it is proper to settle somewhere to dive down into practice. When all the ideas of

body and the like are dissolved of themselves, a person may then pursue whatever state comes to him. Otherwise, it is baneful for a practising aspirant to be always wandering.

4. So in pursuance of this his commandment, his group of Sannyasins are now assembled in a dilapidated house at Baranagore, and two of his lay disciples, Babu Suresh Chandra Mitra and Babu Balaram Bose, so long provided for their food and house-rent.

5. For various reasons, the body of Bhagavan Ramakrishna had to be consigned to fire. There is no doubt that this act was very blamable. His ashes have been preserved, and if they be now properly enshrined somewhere on the banks of the Ganges, I presume we shall be able in some measure to expiate the sin lying on our head. These sacred remains, his seat and his picture are every day worshipped in our Math in proper form, and it is known to you that a brother-disciple of mine, of Brahmin parentage, is occupied day and night with the task. The expenses of the worship used also to be borne by the two great souls mentioned above.

6. What greater regret can there be than this that no memorial could yet be raised in this land of Bengal in the neighbourhood of the place where he lived his life of Sadhana—he by whose birth the race of Bengalees has been sanctified, the land of Bengal has become hallowed, he who came on earth to save the Indians from the spell of the worldly gamour of Western culture and who theerfore chose most of his all-renouncing disciples from university men?

7. The two gentlemen mentioned above had a strong desire to have some land purchased on the banks of the Ganges and see the sacred remains enshrined on it with the disciples living there together; and Suresh Babu had offered a sum of Rs. 1,000 for the purpose, promising to give more,

but for some inscrutable purpose of God he left this world yesternight! And the news of Balaram Babu's death is already known to you.

8. Now there is no knowing as to where his disciples would stand with his sacred remains and his seat (and you know well, people here in Bengal are profuse in their professions, but do not stir out an inch in practice). The disciples are Sannyasins and are ready forthwith to depart anywhere their way may lie. But I, their servant, am in agony, and my heart is breaking to think that a small piece of land could not be had in which to install the remains of Bhagavan Ramakrishna.

9. It is impossible with a sum of Rs. 1,000 to secure a land and raise a temple near Calcutta. Some such land would at least cost about five to seven thousands.

10. You remain now the only friend and patron of Sri Ramakrishna's disciples. In the North-Western Province, great indeed is your fame, your position and your circle of acquaintance. I request you to consider, if you feel like it, the propriety of your getting the affair through by raising subscriptions from well-to-do pious men known to you in your province. If you deem it proper to have some shelter erected on the banks of the Ganges in Bengal for Bhagavan Ramakrishna's sacred remains and for his disciples, I shall with your leave report myself to you and I have not the slightest qualm to beg from door to door for this noble cause, for the sake of my Lord and his children. Please give this proposal your best thoughts with prayers to Vishwanatha. To my mind, if all these sincere, educated youthful Sannyasins of good birth fail to live up to the ideals of Sri Ramakrishna owing to want of an abode and help, then alas for our country!

11. If you ask, "You are a Sannyasin, so why do you trouble over these desires?" I would then reply, I am Ramakrishna's servant and I am willing even to steal and

rob, if by doing so I can perpetuate his name on the land of his birth and Sadhana and help even a little his disciples to practise his great ideals. I know you to be my closest in kinship and I lay my mind bare to you. I have returned to Calcutta for this reason. I had told you this before I left, and now I leave it to you to do what you think best.

12. If you argue that it is better to have the thing done in some place like Kashi, my point is, as I have told you, it would be the greatest pity if the memorial shrine could not be raised on the land of his birth and Sadhana! The condition of Bengal is pitiable. The people here cannot even dream what renunciation truly means—luxury and sensuality have been so much eating into the vitals of the race. May God send renunciation and unworldliness into this land! They have here nothing to speak of, while the people of the North-Western Province, specially the rich there, as I believe, have great zeal in noble causes like this. Please send me some reply you think best. Gangadhar has not reached to-day yet, and may do so to-morrow. I am so keen on seeing him again.

Please write to the address given above.—Yours etc.,
VIVEKANANDA.

(42)

To Swami Saradananda

BAGHBAZAR, CALCUTTA,
6th July, 1890.

DEAR Sarat and Kripananda,—Your letters have duly reached us. They say Almora is healtiest at this time of the year, yet you are taken ill! I hope it is nothing malarious. . . .

I find Gangadhar the same pliant child with his turbulence moderated by his wanderings, and with a greater love for us and for our Lord. He is bold, brave, sincere, and steadfast. The only thing needed is a guiding mind to which he would instinctively submit with reverence, and a fine man would be the result.

I had no wish to leave Ghazipur this time, and certainly not to come to Calcutta, but Kali's illness made me go to Benares and Balaram's sudden death brought me to Calcutta. So Suresh Babu and Balaram Babu have both gone! G. C. Ghose is supporting the Math. . . . I intend shortly, as soon as I can get my fare, to go up to Almora and thence to some place in Gharwal on the Ganges where I can settle down for a long meditation. Gangadhar is accompanying me. Indeed it was with this desire and intention that I brought him down from Kashmir.

I don't think you ought to be in any hurry about coming down to Calcutta. You have done with roving; that's good, but you have not yet attempted the one thing you should do, that is, be resolved to sit down and meditate. I don't think Jnana is like rousing a maiden suddenly from sleep by saying, "Get up, dear girl, your marriage ceremony is waiting for you!" as we say. I am strongly of opinion that very few persons in any Yuga attain Jnana, and therefore we should go on striving and striving even unto death. That's my old-fashioned way, you know. About the humbug of modern *Sannyasi* Jnana I know too well. Peace be unto you and strength! Daksha who is staying at Brindaban with Rakhal, has learnt to make gold and has become a *pucca* Jnani, so writes Rakhal. God bless him and you may say, amen!

I am in fine health now, and the good I gained by my stay in Ghazipur will last, I am sure, for some time. I am longing for a flight to the Himalayas. This time I shall not go to Pavhari Baba or any other saint—they divert one from one's highest purpose. Straight up!

How do you find the climate at Almora? Neither of

you need come down. What is the use of so many living together in one place and doing no good to one's soul? Don't be fools always wandering from place to place—that's all very good—but be heroes.

निर्मानमोहा जितसंगदोषा
अध्यात्मनित्या विनिवृत्तकामाः।
द्वंद्वैर्विमुक्ताः सुखदुःखसंज्ञै-
र्गच्छन्त्यमूढाः पदमव्ययं तत्॥

(Gita, XV. 5.)

"Free from pride and delusion, with the evil of attachment conquered, ever dwelling in the Self, with desires completely receded, liberated from the pairs of opposites known as pleasure and pain, the undeluded reach that Goal Eternal."

Who advises you to jump into fire? If you don't find the Himalayas a place for Sadhana, go somewhere else then.

So many gushing inquiries simply betray a weak mind. Arise, ye mighty one, and be strong! Work on and on, struggle on and on! Nothing more to write.—Yours affectionately, VIVEKANANDA.

(43)

To Lala Govinda Sahay

AJMERE,
14th April, 1891.

DEAR Govinda Sahay—. . . . Try to be pure and unselfish—that is the whole of religion. . . . —Yours with love, VIVEKANANDA.

(44)

To The Same

ABU,
30th April, 1891.

DEAR Govinda Sahay—Have you done the Upanayana of that Brahmin boy? Are you studying Sanskrit? How far have you advanced? I think you must have finished the first part. . . . Are you diligent in your Shiva Puja? If not, try to be so. "Seek ye first the kingdom of God and all good things will be added unto you." Follow God and you shall have whatever you desire. . . . To the two Commander Sahebs my best regards; they being men of high position were very kind to a poor Fakir like me. My children, the secret of religion lies not in theories but in practice. To be good and to do good—that is the whole of religion. "Not he that crieth 'Lord,' 'Lord,' but he that doeth the will of the Father." You are a nice band of young men, you Alwaris, and I hope in no distant future many of you will be ornaments of the society and blessings to the country you are born in.—Yours with blessings, VIVEKANANDA.

P. S. Don't be ruffled if now and then you get a brush from the world; it will be over in no time, and everything will be all right.

(45)

To The Same

MOUNT ABU,
1891.

DEAR Govinda Sahay—You must go on with your Japam whatever direction the mind takes. Tell Harbux that he is to begin with the Prânâyâma in the following way. . . . .

Try hard with your Sanskrit studies.—Yours with love, VIVEKANANDA.

(46)

To Pandit Shankarlal

BOMBAY,
20th September, 1892.

DEAR PANDITJI MAHARAJ—Your letter has reached me duly. I do not know why I should be undeservingly praised. "None is good, save One, that is, God," as the Lord Jesus hath said. The rest are only tools in His hands. "Gloria in Excelsis," "Glory unto God in the highest," and unto men that deserve, but not to such an undeserving one like me. Here, "The servant is *not* worthy of the hire," and a Fakir, especially, has no right to any praise whatsoever, for, would you praise your servant for simply doing his duty?

. . . My unbounded gratitude to Pandit Sundarlalji, and to my Professor[1] for this kind remembrance of me.

Now I would tell you something else. The Hindu mind was ever deductive and never synthetic or inductive. In all our philosophies, we always find hair-splitting arguments, taking for granted some general proposition, but the proposition itself may be as childish as possible. Nobody ever asked or searched the truth of these general propositions. Therefore, independent thought we have almost none to speak of, and hence the dearth of those sciences which are the results of observation and generalisation. And why was it thus?—From two causes;—the tremendous heat of the climate forcing us to love rest

[1] Swamiji used to call him 'Professor,' for he read Patanjali's Mahâ-Bhâshya of Pânini with him.

and contemplation better than activity, and the Brahmins as priests never undertaking journeys or voyages to distant lands. There were voyagers and people who travelled far; but they were almost always traders, i.e., people from whom priestcraft, and their own sole love for gain, had taken away all capacity for intellectual development. So their observations, instead of adding to the store of human knowledge, rather degenerated it. For their observations were bad, and their accounts exaggerated and tortured into fantastical shapes, until they passed all recognition.

So you see, we must travel, we must go to foreign parts. We must see how the engine of society works in other countries, and keep free and open communication with what is going on in the minds of other nations, if we really want to be a nation again. And over and above all, we must cease to tyrannise. To what a ludicrous state are we brought! If a Bhângi comes to anybody, as a Bhângi, he would be shunned as the plague; but no sooner does he get a cupful of water poured upon his head with some mutterings of prayers by a Pâdri, and get a coat to his back, no matter how threadbare, and come into the room of the most orthodox Hindu—I don't see the man who then dares refuse him a chair and a hearty shake of the hands!! Irony can go no farther. And come and see what they, the Padris, are doing here in the Dakshin (Deccan). They are converting the lower classes by lakhs; and in Travancore, the most priest-ridden country in India—where every bit of land is owned by the Brahmins, and where the females, even of the *royal family*, hold it as high honour to live in concubinage with the Brahmins—nearly one-fourth has become Christian! And I cannot blame them; what part have they in David and what in Jesse? When, when, O Lord, shall man be brother to man?—Yours etc., VIVEKANANDA.

(47)

To Śj. Alasinga Perumal

HYDERABAD,
21st Feb., 1893.

DEAR Alasinga—Your friend, the young graduate, came to receive me at the station, so also a Bengali gentleman. At present I am living with the Bengali gentleman; to-morrow I go to live with your young friend for a few days, and then I see the different sights here, and in a few days you may expect me at Madras. For I am very sorry to tell you that I cannot go back at present to Rajputana. It is so very dreadfully hot here already. I do not know how hot it would be at Rajputana and I cannot bear heat at all. So the next thing I would do would be to go back to Bangalore and then to Ootacamund to pass the summer there. My brain boils in heat.

So all my plans have been dashed to the ground. That is why I wanted to hurry off from Madras early. In that case I would have left months in my hands to seek out for somebody amongst our northern princes to send me over to America. But alas, it is now too late. First, I cannot wander about in this heat—I would die. Secondly, my fast friends in Rajputana would keep me bound down to their sides if they get hold of me and would not let me go over to Europe. So my plan was to get hold of some new person without my friends' knowledge. But this delay at Madras has dashed all my hopes to the ground, and with a deep sigh I give it up and the Lord's will be done! However, you may be almost sure that I shall see you in a few days for a day or two in Madras and then go to Bangalore and thence to Ootacamund to see "if" the M— Maharaja sends me up. "If"—because you see I cannot be sure of any promise of a D— Raja. They are not Rajputs. A Rajput would rather die than break his promise. However, man learns as he lives and experience is the greatest teacher in the world.

"Thy will be done on earth as it is in heaven, for Thine is the glory and the kingdom for ever and ever." My compliments to you all.—Yours etc., SACCHIDANANDA.[1]

(48)

To Dr. Nanjunda Rao, M.D.

KHETRI,
27th April, 1893.

DEAR DOCTOR—Your letter has just reached me. I am very much gratified by your love for my unworthy self. So, so sorry to learn, that poor Balaji has lost his son. "The Lord gave and the Lord hath taken away; blessed be the name of the Lord." We only know that nothing is lost or can be lost. For us is only submission, calm and perfect. The soldier has no right to complain, nay murmur, if the general orders him into the cannon's mouth. May He comfort Balaji in his grief, and may it draw him closer and closer to the breast of the All-merciful Mother!

As to my taking ship I have already made arrangements from Bombay. Tell Mr. Bhattacharya that the Raja[2] or my Gurubhais would be the last men to put any obstacles in my way. As for the Rajaji, his love for me is simply without limit.

May the Giver of all good bless you all here and hereafter, will be the constant prayer of—VIVEKANANDA.

[1] Swamiji used to call himself such in those days.
[2] The Maharaja of Khetri, Rajputana.

(49)

To Sj. Haridas Viharidas Desai

BOMBAY,
22nd May, 1893.

DIWANJI SAHEB—Reached Bombay a few days ago and would start off in a few days. Your friend, the Banya gentleman to whom you wrote for the house accommodation, writes to say that his house is already full of guests and some of them are ill and that he is very sorry he cannot accommodate me. After all we have got a nice, airy place.

. . . The Private Secretary to H. H. of Khetri and I are now residing together. I cannot express my gratitude to him for his love and kindness to me. He is what they call a Tazimi Sardar in Rajputana, i.e., one of those whom the Rajas rise and receive. Still he is so simple and his service sometimes for me makes me almost ashamed.

. . . Often and often, we see that the very best of men even are troubled and visited with tribulations in this world; it may be inexplicable, but it is also the experience of my life that the heart and core of everything here is good, that whatever may be the surface waves, deep down and underlying everything there is an infinite basis of goodness and love; and so long we do not reach that basis we are troubled but once reached that zone of calmness, let winds howl and tempests rage, the house which is built on a rock of ages cannot shake.

I thoroughly believe that a good, unselfish and holy man like you, whose whole life has been devoted to doing good to others, has already reached this basis of firmness which the Lord Himself has styled as "rest upon Brahma" in the Gita.

May the blows you have received draw thee closer to that Being who is the only one to be loved here and hereafter, so that you may realise Him in everything past, present and future, and find everything present or lost in Him and Him alone. Amen.—Yours affectionately, VIVEKANANDA.

(50)

To Srimati Indumati Mitra

BOMBAY,*
24th May, 1893.

DEAR MOTHER—Very glad to receive your letter and that of dear Haripada. Please be not sorry that I could not write to you very often. I am always praying to the Lord for your welfare. I cannot go to Belgaum now as arrangements are all ready for my starting for America on the 31st next. The Lord willing, I shall see you on returning from my travels in America and Europe. Always resign yourselves to Lord Sri Krishna. Always remember that we are but puppets in the Lord's hands. Remain pure always. Please take care not to become impure even in thought, as in speech and action; always try to do good to others as far as in you lies. And remember that the paramount duty of a woman is to serve her husband by thought, word and deed. Please read the Gita every day to the best of your opportunity. Why have you signed yourself as Indumati *Dasi*? The Vaishya and the Shudra should sign as *Dâsa* and *Dâsi*, but the Brahmin and Kshatriya should write *Deva* and *Devi*. Moreover, these distinctions of caste and the like have been the invention of our modern sapient Brahmins. Who is a servant and to whom? Everyone is a servant of the Lord Hari. Hence a woman should use her patronymic, that is, the surname of her husband. This is the ancient Vedic custom, as for example, such and such *Mitra* or the like. It is needless to write much, dear mother; always know that I am constantly praying for your well-being. From America I shall now and then write to you letters with descriptions of the wonderful things there. I am now at Bombay, and shall stay here up to the 31st. The Private Secretary to the Maharaja of Khetri has come here to see me off. With blessings,—Yours sincerely, VIVEKANANDA.

(*51*)

To Sj. Alasinga Perumal

YOKOHAMA,
10th July, 1893.

DEAR Alasinga, Balaji, G. G., . . . and all my Madras friends—Excuse my not keeping you constantly informed of my movements. One is so busy every day, and specially myself who am quite new to the life of possessing things and taking care of them. That consumes so much of my energy. It is really an awful botheration.

From Bombay we reached Colombo. Our steamer remained in port for nearly the whole day, and we took the opportunity of getting off to have a look at the town. We drove through the streets, and the only thing I remember, was a temple in which was a very gigantic Murti of the Lord Buddha in a reclining posture entering Nirvana. . . .

The next station was Penang, which is only a strip of land along the sea in the body of the Malay Peninsula. The Malays are all Mohammedans, and in old days were noted pirates and quite a dread to merchantmen. But now the leviathan guns of modern turreted battleships have forced the Malays to look about for more peaceful pursuits. On our way from Penang to Singapore, we had glimpses of Sumatra with its high mountains, and the Captain pointed out to me several places as the favourite haunts of pirates in days gone by. Singapore is the capital of the Straits Settlements. It has a fine botanical garden with the most splendid collection of palms. The beautiful fan-like palm called the traveller's paom grows here in abundance, and the bread-fruit tree everywhere. The celebrated mangosteen is as plentiful here as mangoes in Madras, but mango is nonpareil. The people here are not half so dark as the people of Madras, although so near the line. Singapore possesses a fine museum too.

Hongkong next. You feel that you have reached China, the Chinese element predominates so much. All labour, all trade seems to be in their hands. And Hongkong is real China. As soon as the steamer casts anchor, you are besieged with hundreds of Chinese boats to carry you to the land. These boats with two helms are rather peculiar. The boatman lives in the boat with his family. Almost always, the wife is at the helms, managing one with her hands and the other with one of her feet. And in ninety per cent cases, you find a baby tied to her back, with the hands and feet of the little Chin left free. It is a quaint sight to see the little John Chinaman dangling very quietly from his mother's back, whilst she is now setting with might and main, now pushing heavy loads, or jumping with wonderful agility from boat to boat. And there is such a rush of boats and steam launches coming in and going out! Baby John is every moment put into the risk of having his little head pulverised, pigtail and all; but he does not care a fig. This busy life seems to have no charm for him, and he is quite content to learn the anatomy of a bit of rice-cake given to him from time to time by the madly busy mother. The Chinese child is quite a philosopher and calmly goes to work at an age when your Indian boy can hardly crawl on all fours. He has learned the philosophy of necessity too well. Their extreme poverty is one of the causes why the Chinese and the Indians have remained in a state mummified civilisation. To an ordinary Hindu or Chinese, everyday necessity is too hideous to allow him to think of anything else.

Hongkong is a very beautiful town. It is built on the slopes of hills and on the tops too, which are much cooler than the city. There is an almost perpendicular tramway going to the top of the hill, dragged by wire rope and steam power.

We remained three days at Hongkong and went to see Canton, which is eighty miles up a river. What a scene of bustle and life! What an immense number of boats almost covering the waters! And not only those that are carrying on the trade, but hundreds of others which serve as houses to live in. And quite a lot of them, so nice and big. In fact they are big houses two or three stories high, with verandahs running round, and streets between, and all floating!

We landed on a strip of ground given by the Chinese Government to foreigners to live in. Around us on both sides of the river for miles and miles is the big city—a wilderness of human beings, pushing, struggling, surging, roaring. But with all its population, all its activity, it is the dirtiest town I saw, not in the sense in which a town is called dirty in India, for as to that not a speck of filth is allowed by the Chinese to go waste; but because of the Chinaman, who has, it seems, taken a vow never to bathe! Every house is a shop, people living only on the top floor. The streets are very very narrow, so that you almost touch the shops on both sides as you pass. At every ten paces you find meat stalls, and there are shops which sell cat's and dog's meat. Of course only the poorest classes of Chinamen eat dog or cat.

The Chinese lady can never be seen. They have got as strict a Zenana as the Hindus of Northern India; only the women of the labouring classes can be seen. Even amongst these, one sees now and then a woman with feet smaller than those of your youngest child, and of course they cannot be said to walk, but hobble.

I went to see several Chinese temples. The biggest in Canton is dedicated to the memory of the first Buddhistic Emperor and the five hundred first disciples of Buddhism. The central figure is of course Buddha, and next beneath him is seated the Emperor, and ranging on both sides are the statues of the disciples, all beautifully carved out of wood.

From Canton back to Hongkong, and from thence to Japan. The first port we touched was Nagasaki. We landed for a few hours and drove through the town. What a contrast! The Japanese are one of the cleanliest peoples on earth. Everything is neat and tidy. Their streets are nearly all broad, straight and regularly paved. Their little houses are cage-like and their pine-covered evergreen little hills form the background of almost every town and village. The short-statured, fair-skinned, quaintly-dressed Japs, their movements, attitudes, gestures, everything is picturesque. Japan is the land of the picturesque! Almost every house has a garden at the back, very nicely laid out according to Japanese fashion with small shrubs, grass-plots, small artificial waters and small stone bridges.

From Nagasaki to Cobe. Here I gave up the steamer and took the land route to Yokohama, with a view to see the interior of Japan.

I have seen three big cities in the interior, Osaka, a great manufacturing town, Kioto, the former capital, and Tokio, the present capital. Tokio is nearly twice the size of Calcutta with nearly double the population.

No foreigner is allowed to travel in the interior without a passport.

The Japanese seem now to have fully awakened themselves to the necessity of the present times. They have now a thoroughly organised army equipped with guns, which one of their own officers has invented, and which is said to be second to none. Then they are continually increasing their navy. I have seen a tunnel nearly a mile long bored by a Japanese engineer.

The match factories are simply a sight to see, and they are bent upon making everything they want in their own country. There is a Japanese line of steamers plying between China and Japan, which shortly intends running between Bombay and Yokohama.

I saw quite a lot of temples. In every temple there are some Sanskrit Mantras written in old Bengali characters. Only a few of the priests know Sanskrit. But they are an intelligent sect. The modern rage for progress has penetrated even the priesthood. I cannot write what I have in my mind about the Japs in one short letter. Only I want that numbers of our young men should pay a visit to Japan every year. To the Japanese, India is still the dreamland of everything high and good. And you, what are you? . . . talking twaddle all your lives, vain talkers, what are you? Come, see these people and then go and hide your faces in shame. A race of dotards, you lose your caste if you come out! Sitting down these hundreds of years with an ever-increasing load of crystallised superstition on your heads, for hundreds of years spending all your energy upon discussing the touchableness or untouchableness of this food or that, with all humanity crushed out of you by the continuous social tyranny of ages—what are you? And what are you doing now? . . . promenading the sea-shores with books in your hands—repeating undigested stray bits of European brain-work, and the whole soul bent upon getting a thirty rupees clerkship or at best becoming a lawyer—the height of young India's ambition—and every student with a whole brood of hungry children cackling at his heels and asking for bread! Is there not water enough in the sea to drown you, books, gowns, university diplomas, and all?

Come, be men! Kick out the priests who are always against progress. Because they would never mend; their hearts would never become big. They are the offspring of centuries of superstition and tyranny. Root out priest-craft first. Come, be men. Come out of your narrow holes and have a look abroad. See how nations are on the march. Do you love man? Do you love your country? Then come, let us struggle for higher and better things, look not back, no, not even if you see the dearest and nearest cry. Look not back, but forward!

India wants the sacrifice of at least a thousand of her young men—men, mind, and not brutes. The English Government has been the instrument brought over here by the Lord, to break your crystallised civilisation, and Madras supplied the first men who helped in giving the English a footing. How many men, unselfish, thorough-going men, is Madras ready now to supply, to struggle unto life and death to bring about a new state of things—sympathy for the poor—and bread to their hungry mouths—enlightenment to the people at large—and struggle unto death to make men of them who have been brought to the level of beasts, by the tyranny of your forefathers?—Yours etc., VIVEKANANDA.

P. S. Calm and silent and steady work, and no newspaper humbug, no name-making, you must always remember.

—V.

(52)

To The Same

Breezy Meadows,
Metcalf, Mass.,
20th August, 1893.

Dear Alasinga—Received your letter yesterday. Perhaps you have by this time got my letter from Japan. From Japan I reached Vancouver. The way was by the Northern Pacific. It was very cold and I suffered much for want of warm clothing. However, I reached Vancouver anyhow, and thence went through Canada to Chicago. I remained about twelve days in Chicago. And almost every day I used to go to the Fair. It is a tremendous affair. One must take at least ten days to go through it. The lady to whom Varada Rao introduced me, and her husband, belong to the highest Chicago society, and they were so very kind to me. I took my departure from Chicago and came to Boston. Mr. Lulloobhoy was with me up to Boston. He was very kind to me.

The expense I am bound to run into here is awful. . . . On an average it costs me £1 every day; a cigar costs eight annas of our money. The Americans are so rich that they spend money like water, and by forced legislation keep up the price of everything so high that no other nation on earth can approach it. Every common coolie earns nine or ten rupees a day, and spends it. All those rosy ideas we had before starting have melted, and I have now to fight against impossibilities. A hundred times I had a mind to go out of the country and go back to India. But I am determined and I have a call from above; I see no way, but His eyes see. And I must stick to my guns, life or death. . . .

Just now I am living as the guest of an old lady in a village near Boston. I accidentally made her acquaintance in the railway train, and she invited me to come over and live with her. I have an advantage in living with her, in saving for some time my expenditure of £1 per day, and she has the advantage of inviting her friends over here, and showing them a curio from India! And all this must be borne. Starvation, cold, hooting in the streets on account of my quaint dress, these are what I have to fight against. But, my dear boy, no great things were ever done without great labour.

. . . Know then that this is the land of Christians, and any other influence than that is almost zero. Nor do I care a bit for the enmity of any 'ists' in the world. I am here amongst the children of the son of Mary, and the Lord Jesus will help me. They like much the broad views of Hinduism and my love for the prophet of Nazareth. I tell them that I preach nothing against the great One of Galilee. I only ask the Christians to take in the great Ones of Ind along with the Lord Jesus, and they appreciate it.

Winter is approaching and I shall have to get all sorts of warm clothing, and we require more warm clothing than the natives. . . . Look sharp, my boy, take courage. We are destined by the Lord to do great things in India. Have faith. We will do. We the poor and the despised who really feel, and not those . . . .

In Chicago, the other day a funny thing happened. The Raja of Kapurthala was here and he was being lionised by some portion of Chicago society. I once met the Raja in the Fair grounds, but he was too big to speak with a poor Fakir. There was an eccentric Mahratta Brahmin selling nail-made pictures in the Fair, dressed in a *dhoti*. This fellow told the reporters all sorts of things against the Raja—that he was a man of low caste, that those Rajas were nothing but slaves, and that they generally led immoral lives, etc., etc. And these truthful (?) editors for which America is famous, wanted to give to the boy's stories some weight; and so the next day they wrote huge columns in the papers about the description of a man of wisdom from India, meaning me —extolling me to the skies, and putting all sorts of words in my mouth, which I never even dreamt of, and ascribing to me all those remarks made by the Mahratta Brahmin about the Raja of Kapurthala. And it was such a good brushing that Chicago society gave up the Raja in hot haste. . . . . The newspaper editors made capital out of me to give my countryman a brushing. That shows also that in this country intellect carries more weight than all the pomp of money and title.

Yesterday, Mrs. Johnson, the lady superintendent of the women's prison, was here. They don't call it prison but reformatory here. It is the grandest thing I have seen in America. How the inmates are benevolently treated, how they are reformed and sent back as useful members of society; how grand, how beautiful, you must see to believe! And, oh, how my heart ached to think of what we think of the poor, the low in India. They have no chance, no escape, no way to climb up. The poor, the low, the sinner in India have no friends, no help—they cannot rise, try however they may. They sink lower and lower every day, they feel the blows showering upon them by a cruel society, and they do not know whence the blow comes. They have forgotten that they too are men. And the result is slavery. Thoughtful people within the last few years have seen it, but unfortunately laid it at the door of the Hindu religion, and to them the only way of bettering is by crushing this grandest religion of the world. Hear me, my friend, I have discovered the secret through the grace of the Lord. Religion is not at fault. On the other hand, your religion teaches you that every being is only your own self multiplied. But it was the want of practical application, the want of sympathy—the want of heart. The Lord once more came to you as Buddha and taught you how to feel, how to sympathise with the poor, the miserable, the sinner, but you heard him not. Your priests invented the horrible story that the Lord was here for deluding demons with false doctrines! True, indeed, but we are the demons, not those that believed. And just as the Jews denied the Lord Jesus and are since that day wandering over the world as homeless beggars, tyrannised over by everybody, so you are bond-slaves to any nation that thinks it worth while to rule over you. Ah, tyrants! you do not know that the obverse is tyranny and the reverse slavery. The slave and the tyrant are synonymous.

Balaji and G. G. may remember, one evening at Pondicherry, we were discussing the matter of sea-voyage with a Pandit, and I shall always remember his brutal gestures and his *Kadâpi na* (never)! They do not know that India is a very small part of the world, and the whole world looks down with contempt upon the three hundred millions of earthworms crawling upon the fair soil of India and trying to oppress each other. This state of things must be removed, not by destroying religion but by following the great teachings of the Hindu faith, and joining with it the wonderful sympathy of that logical development of Hinduism—Buddhism.

A hundred thousand men and women, fired with the zeal of holiness, fortified with the eternal faith in the Lord, and nerved to lion's courage by their sympathy for the poor and the fallen and the downtrodden, will go over the length and breadth of the land, preaching the gospel of salvation, the gospel of self; the gospel of social raising-up—the gospel of Equality.

No religion on earth preaches the dignity of humanity in such a lofty strain as Hinduism, and no religion on earth treads upon the necks of the poor and the low in such a fashion as Hinduism. The Lord has shown me that religion is not at fault, but it is the Pharisees and Sadducees in Hinduism, hypocrites, who invent all sorts of engines of tyranny in the shape of doctrines of Pâramârthika and Vyavahârika (absolute and relative truth).

Despair not, remember the Lord says in the Gita, "To work you have the right but not to the result." Gird up your loins, my boy. I am called by the Lord for this. I have been dragged through a whole life full of crosses and tortures, I have seen the nearest and dearest die, almost of starvation—I have been ridiculed, distrusted, and have suffered for my sympathy for the very men who scoff and scorn. Well, my boy, this is the school of misery, which is also the school for great souls and prophets for the cultivation of sympathy, of patience, and above all, of an indomitable iron-will which quakes not even if the universe be pulverised at our feet. I pity them. It is not their fault. They are children, yea, veritable children, though they be great and high in society. Their eyes see nothing beyond their little horizon of a few yards—the routine work, eating, drinking, earning and begetting, following each other in mathematical precision. They know nothing beyond happy little souls! Their sleep is never disturbed. Their nice little brown-studies of lives never rudely shocked by the wail of woe, of misery, of degradation and poverty, that has filled the Indian atmosphere—the result of centuries of oppression. They little dream of the ages of tyranny, mental, moral and physical, that has reduced the image of God to a mere beast of burden; the emblem of the divine Mother, to a slave to bear children; and life itself, a curse. But there are others who see, feel, and shed tears of blood in their hearts, who think that there is a remedy for it, and who are ready to apply this remedy at any cost, even to the giving up of life. And "Of such is the kingdom of Heaven." Is it not then natural, my friends, that they have no time to look down from their heights to the vagaries of these contemptible little insects, ready every moment to spit their little venoms?

Trust not to the so-called rich, they are more dead than alive. The hope lies in you—in the meek, the lowly, but the faithful. Have faith in the Lord; no policy, it is nothing. Feel for the miserable and look up for help—it *shall come*. I have travelled twelve years with this load in my heart and this idea in my head. I have gone from door to door of the so-called rich and great. With a bleeding heart I have crossed half the world to this strange land, seeking for help. The Lord is great. I know He will help me. I may perish of cold or hunger in this land, but I bequeath to you, young men, this sympathy, this struggle for the poor, the ignorant, the oppressed. Go now this minute to the temple of Pârthasârathi, and before Him who was friend to the poor and lowly cowherds of Gokul, who never shrank to embrace the pariah Guhak, who accepted the invitation of a prostitute in preference to that of the nobles and saved her in His incarnation as Buddha—yea, down on your faces before Him, and make a great sacrifice; the sacrifice of a whole life for them, for whom He comes from time to time, whom He loves above all, the poor, the lowly, the oppressed. Vow then to devote your whole lives to the cause of the redemption of these three hundred millions, going down and down every day.

It is not the work of a day, and the path is full of the most deadly thorns. But Parthasarathi is ready to be our Sarathi, we know that, and in His name and with eternal faith in Him, set fire to the mountain of misery that has been heaped upon India for ages—and it shall be burned down. Come then, look it in the face, brethren, it is a grand task and we are so low. But we are the sons of Light and children of God. Glory unto the Lord, we will succeed. Hundreds will fail in the struggle—hundreds will be ready to take it up. I may die here unsuccessful, another will take up the task. You know the disease, you know the remedy, only have faith. Do not look up to the so-called rich and great; do not care for the heartless intellectual writers, and their cold-blooded newspaper articles. Faith—sympathy, fiery faith, and fiery sympathy! Life is nothing, death is nothing, —hunger nothing, cold nothing. Glory unto the Lord—march on, the Lord is our General. Do not look back to see who falls—forward—onward! Thus and thus we shall go on, brethren. One falls, and another takes up the work.

From this village I am going to Boston to-morrow. I am going to speak at a big ladies' club here, which is helping Ramabai. I must first go and buy some clothing in Boston. If I am to live longer here, my quaint dress will not do. People gather by hundreds in the streets to see me. So what I want is to dress myself in a long black coat, and keep a red robe and turban to wear when I lecture. This is what they advise me to do. . . . It is necessary to remain here for some time to gain any influence. . . .

In America, there are no classes in the railway except in Canada. So I have to travel first-class, as that is the only class; but I do not venture in the Pullmans. They are very comfortable—you sleep, eat, drink, even bathe in them, just as if you were in a hotel—but they are too expensive.

It is very hard work getting into society and making yourself heard. Now nobody is in the towns, they are all away in summer places. They will all come back in winter. Therefore I must wait. After such a struggle I am not going to give up easily. Rome was not built in a day. If you can keep me here for six months at least, I hope everything will come right. In the meantime I am trying my best to find any plank I can float upon.

Even now it is so cold in New England that every day we have fires night and morning. Canada is still colder. I never saw snow on such low hills as there.

Gradually I can make my way; but that means a longer residence in this horribly expensive country. Just now the raising of the Rupee in India has created a panic in this country, and lots of mills have been stopped. . . I must wait.

I must try to the end, and even if I die of cold or disease or hunger here, you take up the task. Holiness, sincerity and faith. First, I will try in America and if I fail, I will try in England; if I fail there too, I can go back to India and wait for further commands from On High.—Yours, VIVEKANANDA.

(53)

To The Same

CHICAGO,
2nd Nov., 1893.

DEAR Alasinga—I am so sorry that a moment's weakness on my part should cause you so much trouble; I was out of pocket at that time. Since then the Lord sent me friends. At a village near Boston I made the acquaintance of Dr. Wright, Professor of Greek in the Harvard University. He sympathised with me very much and urged upon me the necessity of going to the Parliament of Religions, which he thought would give me an introduction to the nation. As I was not acquainted with anybody, the Professor undertook to arrange everything for me, and eventually I came back to Chicago. Here I, together with the oriental and occidental delegates to the Parliament of Religions, were all lodged in the house of a gentleman.

On the morning of the opening of the Parliament, we all assembled in a building called the Art Palace, where one huge, and other smaller temporary halls were erected for the sittings of the Parliament. Men from all nations were there. From India, were Mazoomdar of the Brahmo Samaj, and Nagarkar of Bombay, Mr. Gandhi representing the Jains and Mr. Chakravarti representing Theosophy with Mrs. Annie Besant. Of these men, Mazoomdar and I were, of course, old friends, and Chakravarti knew me by name. There was a grand procession, and we were all marshalled on to the platform. Imagine a hall below and a huge gallery above, packed with six or seven thousand men and women representing the best culture of the country, and on the platform learned men of all the nations of the earth. And I, who never spoke in public in my life, to address this august assemblage!! It was opened in great form with music and ceremony and speeches; then the delegates were introduced one by one, and they stepped up and spoke. Of course my heart was fluttering and my tongue nearly dried up; I was so nervous, and could not venture to speak in the morning. Mazoomdar made a nice speech —Chakravarti a nicer one, and they were much applauded. They were all prepared and came with ready-made speeches. I was a fool and had none, but bowed down to Devi Sarasvati and stepped up, and Dr. Barrows introduced me. I made a short speech. I addressed the assembly as, "Sisters and Brothers of America"—a deafening applause of two minutes followed, and then I proceeded, and when it was finished I sat down, almost exhausted with emotion. The next day all the papers announced that my speech was the hit of the day, and I became known to the whole of America. Truly has it been said by the great commentator Shridhara मूकं करोति वाचालं—"Who maketh the dumb a fluent speaker." His name be praised! From that day I became a celebrity, and the day I read my paper on Hinduism, the hall was packed as it had never been before. I quote to you from one of the papers: "Ladies, ladies, ladies packing every place—filling every corner, they patiently waited and waited while the papers that separated them from Vivekananda were read," etc. You would be astonished if I sent over to you the newspaper cuttings, but you already know that I am a hater of celebrity. Suffice it to say, that whenever I went on the platform a deafening applause would be raised for me. Nearly all the papers paid high tributes to me, and even the most bigoted had to admit that "This man with his handsome face and magnetic presence and wonderful oratory is the most prominent figure in the Parliament." etc., etc.

And how to speak of their kindness! I have no more wants now, I am well-off, and all the money that I require to visit Europe I shall get from here. . . . A boy called ——Acharya has cropped up in our midst. He has been loafing about the city for the last three years. Loafing or no loafing, I like him, but please write to me all about him, if you know anything. He knows you. He came in the year of the Paris Exhibition to Europe.

I am now out of want. Many of the handsomest houses in this city are open to me. All the time I am living as a guest of somebody or other. There is a curiosity in this nation, such as you meet with nowhere else. They want to know everything, and their women—they are the most advanced in the world. The average American woman is far more cultivated than the average American man. The men slave all their life for money, and the women snatch every opportunity to improve themselves. And they are a very kind-hearted, frank people. Everybody who has a fad to preach comes here, and I am sorry to say that most of these are not sound. The Americans have their faults too, and what nation has not? But this is my summing up. Asia laid the germs of civilisation, Europe developed man, and America is developing woman and the masses. It is the paradise of the woman and the labourer. Now contrast the American masses and women with ours, and you get the idea at once. Americans are fast becoming liberal. Judge them not by the specimens of *hard-shelled Christians* (it is their own phrase), that you see in India. There are those here, too, but their number is decreasing rapidly, and this great nation is progressing fast towards that spirituality which is the standard boast of the Hindu.

The Hindu must not give up his religion, but must keep religion within its proper limits and give freedom to society to grow. All the reformers in India made the serious mistake of holding religion accountable for all the horrors of priestcraft and degeneration, and went forthwith to pull down the indestructible structure, and what was the result? Failure!! Beginning from Buddha down to Ram Mohan Roy, everyone made the mistake of holding caste to be a religious institution and tried to pull down religion and caste altogether, and failed. But in spite of all the ravings of the priests, caste is simply a crystallised social institution, which after doing its service is now filling the atmosphere of India with its stench, and it can only be removed by giving back to the people their lost social individuality. Every man born here knows that he is a *man*. Every man born in India knows that he is a slave of society. Now, freedom is the only condition of growth; take that off, the result is degeneration. With the introduction of modern competition see how caste is disappearing fast! No religion is now necessary to kill it. The Brahmin shopkeeper, shoemaker and wine-distiller are common in Northern India. And why? Because of competition. No man is prohibited from doing anything he pleases for his livelihood under the present government, and the result is neck and neck competition, and thus thousands are seeking and finding the highest level they were born for, instead of vegetating at the bottom.

I must remain in this country at least through the winter, and then go to Europe. The Lord will provide everything for me. You need not disturb yourself about it. I cannot express my gratitude for your love.

Day by day I am feeling that the Lord is with me, and I am trying to follow His direction. His will be done. . . . We will do great things for the world, and that for the sake of doing good and not for name and fame.

"Ours not to reason why, ours but to do and die." Be of good cheer and believe that we are selected by the Lord to do great things, and we will do them. Hold yourself in readiness, i.e., be pure and holy, and love for love's sake. Love the poor, the miserable, the downtrodden, and the Lord will bless you.

See the Raja of Ramnad and other friends from time to time, and urge them to sympathise with the masses of India. Tell them how they are standing on the neck of the poor, and that they are not fit to be called men if they do not try to raise them up. Be fearless, the Lord is with you, and He will yet raise the starving and ignorant millions of India. A railway porter here is better educated than many of your young men and most of your princes. Every American woman has far better education than can be conceived of by the majority of Hindu women. Why cannot we have the same education? We must.

Think not that you are poor; money is not power, but goodness, holiness. Come and see how it is so all over the world.—Yours etc., VIVEKANANDA.

P.S. By the bye,—'s paper was the most curious phenomenon I ever saw. It was like a tradesman's catalogue and it was not thought fit to be read in the Parliament. So N—read a few extracts from it in a side-hall and nobody understood a word of it. Do not tell him of it. It is a great art to press the largest amount of thought into the smallest number of words. Even —'s paper had to be cut very short. More than a thousand papers were read, and there was no time to give to such wild perorations. I had a good long time given to me over the ordinary half hour, because the most popular speakers were always put down last, to hold the audience. And Lord bless them, what sympathy they have, and what patience! They would sit from ten o'clock in the morning to ten o'clock at night—only a recess of half an hour for a meal, and paper after paper read, most of them very trivial, but they would wait and wait to hear their favourites.

Dharmapala of Ceylon was one of the favourites. . . . He is a very sweet man, and we became very intimate during the Parliament.

A Christian lady from Poona, Miss Sorabji and the Jain representative, Mr. Gandhi, are going to remain longer in the country and make lecture tours. I hope they will succeed. Lecturing is a very profitable occupation in this country and sometimes pays well.

Mr. Ingersoll gets five to six hundred dollars a lecture. He is the most celebrated lecturer in this country.—V.

(54)

To Sj. Haripada Mitra

C/o George W. Hale, Esq.,*
541, Dearborn Avenue, Chicago,
28th December, 1893.

Dear Haripada—It is very strange that news of my Chicago lectures has appeared in the Indian papers; for whatever I do, I try my best to avoid publicity. Many things strike me here. It may be fairly said that there is no poverty in this country. I have never seen women elsewhere, as cultured and educated as they are here. Well-educated men there are in our country, but you will scarcely find anywhere women like those here. It is indeed true, that goddesses themselves live in the houses of virtuous men. I have seen thousands of women here whose hearts are as pure and stainless as snow. Oh, how free they are! It is they who control social and civic duties. Schools and colleges are full of women, and in our country women cannot be safely allowed to walk in the streets! Their kindness to me is immeasurable. Since I came here I have been welcomed by them to their houses. They are providing me with food, arranging for my lectures, taking me to market, and doing everything for my comfort and convenience. I shall never be able to repay in the least, the deep debt of gratitude I owe to them.

Do you know who is the real "Shakti-worshipper"? It is he who knows that God is the Omnipresent Force in the Universe, and sees in women the manifestation of that Force. Many men here look upon their women in this light. Manu, again, has said that gods bless those families where women are happy and well-treated. Here men treat their women as well as can be desired, and hence they are so prosperous, so learned, so free and so energetic.

But why is it that we are slavish, miserable and dead? The answer is obvious.

And how pure and chaste are they here! Few women are married before twenty or twenty-five, and they are as free as the birds in the air. They go to market, school and college, earn money, and do all kinds of work. Those who are well-to-do devote themselves to doing good to the poor. And what are we doing? We are very regular in marrying our girls at eleven years of age, lest they should become corrupt and immoral. What does our Manu enjoin? "Daughters should be supported and educated with as much care and attention as the sons." As sons should be married after observing Brahmacharya up to the thirtieth year, so daughters also must observe Brahmacharya and be educated by their parents. But what are we actually doing? Can you better the condition of your women? Then there will be hope for your well-being. Otherwise you will remain as backward as you are now.

If anybody is born of a low caste in our country he is gone for ever, there is no hope for him. Why, what a tyranny it is! There are possibilities, opportunities and hope for every individual in this country. To-day he is poor, to-morrow he may become rich and learned and respected. Here everyone is anxious to help the poor. In India there is a howling cry that we are very poor, but how many charitable associations are there for the well-being of the poor? How many people really weep for the sorrows and sufferings of the millions of poor in India? Are we *men*? What are we doing for their livelihood, for their improvement? We do not touch them, we avoid their company! Are we men? Those thousands of Brahmins—what are they doing for the low, downtrodden masses of India? "Don't-touch," "Don't-touch," is the only phrase that plays upon their lips! How mean and degraded has our eternal religion become at their hands!

Wherein does our religion lie now? In "Don't-touchism" alone, and nowhere else!

I came to this country not to satisfy my curiosity, nor for name or fame, but to see if I could find any means for the support of the poor in India. If God helps me, you will know by and by what those means are.

As regards spirituality, the Americans are far inferior to us, but their society is far superior to ours. We will teach them our spirituality, and assimilate what is best in their society. With love and best wishes,—Yours, VIVEKANANDA.

(55)

To Sj. D. R. Balaji Rao

a Madras friend

who just had a severe domestic affliction

1893.

MY DEAR BALAJI—" Naked came I out of my mother's womb, and naked shall I return thither; the Lord gave and the Lord hath taken away; blessed be the name of the Lord." Thus said the old Jewish saint when suffering the greatest calamities that could befall man, and he erred not. Herein lies the whole secret of Existence. Waves may roll over the surface and tempests rage, but deep down there is the stratum of infinite calmness, infinite peace, and of infinite bliss. " Blessed are they that mourn, for they shall be comforted." And why? Because it is during these moments of visitations, when the heart is wrung by hands which never stop for the father's cries or the mother's wail, when under the load of sorrow, dejection and despair, the world seems to be cut off from under our feet, and when the whole horizon seems to be nothing but an impenetrable sheet of misery and utter despair, that the internal eyes open, light flashes all of a sudden, the dream vanishes, and intuitively we come face to face with the grandest mystery in nature—Existence. Yes, then it is—when the load would be sufficient to sink a lot of frail vessels—that the man of genius, of strength, the hero, sees that infinite, absolute, ever-blissful Existence *per se*, that infinite Being who is called and worshipped under different names, in different climes. Then it is, the shackles that bind the soul down to this hole of misery, break, as it were, for a time, and unfettered, it rises and rises until it reaches the throne of the Lord, "where the wicked cease from troubling and the weary are at rest." Cease not, brother, to send up petitions day and night, cease not to say day and night, THY WILL BE DONE.

> " Ours not to question why,
> Ours but to do and die."

Blessed be Thy name, O Lord! And Thy will be done. Lord, we know that we are to submit; Lord, we know that it is the Mother's hand that is striking, and "the spirit is willing but the flesh is weak." There is, Father of Love, an agony at the heart which is fighting against that calm resignation which Thou teachest. Give us strength, O Thou who saw Thy whole family destroyed before Thine eyes, with Thine hands crossed on Thy breast. Come, Lord, Thou Great Teacher, who hast taught us that the soldier is only to obey and speak not. Come Lord, come, Arjuna's charioteer, and teach me, as Thou once taughtest him, that resignation in *Thyself* is the highest end and aim of this life, so that with those great ones of old, I may also firmly and resignedly cry, *Om Sri Krishnârpanamastu*. May the Lord send you peace is the prayer, day and night, of—VIVEKANANDA.

(56)

To Madras Disciples

541, Dearborn Avenue, Chicago,

24th January, 1894.

Dear Friends—Your letters have reached me. I am surprised that so much about me has reached you. That criticism of the paper you mention is not to be taken as the attitude of the American people. That paper is almost unknown here, and belongs to what they call a "blue-nose Presbyterian paper," very bigoted. Still all the "blue-noses" are not ungentlemanly. The American people, and many of the clergy are very hospitable to me. That paper wanted a little notoriety by attacking a man who was being lionised by society. That trick is well known here, and they do not think anything of it. Of course our Indian missionaries may try to make capital out of it. If they do, tell them, "Mark, Jew, a judgment has come upon you!" Their old building is tottering to its foundation and must come down in spite of their hysterical shrieks. I pity them—if their means of living fine lives in India is cut down by the influx of oriental religions here. But not one of their leading clergy is ever against me. Well, when I am in the pond I must bathe thoroughly.

I send you a newspaper cutting of the short sketch of our religion which I read before them. Most of my speeches are extempore. . . . I do not require any help from India, I have plenty here. Employ the money you have in printing and publishing this short speech, and translating it into the vernaculars, throw it broadcast; that will keep before us the national mind. In the meantime do not forget our plan of a central college and the starting from it to all directions in India. Work hard . . .

About the women of America, I cannot express my gratitude for their kindness. Lord bless them. In this country women are the life of every movement, and represent all the culture of the nation, for men are too busy to educate themselves.

I have received Kidi's letters. With the question whether caste shall go or come I have nothing to do. My idea is to bring to the door of the meanest, the poorest, the noble ideas that the human race has developed both in and out of India, and let them think for themselves. Whether there should be caste or not, whether women should be perfectly free or not, does not concern me. "Liberty of thought and action is the only condition of life, of growth and well-being." Where it does not exist, the man, the race, the nation must go down.

Caste or no caste, creed or no creed, any man or class, or caste, or nation, or institution which bars power of free thought and action of an individual—even so long as that power does not injure others—is devilish and must go down.

My whole ambition in life is to set in motion a machinery which will bring noble ideas to the door of everybody, and then let men and women settle their own fate. Let them know what our forefathers as well as other nations have thought on the most momentous questions of life. Let them see specially what others are doing now, and then decide. We are to put the chemicals together, the crystallisation will be done by nature according to her laws. Work hard, be steady and have faith in the Lord. Set to work, I am coming sooner or later. Keep the motto before you, "Elevation of the masses without injuring the religion."

Remember that the nation lives in the cottage. But alas! nobody ever did anything for them. Our modern reformers are very busy about widow remarriage. Of course I am a sympathiser in every reform, but the fate of a nation does not depend upon the number of husbands their widows get, but upon the *condition of the masses.* Can you raise them? Can you give them back their lost individuality without making them lose their innate spiritual nature? Can you become an occidental of occidentals in your spirit of equality, freedom, work and energy, and at the same time a Hindu to the very backbone in religious culture and instincts? This is to be done and *we will do it.* You are all *born to do it.* Have faith in yourselves, great convictions are the mothers of great deeds. Onward for ever! Sympathy for the poor, the downtrodden, even unto death—this is our motto.

Onward, brave lads!—Yours affectionately, VIVEKANANDA.

P.S. Preach the idea of elevating the masses by means of a central college, and bringing education as well as religion to the door of the poor by means of missionaries trained in this college. Try to interest everybody.—V.

(57)

To Sj. Haridas Viharidas Desai

CHICAGO,
29th January, 1894.

DEAR DIWANJI SAHEB—Your last letter reached me a few days ago. You have been to see my poor mother and brothers. I am glad you did. But you have touched the only soft place in my heart. You ought to know, Diwanji, that I am no hard-hearted brute. If there is any being I love in the whole world, it is my mother. Yet I believed and still believe that without my giving up the world, the great mission which Ramakrishna Paramahamsa, my great Master, came to preach would not see the light, and where would those young men be who have stood as bulwarks against the surging waves of materialism and luxury of the day? These have done a great amount of good to India, especially to Bengal, and this is only the beginning. With the Lord's help they will do things for which the whole world will bless them for ages. So on the one hand my vision of the future of Indian religion and that of the whole world, my love for the millions of beings sinking down and down for ages with nobody to help them, nay, nobody with even a thought for them; on the other hand making those who are nearest and dearest to me miserable: I choose the former, "Lord will do the rest." He is with me, I am sure of that if of anything. So long as I am sincere, nothing can resist me because He will be my help. Many and many in India could not understand me, and how could they, poor men, their thoughts never strayed beyond the everyday routine business of eating and drinking? I know only a few noble souls like yourself appreciate me. Lord bless your noble self. But appreciation or no appreciation, I am born to organise these young men, nay, hundreds more in every city are ready to join me, and I want to send them rolling like irresistible waves over India bringing comfort, morality, religion, education to the doors of the meanest and the most downtrodden. And this I will do or die.

Our people have no idea, no appreciation. On the other hand that horrible jealousy and suspicious nature which is the natural outcome of a thousand years of slavery make them stand as enemies to every new idea. Still the Lord is great.

About the Arati as well as other things you speak of, it is the form in every one of the monasteries in all parts of India, and the worshipping of Guru is the first duty inculcated in the Vedas. It has its bad and good sides, but you must remember we are a unique company, nobody amongst us has a right to force his faith upon the others. Many of us do not believe in any form of idolatry, but they have no right to object when others do it because that would break the first principle of our religion. Again God can only be known in and through man. Vibrations of light are everywhere, even in the darkest corners, but it is only in the lamp that it becomes visible to man. Similarly, God though everywhere, we can only conceive Him as a big man. All ideas of God such as merciful preserver, helper, protector—all these are human ideas, anthropomorphic, and again these ideas must cling to a man, call him a Guru or a Prophet or an Incarnation. Man cannot go beyond his nature, no more than you can jump out of your body. What harm is there in some people worshipping their Guru when that Guru was a hundred times more holy than even your historical prophets all taken together. If there is no harm in worshipping Christ, Krishna or Buddha, why should there be in worshipping this man who never did or thought anything unholy, whose intellect only through intuition stands head and shoulders above all the other prophets because they were all one-sided? It was he that brought first to the world this idea of the truth, not in but of every religion, which is gaining ground all over the world, and that without the help of science or philosophy or any other acquirement.

But even this is not compulsory, none of the brethren has told you that all must worship his Guru, No-No-No. But again none of us has a right to object when another worships. Why? Because that would overthrow this unique society the world has ever seen, ten men of ten different notions and ideas living in perfect harmony. Wait, Diwanji, the Lord is great and merciful, you will see more.

We do not only tolerate but accept every religion, and

with the Lord's help I am trying to preach it to the whole world.

Three things are necessary to make every man great, every nation great:—

1. Conviction of the powers of goodness.

2. Absence of jealousy and suspicion.

3. Helping all who are trying to be and do good.

Why should the Hindu nation with all its wonderful intelligence and other things have gone to pieces? I would answer you, *Jealousy*. Never were there people more wretchedly jealous of one another, more envious of one another's fame and name than this wretched Hindu race. And if you ever come out in the West, the absence of this is the first feeling which you will see in the Western nations.

Three men cannot act in concert together in India for five minutes. Each one struggles for power and in the long run the whole organisation comes to grief. Lord! Lord! When will we learn not to be jealous! In such a nation, and especially in Bengal, to create a band of men who are tied and bound together with a most undying love in spite of difference, is it not wonderful? This band will increase. This idea of wonderful liberality joined with eternal energy and progress must spread over India, it must electrify the whole nation and must enter the very pores of society in spite of the horrible ignorance, spite, caste-feeling, old boobyism, and jealousy which are the heritage of this nation of slaves.

You are one of the few noble natures who stand out as rocks out of water in this sea of universal stagnation. Lord bless you for ever and ever!—Yours ever faithfully,
VIVEKANANDA.

(58)

To " Kidi ".

541, Dearborn Avenue,
Chicago,
3rd March, 1894.

Dear Kidi—. . . I agree with you so far that faith is a wonderful insight and that it alone can save, but there is the danger in it of breeding fanaticism barring further progress.

Jnanam is all right, but there is the danger of its becoming dry intellectualism. Love is great and noble, but it may die away in meaningless sentimentalism. A harmony of all these is the thing required. Ramakrishna was such a harmony. Such beings are few and far between; but keeping him and his teachings as the ideal we can move on. And if amongst us, each one may not individually attain to that perfection, still we may get it collectively by counteracting, equipoising, adjusting and fulfilling one another. This would be *harmony* by a number of persons, and a decided advance on all other forms and creeds.

For a religion to be effective, enthusiasm is necessary. At the same time we must try to avoid the danger of multiplying creeds. We avoid that by being a non-sectarian sect, having all the advantages of a sect and the broadness of a universal religion.

God, though everywhere, can be known to us in and through human character. No character was ever so perfect as Ramakrishna, and that should be the centre round which we ought to rally; at the same time allowing everybody to regard him in his own light, either as God, Saviour, teacher, model or a great man, just as he pleases.

We preach neither social equality nor inequality, but

that every being has the same rights, and insist upon freedom of thought and action in every way.

We reject none, neither theist, nor pantheist, monist, polytheist, agnostic, nor atheist; the only condition of being a disciple is modelling a character at once the broadest and the most intense.

Nor do we insist upon particular codes of morality as to conduct, or character, or eating and drinking, except so far as it injures others.

Whatever retards the onward progress or helps the downward fall is vice; whatever helps in coming up and becoming harmonised is *virtue*.

We leave everybody free to know, select and follow whatever suits and helps him. Thus, for example, eating meat may help one, eating fruit another. Each is welcome to his own peculiarity, but he has no right to criticise the conduct of others, because that would, if followed by him, injure him, much less to insist that others should follow his way. A wife may help some people in this progress, to others she may be a positive injury. But the unmarried man has no right to say that the married disciple is wrong, much less to force his own ideal of morality upon his brother.

We believe that every being is divine, is God. Every soul is a sun covered over with clouds of ignorance; the difference between soul and soul is due to the difference in density of these layers of clouds. We believe that this is the conscious or unconscious basis of all religions, and that this is the explanation of the whole history of human progress either in the material, intellectual, or spiritual plane—the same spirit is manifesting through different planes.

We believe that this is the very essence of the Vedas.

We believe that it is the duty of every *soul* to treat,

think of, and behave to other *souls* as such, i.e., as *Gods*, and not hate or despise, or vilify, or try to injure them by any manner or means. This is the duty not only of the Sannyasin but of all men and women.

The soul has neither sex, nor caste, nor imperfection.

We believe that nowhere throughout the Vedas, Darshanas, or Purânas, or Tantras, it is ever said that the soul has any sex, creed, or caste. Therefore we agree with those who say, "What has religion to do with social reforms?" But they must also agree with us when we tell them that religion has no business to formulate social laws and insist on the difference between beings. Because its aim and end is to obliterate all such fictions and monstrosities.

If it be pleaded that through this difference we would reach the final equality and unity, we answer that the same religion has said over and over again, that mud cannot be washed with mud.

As if a man can be moral by being immoral!

Social laws were created by economic conditions under the sanction of religion. The terrible mistake of religion was to interfere in social matters. But how hypocritically it says and thereby contradicts itself—"Social reform is not the business of religion!" True, what we want is that religion should not be a social reformer, but we insist at the same time that religion has no right to become a social law-giver. Hands off! Keep yourself to your own bounds and everything would come right.

1. Education is the manifestation of the perfection already in man.

2. Religion is the manifestation of the Divinity already in man.

Therefore the only duty of the teacher in both cases

is to remove all obstructions from the way. Hands off! as I always say, and everything will be right. That is, our duty is to clear the way. The Lord does the rest.

Specially therefore you must bear in mind that religion has to do only with the soul and has no business to interfere in social matters—you must also bear in mind that this applies completely to the mischief which has already been done. It is as if a man after forcibly taking possession of another's property cries through the nose when that man tries to regain it—and preaches the doctrine of the sanctity of human right!

What business had the priest to interfere (to the misery of millions of human beings) in every social matter?

You speak of the meat-eating Kshatriya; meat or no meat, it is they who are the fathers of all that is noble and beautiful in Hinduism. Who wrote the Upanishads? Who was Rama? Who was Krishna? Who was Buddha? Who were the Tirthankaras of the Jains? Whenever the Kshatriyas have preached religion, they have given it to everybody, and whenever the Brahmins wrote anything they would deny all right to others. Read the Gita and the Sutras of Vyasa, or get some one to read them to you. In the Gita the way is laid open to all men and women, to all caste and colour, but Vyasa tries to put meanings upon the Vedas to cheat the poor Shudras. Is God a nervous fool like you that the flow of His river of mercy would be dammed up by a piece of meat? If such be He, His value is not a pie!

Hope nothing from me, but I am convinced, as I wrote to you, and had spoken to you, that India is to be saved by the Indians themselves. So you, young men of the motherland, can dozens of you become almost fanatics over this new ideal? Take thought, get materials, write a sketch of the life of Ramakrishna, *studiously avoiding all miracles*. The life should be written as an illustration of the doctrines he preached. Only his—do not bring me or any living persons into that. The main aim should be to give to the world what he taught, and the life as illustrating that. I, unworthy though I am, had one commission—to bring out the casket of jewels that was placed in my charge, and make it over to you. Why to you? Because the hypocrites, the jealous, the slavish, and the cowardly, those who believe in matter only, can never do anything. Jealousy is the bane of our national character, natural to slaves. Even the Lord with all His power can do nothing on account of the jealousy. . . .

Think of me as one who has done all his duty and is now dead and gone. Think that the whole work is upon your shoulders . . . . Think that you, young men of our motherland were destined to do this. Put yourself to the task. Lord bless you. Leave me, throw me quite out of sight. Preach the new ideal, the new doctrine, the new life. Preach against nobody, against no custom. Preach neither for nor against caste or any other social evil; preach to let "Hands off," and everything will come right.

With my blessings on you all, my brave steadfast and loving souls.—Yours, VIVEKANANDA.

(59)

To an American friend

DETROIT,
15th March, 1894.

I am wearied of lecturing and all that nonsense. This mixing with hundreds of varieties of the human animals has disturbed me. I will tell you what is to my taste: I cannot write and I cannot speak, but I can think deep, and when I am heated, can speak fire. It should be however to a select, a very select, few. Let them, if they will, carry and scatter my ideas broadcast—not I. This is only a just division of labour. The same man never succeeded both in thinking and in scattering his thoughts. Thoughts so given are not worth anything. A man should be free to think especially spiritual thoughts.

Just because this assertion of independence, this proving that man is *not a machine*, is the essence of all religious thought, for that very reason it is impossible to think it in the routine mechanical way. It is this tendency to bring everything down to the level of a machine that has given the West its wonderful prosperity. And it is this which has driven away all religion from its doors. Even the little that is left, the West has reduced to a systematic drill.

I am really not "cyclonic" at all. Far from it. The thing that I want it not here, nor can I longer bear this "cyclonic" atmosphere. This is the way to perfection, to strive to be perfect, and to strive to make perfect a few men and women. My idea of doing good is only this—to evolve a few giants, and not to strew pearls before swine, and so lose time, health and energy.

How I should like to become dumb for some years, and not talk at all! I was not made for these worldly fights and struggles. I am naturally dreamy and slothful. I am a born idealist, and can only live in a world of dreams. The touch of material things disturbs my visions and makes me unhappy. But Thy will be done!

(60)

To Swami Brahmananda

C/o George W. Hale,*
541, Dearborn Avenue,
Chicago,
19th March, 1894.

My Dear Rakhal—I have not written to you since coming to this country. But Haridas Bhai's[1] letter gives me all the news. It is excellent that G. C. Ghose and all of you have treated him with due consideration.

I have no wants in this country, but mendicancy has no vogue here and I have to labour, that is, lecture in places. It is as cold here as it is hot. The summer is not a bit less hot than in Calcutta. And how to describe the cold in winter! The whole country is covered with snow, three or four feet deep, nay, six or seven feet, at places! In the Southern parts there is no snow. Snow, however, is a thing of little consideration here. For it snows when the mercury stands at 32°F. In Calcutta it scarcely comes down to 60° and it rarely approaches zero in England. But here, your mercury sinks to *minus* 40° or 50°. In Canada, in the North, mercury becomes condensed, when they have to use the alcohol thermometer. When it is too cold, that is, when the mercury stands even below 20°F, it does not snow. I used to think that it must be an exceedingly cold day on which the snow falls. But it is not so, it snows on comparatively warm days. Extreme cold produces a sort of intoxication. No carriages would run; only the sledge, which is without wheels, slides on the ground! Everything is frozen stiff—even an elephant can walk on rivers and

[1] Haridas Bhai—ex-Dewan of Junagarh Shortly before Swamiji left India for America, he became intimately acquainted with this gentleman, and was introduced by him to many Indian princes.

canals and lakes. The massive Falls of Niagara, of such tremendous volocity, are frozen to marble!! But I am doing nicely. I was a little afraid at first, but later on, necessity makes me travel by rail to the borders of Canada one day, and the next day finds me lecturing in South America! The carriages are kept quite warm, like your own room, by means of steam pipes, and all around are masses of snow, spotlessly white—oh, the beauty of it!

I was mortally afraid that my nose and ears would fall off, but to this day they are all right. I have to go out, however, dressed in a heap of warm clothing, surmounted by a fur-coat, with boots, encased in a woollen jacket, and so on. No sooner do you breathe out than the breath freezes among the beard and moustache! Notwithstanding all this, the fun of it is that they won't drink water indoors without putting a lump of ice into it. This is, because it is warm indoors. Every room and the staircase are kept warm by steam pipes. They are first and foremost in arts and appliances, foremost in enjoyment and luxury, foremost in making money, and foremost in spending it. The daily wages of a coolie are six rupees, as also are those of a servant; you cannot hire a cab for less than three rupees, nor get a cigar for less than four annas. A decent pair of shoes costs twenty-four rupees, and a suit, rupees five hundred. As they earn, so they spend. A lecture fetches from two hundred up to three thousand rupees. I have got up to five hundred.[1] Of course now I am in the very heyday of fortune. They like me, and thousands of people come to hear me speak.

As it pleased the Lord, I met here Mr. M—r. He was very cordial at first, but when the whole Chicago popula-

[1] For some time after the Chicago Address Swamiji lectured on behalf of a Lecture Bureau, which task, however, he soon gave up as curtailing his independence, and devoted most of the money thus earned to various charitable works in different parts of India.

tion began to flock to me in overwhelming numbers, then grew the canker in M—r's mind! . . . The priests tried their utmost to snub me. But the Guru is with me, what could anybody do? And the whole American nation loves and respects me, pays my expenses, and reveres me as a Guru. . . . It was not in the power of your priests to do anything against me. Moreover, they are a nation of scholars. Here it would no longer do to say, "We marry our widows," "We do not worship idols," and things of that sort. What they want is philosophy, learning, and empty talk will no more do.

Dharmapal is a nice boy. He has not much of learning, but is very gentle. He had a good deal of popularity in this country.

Brother, I have been brought to my senses. . . . . के निघ्नन्ति परहितं निरर्थकं ते के न जानीमहे।—"We do not know what sort of people they are who for nothing hinder the welfare of others. (Bhartrihari). Brother, we can get rid of everything, but not of that cursed jealousy. . . . That is a national sin with us, speaking ill of others, and burning at heart at the greatness of others. Mine alone is the greatness, none else should rise to it!!

Nowhere in the world are women like those of this country. How pure, independent, self-relying and kind-hearted! It is the women who are the life and soul of this country. All learning and culture are centred in them. The saying या श्रीः स्वयं सुकृतीनां भवनेषु—"Who is the Goddess of Fortune Herself in the families of the meritorious"—holds good in this country, while that other, पापात्मनां हृदयेष्वलक्ष्मी —"The Goddess of ill-luck in the hearts of the sinful"—applies to ours. Just think on this. Great God! I am struck dumb with wonderment at seeing the women of America—त्वं श्रीस्त्वमीश्वरी त्वं ह्रीः:—"Thou art the Goddess of Fortune,

Thou art the supreme Goddess, Thou art Modesty." या देवी सर्वभूतेष शक्तिरूपेण संस्थिता—" The Goddess who resides in all beings as Power." All this holds good here. There are thousands of women here, whose minds are as pure and white as the snow of this country. And look at our girls, becoming mothers below their teens! Good Lord! I now see it all. Brother, यत्र नार्यस्तु पूज्यन्ते नन्दन्ते तत्र देवताः—"The gods are pleased where the women are held in esteem"—says the old Manu. We are horrible sinners; and our degradation is due to our calling women "despicable worms," "gateways to hell," and so forth. Goodness gracious! There is all the difference between heaven and hell!! याथातथ्यतोऽर्थान् व्यदधाति।—" He adjudges gifts according to the merits of the case." Is the Lord to be hoodwinked by idle talk? The Lord has said, त्वं स्त्री त्वं पुमानसि त्वं कुमार उत वा कुमारी—"Thou art the woman, Thou art the man. Thou art the boy and the girl as well." (Shvetashvatara Upa.). And we on our part are crying, दूरमपसर रे चण्डाल—"Be off, thou outcast!" केनैषा निर्मिता नारी मोहिनी—" Who has made the bewitching woman?" My brother, what experiences I have had in the South of the upper classes torturing the lower! What Bacchanalian orgies within the temples! Is it a religion that fails to remove the misery of the poor and turn men into gods? Do you think our religion is worth the name? Ours is only Don't-touchism, only "Touch me not," "Touch me not." Good heavens! A country, the big leaders of which have for the last two thousand years been only discussing whether to take food with the right hand or the left, whether to take water from the right-hand side or from the left, . . . if such a country does not go to ruin what other will? कालः सुप्तेषु जागर्ति कालो हि दुरतिक्रमः—" Time keeps wide awake when all else sleeps; Time is invincible indeed!" He knows it; who is there to throw dust in His eyes, my friend?

A country where millions of people live on flowers of the *mohua* plant, and a million or two of Sadhus and a hundred million or so of Brahmins such the blood out of these poor people, without even the least effort for their amelioration—is that a country or hell? Is that a religion, or the devil's dance? My brother, here is one thing for you to understand fully—I have travelled all over India, and seen this country too—can there be an effect without cause? Can there be punishment without sin?

सर्वशास्त्रपुराणेषु व्यासस्य वचनं ध्रुवं ।
परोपकारः पुण्याय पापाय परपीडनम् ॥

—"Amidst all the scriptures and Purânas, know this statement of Vyasa to be true, that doing good to others conduces to merit, and doing harm to them leads to sin."

Isn't it true?

My brother, in view of all this, specially, of the poverty and ignorance, I had no sleep. At Cape Comorin sitting in Mother Kumari's temple, sitting on the last bit of Indian rock—I hit upon a plan. We are so many Sannyasins wandering about, and teaching the people metaphysics—it is all madness. Did not our Gurudeva use to say, "An empty stomach is no good for religion"? That those poor people are leading the life of brutes, is simply due to ignorance. We have for all ages been sucking their blood and trampling them under foot.

. . . Suppose some disinterested Sannyasins, bent on doing good to others, go from village to village, disseminating education, and seeking in various ways to better the condition of all down to the Chandâla, through oral teaching, and by means of maps, cameras, globes and such other accessories—can't that bring forth good in time? All these plans I cannot write out in this short letter. The long and short of it is—if the mountain does not come to

Mohammed, Mohammed must go to the mountain. The poor are too poor to come to schools and Pâthshâlâs, and they will gain nothing by reading poetry and all that sort of thing. We as a nation have lost our individuality, and that is the cause of all mischief in India. We have to give back to the nation its lost individuality and *raise the masses*. The Hindu, the Mohammedan, the Christian, all have trampled them under foot. Again the force to raise them must come from inside, that is, from the orthodox Hindus. In every country the evils exist not with, but against Religion. Religion therefore is not to blame, but men.

To effect this, the first thing we need is men, and the next is funds. Through the grace of our Guru I was sure to get from ten to fifteen men in every town. I next travelled in search of funds, but do you think the people of India were going to spend money!!. . . Selfishness personified—are they to spend anything? Therefore I have come to America, to earn money myself, and then return to my country and devote the rest of my days to the realisation of this one aim of my life.

As our country is poor in social virtues, so this country is lacking in spirituality. I give them spirituality and they give me money. I do not know how long I shall take to realise my end . . . These people are not hypocrites, and jealousy is altogether absent in them. I depend on no one in Hindusthan. I shall try to earn the wherewithal myself to the best of my might and carry out my plans, or die in the attempt. सन्निमित्ते वरं त्यागो विनाशे नियते सति —"When death is certain, it is best to sacrifice oneself for a good cause."

You may perhaps think what Utopian nonsense all this is! You little know what is in me. If any of you help me in my plans, all right, or Gurudeva will show me the way out. . . . We cannot give up jealousy and rally together. That is our national sin! It is not to be met with in this country, and this is what has made them so great.

Nowhere in the world have I come across such "frogs-in-the-well" as we are. Let anything new come from some foreign country, and America will be the first to accept it. But we?—oh, there are none like us in the world, we men of Aryan blood!! Where that heredity really expresses itself, I do not see. . . . Yet they are descendants of the Aryans!—Ever yours, VIVEKANANDA.

(61)

To Sj. Alasinga Perumal

NEW YORK,
9th April, 1894.

DEAR ALASINGA—. . . Secretary Saheb writes me that I must come back to India because that is my field. No doubt of that. But, my brother, we are to light a torch which will shed a lustre over all India. So let us not be in a hurry; everything will come by the grace of the Lord. I have lectured in many of the big towns of America. . . . I have made a good many friends here, some of them very influential. Of course the orthodox clergymen are against me and seeing that it is not easy to grapple with me they try to hinder, abuse and vilify me in every way. . . . Lord bless them! My brother, no good thing can be done without obstruction. It is only those who persevere to the end that succeed. . . . I believe that the Satya-yuga will come when there will be one caste, one Veda, and peace and harmony. This idea of Satya-yuga is what would revivify India. Believe it. . . . .

Up boys, and put yourselves to the task! . . .

Old Hinduism for ever! . . . Up, up, my boys, we are sure to win!

. . . When once we begin to work we shall have a tremendous "boom," but I do not want to talk without working. . . . Yours, with all blessings, VIVEKANANDA.

(62)

To The Same

CHICAGO,
28th May, 1894.

DEAR ALASINGA—I could not reply to your note earlier because I was whirling to and fro from New York to Boston. I do not know when I am going back to India. It is better to leave everything in the hands of Him who is at my back directing me. Try to work without me, as if I never existed. Do not wait for anybody or anything. Do whatever you can. Build your hope on none. . . .

I have done a good deal of lecturing here . . . . . The expenses here are terrible; money has to fly, although I have been almost always taken care of everywhere by the nicest and the highest families.

I do not know whether I shall go away this summer or not. Most probably not. In the meantime try to organise and push on our plans. Believe you can do everything. Know that the Lord is with us, and so, onward, brave souls!

I have had enough appreciation in my own country. Appreciation or no appreciation, sleep not, slacken not. You must remember that not a bit even of our plans has been as yet carried out.

Act on the educated young men, bring them together and organise them. Great things can be done by great sacrifices only. No selfishness, no name, no fame, yours or mine, nor my Master's even. Work, work the idea, the plan, my boys, my brave, noble, good souls—to the wheel, to the wheel put your shoulders! Stop not to look back for name, or fame, or any such nonsense. Throw self overboard and work. Remember, "The grass when made into a rope by being joined together can even chain a mad elephant." The Lord's blessings on you all! His power be in you all—as I believe it is *already*. "Wake up, stop not until the goal is reached," say the Vedas. Up, up, the long night is passing, the day is approaching, the wave has risen, nothing will be able to resist its tidal fury. The spirit, my boys, the spirit; the love, my children, the love; the faith, the belief; and fear not! The greatest sin is fear.

My blessings on all. Tell all the noble souls there who helped our cause, that I send them my eternal love and gratitude, but I beg of them not to slacken. Throw the idea broadcast. Do not be proud; do not insist upon anything dogmatic; do not go against anything—ours is to put chemicals together, the Lord knows how and when the crystal will form. Above all, be not inflated with my success or yours. Great works are to be done; what is this small success in comparison with what is to come? Believe, believe, the decree has gone forth, the fiat of the Lord has gone forth—India must rise, the masses and the poor are to be made happy. Rejoice. . . . The flood of spirituality has risen. I see it is rolling over the land, resistless, boundless, all-absorbing. Every man to the fore, every good will be added to its forces, every hand will smooth its way, and glory be unto the Lord! . . .

I do not require any help. Try to get up a fund, buy some magic-lanterns, maps, globes, etc., and some chemicals. Get every evening a crowd of the poor and the low, even the pariahs, and lecture to them about religion first, and then teach them through the magic-lantern and other things, astronomy, geography, etc., in the dialect of the people. Train up a band of fiery young men. Put your fire in them and gradually increase the organisation letting it widen and widen its circle. Do the best you can, do not wait to cross the river when the water has all run down. Printing magazines, papers, etc., is good, no doubt, but actual work, my boys, even if infinitesimal, is better than eternal scribbling and talking. Call a meeting at Bhattacharya's, get a little money and buy those things I have just now stated, hire a hut and go to work. Magazines are *secondary*, but this is primary. You must have a hold on the masses. Do not be afraid of a small beginning, great things come afterwards. Be courageous. Do not try to lead your brethren, but serve them. The brutal mania for leading has sunk many a great ship in the waters of life. Take care especially of that, i.e., be unselfish even unto death, and work. I could not write all I was going to say, but the Lord will give you all understanding, my brave boys. At it, my boys! Glory unto the Lord!—Yours affectionately, VIVEKANANDA.

(63)

To Sj. Haridas Viharidas Desai

CHICAGO,
20th June, 1894.

DEAR DIWANJI SAHEB—Your very kind note came to-day. I am so sorry that I could have caused pain to such a noble heart as yours with my rash and strong words. I bow down to your mild corrections. "Thy son am I, teach me thus bowing."—Gita. But you well know, Diwanji Saheb, it was my love that prompted me to say so. The backbiters, I must tell you, have not indirectly benefited me, on the other hand, they have injured me immensely in view of the fact that our Hindu people did not move a finger to tell the Americans that I represented them. Did our people send some words thanking the American people for their kindness to me and stating that I was representing them? . . . have been telling the American people that I have donned the Sannyasin's garb only in America and that I was a cheat, pure and simple. So far as reception goes, it has no effect on the American nation, but so far as helping me with funds goes, it has a terrible effect in making them take off their helping hands from me. And it is one year since I have been here, and not one man of note from India has thought it fit to make the Americans know that I am no cheat. Then again, the missionaries are always seeking for something against me, and they are busy picking up anything said against me by the Christian papers of India and publishing it here. Now you must know that the people here know very little of the distinction in India between the Christian and the Hindu.

Primarily my coming has been to raise funds for an enterprise of my own. Let me tell it all to you again.

The whole difference between the West and the East is in this: they are nations, we are not. That is, civilisation, education here is general, it penetrates into the masses. The higher classes in India and America are the same, but the distance is infinite between the lower classes of the two countries. Why was it so easy for the English to conquer India? It was because they are a nation, we are not. When one of our great men dies, we must sit for centuries to have another—they can produce them as fast as they die. When our Diwanji Saheb will pass away (which the Lord may delay long for the good of my country), the nation will see the difficulty at once of filling his place—which is seen even now why they cannot dispense with your services. It is the dearth of great ones.

Why so? Because they have such a bigger field of recruiting their great ones, we have so small. A nation of 300 millions has the smallest field of recruiting its great ones compared with nations of thirty, forty or sixty millions, because the number of educated men and women in those nations is so great. Now do not mistake me, my kind friend, this is the great defect in our nation and must be removed.

Educate and raise the masses, and thus alone a nation is possible. Our reformers do not see where the wound is, they want to save the nation by marrying the widows; do you think that a nation is saved by the number of husbands its widows get? Nor is our religion to blame, for an idol more or less makes no difference. The whole defect is here, the real nation who live in cottages have forgotten their manhood, their individuality. Trodden under the foot of the Hindu, Mussalman, or Christian, they have come to think that they are born to be trodden under the foot of everybody who has money enough in his pocket. They are to be given back their lost individuality. They are to be educated. Whether idols will remain or not, whether widows will have husbands enough or not, whether caste is good or bad, I do not bother myself with such questions. Everyone must work out his own salvation. Our duty is to put chemicals together, the crystallisation will come through God's laws. Let us put ideas into their heads, and they will do the rest. Now this means educating the masses. Here are these difficulties. A pauper government cannot, will not do anything, so no help from that quarter.

Even supposing, we are in a position to open schools in each village free, still the poor boys would rather go to the plough to earn their living than come to your school. Neither have we the money nor can we make them come to education. The problem seems hopeless. I have found a way out. It is this. If the mountain does not come to

Mohammed, Mohammed must go to the mountain. If the poor cannot come to education, education must reach them at the plough, in the factory, everywhere. How? You have seen my brethren. Now I can get hundreds of such, all over India, unselfish, good and educated. Let these men go from village to village bringing not only religion to the door of everyone but also education. So I have a nucleus of organising the widows also as instructors to our women.

Now suppose the villagers after their day's work have come to their village, and sitting under a tree or somewhere are smoking and talking the time away. Suppose two of these educated Sannyasins get hold of them there and with a camera throw astronomical or other pictures, scenes from different nations, histories, etc. Thus with globes, maps, etc.—and all this orally—how much can be done that way, Diwanji! It is not that the eye is the only door of knowledge, the ear can be the same. So they would have ideas and morality and hope for better. Here our work ends. Let them do the rest. What would make the Sannyasins do this sacrifice, undertake such a task?—religious enthusiasm. Every new religious wave requires a new centre. The old religion can be revivified only by a new centre. Hang your dogmas or doctrines, they never pay. It is a character, a life, a centre, a God-man that must lead the way, that must be the centre round which all other elements will gather themselves and then fall like a tidal wave upon the society, carrying all before them, washing away all impurities. Again, a piece of wood can be easily cut only along the grains. So the old Hinduism can be reformed only through Hinduism, and not through the new-fangled reform movements. At the same time, the reformers must be able to unite in themselves the culture of both the East and the West. Now, do you not think that you have already seen the nucleus of such a great movement, that you have heard the low rumblings of the coming tidal wave? That centre, that God-man to lead, was born in India. He was the great Ramakrishna Paramahamsa, and round him this band is slowly gathering. They will do the work. Now, Diwanji Maharaj, this requires an organisation and money—a little at least to set the wheel in motion. Who would have given us money in India? . . . So, Diwanji Maharaj, I crossed over to America. You may remember I begged all the money from the poor, and the offers of the rich I would not accept because they could not understand my ideas. Now lecturing for a year in this country, I could not succeed at all (of course, I have no wants for myself) in my plan of raising some funds for setting up my work. First, this year is a very bad year in America: thousands of their poor are without work. Secondly, the missionaries and the . . . try to thwart all my views. Thirdly, a year has rolled by, and our countrymen could not do even so much for me as to say to the American people that I was a real Sannyasin and no cheat, and that I represented the Hindu religion. Even this much, the expenditure of a few words, they could not do! Bravo, my countrymen! I love them, Diwanji Saheb. Human help I spurn with my foot. He who has been with me through hills and dales, through deserts or forests, will be with me, I hope; if not, some heroic soul would arise sometime or other in India, far abler than myself and carry it out. So I have told you all about it. Diwanji, excuse my long letter, my noble friend, one of the few who really feel for me, have real kindness for me. You are at liberty, my friend, to think that I am a dreamer, a visionary; but believe at least that I am sincere to the backbone, and my greatest fault is that I love my country only too, too well. May you and yours be blessed ever and ever, my noble, noble friend. May the shadow of the Almighty ever rest on all those you love. I offer my eternal gratitude to you. My debt to you is immense, not only because you are my friend, but also because you have all your life served the Lord and your motherland so well.—Ever yours in gratitude, VIVEKANANDA.

(64)

To H. H. The Maharaja of Mysore

CHICAGO,
23rd June, 1894.

YOUR HIGHNESS—Sri Narayana bless you and yours. Through your Highness' kind help, it has been possible for me to come to this country. Since then I have become well known here, and the hospitable people of this country have supplied all my wants. It is a wonderful country and this is a wonderful nation in many respects. No other nation applies so much machinery in their everyday work as do the people of this country. Everything is machine. Then again, they are only one-twentieth of the whole population of the world. Yet they have fully one-sixth of all the wealth of the world. There is no limit to their wealth and luxuries. Yet everything here is so dear. The wages of labour are the highest in the world; yet the fight between labour and capital is constant.

Nowhere on earth have women so many privileges as in America. They are slowly taking everything into their hands and, strange to say, the number of cultured women is much greater than that of cultured men. Of course the higher geniuses are mostly from the rank of males. With all the criticism of the Westerners against our caste, they have a worse one—that of money. The almighty dollar, as the Americans say, can do anything here. . . .

No country on earth has so many laws, and in no country are they so little regarded. On the whole our poor Hindu people are infinitely more moral than any of the Westerns. In religion they practise either hypocrisy or fanaticism. Sober-minded men have become disgusted with their superstitious religions and are looking forward to India for new light. Your Highness cannot realise without seeing, how eagerly they take in any little bit of the grand thoughts of the holy Vedas, which resist and are unharmed by the terrible onslaughts of modern science. The theories of creation out of nothing, of a created soul, and of the big tyrant of a God sitting on a throne in a place called heaven, and of the eternal hell-fires, have disgusted all the educated; and the noble thoughts of the Vedas about the eternity of creation and of the soul, and about the God in our own soul, they are imbibing fast in one shape or other. Within fifty years the educated of the world will come to believe in the eternity of both soul and creation, and in God as our highest and perfect nature, as taught in our holy Vedas. Even now their learned priests are interpreting the Bible that way. My conclusion is, that they require more spiritual civilisation, and we, more material.

The one thing that is at the root of all evils in India is the condition of the poor. The poor in the West are devils; compared with them ours are angels, and it is therefore so much the easier to raise our poor. The only service to be done for our lower classes, is to give them education, *to develop their lost individuality*. That is the great task between our people and princes. Up to now nothing has been done in that direction. Priest-power and foreign conquest have trodden them down for centuries, and at last the poor of India have forgotten that they are human beings. They are to be given ideas; their eyes are to be opened to what is going on in the world around them, and then they will work out their own salvation. Every nation, every man, every woman, must work out one's own salvation. Give them ideas—that is the only help they require, and then the rest must follow as the effect. Ours is to put the chemicals together, the crystallisation comes in the law of nature. Our duty is to put ideas into their heads, they will do the rest. This is what is to be done in India. It is this idea that has been in my mind for a long time. I could not accomplish it in India, and that was the reason of my coming to this country. The great difficulty in the way of educating the poor is this. Supposing even your Highness opens a free school in every village, still it would do no good, for the poverty in India is such, that the poor boys would rather go to help their fathers in the fields, or otherwise try to make a living, than come to the school. Now, if the mountain does not come to Mohammed, Mohammed must go to the mountain. If the poor boy cannot come to education, education must go to him. There are thousands of single-minded, self-sacrificing Sannyasins in our own country, going from village to village, teaching religion. If a part of them can be organised as teachers of secular things also, they will go from place to place, from door to door, not only preaching but teaching also. Suppose two of these men go to a village in the evening with a camera, a globe, some maps, etc. They can teach a great deal of astronomy and geography to the ignorant. By telling stories about different nations, they can give the poor a hundred times more information through the ear than they can get in a life-time through books. This requires an organisation, which again means money. Men enough there are in India to work out this plan, but alas! they have no money. It is very difficult to set a wheel in motion, but when once set, it goes on with increasing velocity. After seeking help in my own country and failing to get any sympathy from the rich, I came over to this country through your Highness' aid. The Americans do not care a bit whether the poor of India die or live.

And why should they, when our own people never think of anything but their own selfish ends?

My noble prince, this life is short, the vanities of the world are transient, but they alone live who live for others, the rest are more dead than alive. One such high, noble-minded and royal son of India as your Highness, can do much towards raising India on her feet again, and thus leave a name to posterity which shall be worshipped. That the Lord may make your noble heart feel intensely for the suffering millions of India sunk in ignorance, is the prayer of—VIVEKANANDA.

(65)

To Rao Bahadur Narasimhachariar

CHICAGO,
23rd June, 1894.

DEAR SIR—Your kindness to me makes me venture to take a little advantage of it. Mrs. Potter Palmer is the chief lady of the United States. She was the lady President of the World's Fair. She is much interested in raising the women of the world and is at the head of a big organisation for women. She is a particular friend of Lady Dufferin and has been entertained by the Royalties of Europe on account of her wealth and position. She has been very kind to me in this country. Now she is going to make a tour in China, Japan, Siam and India. Of course she will be entertained by the Governors and other high people in India. But she is particularly anxious to see our society apart from English official aid. I have on many occasions told her about your noble efforts in raising the Indian women, of your wonderful College in Mysore. I think it is our duty to show a little hospitality to such personages from America in return for their kindness to our countrymen who come here. I hope she will find a warm reception at your hands and be helped to see a little of our women as they are. And I assure you she is no missionary, nor Christian, even as to that. She wants to work apart from all religions to ameliorate the condition of women all over the world. This would also be helping me a great deal in this country.

May the Lord bless you.—Yours for ever and ever affectionate, VIVEKANANDA.

(66)

To Misses Mary and Harriet Hale

GREENACRE INN, ELIOT, MAINE,
26th June, 1894.

DEAR SISTERS—, . . . This is a big fun and farm house where the Christian Scientists are holding a session. Last spring in New York I was invited by the lady projector of the meeting to come here, and here I am. It is a beautiful and cool place, no doubt, and many of my old friends of Chicago are here. Mrs. Mills, Miss Stockham and several other ladies and gentlemen live in tents which they have pitched on the open ground by the river. They have a lively time and sometimes all of them wear what you call your scientific dress the whole day. They have lectures almost everyday. One Mr. Colville from Boston is here; he speaks every day, it is said, under spirit control. The Editor (?) of the *Universal Truth* has settled herself down here. She is conducting religious services and holding classes to heal all manner of diseases, and very soon I expect them to be giving eyes to the blind, and the like! After all, it is a queer gathering. They do not care much about social laws and are quite free and happy. Mrs. Mills is quite brilliant and so are many other ladies. . . . A very cultured lady from Detroit is going to take me to an Island fifteen miles into the sea. I hope we shall have a nice time. . . . I may go over to Amisquan from here, I suppose. This is a beautiful and nice place and the bathing is splendid. Cora Stockham has made a bathing dress for me, and I am having as good a time in the water as a duck—this is delicious even for the denizens of Mud ville. . . .

There is here Mr. Wood of Boston, who is one of the great lights of your sect. But he objects to belong to the sect of Mrs. Whirlpool. So he calls himself a mental healer of metaphysical-chemico-physico-religiosio what-not! Yesterday there was a tremendous cyclone which gave a good "treatment" to the tents. The big tent under which they had the lectures, had developed so much spirituality, under the "treatment", that it entirely disappeared from mortal gaze and about two hundred chairs were dancing about the grounds under spiritual ecstasy! Mrs. Figs gives a class every morning; and Mrs. Mills is jumping all about the place, they are all in high spirits. I am especially glad for Cora, for they have suffered a good deal last winter and a little hilarity would do her good. You will be astounded with the liberty they enjoy in the camps, but they are very good and pure people there—a little erratic and that is all.

I shall be here till Saturday next. . . . The other night the camp people went to sleep beneath a pine tree under which I sit every morning *à la* Hindu and talk to them. Of course I went with them, and we had a nice night under the stars, sleeping on the lap of mother earth, and I enjoyed every bit of it. I cannot describe to you that night's glories—after a year of brutal life that I have led, to sleep on the ground, to meditate under the tree in the forest! The inn people are more or less well-to-do, and the camp people are healthy, young, *sincere* and holy men and women. I teach them *Shivoham, Shivoham*, and they all repeat it, innocent and pure as they are and brave beyond all bounds. And so I am happy and glorified. Thank God for making me poor, thank God for making these children in the tents poor. The Dudes and Dudines are in the Hotel, but iron-bound nerves and souls of triple steel and spirits of fire are in the camp. If you had seen them yesterday, when the rain was falling in torrents and the cyclone was overturning everything, hanging by their tent strings to keep them from being blown down, and standing on the majesty of their souls—these brave ones—it would have done your hearts good—I will go a hundred miles to see the like of them. Lord bless them. I hope you are enjoying your nice village life. Never be anxious for a moment. I *will* be taken care of, and if not, I *will* know my time has come and shall pass out.

"Sweet One! Many people offer to You many things. I am poor—but I have the body, mind and soul. I give them over to You. Deign to accept, Lord of the Universe, and refuse them not." So have I given over my life and soul once for all. One thing—they are a dry sort of people here—and as to that very few in the whole world are there that are not. They do not understand "Madhava," the Sweet One. They are either intellectual or go after faith cure, table turning, witchcraft, etc., etc. Nowhere have I heard so much about "love, life and liberty" as in this country, but nowhere is it less understood. Here God is either a terror or a healing power, vibration, and so forth. Lord bless their souls! And these parrots talk day and night of love and love and love!

Now, good dreams, good thoughts for you. You are good and noble. Instead of materialising the spirit, i.e., dragging the spiritual to the material plane as these folks do, convert the matter into spirit, catch a glimpe at least, every day, of that world of infinite beauty and peace and purity—the spiritual, and try to live in it day and night. Seek not, touch not with your toes even, anything that is uncanny. Let your souls ascend day and night like an "unbroken string" unto the feet of the Beloved whose throne is in your own hearts and let the rest take care of themselves, i.e., the body and everything else. Life is evanescent, a fleeting dream; youth and beauty fade; say day and night, "Thou art my father, my mother, my husband, my love, my lord, my God—I want nothing but Thou, nothing but Thee, nothing but Thee. Thou in me, I in Thee, I am Thee, Thou art me." Wealth goes, beauty vanishes, life flies, powers fly—but the Lord abideth for ever, love abideth for ever. If there is glory in keeping the machine in good trim, it is more glorious to withhold the soul from suffering with the body—that is the only demonstration of your being "not matter" by letting the matter alone.

Stick to God! Who cares what comes to the body or to anything else. Through the terrors of evil, say—my God, my love! Through the pangs of death, say—my God, my love! Through all the evils under the sun, say—my God, my love! Thou art here, I see Thee. Thou art with me, I feel Thee. I am Thine, take me. I am not of the world's but Thine, leave not then me. Do not go for glass beads leaving the mine of diamonds! This life is a great chance. What, seekest thou the pleasures of the world?—He is the fountain of all bliss. Seek for the highest, aim at that highest and you *shall* reach the highest.—Yours with all blessings, VIVEKANANDA.

(*67*)

C/O GEORGE W. HALE, ESQ.,
541, DEARBORN AVENUE, CHICAGO,
26th June, 1894.

DEAR—, The great Hindi poet Tulsidas, in his benediction to the translation of the Ramayana, says, "I bow down to both the wicked and holy, but alas! for me, they are both equally torturers—the wicked begin to torture me as soon as they come in contact with me—the good, alas! take my life away when they leave me."

I say amen to this. To me, for whom the only thing left in the world is to love the holy ones of God, it is a mortal torture to separate myself from them. But these things must come. Thou Music of my Beloved's flute, lead on, I am following. It is impossible to express my pain, my anguish at being separated from you, noble and sweet and generous and holy ones. Oh! how I wish I had succeeded in becoming a Stoic!

Hope you are enjoying the beautiful village scenery. "Where the world is awake, there the man of self-control is sleeping. Where the world sleeps, there he is waking."

May even the dust of the world never touch you, for after all, the poets say, it is only a piece of carrion covered over with garland. Touch it not—if you can. Come up, young ones of the bird[1] of Paradise, before your feet touch the cesspool of corruption, this world, and fly upwards.

"Oh, thou that art awake, do not go to sleep again."

"Let the world love its many, we have but one Beloved—the Lord. We care not what they say; we are only afraid when they want to paint our Beloved and give Him all sorts of monstrous qualities. Let them do what-

[1] The Swami rather means here a bird of Bengalee folklore, which is fabled to live exclusively in the atmosphere, and whose eggs, laid high up in the air, are hatched during the steep fall towards the ground, so that the young ones, who fly upwards the very moment, have never to touch the earth. Sri Ramakrishna used to compare the Nitya-siddhas, or the eternally liberated souls, to these young birds, because they also soar high up away from Maya before its entanglements can touch them in their earthly life.

ever they please,—for us He is only the beloved—my love, my love, and nothing more."

"Who cares to know how much power, how much quality He has—even that of doing good? We will say once for all, we love not for the long purse, we never sell our love, we want not, we give."

"You, philosopher, come to tell us of His essence, His powers, His attributes—fool! we are here dying for a kiss of His lips."

"Take your nonsense back to your own home and send me a kiss of my Love—can you?"

"Fool! whom art thou bending thy tottering knees before, in awe and fear? I took my necklace and put it round his neck, and tying a string to it as to a collar I am dragging Him along with me, for fear He may fly away even for a moment—that necklace was the collar of love, that string the ecstasy of love. Fool! you know not the secret—the Infinite One comes within my hand under the bondage of love. Knowest thou not that the Mover of the Universe used to dance to the music of the ringing bracelets of the shepherdesses of Brindaban?"

Excuse my mad scribbling, excuse my foolery in trying to express the inexpressible. It is to be felt only.—Ever with blessings, your brother, VIVEKANANDA.

(68)

To a Madrasi disciple

541, DEARBORN AVE.,
CHICAGO,
29th June, 1894.

DEAR—, . . .On the whole the Americans are a million times nobler than the Hindus, and I can work more good here than in the country of the ingrate and the heartless. . . The number of T—s in all America is only 625 by the last census. Mixing up with them will smash me in a minute than help me in any way. . . . The Madras people have done for me more than I deserved and more than was in their power. . . . America is the best field in the world to carry on any idea, so I do not think of leaving America soon. And why? Here I have food and drink and clothes, and everybody so kind, and all this for a few good words!! Why should I give up such a noble nation to go to the land of brutes and the ingrates and the brainless boobies held in the eternal thraldom of superstition, merciless, pitiless wretches? . . .—Yours truly, VIVEKANANDA.

(69)

To Sj. Alasinga Perumal

U. S. A.,
11th July, 1894.

DEAR ALASINGA—, . . . Learn business, my boy. We will do great things yet! Last year I only sowed the seeds; this year I mean to reap. In the meanwhile, keep up as much enthusiasm as possible in India. Let Kidi go his own way. He will come out all right in time. I have taken his responsibility. He has a perfect right to his own opinion. Make him write for the paper; that will keep him in good temper! My blessings on him.

. . . You must send a paper and a letter to Professor J. H. Wright of Harvard University, Boston, thanking him as having been the first man who stood as my friend.

. . . In the Detroit lecture I got $900, i.e., Rs. 2,700. In other lectures, I earned in one, $2,500, i.e., Rs. 7,500, in one hour, but got only 200 dollars! I was cheated by a roguish lecture bureau. I have given them up. . . .

I shall have to print much matter next year. I am going regularly to work. . . . The sheer power of the *will*, will do everything. . . . You must organise a society which should regularly meet, and write to me about it as often as you can. In fact, get up as much enthusiasm as you can. Only, *beware* of falsehood. Go to work, my boys, the fire will come to you! The faculty of organisation is entirely absent in our nature, but this has to be infused. The great secret is—absence of jealousy. Be always ready to concede to the opinions of your brethren, and try always to conciliate. That is the whole secret. Fight on bravely! Life is short! Give it up to a great cause. . . We must not join any sect, but we must sympathise and work with each. . . . Work, work—conquer all by your love! . . .

Try to expand. Remember, the only *sign of life* is motion and growth . . . Keep on steadily. So far we have done wonderful things. Onward, brave souls, we will gain! Organise and found societies and go to work, that is the only way.

At this time of the year there is not much lecturing to be done here, so I will devote myself to my pen, and write. I shall be hard at work all the time, and then when the cold weather comes and people return to their homes, I shall begin lecturing again, and at the same time organise societies.

My love and blessings to you all. I never forget anybody, though I do not write often. Then again, I am now continuously travelling, and letters have to be redirected from one place to another.

Work hard. Be holy and pure, and the fire will come. —Yours affectionately, VIVEKANANDA.

(70)

To The Same

U. S. A.,
31st August, 1894.

DEAR ALASINGA—. . . I have received a letter from *Cat*, but it requires a book to answer all his queries. So, I send him my blessings through you and ask you to remind him, that we agree to differ—and see the harmony of contrary points. So it does not matter what he believes in; he must act.

Give my love to Balaji, G. G., Kidi, Doctor, and to all our friends and all the great and patriotic souls, who were brave and noble enough to sink their differences for their country's cause.

. . . Now organise a little society . . . . You will have to take charge of the whole movement, not as a *leader*, but as a *servant*. Do you know, the least show of leading destroys everything by rousing jealousy! . . . Work slowly by disseminating the ideas broadcast . . . . Mysore will in time be a great stronghold of our Mission. . . . Try to collect funds from Mysore and elsewhere to build a temple in Madras, which should have a library and some rooms for the office and the preachers who should be Sannyasins, and for Vairâgis who may chance to come. Thus we shall progress inch by inch . . . . So far you have done well indeed, my brave boy. All strength shall be given to you. . . .

This is a great field for my work, and everything done here prepares the way for my coming work in England. . . .

You know the greatest difficulty with me is to keep or even to touch money. It is disgusting and debasing. So you must organise a society to take charge of the practical and pecuniary part of it. I have friends here who take care of all my monetary concerns. Do you see? It will be a wonderful relief to me to get rid of horrid money affairs. So, the sooner you organise yourselves and you be ready as secretary and treasurer to enter into direct communication with my friends and sympathisers here, the better for you and me. Do that quickly, and write to me. Give the society a non-sectarian name.

. . . Great things are in store for you. . . . By and by I hope to make you independent of your college work, so that you may, without starving yourself and family, devote your whole soul to the work. So work, my boys, work! The rough part of the work has been smoothened and rounded; now it will roll on better and better every year. And if you can simply keep it going well until I come to India, the work will progress by leaps and bounds. Rejoice that you have done so much. When you feel gloomy, think what has been done within the last year. How, rising from nothing, we have the eyes of the world fixed upon us now. Not only India, but the world outside is expecting great things of us.

. . . Nothing will be able to resist truth and love and sincerity. Are you sincere? Unselfish even unto death? —and loving? Then fear not, not even death. Onward, my lads! The whole world requires Light. It is expectant! India alone has that Light, not in magic, mummeries and charlatanism, but in the teaching of the glories of the spirit of real religion—of the highest spiritual truth. That is why the Lord has preserved the race through all its vicissitudes unto the present day. Now the time has come. Have faith that you are all, my brave lads, born to do great things! Let not the barks of puppies frighten you, no, not even the thunderbolts of heaven, but stand up and work!—Ever yours affectionately, VIVEKANANDA.

(71)

To a Sannyasin—an American disciple

BELLE VUE HOTEL,
BOSTON,
13th September, 1894.

Forgive me, but I have the right, as your Guru, to advise you, and I insist that you buy some clothes for yourself, *as the want of them stands in the way of your doing anything in this country.* Once you have a start, you may dress in whatever way you like. People do not object.

You need not thank me, for this is only a duty. According to Hindu law, if a Guru dies his heir is his disciple, and not even his son—supposing him to have had one, before becoming a Sannyasin. This is, you see, an actual spiritual relationship, and none of your Yankee " tutor " business!

With all blessings and prayers for your success,—Yours, VIVEKANANDA.

(72)

To Mrs. Ole Bull

HOTEL BELLE VUE,
BEACON STREET, BOSTON,
19th September, 1894.

DEAR MOTHER SARA—I did not forget you at all. You do not think I will be ever as ungrateful as that. You did not give me your address, still I have been getting news about you from Landsberg through Miss Philips. Perhaps you have seen the memorial and address sent to me from Madras. I send some to be sent to you to Landsberg.

A Hindu son never lends to his mother, but the mother has every right over the son and so the son in the mother. I am very much offended at your offering to repay me the nasty few dollars. I can never repay my debts to you.

I am at present lecturing in several places in Boston. What I want is to get a place where I can sit down and write down my thoughts. I had enough of speaking; now I want to write. I think I will have to go to New York for it. Mrs. Guernsey was so kind to me and she is ever willing to help me. I think I will go to her and sit down and write my book. Yours ever affectionately, VIVEKANANDA.

P.S. Kindly write me whether the Guernseys have returned to town or are still in Fishskill.—V.

(73)

To Sj. Alasinga Perumal

U. S. A.,
21st September, 1894.

DEAR ALASINGA—. . . have been continuously travelling from place to place and working incessantly, giving lectures and holding classes etc.

I have not been able to write a line yet for my proposed book. Perhaps I may be able to take it in hand later on. I have made some nice friends here amongst the liberal people, and a few amongst the orthodox. I hope soon to return to India. I have had enough of this country, and especially as too much work is making me nervous. The giving of too many public lectures and constant hurry have brought on this nervousness. . . . So you see, I will soon return. Of course, there is a growing section with whom I am very popular, and who will like to have me here all the time. But I think I have had enough of newspaper blazoning, and humbugging of a public life. I do not care the least for it.

. . . No large number of men in any country do good out of mere sympathy. A few who give money in Christian lands often do so through policy or fear of hell. So it is as in our Bengali proverb, "Kill a cow and make a pair of shoes out of the leather and give them in charity to a Brahmin." So it is here, and so everywhere; and then, the Westerners are miserly in comparison to our race. I sincerely believe that the Asiatics are the most charitable race in the world, only they are very poor.

I am going to live for a few months in New York. That city is the head, hand and purse of the country. Of course, Boston is called the Brahminical city, and here in America there are hundreds of thousands that sympathise with me. . . . The New York people are very open. I will see what can be done there, as I have some very influential friends. After all, I am getting disgusted with this lecturing business. It will take a long time for the Westerners to understand the higher spirituality. Everything is £ s. d. to them. If a religion brings them money or health or beauty, or long life, they will all flock to it, otherwise not. . . .

Give to Balaji, G. G., and all of our friends my best love.—Yours with everlasting love, VIVEKANANDA.

(74)

To "Kidi"

U. S. A.,
21st September, 1894.

DEAR KIDI—I am very sorry to hear your determination of giving up the world so soon. The fruit falls from the tree when it gets ripe. So wait for the time to come. Do not hurry. Moreover, no one has the right to make others miserable by his foolish acts. Wait, have patience, everything will come right in time. . . . . —Yours with blessings, VIVEKANANDA.

(75)

NEW YORK,*
25th September, 1894.

MY DEAR—, Glad to receive some letters from you. If gives me great pleasure to learn that Sasi and others are making a stir. We must create a stir, nothing short of this will do. You will be throwing the whole world into convulsions.—Victory to the Guru! You know, श्रेयांसि बहुविघ्नानि—"Great undertakings are always fraught with many obstacles." It is these obstacles which knock and shape great characters. . . . Is it in the power of missionaries and people of that sort to withstand this shock? . . . Should a fool succeed where scholars have failed? It is no go, my boy, set your mind at ease about that. In every attempt there will be one set of men who will applaud, and another who will pick holes. Go on doing your own work, what need have you to reply to any party? सत्यमेव जयते नानृतं सत्येनैव पन्था विततो देवयानः।—"Truth alone triumphs, not falsehood. Through Truth lies the path of Devayana." . . . Everything will come about by degrees.

Here in summer they go to the seaside—I also did the same. They have got almost a mania for boating and yachting. The yacht is a kind of light vessel which everyone, young and old, who has the means, possesses. They set sail in them every day to the sea, and return home, to eat and drink and dance—while music continues day and night. Pianos render it a botheration to stay indoors!

I shall now tell you something of the Hales to whose address you direct my letters. He and his wife are an old couple, having two daughters, two nieces and a son. The son lives abroad where he earns a living. The daughters live at home. In this country relationship is through the girls. The son marries and no longer belongs to the family, but the daughter's husband pays frequent visits to his father-in-law's house. They say,

"Son is son till he gets a wife,
The daughter is daughter all her life."

All the four are young and not yet married. Marriage is a very troublesome business here. In the first place one must have a husband after one's heart. Secondly, he must be a moneyed man. . . . They will probably live unmarried; besides, they are now full of renunciation through my contact and are busy with thoughts of Brahman!

The two daughters are blondes, that is, have golden hair, while the two nieces are brunettes, that is, of dark hair. They know all sorts of occupations. The nieces are not so rich, they conduct a kindergarten school; but the daughters do not earn. Many girls of this country earn their living. Nobody depends upon others. Even millionaires' sons earn their living, but they marry and have separate establishments of their own. The daughters call me brother, and I address their mother as mother. All my things are at their places, and they look after them, wherever I may go. Here the boys go in search of a living while quite young, and the girls are educated in the universities. So you will find that in a meeting there will be ninety-nine per cent of girls. The boys are nowhere in comparison with them.

There are a good many spiritualists in this country. The medium is one who induces the spirit. He goes behind a screen, and out of the latter come ghosts, of all sizes and all colours. I have witnessed some cases, but they seemed to be a hoax. I shall test some more before I come to a final conclusion. Many of the spiritualists respect me.

Next comes Christian Science. They form the most influential party, nowadays, figuring everywhere. They are spreading by leaps and bounds, and causing heart-burn to the orthodox. They are Vedantins; I mean, they have picked up a few doctrines of the Advaita and grafted them upon the Bible. And they cure diseases by proclaiming, सोऽहं सोऽहं—"I am He! I am He!"—through strength of mind. They all admire me highly.

Nowadays the orthodox section of this country are crying for help. "Devil worship"[1] is but a thing of the past. They are mortally afraid of me and exclaim, "What a pest! Thousands of men and women follow him! He is going to root out orthodoxy!" Well, the torch has been applied and the conflagration that has set in through the grace of the Guru will not be put out. In course of time the bigots will have their breath knocked out of them. . . . .

The Theosophists have not much power. But they, too, are dead set against the orthodox section.

This Christian Science is exactly like our Kartâbhajâ[2] sect: Say, "I have no disease," and you are whole; and say, "I am He"— सोऽहं —and you are quits—be at

[1] The Orthodox Christians brand Hindus and people of other religion with this name and look upon them with scorn.

[2] An offshoot of Vaishnavism during its degeneracy. They call God "Kartâ," or Master, and are noted for their efficiency in faith-cure.

large. This is a thoroughly materialistic country. The people of this Christian land will recognise religion if only you can cure diseases, work miracles, and open up avenues to money, and understand little of anything else. But there are honourable exceptions. . . .

People here have found a new type of man in me. Even the orthodox are at their wit's end. And people are now looking up to me with an eye of reverence. Is there a greater strength than that of Brahmacharyam—purity, my boy?

I am now busy writing a reply to the Madras Address, which was published in all the newspapers here and created a sensation. If it be cheap, I shall send it in print, but if dear, I shall send a type-written copy. To you also I shall send a copy, have it published in the *Indian Mirror*. The unmarried girls of this country are very good and have a good deal of self-respect. . . . These (the people) are come of Virochana's[1] race. To them ministering to the body is a great thing: they would trim and polish and give their whole attention to that. A thousand instruments for paring nails, ten thousand for hair-cutting, and who can count the varieties of dress and toilet and perfumery?

. . . They are good-natured, kind, and truthful. All is right with them but that enjoyment is their God. It is a country where money flows like rivers, with beauty as its ripple, and learning its waves, and which rolls in luxury.

कांक्षन्तः कर्मणां सिद्धिं यजन्त इह देवताः।
क्षिप्रं हि मानुषे लोके सिद्धिर्भवति कर्मजा ॥

[1] The King of the Asuras and son of the saintly Prahlâda. He went to Brahmâ for self-knowledge, but misunderstanding his teachings turned a materialist. (Chhândogya Upa., Chap. VIII.)

—"Longing for success in action in this world, (men) worship the deities. For success is quickly attained through action in this world of man." (Gita).

Here you have a wonderful manifestation of grit and power—what strength, what practicality, and what manhood! Horses huge as elephants are drawing carriages that are as big as houses. You may take this as a specimen of gigantic proportions in other things also. Here is a manifestation of tremendous energy. . . . They look with veneration upon women, who play a most prominent part in their lives. Here this form of worship has attained its perfection—this is the long and short of it. But to come to the point. Well, I am almost at my wit's end to see the women of this country! They take me to the shops and everywhere, as if I were a child. They do all sorts of work—I cannot do even a sixteenth part of what they do. They are like Lakshmi (the Goddess of Fortune) in beauty, and like Saraswati (the Goddess of Learning) in virtues—they are the Divine Mother incarnate, and worshipping them, one verily attains perfection in everything. Great God! Are we to be counted among men? If I can raise a thousand such Madonnas—Incarnations of the Divine Mother—in our country, before I die, I shall die in peace. Then only will your countrymen become worthy of their name. . . .

I am really struck with wonder to see the women here. How gracious the Divine Mother is on them! Most wonderful women, these! They are about to corner the men who have been nearly worsted in the competition. It is all through Thy grace, O Mother!. . . I shall not rest till I root out this distinction of sex. Is there any sex-distinction in the Atman? Out with the differentiation between man and woman—all is Atman! Give up the identification with the body, and stand up! Say, अस्ति अस्ति,

—" Everything is !"—cherish positive thoughts. By dwelling too much upon नास्ति नास्ति—" It is not! It is not!" (negativism), the whole country is going to ruin! सोऽहं, सोऽहं, शिवोऽहं —" I am He! I am He! I am Shiva!" What a botheration! In every soul is infinite strength; and should you turn yourselves into cats and dogs by harbouring negative thoughts? Who dares to preach negativism? Whom do you call weak and powerless? शिवोऽहं, शिवोऽहं —" I am Shiva! I am Shiva!" I feel as if a thunderbolt struck me on the head when I hear people dwell on negative thoughts. That sort of self-depreciating attitude is another name for disease—do you call that humility? It is vanity in disguise—न लिङ्गं धर्मकारणं, समता, सर्वभूतेषु एतन्मुक्तस्य लक्षणं,—" The external badge does not confer spirituality. It is same-sightedness to all beings which is the test of a liberated soul." अस्ति अस्ति, सोऽहं सोऽहं चिदानन्दरूपः शिवोऽहं शिवोऽहं।—"I am He!" "I am Shiva, of the essence of Knowledge and Bliss!" निगच्छति जगज्जालात् पिञ्जरादिव केशरी —"He frees himself from the meshes of this world as a lion from its cage!" नायमात्मा बलहीनेन लभ्यः।—"This Atman is not accessible to the weak." . . . Hurl yourselves on the world like an avalanche—let the world crack in twain under your weight! Hara! Hara! Mahadeva! उद्धरेदात्मनात्मानम् —" One must save the self by his own self—by personal prowess."

. . . Will such a day come when this life will go for the sake of other's good? The world is not a child's play —and great men are those who build highways for others with their heart's blood. This has been taking place through eternity, that one builds a bridge by laying down his own body and thousands of others cross the river through its help. एवमस्तु, एवमस्तु, शिवोऽहं, शिवोऽहं —" Be it so! Be it so! I am Shiva! I am Shiva!" . . .

It is welcome news that Madras is in a stir.

Were you not going to start a paper or something of that sort, what about that? We must mix with all, and alienate none. All the powers of good against all the powers of evil—this is what we want. Do not insist upon everybody's believing in our Guru. . . . You shall have to edit a magazine, half Bengali and half Hindi—and, if possible, another in English. . . . It won't do to be roaming aimlessly. Wherever you go, you must start a permanent preaching centre. Then only will people begin to change. I am writing a book. As soon as it is finished, I run for home! . . . Always remember that Sri Ramakrishna came for the good of the world—not for name or fame. *Spread only what he came to teach. Never mind for his name—it will spread of itself.* Directly you insist on everybody's accepting your Guru, you will be creating a sect, and everything will come to the ground—so beware! Have a kind word for all—it spoils work to show temper. Let people say whatever they like, stick to your own convictions, and rest assured, the world will be at your feet. They say, "Have faith in this fellow or that fellow," but I say, "Have faith in yourself first," that's the way. Have faith in yourself—all power is in you,—be conscious and bring it out. Say, "I can do everything." "Even the poison of a snake is powerless if you can firmly deny it." Beware! No saying "nay," no negative thoughts! Say, "Yea, yea," सोऽहं, सोऽहं—"I am He! I am He!"

किन्नाम रोदिषि सखे त्वयि सर्वशक्तिः
आमन्त्रयस्व भगवन् भगदं स्वरूपम् ।
त्रैलोक्यमेतदखिलं तव पादमूले
आत्मैव हि प्रभवते न जडः कदाचित् ॥

"What makes you weep, my friend? In you is all power. Summon up your all-powerful nature, O mighty one, and this whole universe will lie at your feet. It is the Self alone that predominates, and not matter."

To work with undaunted energy! What fear! Who is powerful enough to thwart you! कुर्मस्तारकचर्वणं त्रिभुवनमुत्पाटयामः बलात् किं भो न विजानास्यस्मान्, रामकृष्णदासा वयम् —"We shall crush the stars to atoms, and unhinge the universe. Don't you know who we are? We are the servants of Sri Ramakrishna." Fear! Whom to fear, forsooth!

क्षीणाः स्म दीनाः सकरुणाः जल्पन्ति मूढ़ा जनाः
नास्तिक्यन्त्विदन्तु अहह देहात्मवादातुराः।
प्राप्ताः स्म वीरा गतभया अभयं प्रतिष्ठां यदा
आस्तिक्यन्त्विदन्तु चिनुमः रामकृष्णदासा वयम्॥
पीत्वा पीत्वा परमममृतं वीतसंसाररागाः
हित्वा हित्वा सकलकलहप्रापिणीं स्वार्थसिद्धिं।
ध्यात्वा ध्यात्वा गुरुवरपदं सर्वकल्याणरूपं
नत्वा नत्वा सकलभुवनम् पातुमामन्त्रयामः॥
प्राप्तं यद्वै त्वनादिनिधनं वेदोदधिं मथित्वा
दत्तं यस्य प्रकरणे हरिहरब्रह्मादिदेवैर्बलं।
पूर्णं यत्तु प्राणसारैर्भौमनारायणानां
रामकृष्णस्तनुं धत्ते तत्पूर्णपात्रमिदं भोः॥

—"It is those foolish people who identify themselves with their bodies, and piteously cry 'we are weak, we are low.' All this is atheism. Now that we have attained the state beyond fear, we shall have no more fear and become heroes. This indeed is theism which we will choose, the servants of Sri Ramakrishna.

"Giving up the attachment for the world and drinking constantly the supreme nectar of immortality, for ever discarding that self-seeking spirit which is the mother of all dissension, and ever meditating on the blessed feet of our Guru which are the embodiment of all well-being, with repeated salutations we invite the whole world to participate in drinking the nectar.

"That nectar which has been obtained by churning the infinite ocean of the Vedas, into which Brahmâ, Vishnu, Shiva and the other gods have poured their strength, which is charged with the life-essence of the Avatars—Gods (Incarnate on earth)—Sri Ramakrishna holds that nectar in his person, in its fullest measure!"

We must work among the English-educated young men. त्यागेनैके अमृतत्वमानशुः "Through renunciation alone they attained immortality." Renunciation!—Renunciation!—you must preach this above everything else. There will be no spiritual strength unless one renounces the world. . . .

Why are Baburam and Jogen suffering so much? It is owing to their negative, their self-abasing spirit. Tell them to brush aside their illness by mental strength, and in an hour it will disappear! Is the Atman smitten with disease? Off with it! Tell them to meditate for an hour at a stretch, "I am the Atman, how can I be affected by disease!"—and everything will vanish. Think all of you that you are the infinitely powerful Atman, and see what strength comes out. . . . Self-depreciating! What is it for? I am the child of the infinite, the all-powerful Divine Mother. What means disease, or fear, or want, to me? Stamp out the negative spirit as if it were a pestilence, and it will conduce to your welfare in every way. No negative, all positive, affirmative. I am, God is, everything is in me. I *will* manifest health, purity, knowledge, whatever I want. Well, these foreign people could grasp my teachings and you are suffering from illness owing to your negative spirit! Who says you are ill—what is disease to you? Brush it aside!. . . वीर्यमसि वीर्यं, बलमसि बलं, ओजोऽसि ओजो, सहोऽसि सहो मयि धेहि।—" Thou art Energy, impart energy unto me. Thou art Strength, impart strength unto me. Thou art Spirituality, impart spirituality unto me. Thou art Fortitude, impart fortitude unto me!" The ceremony of steadying one's seat (âsana-pratishthâ) that you perform every day when you sit down to worship the Lord आत्मानमच्छिद्रं भावयेत्—" One must think of himself strong and invulnerable " and so forth—what does it all mean? Say, "Everything is in me, and I can manifest it at will." Repeat to yourself that such and such are Atman, that they are infinite, and how can they have any disease? Repeat this an hour or so, on a few successive days, and all disease and trouble will vanish into nought. --Yours ever, VIVEKANANDA.

(76)

To Mrs. Ole Bull

BOSTON,

26th Sept., 1894.

DEAR MRS. BULL—I have received both of your kind notes. I cannot express my gratitude for your kindness. I will have to go back to Melrose on Saturday and remain there till Monday. On Tuesday I will come over to your place. . . . For that is exactly what I wanted, a quiet place to write. Of course much less space will suffice me than what you have kindly proposed to put at my disposal. I can bundle myself up anywhere and feel quite comfortable.—Yours very sincerely, VIVEKANANDA.

(77)

To Sj. Alasinga Perumal

U. S. A.,
27th September, 1894.

Dear Alasinga—. . . One thing I find in the books of my speeches and sayings published in Calcutta. Some of them are printed in such a way as to savour of political views; whereas I am no politician, or political agitator. I care only for the spirit—when that is right everything will be righted by itself. . . . So you must warn the Calcutta people that no political significance be ever attached falsely to any of my writings or sayings. What nonsense! . . . I heard that Rev. Kali Charan Banerji in a lecture to Christian missionaries said that I was a political delegate. If it was said publicly, then publicly ask the Babu from me, to write to any of the Calcutta papers and prove it, or else take back his foolish assertion. This is their trick! I have said a few harsh words in honest criticism of Christian Governments in general, but that does not mean that I care for, or have any connection with politics or that sort of thing. Those who think it very grand to print extracts from those lectures, and want to prove that I am a political preacher, to them I say, "Save me from my friends." . . .

. . . Tell my friends that a uniform silence is all my answer to my detractors. If I give them tit for tat, it would bring us down to a level with them. Tell them that truth will take care of itself, and that they are not to fight anybody for me. They have much to learn yet, and they are only children. They are still full of foolish golden dreams—mere boys!

. . . This nonsense of public life and newspaper blazoning has disgusted me thoroughly. I long to go

back to the Himalayan quiet. Ever yours affectionately,
VIVEKANANDA.

(78)

To The Same

U. S. A.,
29th September, 1894.

DEAR ALASINGA—You all have done well, my brave unselfish children. I am so proud of you. . . . Hope and do not despair. After such a start, if you despair you are a fool. . . .

Our field is India, and the value of foreign appreciation is in rousing India up. That is all. . . . We must have a strong base from which to spread. . . . Do not for a moment quail. Everything will come all right. It is will that moves the world.

You need not be sorry, my son, on account of the young men becoming Christians. What else can they be under the existing social bondages, specially in Madras? Liberty is the first condition of growth. Your ancestors gave every liberty to the soul, and religion grew. They put the body under every bondage, and society did not grow. The opposite is the case in the West—every liberty to society, none to religion. Now are falling off the shackles from the feet of Eastern society as from those of Western religion.

Each again will have its type: the religious or introspective in India, the scientific or out-seeing in the West. The West wants every bit of spirituality through social improvement. The East wants every bit of social power through spirituality. Thus it was that the modern reformers saw no way to reform but by first crushing out the religion of India. They tried and they failed. Why?

Because few of them ever studied their own religion, and not *one* ever *underwent* the training necessary to understand the *mother of all religions*. I claim that no destruction of religion is necessary to improve the Hindu society, and that this state of society exists not on account of religion, but because that religion has not been applied to society as it should have been. This I am ready to prove from our old books, every word of it. This is what I teach and this is what we must struggle all our lives to carry out. But it will take time, a long time to study. Have patience and work. उद्धरेदात्मनात्मानम्—"Save yourself by yourself."—Yours etc., VIVEKANANDA.

P. S. The present Hindu society is organised only for spiritual men, and hopelessly crushes out everybody else. Why? Where shall they go who want to enjoy the world a little with its frivolities? Just as our religion takes in all, so should our society. This is to be worked out by first understanding the true principles of our religion, and then applying them to society. This is the slow but sure work to be done.

—V.

(79)

To Sj. Haridas Viharidas Desai

CHICAGO,
September, 1894.

DEAR DIWANJI SAHEB.—Your kind letter reached long ago, but as I had not anything to write I was late in answering.

Your kind note to G. W. Hale has been very gratifying as I owed them that much. I have been travelling all over this country all this time and seeing everything. I have come to this conclusion that there is only one country in the world which understands religion—it is India;—that with all their faults the Hindus are head and shoulders above all other nations in morality and spirituality and that with proper care and attempt and struggle of all her disinterested sons, by combining some of the active and heroic elements of the West with calm virtues of the Hindus, there will come a type of men far superior to any that have ever been in this world.

I do not know when I come back but I have seen enough of this country, I think, and so soon will go over to Europe and then to India.

With my best love, gratitude to you and all your brothers,—I remain, Yours faithfully, VIVEKANANDIA.

(*80*)

To The Same

DEAR DIWANJI SAHEB—Very kind of you to send up a man inquiring about my health and comfort. But that's quite of a piece to your fatherly character. I am all right here. Your kindness has left nothing more to be desired here. I hope soon to see you in a few days. I don't require any conveyance while going down. Descent is very bad and the ascent is the worst part of the job, that's the same in everything in the world. My heart-felt gratitude to you.—Yours faithfully, VIVEKANANDA.

(*81*)

To Swami Brahmananda

BALTIMORE, U. S. A.,*
22nd October, 1894.

DEAR RAKHAL—Glad to receive your letter and go through the contents. I received to-day a letter of Akshay Kumar Ghosh from London, which also gives me some information.

Now you have come to know your own powers. Strike the iron while it is hot. Idleness won't do. Throw overboard all idea of jealousy and egotism, once for all. Come on to the practical field with tremendous energy; to work, in the fulness of strength! As to the rest, the Lord will point out the way. The whole world will be deluged by a tidal wave. Work, work, work—let this be your motto. I cannot see anything else. There is no end of work here—I am careering all over the country. Wherever the seed of his power will find its way, there it will fructify—अद्य वाब्दशतान्ते वा—be it to-day, or in a hundred years. You must work in sympathy with all, then only will it lead to quick results.

. . . Our object is to do good to the world, and not the trumpeting of our own names. Why doesn't Niranjan learn Pali, in Ceylon, and study Buddhist books? I cannot make out what good will come of aimless rambling. . . . Those that have come under his protection, have virtue, wealth, desires and freedom lying at their feet. माभैः माभैः—courage! Everything will come about by degrees. From all of you I want this that you must discard for ever self-aggrandisement, faction-mongering and jealousy. You must be all-forbearing, like Mother Earth. If you can achieve this, the world will be at your feet.

. . . Try to give less of material food in the anniversary celebrations, and give some food for the brain instead. . . . —VIVEKANANDA.

(82)

To Sj. Vehemia Chand

WASHINGTON,
23rd October, 1894.

DEAR VEHEMIA CHAND—. . . By this time I have become one of their own teachers. They all like me and my teachings. . . . I travel all over the country from one place to another, as was my habit in India, preaching and teaching. Thousands and thousands have listened to me and taken my ideas in a very kindly spirit. It is the most expensive country, but the Lord provides for me everywhere I go.

With my love to you and all my friends there (Limbdi, Rajputana),—Yours, VIVEKANANDA.

(*83*)

To Mrs. Ole Bull

WASHINGTON,
27th October, 1894.

DEAR MRS. BULL—Many thanks for your kindness in sending me the introduction to Mr. Frederic Douglas. You need not be sorry on account of the ill-treatment I received at the hands of a low class hotel-keeper at Baltimore. It was the fault of Vrooman Brothers. Why should they take me to a low hotel?

And then the American women as everywhere came to my rescue, and I had very good time.

In Washington I am the guest of Mrs. E. Totten who is an influential lady here and a metaphysician. . . . Everything is going on all right. . . . With eternal love and gratitude for you,—I remain, Yours etc., VIVEKANANDA.

(*84*)

To Sj. Alasinga Perumal

WASHINGTON,
27th October, 1894.

DEAR ALASINGA—. . . I am doing here exactly what I used to do in India. Always depending on the Lord and making no plans ahead. . . . Moreover, you must remember that I have to work incessantly in this country and that I have no time to put together my thoughts in the form of a book, so much so, that this constant rush has worn my nerves, and I am feeling it. I cannot express my obligation to you, and all my friends in Madras, for the most unselfish and heroic work you did for me. I am not an organiser, my nature tends towards scholarship and meditation. I think I have worked enough, now I want rest and to teach a little to those that have come to me from my Gurudeva. You have known now what you can do, for it is really you, young men of Madras, that have done all; I am only the figurehead. I am a Tyâgi, I only want one thing. I do not believe in a religion or God which cannot wipe the widow's tears or bring a piece of bread to the orphan's mouth. However sublime be the theories, however well-spun may be the philosophy—I do not call it religion so long as it is confined to books and dogmas. The eye is in the forehead and not in the back. Move onward and carry into practice that which you are very proud to call your religion, and God bless you!

Look not to me, look to yourselves. I am happy to have been the occasion of rousing an enthusiasm. Take advantage of it, float along with it, and everything will come right. Love never fails, my son; to-day or to-morrow or ages after, truth will conquer! Love shall win the victory. Do you love your fellowmen? Where should you go to seek for God; are not all the poor, the miserable, the weak Gods? Why not worship them first? Why go to dig a well on the shores of the Ganges? Believe in the omnipotent power of love. Who cares for these tinsel puffs of name? I never keep watch of what the newspapers are saying. Have you love? You are omnipotent. Are you perfectly unselfish? If so, you are irresistible. It is character that pays everywhere. It is the Lord who protects His children in the depths of the sea. Your country requires heroes; be heroes!

Everybody wants me to come over to India. They think we shall be able to do more if I come over. They are mistaken, my friend. The present enthusiasm is only a little patriotism, it means nothing. If it is true and genuine you will find in a short time hundreds of heroes coming forward and carrying on the work. Therefore know that you have really done all, and go on. Look not for me. Here is a grand field. What have I to do with this "ism" or that "ism"? I am the servant of the Lord, and where on earth is there a better field than here for propagating all high ideas? Here, where if one man is against me, a hundred hands are ready to help me; here, where man feels for man, and women are goddesses! Even idiots may stand up to hear themselves praised, and cowards assume the attitude of the brave when everything is sure to turn out well, but the true hero works in silence. How many Buddhas die before one finds expression! My son, I believe in God and I believe in man. I believe in helping the miserable, I believe in going even to hell to save others. Talk of the Westerners, they have given me food, shelter, friendship, protection—even the most orthodox Christians! What do our people do when any of their priests go to India? You do not touch them even, they are Mlechchhas! No man, no nation, my son, can hate others and live. India's doom was sealed the very day they invented the word Mlechchha and stopped from communion with others. Take care how you foster that idea. It is good to talk glibly about the Vedanta, but how hard to carry out even its least precepts!—Ever yours with blessings,

VIVEKANANDA.

P.S. Take care of these two things--love of power and jealousy. Cultivate always "faith in yourself."

—V.

(85)

To Sj. Haridas Viharidas Desai

CHICAGO,
15th November, 1894.

DEAR DIWANJI SAHEB—I have received your kind note. So very kind of you to remember me even here, I have not seen your Narayan Hemchandra. He is not in America, I believe. I have seen many strange sights and grand things. I am glad that there is a good chance of your coming over to Europe. Avail of it by any means. The fact of our isolation from all the other nations of the world is the cause of our degeneration and its only remedy is getting back into the current of the rest of the world. Motion is the sign of life. America is a grand country. It is a paradise for the poor and women. There is almost no poor in the country and nowhere else in the world women are so free, so educated, so cultured. They are everything in society.

This is a great lesson. The Sannyasin has not lost a bit of his Sannyasiship, even his mode of living. And in this most hospitable country, every home is open to me. The Lord who guides me in India, would He not guide me here? And He has.

You may not understand why a Sannyasin should be in America, but it was necessary. Because the only claim you have to be recognised by the world is your religion, and good specimens of our religious men are required to be sent abroad, to give other nations an idea that India is not dead.

Some representative men must come out of India and go to all the nations of the earth to show at least that you are not savages. You may not feel the necessity of it from your Indian home, but believe me, much depends upon that for your nation. And a Sannyasin who has no idea of doing good to his fellows is a brute, not a Sannyasin.

I am neither a sight-seer nor an idle traveller, but you will see, if you live to see, and bless me all your life.

Mr. Dwivedi's papers were too big for the Parliament, and they had to be cut short.

I spoke at the Parliament of Religions, and with what effect I may quote to you from a few newspapers and magazines ready at hand. I need not be self-conceited, but to you in confidence I am bound to say, because of your love, that no Hindu made such an impression in America, and if my coming has done nothing, it has done this that Americans have come to know that India even to-day produces men at whose feet even the most civilised nations may learn lessons of religion and morality. Don't you think that is enough to say for the Hindu nation sending over here their Sannyasin? You would hear the details from Virchand Gandhi.

These I quote from the journals:—"But eloquent as were many of the brief speeches, no one expressed as well the spirit of the Parliament (of religions) and its limitations as the Hindu monk. I copy his address in full but I can only suggest its effect upon the audience, for he is an orator by Divine right and his strong intelligent face in its picturesque setting of yellow and orange was hardly less interesting than these earnest words and the rich rhythmical utterance he gave them." (Here the speech is quoted in extenso). *New York Critique.*

"His culture, his eloquence and his fascinating personality have given us *a new idea of Hindu civilisation.* His fine intelligent face and his deep musical voice prepossessing one at once in his favour has preached in clubs and churches until his faith has become familiar to us. He speaks without notes, presenting his facts and his conclusion with the greatest art, the most convincing sincerity and rising often to rich inspiring eloquence." *Ibid.*

"Vivekananda is undoubtedly the greatest figure in the Parliament of Religions. After hearing him we feel how foolish it is to send missionaries to this learned nation." *Herald* (The greatest paper here).

I cease from quoting more lest you think me conceited, but this was necessary to you who have become nearly frogs in the well and would not see how the world is going on elsewhere. I do not mean you personally, my noble friend, but our nation in general.

I am the same here as in India; only here in this highly cultured land there is an appreciation, a sympathy which our ignorant fools never dream of. There our people grudge us monks a crumb of bread; here they are ready to pay one thousand rupees a lecture and remain grateful for the instructions for ever.

I am appreciated by these strangers more than I was ever in India. I can, if I will, live here all my life in the greatest luxury, but I am a Sannyasin, and "India, with all thy faults I love thee still." So I am coming back after some months, and shall go on sowing the seeds of religion and progress from city to city as I was doing so long, although amongst a people who know not what appreciation and gratefulness are.

I am ashamed of my own nation when I compare their beggarly, selfish, unappreciative, ignorant ungratefulness with the help, hospitality, sympathy and respect which the Americans have shown to me, a representative of a foreign religion. Therefore come out of the country, see others and compare.

Now after these quotations do you think it was worthwhile to send a Sannyasin to America?

Please do not publish it. I hate notoriety in the same manner as I did in India.

I am doing the Lord's work and wherever He leads I follow. मूकं करोति वाचालं etc.—He who makes the dumb eloquent and the lame cross a mountain, He will help me. I do not care for human help. He is ready to help me in India, in America, in the North Pole, if He thinks fit. If He does not, none else can help me. Glory unto the Lord for ever and ever.—Yours with blessings, VIVEKANANDA.

(86)

To The Same

CHICAGO,
541, DEARBORN AVENUE,
Nov., 1894.

DEAR DIWANJI—Your letter pleased me extremely. I, of course, understand the joke, but I am not the baby to be put off with a joke; now take more.

The secret of success of the Westerners is the power of organisation and combination. That is only possible with mutual trust and co-operation and help. Now here is Virchand—Gandhi, the Jain, whom you well knew in Bombay. This man never takes anything but pure vegetable even in this terrible cold climate, and tooth and nail tries to defend his countrymen and religion. The people of this country like him very well, but what are they doing who sent him over? They are trying to outcast him. Jealousy is a vice necessarily generated in slaves. Again it is jealousy that holds them down.

Here were . . . ; they were all trying to lecture and get money thereby. They did something, but I succeeded better than they—why, I did not put myself as a bar to their success. It was the will of the Lord. But all these . . . except . . . have fabricated and circulated the most horrible lies about me in this country, and at my back. Americans will never stoop to such meanness.

. . . If any man tries to move forward, here everybody is ready to help him. In India you may try tomorrow by writing a single line of praise for me in any one of our papers (Hindu), and next day they would be all against me. Why? It is the nature of slaves. They cannot suffer to see anyone of their brethren putting his head the least above their rank. . . . Do you mean to compare such stuff with these children of liberty, self-help and brotherly love? The nearest approach to our people are the freed slaves of the U. S. A., the Negroes. Why, in the South they are about twenty millions and are now free. The whites are a handful, still the whites hold them down all the same. Why, even when they have every right by law, has a bloody war between the brothers been fought to free these slaves? The same defect—jealousy. Not one of these Negroes would bear to see his brother-Negro praised or pushing on. Immediately they would join the whites to crush him down. You can have no idea about it until you come out of India. It is all right for those who have plenty of money and position to let the world roll on as such, but I call him a traitor who, having been educated and nursed in luxury by the heart's blood of the downtrodden millions of the toiling poor, never even takes a thought for them. Where, in what period of history did your rich men and noble men, your priests and potentates take any thought for the poor—the grinding of whose faces is the very life-blood of their power?

But the Lord is great. The vengeance came sooner or later, and they who sucked the life-blood of the poor, whose very education was at their expense, whose very power was built on their poverty, were in their turn sold as slaves by hundreds and thousands, their wives and daughters dishonoured, their property robbed for the last one thousand years, and do you think it was for no cause?

Why amongst the poor of India are so many Mohammedans? It is nonsense to say they were converted by the sword. It was to gain their liberty from the . . . zemindars and from the . . . priests. And as a consequence you find in Bengal there are more Mohammedans than Hindus amongst the cultivators, because there were so many zemindars there. Who thinks of raising these sunken downtrodden millions? A few thousand graduates do not make a nation; a few rich men do not make a nation. True, our opportunities are fewer, but still there are enough to feed and clothe and make three hundred millions more comfortable, nay, luxurious. Ninety per cent of our people are without education—who thinks of that? These Babus, the so-called patriots?

Now, let me tell you—still there is a God, no joke. He is ordering our lives, and although I know a nation of slaves cannot but try to bite at the hand that wants to give them medicine, yet, pray with me, you—one of the few that have real sympathy for everything good, for everything great, one at least whom I know to be a man of true ring, nobility of nature and a thorough sincerity of head and heart—pray with me:

"Lead, Kindly Light,
amid the encircling gloom."

I do not care what they say. I love my God, my religion, my country, and above all, myself, a poor beggar. I love the poor, the ignorant, the downtrodden. I feel for them. The Lord knows how much. He will show me the way. I do not care a fig for human approbation or criticism. I think of most of them as ignorant, noisy children—they have not penetrated into the inner nature of sympathy, into the spirit which is all love.

I have that insight through the blessings of Ramakrishna. I am trying to work with my little band, all of these poor beggars like me. You have seen them. But the Lord's works have been always done by the lowly, by the poor. You bless me that I may have faith in my Guru, in my God, and in myself.

The only way is love and sympathy. The only worship is love.

May He help you and yours ever and ever!—With prayers and blessings, VIVEKANANDA.

(87)

To Raja Pyari Mohan Mukherjee

NEW YORK,
18th November, 1894.

DEAR SIR—I am in receipt of the resolutions that were passed at the recent Town Hall meeting in Calcutta, and the kind words my fellow-citizens sent over to me.

Accept, sir, my most heart-felt gratitude for your appreciation of my insignificant services.

I am thoroughly convinced that no individual or nation can live by holding itself apart from the community of others, and whenever such an attempt has been made under false ideas of greatness, policy or holiness—the result has always been disastrous to the secluding one.

To my mind, the one great cause of the downfall and the degeneration of India was the building of a wall of custom—whose foundation was hatred of others—round the nation, and the real aim of which in ancient times was to prevent the Hindus from coming in contact with the surrounding Buddhistic nations.

Whatever cloak ancient or modern sophistry may try to throw over it, the inevitable result—the vindication of the moral law, that none can hate others without degenerating himself—is that the race that was foremost amongst the ancient races is now a byword, and a scorn among nations. We are object-lessons of the violation of that law which our ancestors were the first to discover and discriminate.

Give and take is the law, and if India wants to raise herself once more, it is absolutely necessary that she brings out her treasures and throws them broadcast among the nations of the earth, and in return be ready to receive what others have to give her. Expansion is life, contraction is death. Love is life and hatred is death. We commenced to die the day we began to hate other races, and nothing can prevent our death unless we come back to expansion, which is life.

We must mix, therefore, with all the races of the earth. And every Hindu that goes out to travel in foreign parts renders more benefit to his country than hundreds of men who are bundles of superstitions and selfishness and whose one aim in life seems to be like that of the dog in the manger. The wonderful structures of national life which the Western nations have raised, are supported by the strong pillars of character, and until we can produce numbers of such, it is useless to fret and fume against this or that power.

Do any deserve liberty who are not ready to give it to others? Let us calmly and in a manly fashion go to work, instead of dissipating our energy in unnecessary frettings and fumings. I, for one, thoroughly believe that no power in the universe can withhold from any one anything he really deserves. The past was great no doubt, but I sincerely believe that the future will be more glorious still. May Shankara keep us steady in purity, patience, and perseverance.—Yours faithfully, VIVEKANANDA.

(*88*)

To Sj. Alasinga Perumal

NEW YORK,
19th Nov., 1894.

MY BRAVE BOYS—Push on with the organisation. . . . Nothing else is necessary but these—*Love, Sincerity* and *Patience*. What is life but growth, i.e., expansion, i.e., *love*? Therefore all love is life, it is the only law of life, all selfishness is *death*, and this is true here or hereafter. It is life to do good, it is death not to do good to others. Ninety per cent of human brutes you see are dead, are *ghosts*—for none lives, my boys, but he who loves. Feel, my children, feel: feel for the poor, the ignorant, the downtrodden, feel till the heart stops and the brain reels and you think you will go mad—then pour the soul out at the feet of the Lord and then will come power, help, and indomitable energy. Struggle, struggle was my motto for the last ten years. Struggle, still say I. When it was all dark I used to say, struggle; when light is breaking in, I still say, struggle. Be not afraid, my children. Look not up in that attitude of fear towards that infinite starry vault as if it would crush you. Wait! In a few hours more the whole of it will be under your feet. Wait, money does not pay, nor name; fame does not pay, nor learning.

It is love that pays; it is character that cleaves its way through adamantine walls of difficulties.

Now the question before us is this. There cannot be any growth without *liberty*. Our ancestors freed religious thought, and we have a wonderful religion; but they put a heavy chain on the feet of society, and our society is, in a word, *horrid, diabolical*. In the West, society always had freedom, and look at them. On the other hand, look at their religion.

Liberty is the first condition of growth. Just as man must have liberty to think and speak, so he must have liberty in food, dress and marriage and in every other thing, so long as he does not injure others.

We talk foolishly against material civilisation. The grapes are sour. Even taking all that foolishness for granted, in all India there are, say, a hundred thousand really spiritual men and women. Now, for the spiritualisation of these, must three hundred millions be sunk in savagery and starvation? Why should any starve? How was it possible for the Hindus to have been conquered by the Mohammedans? It was due to the Hindus' ignorance of material civilisation. Even the Mohammedans taught them to wear tailor-made clothes. Would the Hindus had learned from the Mohammedans how to eat in a cleanly way without mixing their food with the dust of the streets! Material civilisation, nay, even luxury, is necessary to create work for the poor. Bread! Bread! I do not believe in a God who cannot give me bread here, giving me eternal bliss in heaven! Pooh! India is to be raised, the poor are to be fed, education is to be spread, and the evil of priestcraft is to be removed. No priestcraft, no social tyranny! More bread, more opportunity for everybody! Our young fools make meetings to get more power from the English. They only laugh. None deserves liberty who is not ready to give liberty. Suppose the English give over to you all the power. Why, the powers that be, then, will hold the people down, and let them not have it. Slaves want power to make slaves.

Now, this is to be brought about slowly and by only insisting on our religion and giving liberty to society. Root up priestcraft from the old religion, and you get the best religion in the world. Do you understand me? Can you make a European society with India's religion? I believe it is possible and must be. . . . The grand plan is to start a colony in Central India, where you can follow your own ideas independently; and then a little leaven will leaven all. In the meanwhile form a Central Association, and go on branching off all over India. Start only on religious grounds now, and do not preach any violent social reform at present; only do not countenance foolish superstitions. Try to revive society on the old grounds of universal salvation and equality as laid down by the old Masters, such as Shankaracharya, Ramanuja and Chaitanya.

Have fire and spread all over. Work, work. Be the servant while leading, be unselfish, and *never listen to one friend in private accusing another.* Have infinite patience, and success is yours. . . . Now take care of this: Do not try to "boss" others, as the Yankees say. Because I always direct my letters to you, you need not try to show your consequence over my other friends. I know you never can be such a fool, but still I think it my duty to warn you. This is what kills all organisation. Work, work, for, to work only for the good of others is life.

I want that there should be no hypocrisy, no Jesuitism, no roguery. I have depended always on the Lord, always on the Truth broad as the light of day. Let me not die with stains on my conscience for having played Jesuitism to get up name or fame, or even to do good. There should not be a breath of immorality, nor a stain of policy which is bad.

No shilly-shally, no *esoteric blackguardism*, no secret humbug, nothing should be done in a corner. No special favouritism of the Master, no Master at that even. Onward, my brave boys—money or no money—men or no men! Have you love? Have you God? Onward, and forward to the breach, you are irresistible.

How absurd! The Theosophical magazines saying that they prepared the way to my success! Indeed!! Pure nonsense! Theosophists prepared the way!! . . .

Take care! Beware of everything that is untrue; stick to truth and we shall succeed, maybe slowly but surely. Work on as if I never existed. Work as if on each of you depended the whole work. Fifty centuries are looking on you, the future of India depends on you. Work on. I do not know when I shall be able to come. This is a great field for work. They can at best praise in India, but they will not give a cent for anything; and where shall they get it, *beggars* themselves? Then they have lost the faculty of doing public good for the last two thousand years or more. They are just learning the ideas of nation, public, etc. So I need not blame them. More afterwards.—With blessings, yours, VIVEKANANDA.

(*89*)

To The Same

30th Nov., 1894.

DEAR ALASINGA—We must organise our forces in the business part of our religious body, but on religious matters must strive not to make a sect. . . .

If anyone can write a real life of Sri Ramakrishna with the idea of showing what he came to do and teach, let him do it, otherwise let him not distort his life and sayings. . . . Now let Kidi translate his love, his knowledge, his teachings, his eclecticism, etc. This is the theme. The life of Sri Ramakrishna was an extraordinary searchlight under whose illumination one is able to really understand the whole scope of Hindu religion. He was the object-lesson of all the theoretical knowledge given in the Shastras. He showed by his life what the Rishis and Avatars really wanted to teach. The books were theories, he was the realisation. This man had in fifty-four years lived the five thousand years of national spiritual life and so raised himself to be an object-lesson for future generations. The Vedas can only be explained and the Shastras reconciled by his theory of *Avasthâ*, or stages. That we must not only tolerate others but positively embrace them, and that Truth is the basis of all religions. Now on these lines a most impressive and beautiful life can be written. Well, everything in good time. . . . Push on with your work independently. "Many come to sit at dinner when it is cooked." Take care and work on.—Yours ever with blessings, VIVEKANANDA.

(*90*)

To "Kidi"

30th Nov., 1894.

DEAR KIDI—. . . As to the wonderful stories published about Sri Ramakrishna, I advise you to keep clear of them and the fools who write them. They are true, but the fools will make a mess of the whole thing, I am sure. He had a whole world of knowledge to teach, why insist upon unnecessary things as miracles really are. They do not prove anything. Matter does not prove spirit. What connection is there between the existence of God, soul, or immortality, and the working of miracles. . . . Preach Sri Ramakrishna. Pass the cup that has satisfied your thirst. . . . Do not disturb your head with metaphysical nonsense, and do not disturb others by your bigotry.—Yours ever with blessings, VIVEKANANDA.

(*91*)

U. S. A.,
30th November, 1894.

DEAR AND BELOVED—Your beautiful letter just came to hand. I am so glad that you have come to know Sri Ramakrishna. I am very glad at the strength of your Vairâgya. It is the one primary necessity in reaching God. I had always great hopes for Madras, and still I have the firm belief that from Madras will come the spiritual wave that will deluge India. I can only say Godspeed to your good intentions, but here, my son, are the difficulties. In the first place, no man ought to take a hasty step. In the second place, you must have some respect for the feelings of your mother and wife. True, you may say that we, the disciples of Ramakrishna, have not always shown great deference to the opinions of our parents. I know and know for sure that great things are done only by great sacrifices. I know for certain that India requires the sacrifice of her highest and best, and I sincerely hope that it will be your good fortune to be one of them.

Throughout the history of the world you find great men make great sacrifices and the mass of mankind enjoy the benefit. If you want to give up everything for your own salvation, it is nothing. Do you want to forgo even your own salvation for the good of the world? You are God, think of that. My advice to you is to live the life of a Brahmacharin, i.e., giving up all sexual enjoyments for a certain time live in the house of your father; this is the "Kutichaka" stage. Try to bring your wife to consent to your great sacrifice for the good of the world. And if you have burning faith and all-conquering love and almighty purity, I do not doubt that you will shortly succeed. Give yourself body and soul to the work of spreading the teachings of Sri Ramakrishna, for work (Karma) is the first stage. Study Sanskrit diligently as well as practise devotion. For you are to be a great teacher of mankind, and my Guru Maharaja used to say, "A penknife is sufficient to commit suicide with, but to kill others one requires guns and swords." And in the fulness of time it will be given unto you when to go forth out of the world and preach His sacred name. Your determination is holy and good. Godspeed to you, but do not take any hasty step. First purify yourself by work and devotion. India has suffered long, the religion eternal has suffered long. But the Lord is merciful. Once more He has come to help His children, once more the opportunity is given to fallen India to rise. India can only rise by sitting at the feet of Sri Ramakrishna. His life and his teachings are to be spread far and wide, are to be made to penetrate every pore of Hindu society. Who will do it? Who are to take up the flag of Ramakrishna and march for the salvation of the world? Who are to stem the tide of degeneration at the sacrifice of name and fame, wealth and enjoyment nay, of every hope of this or other worlds? A few young men have jumped in the breach, have sacrificed themselves. They are a few, we want a few thousands of such as they, and *they will come.* I am glad that our Lord has put it in your mind to be one of them. Glory unto him on whom falls the Lord's choice. Your determination is good, your hopes are high, your aim is the noblest in the world—

to bring millions sunk in darkness to the light of the Lord.

But, my son, here are the drawbacks. Nothing shall be done in haste. Purity, patience and perseverance are the three essentials to success and, above all, *love*. All time is yours, there is no indecent haste. Everything will come right if you are pure and sincere. We want hundreds like you bursting upon society and bringing new life and vigour of the Spirit wherever they go. Godspeed to you.—Yours with all blessings, VIVEKANANDA.

(*92*)

U. S. A.,
26th Dec., 1894.

BLESSED AND BELOVED—. . . In reference to me every now and then, attacks are made in missionary papers (so I hear), but I never care to see them. If you send any of those made in India I should throw them into the waste-paper basket. A little agitation was necessary for our work. We have had enough. Pay no more attention to what people say about me, whether good or bad. You go on with your work and remember that "Never one meets with evil who tries to do good" (Gita).

Every day the people here are appreciating me. Everything must proceed slowly. . . . I have written to you before and I write again, that I shall not pay heed to any criticisms or praises in the newspapers. They are consigned to the fire. Do you do the same. Pay no attention whatsoever to newspaper nonsense or criticism. Be sincere and do your duty. Everything will come all right. Truth must triumph. . . .

Missionary misrepresentations should be beneath your

notice. . . . Perfect silence is the best refutation, and I wish you to maintain the same. . . . Make Mr. Subrahmanyam Ayer the President of your Society. He is one of the sincerest and noblest men I know, and in him, intellect and emotion are beautifully blended. Push on in your work, without counting much on me; work on your own account. . . . As for me, I do not know when I shall go back; I am working here and in India as well. . . . With my love to you all,—Yours ever with blessings, VIVEKANANDA.

(93)

To Lala Govinda Sahay

C/o G. W. HALE, ESQ.,
CHICAGO,
1894.

DEAR GOVINDA SAHAY—Do you keep any correspondence with my Gurubhais of Calcutta? Are you progressing morally, spiritually and in your worldly affairs? . . . Perhaps you have heard how for more than a year I have been preaching Hindu religion in America. I am doing very well here. Write to me as soon as you can and as often as you like.—Yours with love, VIVEKANANDA.

(94)

To The Same

U. S. A.,
1894.

DEAR GOVINDA SAHAY—. . . Honesty is the best policy, and a virtuous man must gain in the end. . . . You must always bear in mind, my son, that however busy or however distant, or living with men however high in position

I may be, I am always praying, blessing and remembering everyone of my friends, even the humblest.—Yours with blessings, VIVEKANANDA.

(95)

To Swami Brahmananda

*1894.**

DEAR RAKHAL—Your letter gives me all the news over there. I am grieved to hear of the bereavement Balaram Babu's wife has sustained. Such is the Lord's will. This is a place for action, not enjoyment, and everyone will go home when his task is done—some earlier, and some later, that is all. F—has gone—well, such is the will of the Lord! It is a welcome news that Sri Ramakrishna's Festival has come off with great *éclat;* the more his name is spread, the better it is. But there is one thing to know —great sages come with special messages for the world, and not for name, but their followers throw their teachings overboard and fight over their names—this is verily the history of the world. I do not take into any consideration whether people accept his name or not, but am ready to lay down my life to help his teachings, his life and his message spread all over the world. What I am most afraid of is the worship-room. It is not bad in itself, but there is a tendency in some to make this all in all and set up that old-fashioned nonsense over again—this is what makes me nervous. I know why they busy themselves with those old, effete ceremonials. Their spirit craves for work, but having got no outlet they waste their energy in ringing bells and all that.

I am giving you a new idea. If you can work it out then I shall know you are men and will be of service . . . . Make an organised plan. A few cameras, some maps, globes, and some chemicals, etc., are needed. The next thing you want is a big hut. Then you must get together a number of poor, indigent folk. Having done all these, show them pictures from astronomy, geography, etc., and preach Sri Ramakrishna to them. Try to have their eyes opened as to what has taken place or is taking place in different countries, what this world is like, and so forth. You have got lots of poor and ignorant folk there. Go to their cottages, from door to door, in the evening, at noon, any time—and open their eyes. Books etc., won't do—give them oral teaching. Then slowly extend your Centres. Can you do all this? Or only bell-ringing?

I have heard everything about Brother Tarak from Madras. They are highly pleased with him. Dear Brother Tarak, if you go to Madras and live there for some time, it will do a lot of work. But before you go, start this work there first. Can't the lady devotees convert some widows into disciples? And can't you put a bit of learning into their heads? And can't you then send them out to preach Sri Ramakrishna from door to door, and impart education along with it? . . .

Come! Apply yourselves heart and soul to it. The day of gossip and ceremonials is gone, my boy, *you must work now*. Now, let me see how far a Bengalee's religion will go. Niranjan writes that Latu needs some warm clothing. The people here import woollen warp from Europe and India. You will get a piece of cloth in Calcutta at one-fourth of the price at which I might buy it here . . . . I don't know when I shall go to Europe, everything is uncertain with me—I am getting on somehow in this country, that is all.

This is a very funny country. It is now summer—this morning it was as hot as April in Bengal, but now it is as cold as February at Allahabad! So much fluctuation within four hours! The hotels of this country beggar description. For instance, there is a hotel in New York where a room can be hired for up to Rs. 5,000 a day, excluding boarding charges. Not even in Europe is there a country like this in point of luxury. It is indeed the richest country in the world, where money is drained off like water. I seldom live in hotels, but am mostly the guest of big people here. To them I am a widely known man. The whole country knows me now, so wherever I go they receive me with open arms into their homes, Mr. H—'s home is my centre in Chicago. I call his wife mother, and his daughters call me brother. I scarcely find a family so highly pure and kind. Or why should God shower His blessings on them in such abundance, my brother? Oh, how wonderfully kind they are! If they chance to learn that a poor man is in a strait at such and such a place, there, they will go, ladies and gentlemen, to give him food and clothing, and find him some job! And what do we do!

In summer they leave their homes to go to foreign lands, or to the seaside. I, too, shall go somewhere, but have not yet fixed a place. In other points, they are just as you see Englishmen. They have got books and things of that sort, but very dear. You can have five times those things in Calcutta for the same price. In other words, these people will not let foreign goods be imported into the country. They set a heavy tax on them, and as a result, the market goes up enormously. Besides, they are not much in the way of manufacturing clothing etc. They construct tools and machinery, and grow wheat, rice, cotton, etc.—which are fairly cheap.

By the bye, nowadays we have plenty of *hilsa* fish here. Eat your fill, but everything digests. There are many kinds of fruits; plantain, lemon, guava, apple, almond, raisin and grape are in abundance; besides many other fruits come from California. There are plenty of pineapples, but there are no mangoes or lichis, or things of that sort.

There is a kind of spinach, which when cooked, tastes just like our *noté* of Bengal, and another class, which they call asparagus, tastes exactly like the tender *dengo* herb, but you can't have our *charchari* made of it here. There is no *kalâi* or any other pulse, they do not even know of them. There is rice, and bread, and numerous varieties of fish and meat, of all descriptions. Their menu is like that of the French. There is your milk, rarely curd, but plenty of whey. Cream is an article of everyday use. In tea, and coffee, and everything there is that cream—not the hardened crust of boiled milk, mind you—and there is your butter, too, and ice-water—no matter whether it is summer or winter, day or night, whether you have got a bad cold or fever—you have ice-water in abundance. These are scientific people and laugh when they are told that ice-water aggravates cold. The more you take, the better. And there is plenty of ice-cream, of all sorts of shapes. I have seen the Niagara Falls seven or eight times, the Lord be praised! Very grand no doubt, but not quite as you have heard them spoken of. One day, in winter, we had the aurora borealis. . . . Only childish prattle! I have not much time to listen to that sort of thing in this life; it will be time enough to see if I can do that in the next.

Jogen has completely rallied by this time, I hope? The vagabond spirit of Sarada is not yet at an end, I see. What is wanted is a power of organisation—do you understand me? Have any of you got that much brain in your head? If you do, let your mind work, Brother Tarak, Sarat and Hari will be able to do it.—has got very little originality, but is a very good workman, and persevering—which is an essential necessity, and is executive to a degree . . . . We want some disciples—fiery young men,—do you see?—intelligent and brave, who dare to go to the jaws of

Death, and are ready to swim the ocean across. Do you follow me? We want hundreds like that, both men and women. Try your utmost for that end alone. Make converts right and left, and put them into our purity-drilling machine.

. . . What made you communicate to the *Indian Mirror* that Paramahamsa Deva used to call Narendra such and such, and all sorts of nonsense?—As if he had nothing else to do but that! Only thought-reading and nonsensical mystery-mongering!. . . It is excellent that Sanyal is visiting you often. Do you write letters to Gupta? Convey to him my love, and take kind care of him. Everything will come right by degrees. I don't find much time to write heaps of letters. As for lectures and so forth, I don't prepare them beforehand. Only one I wrote out, which you have printed. The rest I deliver off-hand whatever comes to my lips—Gurudeva backs me on. I have nothing to do with pen and paper. Once of Detroit I held forth for three hours at a stretch. Sometimes I myself wonder at my own achievement—to think that there was such stuff in this pate! They ask me here to write a book, well, I think I must do something that way, this time. But that's the botheration, who will take the trouble of putting things in black and white and all that! . . .

We must electrify society, electrify the world. Idle gossips and barren ceremonials won't do. Ceremonials are meant for householders, your work is the distribution and propagation of thought-currents. If you can do that, then it is all right. . . .

Let character be formed, and then I shall be in your midst. Do you see? We want two thousand Sannyasins, nay ten, or even twenty thousand—men and women, both. What are our matrons doing? We want converts at any risk. Go and tell them, and try yourselves, heart and soul. Not householder disciples, mind you, we want Sannyasins. Let each one of you have a hundred heads tonsured—young educated men, not fools. Then you are heroes. We must make a sensation. Give up your passive attitude, gird your loins and stand up. Let me see you make some electric circuits between Calcutta and Madras. Start Centres at places, go on always making converts. Convert everyone into the monastic order, whoever seeks for it, irrespective of sex, and then I shall be in your midst. A huge spiritual tidal wave is coming—he who is low shall become noble and he who is ignorant shall become the teacher of great scholars—through his grace. उत्तिष्ठत जाग्रत प्राप्य वरान्निबोधत—"Arise! Awake! and stop not till the goal is reached." Life is ever expanding, contraction is death. The self-seeking man who is looking after his personal comforts and leading a lazy life—there is no room for him even in hell. He alone is a child of Sri Ramakrishna who is moved to pity for all creatures and exerts himself for them even at the risk of incurring personal damnation—इतरे कृपणाः— "others are vulgar people." Whoever, at this great spiritual juncture, will stand up with a courageous heart and go on spreading from door to door, from village to village, his message, is alone my brother, and a son of his. This is the test, he who is Ramakrishna's child, does not seek his personal good. प्राणात्ययेऽपि परकल्याणचिकीर्षवः— "They wish to do good to others even when at the point of death." Those that care for their personal comforts and seek a lazy life, who are ready to sacrifice all before their personal whims, are none of us; let them pack off, while yet there is time. Propagate his character, his teachings, his religion. This is the only spiritual practice, the only worship, this verily is the means, and this the goal. Arise! Arise! A tidal wave is coming! Onward! Men and women, down to the Chandâla—all are pure in his eyes. Onward!

Onward! There is no time to care for name, or fame, or Mukti, or Bhakti! We shall look to these some other time. Now in this life let us infinitely spread his lofty character, his sublime life, his infinite soul. This is the only work—there is nothing else to do. Wherever his name will reach, the veriest worm will attain divinity, nay, *is* actually attaining it, you have got eyes and don't you see it? Is it a child's play? Is it silly prattle? Is it foolery? उत्तिष्ठत जाग्रत—"Arise! Awake!" Great Lord! He is at our back. I cannot write any more.—Onward! I only tell you this that whoever reads this letter, will imbibe my spirit! Have faith! Onward! Great Lord! . . . I feel as if somebody is moving my hand to write in this way. Onward! Great Lord! Everyone will be swept away! Take care, he is coming! Whoever will be ready to serve him—no, not him but his children—the poor and the downtrodden, the sinful and the afflicted, down to the very worm—who will be ready to serve these, in them he will manifest himself. Through their tongue the Goddess of Learning Herself will speak, and the Divine Mother—the Embodiment of all Power—will enthrone Herself in their hearts. Those that are atheists, unbelievers, worthless and foppish, why do they call themselves as belonging to his fold? . . .—Yours affectionately, VIVEKANANDA.

P.S. . . . The term Organisation means division of labour. Each does his own part and all the parts taken together express an ideal of harmony. . . .

(*96*)

To Swami Brahmananda

C/O GEORGE W. HALE,*
541, DEARBORN AVENUE, CHICAGO,
1894.

MY DEAR—, Very glad to receive your letter. I am very sorry to hear of M—r's doings. One always behaves thus in trying to push himself before all others. I am not much to blame. M—r came here ten years ago, and got much reputation and honour; now I am in flying colours. Such is the will of the Guru, what shall I do? It is childishness on M—r's part to be annoyed at this. Never mind उपेक्षितव्यं तद्वचनं भवत्सदृशानां महात्मनाम्। अपि कीटदंशनभीरुका वयं रामकृष्णतनयास्तद्हृदयरुधिरपोषिताः। "अलोकसामान्यमचिन्त्यहेतुकं निन्दन्ति मन्दाश्चरितं महात्मनाम्" इत्यादीनि संस्मृत्य क्षन्तव्योऽयं जाल्मः।—"Great men like you should pay no heed to what he says. Shall we, children of Sri Ramakrishna and nourished with his heart's blood, be afraid of worm-bites? "The wicked criticise the conduct of the magnanimous, which is extraordinary and whose motives are difficult to fathom,"[1]—remember all this and forgive this fool. It is the will of the Lord that people of this land have their power of introspection roused, and does it lie in anybody to check His progress? I want no name—I want to be a voice without a form. I do not require anybody to defend me—कोऽहं तत्पादप्रसरं प्रतिरोद्धुं समर्थयितुं वा, के वान्ये? तथापि मम हृदयकृतज्ञता तान् प्रति—"Who am I to check or to help the course of His march? And who are others also? Still, my heart-felt gratitude to them." यस्मिन्स्थितो न दुःखेन गुरुणापि विचाल्यते—नवः प्राप्तवान् तत्पदवीमिति मत्वा करुणादृष्ट्या द्रष्टव्योऽयमिति—"Established in which state a man is not moved even by great misfortune" (Gita)—that state he has not reached, think of this and look upon him with pity. Through the Lord's will, the desire for name and fame has not yet crept into my heart, and I dare say never will. I am an instrument, and He is the operator. Through this instrument He is rousing the religious instinct in thousands of hearts in this far-off country. Thousands of men and women here love and revere me. . . .

[1] Kalidasa's Kumarasambhavam.

मूकं करोति वाचालं पङ्गुं लङ्घयते गिरिम् —"He makes the dumb eloquent and makes the lame cross mountains." I am amazed at His grace. Whatever town I visit, it is in an uproar. They have named me "the cyclonic Hindu." Remember, it is His will—I am a voice without a form.

The Lord knows whether I shall go to England or any other blessed place. He will arrange everything. Here a cigar costs one rupee. Once you get into a cab, you have to pay three rupees; a coat costs a hundred rupees; the hotel charge is nine rupees a day.—The Lord provides everything. . . . The Lord be praised, I know nothing. सत्यमेव जयते नानृतम् सत्येनैव पन्था विततो देवयानः —"Truth alone triumphs, not falsehood. Through Truth alone lies the path of Devayâna." You must be fearless. It is the coward who fears and defends himself. Let no one amongst us come forward to defend me. I get all news of Madras and Rajputana, from time to time. . . . There are eyes that can see at a distance of fourteen thousand miles. It is quite true. Keep quiet now, everything will see the light in time, as far as He wills it. Not one word of His proves untrue. My brother, do men grieve over the fight of cats and dogs? So, the jealousy, envy and elbowing of common men should make no impression on your mind. For the last six months I have been saying, the curtain is going up, the sum is rising. Yes, the curtain *is* lifting, by degrees, slow but sure, you will come to know it in time. *He* knows. One cannot speak out his mind. These are things not for writing. . . . Never let go your hold of the rudder, grasp it firm. We are steering all right, no mistaking that, but landing on the other shore is only a question of time. That's all. Can a leader be made, my brother? A leader is born. Do you follow me? And it is a very difficult task to take on the role of a leader. One must be दासस्य दासः—a servant of servants, and must accommodate a thousand minds. There must not be a shade of jealousy or selfishness, then you are a leader. First, by birth, and secondly, unselfish—that's a leader. Everything is going all right, everything will come round. He casts the net all right, and winds it up likewise—वयमनुसरामः वयमनुसरामः प्रीतिः परमसाधनम्—ours is but to follow. Love is the best instrument. Love conquers in the long run. It won't do to become impatient—wait, wait,—patience is bound to give success. . . .

I tell you, brother, let everything go on as it is, only take care that no form becomes necessary—unity in variety—see that universality be not hampered in the least. Everything must be sacrificed, if necessary, for that one sentiment, *universality*. Whether I live or die, whether I go back to India or not, remember this specially, that universality—perfect acceptance, not tolerance only—we preach and perform. Take care how you trample on the least rights of others. Many a huge ship has foundered in that whirlpool. Remember, perfect devotion minus its bigotry—this is what we have got to show. Through His grace everything will go all right. . . . Everybody wants to be a leader, but it is the failure to grasp that he is *born*, that causes all this mischief. . . .

Our matrons are all hale and hearty, I hope? Where is Gaur Ma? We want a thousand such Mothers, with that noble stirring spirit. . . . We want all. It is not at all necessary that all would have the same faith in our Lord as we have, but we want to unite all the powers of goodness against all the powers of evil. . . . A besetting sin with Sannyasins is the taking pride in their monastic order. That may have its utility during the first stages, but when they are full grown, they need it no more. One must make no distinction between householders and Sannyasins—then only one is a true Sannyasin. . . .

A movement which half a dozen penniless boys set on

foot and which now bids fair to progress in such an accelerated motion—is it a humbug or the Lord's will? If it is, then let all give up party spirit and jealousy, and unite in action. A universal religion cannot be set up through party faction. . . .

If all understand one day for one minute that one cannot become great by the mere wish, that he only rises whom He raises, and he falls whom He brings down, then all trouble is at an end. But there is that egotism—hollow in itself, and without the power to move a finger: how ludicrous of it to say, "I won't let anyone rise!" That jealousy, that absence of conjoined action is the very nature of enslaved nations. But we must try to shake it off. That terrible jealousy is characteristic of us. . . . You will be convinced of this if you visit some other countries. Our fellows in this respect are the enfranchised Negroes of this country—if but one amongst them rises to greatness, all the others would at once set themselves against him and try to level him down by making a common cause with the Whites. . . .

At any cost, any price, any sacrifice, we must never allow that to creep in among ourselves. Whether we be ten or two, do not care, but, those few must be perfect characters. . . . "It is not good to ask of one's father if the Lord looks after the provision." And the Lord *will* do so, set your minds easy on that score. . . . We must spread his name in Rajputana, Punjab, U. P., Madras and such other provinces—yes, in Rajputana, where still there are people who can say, "Such has ever been the custom with Raghu's line that they keep their word even at the cost of life."

A bird, in the course of its flight, reaches a spot whence it looks on the ground below with supreme calmness. Have you reached that spot? He who has not reached there has no right to teach others. Relax your limbs and float with the current, and you are sure to reach your destination.

Cold is making itself scarce by degrees, and I have been almost through the winter. Here in winter the whole body becomes charged with electricity. In shaking hands one feels a shock, accompanied by a sound. You can light the gas with your finger. And about winter, I have written to you already. I am coursing through the length and breadth of the country, but Chicago is my "Math," where I always return after my wanderings. I am now making for the east. He knows where the bark will reach the shore. . . .

Has Dasu the same sort of love for you? Does he see you frequently? How is Bhavanath and what is he doing? Do you visit him, and look upon him with an eye of regard? Yes, brother, the distinction between Sannyasin and layman is a fiction. मूकं करोति वाचालं etc.—"He makes the dumb fluent etc." My friend, it is difficult to judge what is in a particular individual. He (Sri Ramakrishna) has spoken highly of him, and he deserves our respect. Fie upon you if you have no faith even after so much experience! Does he love you? Please convey to him my hearty love and esteem. My love to Kalikrishna Babu, he is a very noble soul. How is Ramlal? Has he got a little faith and devotion? My love and greetings to him. Sanyal is moving all right with the mill, I suppose? Ask him to have patience, and the mill will go on all right.

My heart's love to all.—Ever yours in love,
VIVEKANANDA.

(97)

To Swami Akhandananda

*1894.**

MY DEAR AKHANDANANDA—I am very glad to receive

your letter. It is a great pleasure to me to learn that you have regained your health to a great extent by your stay at Khetri.

Brother Tarak has done a good deal of work in Madras. Very agreeable news indeed! I heard much praise of him from the people of Madras.

Try to develop spirituality and philanthropy amongst the Thakurs in the different places of Rajputana. We must work, and this cannot be done by merely sitting idle. Make a trip now and then to Malsisar, Alsisar and all the other "sars" that are there. And carefully learn Sanskrit and English. Gunanidhi is in the Punjab, I presume. Convey my special love to him and bring him to Khetri. Learn Sanskrit with his help, and teach him English. Let me have his address by all means.

* * *

Go from door to door amongst the poor and lower classes of the town of Khetri and teach them religion. Also, let them have oral lessons on geography and such other subjects. No good will come of sitting idle and having princely dishes, and saying "Ramakrishna, O Lord!"—unless you can do some good to the poor. Go to other villages from time to time, and teach the people the art of life as well as religion. Work, worship and Jnanam (knowledge)—first work, and your mind will be purified; otherwise everything will be fruitless like pouring oblations on a pile of ashes instead of in the sacred fire. When Gunanidhi comes, move from door to door of the poor and the destitute in every village of Rajputana. If people object to the kind of food you take, give it up immediately. It is preferable to live on grass for the sake of doing good to others. The *geruâ* robe is not for enjoyment. It is the banner of heroic work. You must give your body, mind and speech to "the welfare of the world."

You have read मातृदेवो भव, पितृदेवो भव—"Look upon your mother as God, look upon your father as God,"—but I say, दरिद्रदेवो भव, मूर्खदेवो भव—The poor, the illiterate, the ignorant, the afflicted—let these be your God. Know that service to these alone is the highest religion.—Ever yours, with blessings, VIVEKANANDA.

(98)

To Sj. Alasinga Perumal

541, DEARBORN AVENUE,
CHICAGO,
1894.

DEAR ALASINGA—Your letter just to hand. . . . Money can be raised in this country by lecturing for two or three years. But I have tried a little, and although there is much public appreciation of my work, it is thoroughly uncongenial and demoralising to me. . . .

I have read what you say about the Indian papers, and their criticisms, which are natural. Jealousy is the central vice of every enslaved race. And it is jealousy and the want of combination which cause and perpetuate slavery. You cannot feel the truth of this remark until you come out of India. The secret of Westerner's success is this power of combination, the basis of which is mutual trust and appreciation. The weaker and more cowardly a nation is, so much the more is this sin visible. . . . But, my son, you ought not to expect anything from a slavish race. The case is almost desperate no doubt, but let me put the case before you all. Can you put life into this dead mass—dead to almost all moral aspiration, dead to all future possibilities—and always ready to spring upon those that would try to do good to them? Can you take the position of a physician who tries to pour medicine down the throat of a kicking and refractory child?. . . An American or a European always supports his countrymen in a foreign country. . . .

Let me remind you again, " Thou hast the right to work but not to the fruits thereof." Stand firm like a rock. Truth always triumphs. Let the children of Sri Ramakrishna be true to themselves, and everything will be all right. We may not live to see the outcome, but as sure as we live, it will come sooner or later. What India wants is a new electric fire to stir up a fresh vigour in the national veins. This was ever, and always will be slow work. Be content to work and above all, be true to yourself. Be pure, staunch and sincere, to the very backbone and everything will be all right. If you have marked anything in the disciples of Sri Ramakrishna, it is this—they are sincere to the backbone. My task will be done and I shall be quite content to die, if I can bring up and launch one hundred such men over India. He, the Lord, knows best. Let ignorant men talk nonsense. We neither seek aid nor avoid it—we are the servants of the Most High. The petty attempts of small men should be beneath our notice. Onward! Upon ages of struggle a character is built. Be not discouraged. One word of truth can never be lost; for ages it may be hidden under rubbish, but it will show itself sooner or later. Truth is indestructible, virtue is indestructible, purity is indestructible. Give me a genuine man; I do not want masses of converts. My son, hold fast! Do not care for anybody to help you. Is not the Lord infinitely greater than all human help? Be holy—trust in the Lord, depend on Him always, and you are on the right track; nothing can prevail against you. . . .

Let us pray, "Lead, Kindly Light"—a beam will come through the dark, and a hand will be stretched forth to lead us. I always pray for you: you must pray for me. Let each one of us pray day and night for the downtrodden millions in India, who are held fast by poverty, priest-craft and tyranny—pray day and night for them. I care more to preach religion to them than to the high and the rich. I am no metaphysician, no philosopher, nay, no saint. But I am poor, I love the poor. I see what they call the poor of this country and how many there are who feel for them. What an immense difference in India! Who feels there for the two hundred millions of men and women sunken for ever in poverty and ignorance? Where is the way out? Who feels for them? They cannot find light or education. Who will bring the light to them—who will travel from door to door bringing education to them? Let these people be your God—think of them, work for them, pray for them incessantly—the Lord will show you the way. Him I call a Mahâtman whose heart bleeds for the poor, otherwise he is a Durâtman. Let us unite our wills in continued prayer for their good. We may die unknown, unpitied, unbewailed, without accomplishing anything—but not one thought will be lost. It will take effect, sooner or later. My heart is too full to express my feeling; you know it, you can imagine it. So long as the millions live in hunger and ignorance, I hold every man a traitor, who having been educated at their expense, pays not the least heed to them. I call those men—who strut about in their finery, having got all their money by grinding the poor—wretches, so long as they do not do anything for those two hundred millions who are now no better than hungry savages. We are poor, my brothers, we are nobodies, but such have been always the instruments of the Most High. The Lord bless you all.—With all love, VIVEKANANDA.

(99)

To Anâgarika Dharmapala

U. S. A.,
1894.

DEAR DHARMAPALA—. . . Last winter I travelled a good

deal in this country although the weather was very severe. I thought it would be dreadful but I did not find it so after all. . . . Hope your noble work will succeed. You are a worthy servant of Him who came, *Bahujana Hitâya Bahujana Sukhâya.*

. . . The Christianity that is preached in India is quite different from what one sees here; you will be astonished to hear, Dharmapala, that I have friends in this country amongst the clergy of the Episcopal and even Presbyterian churches, who are as broad, as liberal and as sincere, as you are in your own religion. The real spiritual man is broad everywhere. His love forces him to be so. Those to whom religion in a trade, are forced to become narrow and mischievous by their introduction into religion of the competitive, fighting and selfish methods of the world.—Yours ever in brotherly love, VIVEKANANDA.

(*100*)

To Sj. Alasinga Perumal

U. S. A.,
1894.

DEAR ALASINGA—Listen to an old story. A lazy tramp sauntering along the road saw an old man sitting at the door of his house and stopped to enquire of him the whereabouts of a certain place. " How far is such and such a village?" he asked. The old man remained silent. The man repeated his query several times. Still there was no answer. Disgusted at this, the traveller turned to go away. The old man then stood up and said, "The village of—is only a mile from here." " What " said the tramp, "Why did you not speak when I asked you before?" "Because then," said the old man, "you seemed so halting and careless about proceeding, but now you are starting off in good earnest and you have a right to an answer."

Will you remember this story, my son? Go to work, the rest will come. "Whosoever not trusting in anything else but Me, rests on Me, I supply him with everything he needs."—The Gita. This is no dream.

. . . The work should be in the line of preaching and serving, at the present time. Choose a place of meeting where you can assemble every week holding a service and reading the Upanishads with the commentaries, and so slowly go on learning and working. Everything will come to you if you put your shoulders to the wheel.

* * *

Now, go to work! G. G.'s nature is of the emotional type; you have a level head, so work together; plunge in; this is only the beginning. Every nation must save itself; we must not depend upon funds from America for the revival of Hinduism, for that is a delusion. To have a centre is a great thing; try to secure such a place in a large town like Madras, and go on radiating a living force in all directions. Begin slowly. Start with a few lay missionaries; by and by others will come who will devote their whole lives to the work. Do not try to be a ruler. He is the best ruler, who can serve well. Be true unto death. The work we want. We do not seek wealth, name or fame . . . . Be brave . . . . Endeavour to interest the people of Madras in collecting funds for the purpose and then make a beginning . . . . Be perfectly unselfish and you will be sure to succeed.

* * *

My children must be ready to jump into fire, if needed, to accomplish their work. Now work, work, work. We will stop and compare notes later on. Have patience, perseverance and purity.

. . . I am writing no hook on Hinduism just now.

I am simply jotting down my thoughts. I do not know if I shall publish them. What is in books? The world is too full of foolish things already. If you could start a magazine on Vedantic lines it would further our object. Be positive; do not criticise others. Give your message, teach what you have to teach, and there stop. The Lord knows the rest.

Do not send me any more newspapers, as I do not notice the missionary criticism on myself, and here the public estimation of me is better for that reason.

. . . If you are really my children, you will fear nothing, stop at nothing. You will be like lions. We must rouse India and the whole world. No cowardice. I will take no nay. Do you understand? Be true unto death! . . . The secret of this is Guru Bhakti. Faith in the Guru unto death. Have you that? I believe with all my heart that you have, and you know that I have confidence in you—so go to work. You must succeed. My prayers and benedictions follow every step you take. Work in harmony. Be patient with everybody. Everyone has my love. I am watching you. Onward! Onward! this is just the beginning. My little work here makes a big echo in India, do you know? So I shall not return there in a hurry. My intention is to do something permanent here, and with that object I am working day by day. I am every day gaining the confidence of the American people. . . . Expand your hearts and hopes, as wide as the world. Study Sanskrit, especially the three Bhâshyas on the Vedanta. Be ready, for I have many plans for the future. Try to be a magnetic speaker. Everything will come to you if you have faith. So tell K—, in fact, tell all my children there. In time they will do great things at which the world will wonder. Take heart and work. Let me see what you can do. . . . Be true to your mission. Thus far you promise well, so go on and do better and better still.

. . . Do not fight with people; do not antagonise anyone. Why should we mind if Jack or John become Christians? Let them follow whatever religion suits them. Why should you mix in controversies? Bear with the various opinions of everybody. Patience, purity and perseverance will prevail.—Yours etc., VIVEKANANDA.

(*101*)

To the Maharaja of Khetri

U. S. A.,
1894.

. . . "It is not the building that makes the home, but it is the wife that makes it,"[1] says a Sanskrit poet, and how true it is! The roof that affords you shelter from heat and cold and rain is not to be judged by the pillars that support it—the finest Corinthian columns though they be, but by the real spirit-pillar who is the centre, the real support of the home—the woman. Judged by that standard, the American home will not suffer in comparison with any home in the world.

I have heard many stories about the American home: of liberty running into licence, of unwomanly women smahsing under their feet all the peace and happiness of home-life in their mad liberty-dance, and much nonsense of that type. And now after a year's experience of American homes, of American women, how utterly false and erroneous that sort of judgment appears! American women! A hundred lives would not be sufficient to pay my deep debt of gratitude to you! I have not words enough to express my gratitude to you. "The Oriental hyperbole" alone expresses the depth of Oriental gratitude—" If the Indian Ocean were an inkstand, the highest mountain of the

[1] न गृहं गृहमित्याहुर्गृहिणी गृहमुच्यते ।

Himalaya the pen, the earth the scroll and time itself the writer,[1] still it would not express my gratitude to you!"

Last year I came to this country in summer, a wandering preacher of a far distant country, without name, fame, wealth, or learning to recommend me—friendless, helpless, almost in a state of destitution; and American women befriended me, gave me shelter and food, took me to their homes and treated me as their own son, their own brother. They stood my friends even when their own priests were trying to persuade them to give up the "dangerous Heathen"—even when day after day their best friends had told them not to stand by this "unknown foreigner, may be, of dangerous character." But they are better judge of character and soul—for it is the pure mirror that catches the reflection.

And how many beautiful homes I have seen, how many mothers whose purity of character, whose unselfish love for their children are beyond expression, how many daughters and pure maidens, "pure as the icicle on Diana's temple" and withal with much culture, education and spirituality in the highest sense! Is America then full of only wingless angels in the shape of women? There is good and bad everywhere, true—but a nation is not to be judged by its weaklings called the wicked, as they are only the weeds which lag behind, but by the good, the noble and the pure, who indicate the national life-current to be flowing clear and vigorous.

Do you judge of an apple tree and the taste of its fruits by the unripe, undeveloped, worm-eaten ones that strew the ground, large even though their number be sometimes? If there is one ripe, developed fruit, that *one* would indicate the powers, the possibility and the purpose of the apple tree and not hundreds that could not grow.

[1] Adapted from the Mahimnah Stotra.

And then the modern American women—I admire their broad and liberal minds. I have seen many liberal and broad-minded men too in this country, some even in the narrowest churches, but here is the difference—there is danger with the men to become broad at the cost of religion, at the cost of spirituality—women broaden out in sympathy to everything that is good everywhere without losing a bit of their own religion. They intuitively know that it is a question of positivity and not negativity, a question of addition and not subtraction. They are every day becoming aware of the fact that it is the affirmative and positive side of everything that shall be stored up, and that this very act of accumulating the affirmative and positive and therefore soul-building forces of nature is what destroys the negative and destructive elements in the world.

What a wonderful achievement was that World's Fair at Chicago! And that wonderful Parliament of Religions where voices from every corner of the earth expressed their religious ideas! I was also allowed to place my own ideas through the kindness of Dr. Barrows and Mr. Bonney. Mr. Bonney is such a wonderful man! Think of that mind that planned and carried out with great success that gigantic undertaking, and he, no clergyman, a lawyer presiding over the dignitaries of all the churches, the sweet, learned, patient Mr. Bonney with all his soul speaking through his bright eyes. . . . —Yours etc., VIVEKANANDA.

(*102*)

To Swami Abhedananda

U. S. A.,*
1894.

DEAR KALI—Thanks for all that I come to know from your letter. I had no news of the telegram in question having appeared in the *Tribune*. It is six months since I left Chicago, and have not yet been free to return So I could not keep myself well-posted. You have taken great pains indeed, and for this how can I thank you adequately? You have all evinced a wonderful capacity for work. Well, how can Sri Ramakrishna's words prove false?—You have got wonderful spirit in you. About— I have already written. Nothing remains undetected, through the grace of Sri Ramakrishna. But let him found a sect or whatever he, will, what harm? शिवा वः सन्तु पन्थानः— "May blessings attend your path!" Secondly, I could not catch the drift of your letter. I shall collect my own funds to build a monastery for ourselves, and if people criticise me for it, I see nothing in this to affect us either way. You have your minds pitched high and steady, it will do you no harm. May you have exceeding love for one another among yourselves, and it would be enough to have an attitude of indifference towards public criticism. Kalikrishna Babu has deep love for the cause and is a great man. Please convey my special love to him. So long as there is no feeling of disunion amongst you, through the grace of the Lord, I assure you, there is no danger for you, रणे वने पर्वतमस्तके वा— "be it in battle, in the forest, or on the top of mountains." श्रेयांसि बहुविघ्नानि—"All noble undertakings are fraught with obstacles." It is quite in the nature of things. Keep up the deepest mental poise. Take not even the slightest notice of what puerile creatures may be saying against you. Indifference, indifference, indifference! I have already written to Sasi (Sanyal) in detail. Please do not send newspapers and tracts any more. "Take the husking hammer to heaven, and there it will do its husking," as the Bengali saying goes. The same trudging about here as it was in India, only with the carrying of others' loads added! How can I procure customers for people's books in this land? I am only one amongst the many here and nothing more. Whatever the papers and things of that sort in this country write about me, I make an offering of to the Fire-God. You also do the same. That is the proper course.

A bit of public demonstration was necessary for Guru Maharaja's work. It is done and so far so good. Now you must on no account pay any heed to what the rabble may be prattling about us. Whether I make my pile or do whatever else I am reported to, shall the opinions of the riff-raff stand in the way of HIS WORK? My dear brother, you are yet a boy, while I am growing gray. What regard I have for the pronouncements and opinions of such people, you should guess from this. So long as you gird up your loins and rally behind me, there is no fear even if the whole world combine against us. This much I understand that I shall have to take up a very lofty attitude. I should not, I think, write to anyone except to you. By the bye, where is Gunanidhi? Try to find him out and bring him to the Math with all kindness. He is a very sincere man and highly learned. You must try your best to secure two plots of land, let people say what they will. Let anyone write anything for or against me in the papers; you shouldn't take the slightest notice. And my dear brother, I beseech you repeatedly not to send me any more newspapers by the basketful. How can you talk of rest now? We shall have rest awhile only when we give up this body. Just do once get up the celebration[1], brother, in that spirit, so that all the country around may burn with enthusiasm. Bravo! Capital indeed! The whole band of scoffers will be swept away by the tidal wave of love. You are elephants, forsooth; what do you fear from an ant-bite?

The address you sent reached me long ago and the reply to it has also been despatched to Pyari Babu.

[1] The Ramakrishna Birthday Anniversary.

Bear in mind—the eyes are two in number and so the ears, but the mouth is but one! Indifference, indifference, indifference! न हि कल्याणकृत्कश्चिद्दुर्गतिं तात गच्छति—"The doer of good deeds never comes to grief, my dear." Ah! To fear! and whom are we going to fear, brother? Here the missionaries and their ilk have howled themselves on to silence—and the whole world will but do likewise.

निन्दन्तु नीतिनिपुणा यदि वा स्तुवन्तु
लक्ष्मीः समाविशतु गच्छतु वा यथेष्टम् ।
अद्यैव वा मरणमस्तु शतान्तरे वा
न्याय्यात्पथः प्रविचलन्ति पदं न धीराः ॥

—"Whether people skilled in policy praise or blame, whether the Goddess of Fortune favours or goes her way, whether death befalls to-day or after hundreds of years—persons of steady mind never swerve from the path of righteousness."[1]

You need not even mix with the humdrum people, nor beg of them either. The Lord is supplying everything and will do so in future. What fear, my brother? All great undertakings are achieved through mighty obstacles. हे वीर कुरु पौरुषमात्मनः, उपेक्षितव्या जनाः सुकृपणाः कामकाञ्चनवशगाः—"You valiant one, put forth your manly efforts; wretched people under the grip of lust and gold deserve to be looked upon with indifference." Now I have got a firm footing in this country, and therefore need no assistance. But my one prayer to you all is that you should apply to the service of the Lord that active impulse of manliness which your eagerness to help me through brotherly love has brought out in you. Do not open out your mind, unless you feel it will be positively beneficial. Use agreeable and wholesome language towards even the greatest enemy. The desire for fame, for riches, for enjoyment is quite natural to every mortal,

[1] Bhartrihari.

dear brother, and if that agrees well with serving both ways (i.e., serving both God and mammon), why, all men would exhibit great zeal! It is only the great saint who can work, making a mountain of an atom of virtue in others and cherishing no desire but that of the good of the world—परगुणपरमाणु पर्वतीकृत्य, अपिच, त्रिभुवनमुपकारश्रेणिभिः प्रीयमानः, etc.[1] Therefore let dullards whose intellect is steeped in ignorance and who look upon the non-Self as all in all, play out their boyish pranks. They will of themselves leave off the moment they find it too hot! Let them try to spit upon the moon—it will but recoil upon themselves. शुभं भवतु तेषाम् —Godspeed to them! If they have got anything substantial in them, who can bar their success? But if it be only empty swagger due to jealousy, then all will be in vain. Hara Mohan has sent rosaries. All right. But you should know that religion of the type that obtains in our country has no go here. You must suit it to the taste of the people. If you ask them to become Hindus, they will all give you the wide berth and hate you, as we do the Christian missionaries. They like some of the ideas of the Hindu scriptures—that is all. Nothing more than that, you should know. The men, most of them, do not trouble about religion and all that. The women are a little interested—that is, all, but no large doses of it! A few thousands of people have faith in the Advaita doctrine. But they will give you the go-by if you talk obscure mannerisms about sacred writings, caste or women. Everything proceeds slowly, by degrees. Patience, purity, perseverance.—Yours etc., VIVEKANANDA.

(103)

To Swami Shivananda

U. S. A.,*
1894.

DEAR SHIVANANDA—Your letter just reached me.

[1] Vivekachudamani.

Perhaps by this time you have received my other letters and learnt that it is not necessary to send anything to America any more. Too much of everything is bad. This newspaper booming has given me popularity no doubt, but its effect is more in India than here. Here on the other hand constant booming creates a distaste in the minds of the higher class people; so enough. Now try to organise yourselves in India on the lines of these meetings. You need not send anything more to this country. As to money, I have determined first to build some place for Mother,[1] for women require it first. . . . I can send nearly Rs. 7,000 for a place for Mother. If the place is first secured, then I do not care for anything else. I hope to be able to get Rs. 1,600 a year from this country even when I am gone. That sum I will make over to the support of the women's place and then it will grow. I have written to you already to secure a place. . . .

I would have, before this, returned to India, but India has no money. Thousands honour Ramakrishna Paramahamsa but nobody will give a cent—that is India. . . . In the meanwhile live in harmony at any price. The world cares little for principles. They care for persons. They will hear with patience the words of a man they like, however nonsensical, and will not listen to anyone they do not like. Think of this and modify your conduct accordingly. Everything will come all right. Be the servant if you will lead. That is the real secret. Your love will tell even if your words be harsh. Instinctively men feel the love clothed in whatever language.

My dear brother, that Ramakrishna Paramahamsa was God incarnate, I have not the least doubt, but then you must let people find out for themselves what he used to teach—you cannot thrust these things upon them —this is my only objection.

[1] The Holy Mother.

Let people speak out their own opinions. Why should we object? Without studying Ramakrishna Paramahamsa first, one can never understand the real import of the Vedas, the Vedanta, of the Bhâgavata and the other Purânas. His life is a searchlight of infinite power thrown upon the whole mass of Indian religious thought. He was the living commentary to the Vedas and to their aim. He lived in one life the whole cycle of the national religious existence in India.[1]

Whether Bhagavân Sri Krishna was born at all we are not sure; and Avataras like Buddha and Chaitanya are monotonous; Ramakrishna Paramahamsa is the latest and the most perfect—the concentrated embodiment of knowledge, love, renunciation, catholicity and the desire to serve mankind. So where is anyone to compare with him? He must have been born in vain who cannot appreciate him! My supreme good fortune is that I am his servant through life after life. A single word of his is to me far weightier than the Vedas and the Vedanta. तस्य दासदासदासोऽहम् —Oh, I am the servant of the servants of his servants. But narrow bigotry militates against his principles, and this makes me cross. Rather let his name be drowned in oblivion, and his teachings bear fruit instead! Why, was he a slave to fame? Certain fishermen and illiterate people called Jesus Christ a God, but the literate people killed him. Buddha was honoured in his lifetime by a number of merchants and cowherds. But Ramakrishna has been worshipped in his lifetime—towards the end of this nineteenth century—by the demons and giants of the university as God incarnate. . . . Only a few things have been jotted down in the books about them (Krishna, Buddha, Christ, etc.). "One must be a wonderful house-keeper with whom we have never yet lived," so the Bengali proverb goes. But here is a

[1] The first two paras as well as the last half of this para are in the original.

man in whose company we have been day and night and yet consider him to be a far greater personality than any of them. Can you understand this phenomenon?

You have not yet understood the wonderful significance of Mother's life—none of you. But gradually you will know. Without Shakti (Power) there is no regeneration for the world. Why is it that our country is the weakest and the most backward of all countries? Because Shakti is held in dishonour there. Mother has been born to revive that wonderful Shakti in India; and making her the nucleus, once more will Gargis and Maitreyis be born into the world. Dear brother, you understand little now. But by degrees you will come to know it all. Hence it is her Math that I want first. . . . Without the grace of Shakti nothing is to be accomplished. What do I find in America and Europe?—the worship of Shakti, the worship of Power. Yet they worship Her ignorantly through sense gratification. Imagine, then, what a lot of good they will achieve who will worship Her with all purity, in a Sâttvika spirit, looking upon Her as their mother! I am coming to understand things clearer every day, my insight is opening out more and more. Hence we must first build a Math for Mother. First Mother and her daughters, then Father and his sons—can you understand this? . . . To me, Mother's grace is a hundred thousand times more valuable than Father's. Mother's grace, Mother's blessings are all paramount to me. . . . Please pardon me, I am a little bigoted here, as regards Mother. If but Mother orders, her demons can work anything. Brother, before proceeding to America I wrote to Mother to bless me. Her blessings came, and at one bound I cleared the ocean. There, you see. In this terrible winter I am lecturing from place to place and fighting against odds, so that funds may be collected for Mother's Math. . . . Niranjan has a militant disposition, but he has great devotion to Mother, and all his vagaries

I can easily put up with. He is now doing the most marvellous work. I am keeping myself well-posted. And you too have done excellently in co-operating with the Madrasis. Dear brother, I expect much from you, you should organise all for conjoint work. As soon as you have secured the land for Mother, I go to India straight. It must be a big plot; let there be a mud-house to begin with; in due course I shall erect a decent building, don't be afraid.

The chief cause of malaria lies in water. Why do you not construct two or three filters? If you first boil the water and then filter it, it will be harmless. . . . Please buy two big Pasteur's bacteria-proof filters. Let the cooking be done in that water and use it for drinking purposes also, and you will never hear of malaria any more. . . . On and on; work, work, work; this is only the beginning. —Yours ever, VIVEKANANDA.

(104)

To Mrs. Ole Bull

BROOKLYN,
28th Dec., 1894.

DEAR MRS. BULL—I arrived safely in New York and proceeded at once to Brooklyn where I arrived in time.

We had a nice evening. Several gentlemen belonging to the Ethical Culture Society came to see me.

Next Sunday we will have a lecture. Dr. Janes was as usual very kind and good and Mr. Higgins is as practical as ever. Here alone in New York I find more men interested in religion than in any other city, and do not know why here the interest is more amongst men than women. . . .

Herewith I send a copy of that pamphlet Mr. Higgins has published about me. Hope to send more in the future.

With my love to Miss Farmer and all the holy family, —I am ever sincerely yours, VIVEKANANDA.

(*105*)

*1894.**

Dear and Beloved—. . . Well, do you think there is any religion left in India? The paths of Knowledge, Devotion, and Yoga—all have gone, and now there remains only that of Don't touchism—"Don't touch me!" "Don't touch me!" The whole world is impure, and I alone am pure! Lucid Brahmajnanam! Bravo! Great God! Nowadays Brahman is neither in the recesses of the heart, nor in the highest heaven, nor in all beings—now He is in the cooking-pot. Formerly the characteristic of a noble-minded man was त्रिभुवनमुपकारश्रेणिभिः प्रीयमानः—"to please the whole universe by one's numerous acts of service," but now it is—I am pure and the whole world is impure, —go and get money and set it at my feet. . . . Tell the sapient sage who writes to me to finish my preaching work here and return home, . . . that this country is more my home—what is there in Hindusthan? Who appreciates religion? Who appreciates learning?

To return home! Where is the home! I do not care for liberation, or for devotion, I would rather go to a hundred thousand hells, वसन्तवल्लोकहितं चरन्तः—"doing good to others (silently) like the spring" —this is my religion. I do not want to have any connection with lazy, hard-hearted, cruel and selfish men. He whose good fortune it is, may help in this great cause.

. . . Please convey to all my love, I want the help of everyone. *Neither money pays, nor name, nor fame, nor learning; it is character that can cleave through adamantine walls of difficulties.* Bear this in mind. . . .
—Ever yours in love, Vivekananda.

(*106*)

To Justice Sir S. Subrahmanya Iyer

541, DEARBORN AVENUE,
CHICAGO,

3rd Jan., 1895.

DEAR SIR—It is with a heart full of love, gratitude and trust, that I take up my pen to write to you. Let me tell you first that you are one of the few men that I have met in my life who are thorough in their convictions. You have a whole-souled possession of a wonderful combination of feeling and knowledge, and withal a practical ability to bring ideas into realised forms. Above all you are sincere, and as such I confide to you some of my ideas.

The work has begun well in India, and it should not only be kept up but pushed on with the greatest vigour. Now or never is the time. After taking a far and wide view of things, my mind has now been concentrated on the following plan. First, it would be well to open a Theological College in Madras, and then gradually extend its scope; to give a thorough education to young men in the Vedas and the different Bhâshyas and Philosophies including a knowledge of the other religions of the world. At the same time a paper in English and the vernacular should be started as an organ of the College.

This is the first step to be taken, and huge things grow out of small undertakings. . . . Madras just now is following the golden mean by appreciating both the ancient and modern phases of life.

I fully agree with the educated classes in India, that a thorough overhauling of society is necessary. But how to do it? The destructive plans of Reformers have failed. My plan is this: We have not done *badly* in the past; certainly not. Our society is not *bad* but *good*, only I want it to be better still. Not from error to truth, nor from bad to good, but from truth to higher truth, from good to better, best. I tell my countrymen that so far they have done well—now is the time to do better. Now take the case of caste, in Sanskrit, Jâti, i.e., species. Now this is the first idea of creation. Variation (Vichitratâ), that is to say Jati, means creation. "I am one, I become many" (various Vedas). Unity is before creation, diversity is creation. Now if this diversity stops, creation will be destroyed. So long as any species is vigorous and active it must throw out varieties. When it ceases or is stopped from breeding varieties, it dies. Now the original idea of Jati was this freedom of the individual to express his nature, his Prakriti, his Jati, his caste, and so it remained for thousands of years. Not even in the latest books is inter-dining prohibited; nor in any of the older books is inter-marriage forbidden. Then what was the cause of India's downfall?—the giving up of this idea of caste. As Gita says, with the extinction of caste the world will be destroyed. Now does it seem true that with the stoppage of these variations the world will be destroyed? The present caste is not the real Jati, but a hindrance to its progress. It really has prevented the free action of Jati, i.e., caste or variation. Any crystallised custom or privilege or hereditary class in any shape really prevents caste (Jati), from having its full sway, and whenever any nation ceases to produce this immense variety, it must die. Therefore what I have to tell you, my countrymen, is this: that India fell because you prevented and abolished caste. Every frozen aristocracy or privileged class is a blow to caste and is not-caste. Let Jati have its sway; break down every barrier in the way of caste, and we shall rise. Now look at Europe. When it succeeded in giving free scope to caste and took away most of the barriers that stood in the way of individuals—each developing his caste—Europe rose. In America there is the best scope for caste (real Jati) to develop, and so the people are great. Every Hindu knows that astrologers try to fix the caste of every boy or girl as soon as he or she is born. That is the real caste, the individuality, and Jyotish recognised that. And we can only rise by giving it full sway again. This variety does not mean inequality nor any special privilege. This is my method—to show the Hindus that they have to give up nothing but only to move on in the line laid down by the sages and shake off their inertia, the result of centuries of servitude. Of course we had to stop advancing during the Mohammedan tyranny, for then it was not a question of progress but of life and death. Now that that pressure has gone, we must move forward, not on the lines of destruction directed by renegades and missionaries, but along our own line—our own road. Everything is hideous because the building is unfinished. We had to stop building during centuries of oppression. Now, finish the building and everything will look beautiful in its own place. This is all my plan. I am thoroughly convinced of this. Each nation has a main current in life; in India it is religion. Make it strong and the waters on either side must move along with it. This is one phase of my line of thought. In time, I hope to bring them all out, but at present I find I have a mission in this country also. Moreover, I expect help in this country and from here alone. But up to date I could not do anything except spreading my ideas. Now I want that a similar attempt be made in India. . . . I do not know when I shall go over to India. I obey the leading of the Lord. I am in His hands.

"In this world in search of wealth, Thou art, O Lord, the greatest jewel I have found. I sacrifice myself unto Thee."

"In search of some one to love, Thou art the One Beloved I have found. I sacrifice myself unto Thee." (Yajurveda Samhitâ).

May the Lord bless you for ever and ever!—Yours ever gratefully, VIVEKANANDA.

(*107*)

To Sj. G. G. Narasimhachariar

CHICAGO,
11th Jan., 1895.

DEAR G. G.—Your letter just to hand. . . . The Parliament of Religions was organised with the intention of proving the superiority of the Christian religion over other forms of faith, but the philosophic religion of Hinduism was able to maintain its position notwithstanding. Dr. Barrows and the men of that ilk are very orthodox, and I do not look to them for help. . . . The Lord has sent me many friends in this country and they are always on the increase. . . . The Lord bless them. . . . I have been running all the time between Boston and New York, two great centres of this country, of which Boston may be called the brain and New York, the purse. In both, my success is more than ordinary. I am indifferent to the newspaper reports and you must not expect me to send any of them to you. A little boom was necessary to begin work. We have had more than enough of that.

I have written to Mani Ayer, and I have given you my directions already. Now *show me what you can do*. No foolish talk now, actual work; the Hindus must back their talk with real work; if they cannot, they do not deserve anything; that is all. . . . As for me, I want to teach the truth; I do not care whether here or elsewhere!

In future do not pay any heed to what people say either for or against you or me. Work on, be lions and the Lord will bless you. I shall work incessantly until I die, and even after death I shall work for the good of the world. Truth is infinitely more weighty than untruth; so is goodness. If you possess these, they will make their way by sheer gravity.

. . . Thousands of the best men *do* care for me; you know this, so have faith in the Lord. I am slowly exercising an influence in this land greater than all the newspaper blazoning can do of me. . . .

It is the force of character, of purity and of truth—of personality. So long as I have these things you can feel easy; no one will be able to injure a hair of my head. If they try they will fail, sayeth the Lord. . . . Enough of books and theories. It is the *life* that is the highest and the only way to stir the hearts of people; it carries the personal magnetism. . . . The Lord is giving me a deeper and deeper insight every day. Work, work, work. . . . Truce to foolish talk; talk of the Lord. Life is too short to be spent in talking about frauds and cranks.

You must always remember that every nation must save itself; so must every man; do not look to others for help. Through hard work here, I shall be able now and then to send you a little money for your work; but that is all. If you have to look forward to that, better stop work. Know also that this is a grand field for my ideas, and that I do not care whether they are Hindus or Mohammedans or Christians, but those that love the Lord will always command my service.

. . . I like to work on calmly and silently and the Lord is always with me. Follow me if you will, by being intensely sincere, perfectly unselfish, and, above all, by being perfectly pure. My blessings go with you. In this short life there is no time for the exchange of compliments. We can compare notes and compliment each other to our hearts' content after the battle is finished. Now, do not talk; work, work, work! I do not see anything permanent you have done in India—I do not see any centre you have made—I do not see any temple or hall you have erected—I do not see anybody joining hands with you. There is too much talk, talk, talk! We are great, we are great! Nonsense! We are imbeciles; that is what we are! This hankering after name and fame and all other humbugs—what are they to me? What do I care about them? I should like to see hundreds coming to the Lord! Where are they? I want them, I want to see them. You must seek them out. You only give me name and fame. Have done with name and fame; to work, my brave men, to work! You have not caught my fire yet—you do not understand me! You run in the old ruts of sloth and enjoyments. Down with all sloth, down with all enjoyments here or hereafter. Plunge into the fire and bring the people towards the Lord.

That you may catch my fire, that you may be intensely sincere, that you may die the heroes' death on the field of battle—is the constant prayer of—VIVEKANANDA.

P. S. Tell Alasinga, Kidi, Doctor, Balaji and all the others not to pin their faith on what Tom, Dick and Harry say for or against us, but to concentrate all their energy on work.—VIVEKANANDA.

(*108*)

To Sj. Alasinga Perumal

CHICAGO,
12th Jan., 1895.

DEAR ALASINGA—Now know once and for all that I do not care for name or fame or any humbug of that type. I want to preach my ideas for the good of the world. You have done a great work, but so far as it goes it has only given *me* name and fame. My life is more precious than spending it in getting the admiration of the world. I have no time for such foolery. What work have you done in the way of advancing the ideas and organising in India? *None, none, none.*

An organisation that will teach the Hindus mutual help and appreciation is absolutely necessary. Five thousand people attended that meeting that was held in Calcutta to express an appreciation of my work here—well and good! But if you asked them each to give an anna, would they do it? The whole national character is one of childish dependence. They are all ready to enjoy food if it is brought to their mouth, and even some want it pushed down. . . . You do not deserve to live if you cannot help yourselves. . . .

I have given up at present my plan for the education of the masses. It will come by and by. What I now want is a band of fiery missionaries. We must have a *College* in Madras to teach comparative religions, Sanskrit, the different schools of Vedanta and some European languages; we must have a press, and papers printed in English and in the Vernaculars. When this is done, then I shall know that you have accomplished something. Let the nation show that they are ready to *do*. If you cannot do anything of the kind in India, then let me alone. I have a message to give, let me give it to the people who appreciate it and who will work it out. What care I who takes it? "He who doeth the will of My Father," is my own. . . .

My name should not be made prominent; it is my ideas that I want to see realised. The disciples of all the prophets have always inextricably mixed up the ideas of the Master with the *person*, and at last killed the ideas for the *person*. The disciples of Sri Ramakrishna must guard against doing the same thing. Work for the *idea*, not the person. The Lord bless you.—Yours ever with blessings, VIVEKANANDA.

(*109*)

To Swami Trigunatitananda

228 W. 39,*
NEW YORK,
17th Jan., 1895.

DEAR SARADA—Your two letters are to hand, as also the two of Ramdayal Babu. I have got the bill of lading, but it will be long before the goods arrive. Unless one arranges for the prompt despatch of goods they take about six months to come. It is four months since Haramohan wrote that the Rudrâksha beads and Kusha mats had been despatched, but there is no news of their whereabouts yet. The thing is, when the goods reach England, the agent of the company here gives me notice, and about a month later, the goods arrive. I received your bill of lading about three weeks ago, but no sign of the notice! Only the goods sent by the Raja of Khetri arrive quickly. Most probably he spends a lot of money for them. However, it is a matter of congratulation that goods do arrive without fail in this region of Pâtâla, at the other end of the globe. I shall let you know as soon as the goods come. Now keep quiet for at least three months! . . .

Now is the time for you to apply yourself to start the magazine. Tell Ramdayal Babu that though the gentleman of whom he speaks be a competent person, I am not in a position to have anybody in America at present. . . . What about your article on Thibet? When it is published in the *Mirror*, send me a copy. . . . Come, here is a task for you, conduct that magazine. Thrust it on people and make them subscribe to it, and don't be afraid. What work do you expect from men of little hearts?—Nothing in the world! You must have an iron will if you would cross the ocean. You must be strong enough to pierce mountains. I am coming next winter. We shall set the world on fire—let those who will, join us and be blessed, and those that won't come, can lag behind for ever and ever; let them do so. You gird up your loins and keep yourself ready. . . . Never mind anything! In your lips and hands the Goddess of Learning will make Her seat; the Lord of infinite power will be seated on your chest; you will do works that will strike the world with wonder. By the bye, can't you shorten your name a bit, my boy? What a long, long name!—a single name enough to fill a volume! Well, you hear people say that the Lord's name keeps away death! It is not the simple name "Hari," mind you. It is those deep and sonorous names, such as अघभगनरकविनाशन (Destroyer of Agha, Bhaga and Naraka), त्रिपुरमदभञ्जन (Subduer of the pride of Tripura, demon of the "three cities"), and अशेषनिःशेषकल्याणकर (Giver of infinite and endless blessings) and so forth—that put to rout King Death and his whole party. Won't it look nice if you simplify yours a little? But it is too late, I am afraid, as it has already been abroad. But, believe me, it is a world-entrancing, death-defying name that you have got![1]—Yours affectionately, VIVEKANANDA.

P. S. Throw the whole of Bengal and, for the matter of that, the whole of India into convulsion! Start centres at different places.

The Bhâgavatam has reached me—a very nice edition indeed, but people of this country have not the least inclination for studying Sanskrit, hence there is very little hope for its sale. There may be a little in England, for, there many are interested in the study of Sanskrit. Give my special thanks to the editor. I hope his noble attempt will meet with complete success. I shall try my best to push his book here. I have sent his prospectus to different places. Tell Ramdayal Babu that a flourishing trade can be set on foot with England and America in *mûng dâl*, *arhar dâl*, etc. *Dâl* soup will have a go if properly introduced. There will be a good demand for them if they be sent from house to house, in small packets, with directions for cooking on them and a depot started for storing

[1] The full name which Swami Trigunatita, to whom this letter was addressed, bore at first was "Swami Trigunâtitananda," hence the Swamiji's pleasantry about it.

a quantity of them. Similarly *barhis*[1] too will have a good market. We want an enterprising spirit. Nothing is done by leading idle lives. If anyone forms a company and exports Indian goods here and into England, it will be a good trade. But they are a lazy set. . . .

(*110*)

To Mrs. Ole Bull,

on the occasion of the loss of her father

BROOKLYN,

20th January, 1895.

. . . I had a premonition of your father's giving up the old body, and it is not my custom to write to anyone when a wave of would-be inharmonious Maya strikes him. But these are the great turning-points in life, and I know that you are unmoved. The surface of the sea rises and sinks alternately, but to the observant soul—the child of light—each sinking reveals more and more of the depth, and of the beds of pearls and coral at the bottom. Coming and going is all pure delusion. The soul never comes nor goes. Where is the place to which it shall go, when all space is *in the soul*? When shall be the time for entering and departing, when all time is *in the soul*?

The earth moves, causing the illusion of the movement of the sun; but the sun does not move. So Prakriti, or Maya, or Nature is moving, changing, unfolding veil after veil, turning over leaf after leaf of this grand book—while the witnessing soul drinks in knowledge, unmoved, unchanged. All souls that ever have been, are, or shall be, are all in the present tense, and—to use a material simile —are all standing at one geometrical point. Because the

[1] Made of dal pounded into a paste, beaten and made into pellets.

idea of space does not occur in the soul, therefore all that were ours, are ours, and will be ours *are* always with us, *were* always with us, and *will be* always with us. We are in them. They are in us. Take these cells. Though each separate, they are all nevertheless inseparably joined at AB. There they are one. Each is an individual, yet all are one at the axis AB. None can escape from that axis, and however broken or torn the circumference, yet by standing at the axis, we may enter any one of the chambers. This axis is the Lord. There we are one with Him, all in all, and all in God.

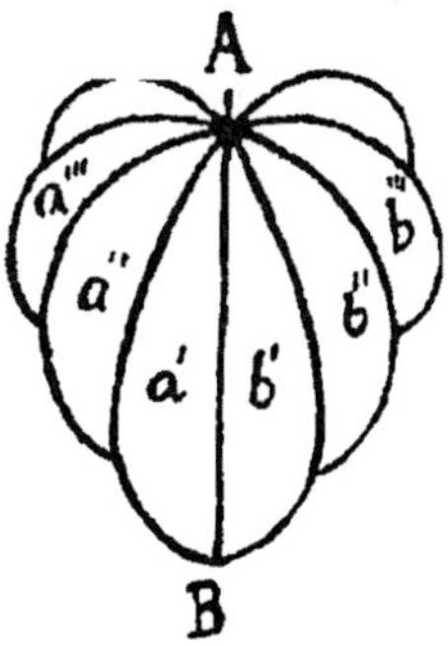

The cloud moves across the face of the moon, creating the illusion that the moon is moving. So nature, body, matter moves on, creating the illusion that the soul is moving. Thus we find at last that that instinct (or inspiration?) which men of every race, whether high or low, have had to feel, viz., the presence of the departed about them, is true intellectually also.

Each soul is a star, and all stars are set in that infinite azure, that eternal sky, the Lord. There is the root, the reality, the real individuality of each and all. Religion began with the search after some of these stars that had passed beyond our horizon, and ended in finding them all in God, and ourselves in the same place. The whole secret is, then, that your father has given up the old garment he was wearing, and is standing where he was through all eternity. Will he manifest another such garment in this or any other world? I sincerely pray that he may not, until he does so in full consciousness. I pray that none may be dragged anywhither by the unseen power of his own past actions. I pray that all may be free, that is to say, may know that they are free. And if they are to dream again, let us pray that their dreams be all of peace and bliss. . . .—Yours etc., VIVEKANANDA.

(*111*)

To Sj. Alasinga Perumal

U. S. A.,

23rd Jan., 1895.

DEAR ALASINGA—. . . I only want men to follow me who will be true and faithful unto death. I do not care for success or non-success. . . . I must keep my movement *pure* or I will have none of it. . . .—Yours, VIVEKANANDA.

(*112*)

To Mrs. Ole Bull

NEW YORK,

24th Jan., 1895.

DEAR MRS. BULL—. . . This year I am afraid I am getting overworked as I feel the strain. I want a rest badly. So it is very good as you say that the Boston work be taken up in the end of March. By the end of April I will start for England.

Land can be had in large plots in the Catskills for very little money. There is a plot of 101 acres for $200. The money I have ready, only I cannot buy the land in my name. You are the only friend in this country in whom I have perfect trust. If you consent I will buy the land in your name. The students will go there in summer and build cottages or camps as they like and practise meditation. Later on if they can collect funds they may build something up.

. . . To-morrow will be the last Sunday lecture of this month. The first Sunday of next month there will be a lecture in Brooklyn; the rest, three in New York, with which I will close this year's New York lectures.

I have worked my best. If there is any seed of truth in it, it will come to life. So I have no anxiety about anything. I am also getting tired of lecturing and having classes. After a few months' work in England I will go to India and hide myself absolutely for some years or for ever. I am satisfied in my conscience that I did not remain an idle Swami. I have a note-book which has travelled with me all over the world. I find these words written seven years ago—" Now to seek a corner and lay myself to die!" Yet all this Karma remained. I hope I have worked them out. I hope the Lord will give me freedom from this preaching and adding good bondages.

" If you have known the Atman as the one existence and that nothing else exists, for whom, for what desire do you trouble yourself?" Through Maya all this doing good etc., came into my brain—now they are leaving me. I get more and more convinced that there is no other object in work except the purification of the soul—to make it fit for knowledge. This world with its good and evil will go on in various forms. Only the evil and good will take new names and new seats. My soul is hankering after peace and rest eternal, undisturbed.

"Live alone, live alone. He who is alone never comes into conflict with others—never disturbs others, is never disturbed by others." I long, oh! I long for my rags, my shaven head, my sleep under the trees and my food from begging! That India is the only place where with all its faults, the soul finds its freedom, its God. All this Western pomp is only vanity, only bondage of the soul. Never more in my life I realised more forcibly the vanity of the world. May the Lord break the bondage of all—may all come out of Maya—is the constant prayer of—
VIVEKANANDA.

(*113*)

To Miss Mary Hale

54, W. 33RD STREET, N. Y.,
1st Feb., 1895.

DEAR SISTER—I just received your beautiful note. . . . Well, sometimes it is a good discipline to be forced to work for work's sake, even to the length of not being allowed to enjoy the fruits of one's labour. . . . I am very glad of your criticisms and am not sorry at all. The other day at Miss Thursby's I had an excited argument with a Presbyterian gentleman, who as usual got very hot, angry and abusive. However, I was afterwards severely reprimanded by Mrs. Bull for this, as such things hinder my work. So, it seems, is your opinion.

I am glad you write about it just now, because I have been giving a good deal of thought to it. In the first place, I am not at all sorry for these things. Perhaps that may disgust you—it may: I know full well how good it is for one's worldly prospects to be *sweet*. . . . I do everything to be *sweet*, but when it comes to a horrible compromise with the truth within, then I stop. I do not believe in *humility*. I believe in *Samadarshitvam*—same state of mind with regard to all. The duty of the ordinary man is to obey the commands of his "God"—society, but the children of Light never do so. This is an eternal law. One accommodates himself to surroundings and social opinion and gets all good things from society, the giver of all good to such. The other stands alone and draws society up towards him. The accommodating man finds a path of roses—the non-accommodating, one of thorns. But the worshippers of "Vox populi" go to annihilation in a moment—the children of truth *live for ever*.

I will compare truth to a corrosive substance of infinite power. It burns its way in wherever it falls—in soft substance at once, hard granite slowly, but it must. What is writ is writ. I am so, sorry, Sister, that I cannot make myself *sweet* and accommodating to every black falsehood. But I cannot. I have suffered for it all my life, but I cannot. I have essayed and essayed, but I cannot. At last I have given it up. The Lord is great. He will not allow me to become a hypocrite. Now let what is in come out. I have not found a way that will please all, and I cannot but be what I am, true to my own self. "Youth and beauty vanish, life and wealth vanish, name and fame vanish, even the mountains crumble into dust. Friendship and love vanish. Truth alone abides." God of Truth, be Thou alone my guide! I am too old to change now into milk and honey. Allow me to remain as I am. "Without fear, without shop-keeping, caring neither for friend nor foe, do thou hold on to truth, Sannyasin, and from this moment give up this world and the next and all that are to come—their enjoyments and their vanities. Truth, be thou alone my guide." I have no desire for wealth or name or fame or enjoyments, Sister, they are dust unto me. I wanted to help my brethren. I have not the *tact to earn money*, bless the Lord. What reason is there for me to conform to the vagaries of the world around me and not obey the voice of Truth within? The mind is still weak, Sister, it sometimes mechanically clutches at earthly help. But I am not afraid. Fear is the greatest sin, my religion teaches.

The last fight with the Presbyterian priest and the long fight afterwards with Mrs. Bull showed me in a clear light what Manu says to the Sannyasin—"Live alone, walk alone." All friendship, all love, is only limitation. There never was a friendship, especially of women, which was not exacting. Oh! great sages! You were right. One cannot serve the God of Truth who leans upon somebody. Be still, my soul! Be alone! and the Lord is with you. Life is nothing! Death is a delusion! All this is not, God alone is! Fear not, my soul! Be alone. Sister, the way is long, the time is short, evening is approaching. I have to go home soon. I have no time to give my manners a finish. I cannot find time to deliver my message. You are good, you are so kind, I will do anything for you; but do not be angry, I see you all as mere children.

Dream no more! Oh, dream no more, my soul! In one word, I have a message to give, I have no time to be sweet to the world, and every attempt at sweetness makes me a hypocrite. I will die a thousand deaths rather than lead a jelly-fish existence and yield to every requirement of this foolish world—no matter whether it be my own country or a foreign country. You are mistaken, utterly mistaken if you think I have a *work* as Mrs. Bull thinks—I have no *work* under or beyond the sun. I have a message and I will give it after my own fashion. I will neither Hinduise my message, nor Christianise it, nor make it any "ise" in the world. I will only *my-ise* it and that is all. Liberty, Mukti is all my religion, and everything that tries to curb it, I will avoid by fight or flight. Pooh! I try to pacify the priests!! Sister, do not take this amiss. But you are babies and babies must submit to be taught. You have not yet drunk of that fountain which makes "reason unreason—mortal immortal—this world a zero, and of man a God." Come out if you can of this network of foolishness they call this *world*. Then I will call you indeed brave and free. If you cannot, cheer those that dare dash this false God, society, to the ground and trample on its unmitigated hypocrisy; if you cannot cheer them, pray, be silent, but do not try to drag them down again into the mire with such false nonsense as *compromise* and becoming nice and sweet.

I hate this world—this dream—this horrible nightmare—with its churches and chicaneries, its books and blackguardisms—its fair faces and false hearts—its howling righteousness on the surface and utter hollowness beneath and, above all, its sanctified shop-keeping. What! measure my soul according to what the bondslaves of the world say!

—Pooh! Sister, you do not know the Sannyasin. "He stands on the head of the Vedas!" say the Vedas, because he is free from churches and sects and religions and prophets and books and all of that ilk! Missionary or no missionary, let them howl and attack me with all they can, I take them as Bhartrihari says, "Go thou thy way, Sannyasin! Some will say, who is this mad man? Others, who is this Chandâla? Others will know thee to be a sage. Be glad at the prattle of the worldlings. But when they attack, know that the elephant passing through the market-place is always beset by curs, but he cares not. He goes straight on *his own way*. So it is always, when a great soul appears there will be numbers to bark after him."

I am living with Landsberg at 54, W. 33rd Street. He is a brave and noble soul, Lord bless him. Sometimes I go to the Guernseys' to sleep.

Lord bless you all ever and ever—and may He lead you quickly out of this big humbug, the world! May you never be enchanted by this old witch, the world! May Shankara help you! May Umâ open the door of truth for you and take away all your delusions!—Yours with love and blessings, VIVEKANANDA.

(*114*)

To Sj. Vaikuntha Nath Sanyal

54, W. 33RD ST., NEW YORK,*

9th February, 1895.

DEAR SANYAL—. . . Paramahamsa Deva was my Guru, and whatever I may think of him in point of greatness. why should the world think after me? And if you press the point hard, you will spoil everything. The idea of worshipping the Guru as God is nowhere to be met with outside Bengal, for other people are not yet ready to take up that ideal. . . .

Henceforth address my letters as above, which is to be my permanent seat from now.

Try to send me an English translation of the Yoga-vâshishtha Ramayana. . . .

Don't forget those books I asked for before, viz., Sanskrit Narada and Shandilya Sutras.

आशा हि परमं दुःखं नैराश्यं परमं सुखम्— "Hope is the greatest of miseries, the highest bliss lies in giving up hope."—

Yours affectionately, VIVEKANANDA.

(*115*)

To Mrs. Ole Bull

54, W. 33RD ST., NEW YORK,
14th February, 1895.

DEAR MRS. BULL—. . . Accept my heart-felt gratitude for your motherly advice.

. . . How can I express my gratitude to you for what you have already done for me and my work, and my eternal gratitude to you for your offering to do something more this year? But I sincerely believe that you ought to turn all your help to Miss Farmer's Greenacre work this year. India can wait as she is waiting centuries and an immediate work at hand should always have the preference.

Again, according to Manu, collecting funds even for a good work is not good for a Sannyasin, and I have begun to feel that the old sages were right. "Hope is the greatest misery, despair is the greatest happiness." I had these childish ideas of doing this and doing that. These appear like a hallucination to me now. I am getting out of them.

"Give up all desire and be at peace. Have neither friends nor foes and live alone. Thus shall we travel having neither friends nor foes, neither pleasure nor pain, neither desire nor jealousy, injuring no creatures, being the cause of injury to no creatures—from mountain to mountain, from village to village preaching the name of the Lord."

"Seek no help from high or low, from above or below. Desire nothing—and look upon this vanishing panorama as a witness and let it pass."

Perhaps these mad desires were necessary to bring me over to this country. And I thank the Lord for the experience.

I am very happy now. Between Mr. Landsberg and me, we cook some rice and lentils or barley and quietly eat it, and write something or read or receive visits from poor people who want to learn something, and thus I feel I am more a Sannyasin now than I ever was in America.

"In wealth is the fear of poverty, in knowledge the fear of ignorance, in beauty the fear of age, in fame the fear of backbiters, in success the fear of jealousy, even in body is the fear of death. Everything in this earth is fraught with fear. He alone is fearless who has given up everything."[1]

I went to see Miss Corbin the other day, and Miss Farmer and Miss Thursby were also there. We had a nice half hour, and she wants me to hold some classes in her home from next Sunday.

I am no more seeking for these things. If they come the Lord be blessed, if not, blessed more be He.

Again accept my eternal gratitude.—Your devoted son, VIVEKANANDA.

(116)

To Sj. Alasinga Perumal

19, W. 38TH ST.,
NEW YORK,
1895.

DEAR ALASINGA—. . . Meddle not with so-called social reform, for there cannot be any reform without spiritual

[1] Bhartrihari's Vairâgya-Shatakam.

reform first. . . . Preach the Lord—say neither good nor bad about the superstitions and evils. . . . Do not lose heart, do not lose faith in your Guru, do not lose faith in God. So long as you possess these three, nothing can harm you, my child. I am growing stronger every day. Work on, my brave boys.—Ever yours with blessings, VIVEKANANDA.

(*117*)

To The Same

6th March, 1895.

DEAR ALASINGA—. . . . Do not for a moment think the "Yankees" are practical in religion. In that the Hindu alone is practical, the Yankee in money-making. . . . Therefore I want to have solid ground under my feet before I depart. Every work should be made thorough. . . . You need not insist upon preaching Sri Ramakrishna. Propagate his ideas first, though I know the world always wants the man first, then the idea. . . . Do not figure out big plans at first, but begin slowly and feel your ground.

. . . Work on my brave boys. We shall see the light some day.

Harmony and peace. . . . Let things slowly grow. Rome was not built in a day. The Maharaja of Mysore is dead—one of our greatest hopes. Well! the Lord is great. He will send others to help.

Send some Kushâsanas if you can.—Yours ever with blessings, VIVEKANANDA.

(*118*)

To Mrs. Ole Bull

54, W. 33RD ST., NEW YORK,
21st March, 1895.

DEAR MRS. BULL—. . . I am astonished to hear the scandals the Ramabai circles are indulging in about me.

. . . Don't you see, Mrs. Bull, that however a man may conduct himself, there will always be persons who invent the blackest lies about him. At Chicago I had such things every day against me!

And these women are invariably the very Christian of Christians! . . . I am going to have a series of paid lectures in my rooms (downstairs), which will seat about a hundred persons, and that will cover the expenses. . . . Miss Hamlin has been very kind to me and does all she can to help me.

My Master used to say that these names as, Hindu, Christian, etc., stand as great bars to all brotherly feelings between man and man. We must try to break them down first. They have lost all their good powers and now only stand as baneful influences under whose black magic even the best of us behave like demons. Well, we will have to work hard and must succeed.

That is why I desire so much to have a centre. Organisation has its faults, no doubt, but without that nothing can be done. And here, I am afraid, I will have to differ from you—that no one ever succeeded in keeping society in good humour and at the same time did great works. One must work as the dictate comes from within, and then if it is right and good, society is bound to veer round, perhaps centuries after one is dead and gone. We must plunge heart and soul and body into the work. And until we be ready to sacrifice everything else to one *Idea* and to *one* alone, we *never, never* will see the Light.

Those that want to help mankind must take their own pleasure and pain, name and fame, and all sorts of interests, and make a bundle of them and throw them into the sea, and then come to the Lord. This is what all the masters said and *did*.

I went to Miss Corbin's last Saturday and told her that I would not be able to come to hold classes any more. Was it ever in the history of the world that any great work was done by the rich? It is the heart and the brain that do it ever and ever and not the purse.

My *idea* and all my life with it—and to *God* for help; to none else! This is the only secret of success. I am sure you are one with me here. . . .—Ever yours in grateful affection, VIVEKANANDA.

(*119*)

To Sj. Alasinga Perumal

U. S. A.,
4th April, 1895.

MY DEAR ALASINGA—Your letter just to hand. You need not be afraid of anybody's attempting to hurt me. So long as the Lord protects me I shall be impregnable. Your ideas of America are very hazy. . . . This is a huge country, the majority do not care much about religion. . . . Christianity holds its ground as a mere patriotism, and nothing more. . . . Now, my son, do not lose courage. . . . Send me the Vedanta-Sutras and the Bhâshyas of all the sects. . . .

I am in His hands. What is the use of going back to India? India cannot further my ideas. This country takes kindly to my ideas. I will go back when I get the command. In the meanwhile, do you all gently and patiently work. If anybody attacks me, simply ignore his existence. . . . My idea is for you to start a society where people could be taught the Vedas and the Vedanta, with the commentaries. Work on this line at present. . . . Know that every time you feel weak, you not only hurt yourself but also the cause. Infinite faith and strength are the only conditions of success.

Be cheerful. . . . Hold on to your own ideal. . . . Above all, never attempt to guide or rule others, or, as the Yankees say, " boss " others. Be the servant of all.—Ever with blessings, VIVEKANANDA.

(*120*)

To Mrs. Ole Bull

54, W. 33RD ST., NEW YORK,
11th April, 1895.

DEAR MRS. BULL—. . . I am going away to the country to-morrow to Mr. L— for a few days. A little fresh air will do me good, I hope.

I have given up the project of removing from this house just now, as it will be too expensive, and moreover it is not advisable to change just now. I am working it up slowly.

. . . I send you herewith the letter from H. H. the Maharaja of Khetri. . . .

. . . Miss Hamlin has been helping me a good deal. I am very grateful to her. She is very kind and, I hope, sincere. She wants me to be introduced to the "right kind of people." This is the second edition of the "Hold yourself steady" business, I am afraid. The only "right sort of people" are those whom the Lord sends—that is what I understand in my life's experience. They alone can and will help me. As for the rest, Lord help them in a mass and save me from them.

Every one of my friends thought it would end in nothing, this my living and preaching in poor quarters all by myself, and that no *ladies will ever come here.* Miss Hamlin especially thought that "she" or "her right sort of people" were *way up* from such things as to go and listen to a man who lives by himself in a poor lodging. But the "right kind" came for all that, day and night, and she too. Lord! how hard it is for man to believe in Thee and Thy mercies! Shiva! Shiva! Where is the right kind and where is the bad, mother? It is all *He*! In the tiger and in the lamb, in the saint and sinner all *He*! In Him I have taken my refuge, body, soul, and Atman. Will

He leave me now after carrying me in His arms all my life? Not a drop will be in the ocean, not a twig in the deepest forest, not a crumb in the house of the god of wealth, if the Lord is not merciful. Streams will be in the desert and the beggar will have plenty if He wills it. He seeth the sparrows fall. Are these but words, mother, or literal, actual life?

Truce to these "right sort of presentation" and the like. Thou art my right, Thou my wrong, my Shiva. Lord, since a child I have taken refuge in Thee. Thou wilt be with me in the tropics or at the poles, on the tops of mountains or in he depth of oceans. My stay—my guide in life—my refuge—my friend—my teacher—my God—my real self. Thou wilt never leave me, *never*. I know it as sure as anything. Sometimes I became weak, being alone and struggling against odds, my God, and I think of human help. Save Thou me for ever from these weaknesses, and may I never, never seek for help from any being but Thee. If a man puts his trust in another good man he is never betrayed, never forsaken. Wilt Thou forsake me, Father of all good, Thou who knowest that *all* my life I am Thy servant and Thine alone? Wilt Thou give me over to be played upon by others, or dragged down by evil?

He will never leave me, I am sure, mother.—Your son, VIVEKANANDA.

(*121*)

To Swami Ramakrishnananda

U. S. A.,*
11th April, 1895.

MY DEAR SASI—. . . You write that you have recovered from your illness, but you must henceforth be very careful. Late dinners, or unwholesome food, or living in a stinking place may bring on a relapse, and make it hard to escape the clutches of malaria. First of all you should hire a small garden-house—you may get one for 30 or 40 rupees. Secondly, see that cooking and drinking water be filtered—a bamboo filter of a big size will do. Water is the cause of all sorts of disease. It is not the clearness or dirtiness of water, but its being full of disease germs, that causes disease. Let the water be boiled and filtered. You must all pay attention to your health first. A cook, a servant, clean beds and timely meals—these are absolutely necessary. Please see that all these suggestions be carried out *in toto*. . . . The success of your undertakings depends wholly upon your mutual love. There is no good in store so long as malice and jealousy and egotism will prevail. . . . Kali's pamphlet is very well written, and has no exaggerations. Know that talking ill of others in private is a sin. You must wholly avoid it. Many things may occur to the mind, but it gradually makes a mountain of a mole-hill if you try to express them. Everything is ended if you forgive and forget. It is welcome news that Sri Ramakrishna's Festival was celebrated with great *eclat*. You must try so that there is a muster of hundred thousand people next year. Put year energies together to start a magazine. Shyness won't do any more. . . . He who has infinite patience and infinite energy at his back, will alone succeed. You must pay special attention to study. Do you understand? You must not huddle together too many fools. I shall be glad if you bring together a few real men. Why, I don't hear even a single one opening his lips. You distributed sweets at the Festival, and there was singing by some parties, mostly idlers. True, but I don't hear what spiritual food you have given. So long as that *nil admirari* attitude is not gone, you will not be able to do anything, and none of you will have courage. Bullies are always cowards.

Take up everyone with sympathy, whether he believes in Sri Ramakrishna or not. If anybody comes to you for vain dispute, politely withdraw yourselves. . . . You must express your sympathy with people of all sects. When these cardinal virtues will be manifested in you, then only you will be able to work with great energy. Otherwise, mere taking the name of the Guru will not do. However, there is no doubt that this year's Festival has been a great success, and you deserve special thanks for it, but you must push forward, do you see? What is Sarat doing? Never shall you be able to know anything if you persist in pleading ignorance. . . . We want something of a higher tone—that will appeal to the intellect of the learned. It won't do merely to get up musical parties and all that. Not only will this Festival be his memorial but also the central union of an intense propaganda of his doctrines. . . . All will come in good time. But at times I fret and stamp like a leashed hound. Onward and forward, my old watchword. I am doing well. No use going back to India in a hurry. Summon all your energies and set yourselves to work, heart and soul; that will really be heroic.—Yours affectionately, VIVEKANANDA.

(*122*)

To Mr. E. T. Sturdy

54, W. 33RD ST., NEW YORK,
24th April, 1895.

I am perfectly aware that although some truth underlies the mass of mystical thought which has burst upon the Western world of late, it is for the most part full of motives unworthy or insane. For this reason, I have never had anything to do with these phases of religion, either in India or elsewhere, and mystics as a class are not very favourable to me. . . .

I quite agree with you that only the Advaita Philosophy can save mankind, whether in East or West, from "devil worship" and kindred superstitions, giving tone and strength to the very nature of man. India herself requires this, quite as much or even more than the West. Yet it is hard uphill work, for we have first to create a taste, then teach, and lastly proceed to build up the whole fabric.

Perfect sincerity, holiness, gigantic intellect, and an all-conquering will. Let only a handful of men work with these, and the whole world will be revolutionised. I did a good deal of platform work in this country last year, and received plenty of applause, but found that I was only working for myself. It is the patient upbuilding of character, the intense struggle to *realise* the truth, which alone will tell, in the future of humanity. So this year I am hoping to work along this line—training up to practical Advaita realisation a small band of men and women. I do not know how far I shall succeed. The West is the field for work, if a man wants to benefit humanity, rather than his own particular sect or country. I agree perfectly as to your idea of a magazine. But I have no business capacity at all, to do these things. I can teach, and preach, and sometimes write. But I have intense faith in Truth. The Lord will send help and hands to work with me. Only let me be perfectly pure, perfectly sincere, and perfectly unselfish.

"Truth alone triumphs, not untruth; through truth alone stretches the way to the Lord" (Yajurveda). He who gives up the little self for the world will find the whole universe his. . . . I am very uncertain about coming to England. I know no one there, and here I am doing some work. The Lord will guide, in His own time.

(*123*)

To The Same

19, W. 38TH ST.,
NEW YORK.

DEAR FRIEND—I received your last duly, and as I had a previous arrangement to come to Europe by the end of this August, I take your invitation as a Divine Call.

"Truth alone triumphs, not untruth. Through truth alone lies the way to Devayânan (the way to God)." Those who think that a little sugar-coating of untruth helps the spread of truth, are mistaken, and will find in the long run that a single drop of poison poisons the whole mass. . . . The man who is pure and who dares, does all things. May the Lord ever protect you from illusion and delusion! I am ever ready to work with you, and the Lord will send us friends by the hundred, if only we be our own friends first. "The Atman alone is the friend of the Atman."

Europe has always been the source of social and Asia, of spiritual power; and the whole history of the world is the tale of the varying combinations of these two powers. Slowly a new leaf is being turned in the story of humanity. The signs of this are everywhere. Hundreds of new plans will be created and destroyed. Only the fit will survive, and what, but the true and the good, is the fit?—Yours etc. VIVEKANANDA.

(*124*)

To Mrs. Ole Bull

54, W. 33RD ST., NEW YORK,
25th April, 1895.

DEAR MRS. BULL—The day before yesterday I received a kind note from Miss F—including a cheque for a hundred dollars for the Barbar House lectures. She is coming to New York next Saturday.

I will of course tell her not to put my name in her circulars as I have arranged to go to the Thousand Islands, wherever that may be. There is a cottage belonging to Miss Dutcher, one of my students, and a few of us will be there in rest and peace and seclusion. I want to manufacture a few "Yogis" out of the materials of the classes, and a busy fair like Greenacre is the last place for that, while the other is quite out of the way, and none of the curiosity-seekers will dare go there.

I am very glad that Miss Hamlin took down the names of the one hundred and thirty persons who came to the Jnana-Yoga class. There were fifty more who came to the Wednesday Yoga class and about fifty more to the Monday class. Mr. Landsberg had all the names, and they will come anyhow, names or no names. . . . If they do not, others will, and so it will go on—the Lord be praised.

Taking down names and giving notices is a big task, no doubt, and I am very thankful to both of them for doing that for me. But I am thoroughly persuaded that it is laziness on my part, and therefore immoral, to depend on others, and always evil comes out of laziness. So henceforth I will do it all myself. . . .

However, I will be only too glad to take in any one of Miss Hamlin's "right sort of persons," but unfortunately for me not one such has as yet turned up. It is the duty of the teacher always to turn the "right sort" out of the most " unrighteous sort " of persons. After all, though I am very, very grateful to the young lady, Miss Hamlin, for the great hope and encouragement she gave me of introducing me to the "right sort of New Yorkers" and for the practical help she has given me, I think I had better do my little work with my own hands. . . .

I am only glad that you have such a great opinion about Miss Hamlin. I for one am glad to know that you will help her, for she requires it. But, mother, through the mercy of Ramakrishna, my instinct "sizes up" almost infallibly a human face as soon as I see it, and the result is this: you may do anything you please with my affairs, *I will not even murmur*—I will be only too glad to take Miss Farmer's advice, in spite of ghosts and spooks. Behind the spooks I *see* a heart of immense love, only covered with a thin film of *laudable* ambition—even that is bound to vanish in a few years. Even I will allow

Landsberg to "monkey" with my affairs from time to time, but here I put a full stop. Help from any other person besides these *frightens* me. That is all I can say. Not only for the help you have given me but from my instinct (or as I call it, inspiration of my Master) I regard you as my mother, and will always abide by any advice you may have for me—but only *personally*. When you select a medium I will beg leave to exercise my choice. That is all.

Herewith I send the English gentleman's letter. I have made a few notes on the margin to explain Hindusthanee words.—Ever your son, VIVEKANANDA.

(*125*)

U. S. A.,
2nd May, 1895.

DEAR S——, So you have made up your mind to renounce the world. I have sympathy with your desire. There is nothing so high as renunciation of self. But you must not forget that to forgo your own favourite desire for the welfare of those that depend upon you is no small sacrifice. Follow the spotless life and teachings of Sri Ramakrishna and look after the comforts of your family. You do your own duty, and leave the rest to Him.

Love makes no distinction between man and man, between an Aryan and a Mlechchha, between a Brahmin and a Pariah, nor even between a man or a woman. Love makes the whole universe as one's own home. True progress is slow but sure. Work among those young men who can devote heart and soul to this one duty—the duty of raising the masses of India. Awake them, unite them, and inspire them with this spirit of renunciation; it depends wholly on the young people of India.

Cultivate the virtue of obedience, but you must not

sacrifice your own faith. No centralisation is possible unless there is obedience to superiors. No great work can be done without this centralisation of individual forces. The Calcutta Math is the main centre; the members of all other branches must act in unity and conformity with the rules of that centre.

Give up jealousy and conceit. Learn to work unitedly for others. This is the great need of our country.—Yours with blessings, VIVEKANANDA.

(*126*)

To Sj. Alasinga Perumal

6th May, 1895.

DEAR ALASINGA—This morning I received your last letter and the first volume of the Bhâshya of Ramanujacharya. . . . Why should I waste my energies defending Hinduism if the Hindus all go to sleep? What are you three hundred millions of people doing there, especially those that are so proud of their learning etc.? Why do you not take up the fight and leave me to teach and preach? Here am I struggling day and night in the midst of strangers. . . . What help does India send? Did the world ever see a nation with less patriotism than the Indian? If you could send and maintain for a few years a dozen well-educated strong men, to preach in Europe and America, you would do immense service to India, both morally and politically. Every man who morally sympathises with India becomes a political friend. Many of the Western people think of you as a nation of half-naked savages, and therefore only fit to be whipped into civilisation. Why don't you show them to the contrary. . . . What can one man do in a far distant land? Even what I have done, you do not deserve. . . .

Hindus that have hitherto come to Western lands have too often criticised their own faith and country in order to get praise or money. You know that I did not come to seek name and fame; it was forced upon me. Why shall I go back to India? Who will help me? Where are the men in Madras who will give up the world to preach religion? I am the one man who dared defend his country and I have given them such ideas as they never expected from a Hindu. There are thousands in the country who are my friends and hundreds who would follow me unto death; every year they will increase, and if I live and work with them, my ideals of life and religion will be fulfilled. Do you see?

I do not hear much now about the Temple Universal that was to be built in America; yet I have a firm footing in New York, the very centre of American life, and so my work will go on. I am taking several of my disciples to a summer retreat to finish their training in Yoga and Bhakti and Jnana, and then they will be able to help carry the work on. Now my boys, go to work.

Within a month I shall be in a position to send some money for the paper. Do not go about begging from the Hindu beggars. I will do it all *myself* with my own brain and strong right hand. I do not want the help of any man here or in India. . . . Do not press too much the Ramakrishna Avatar.

Now I will tell you my discovery. All of religion is contained in the Vedanta, that is, in the three stages of the Vedanta philosophy, the Dvaita, Vishishtâdvaita and Advaita; one comes after the other. These are the three stages of spiritual growth in man. Each one is necessary. This is the essential of religion. The Vedanta applied to the various ethnic customs and creeds of India, is Hinduism. The first stage, Dvaita, applied to the ideas of the ethnic groups of Europe, is Christianity; as applied to the Semitic groups, Mohammedanism. The Advaita as applied in its Yoga-perception form, is Buddhism etc. Now by religion is meant the Vedanta; the applications must vary according to the different needs, surroundings and other circumstances of different nations. You will find that although the philosophy is the same, the Shâktas, Shaivas, etc., apply it to their own special cult and *forms*. Now, in your journal write article after article on these three systems, showing their harmony as one following after the other, and at the same time keeping off the ceremonial forms altogether. That is, preach the philosophy, the spiritual part, and let people suit it to their own forms. I want to write a book on this subject, therefore I wanted the three Bhâshyas, but only one volume of the Ramanuja has reached me as yet.

. . . You know I am not much of a writer. I am not in the habit of going from door to door begging. I sit quiet and let things come to me. . . . Now my children, I could have made a grand success in the way of organising here, if I were a worldly hypocrite. Alas! That is all of religion here; money and name—priest, money and lust—layman, I am to create a new order of humanity here, who are sincere believers in God and care nothing for the world. This must be slow, very slow. In the meantime you go on with your work, and I shall steer my boat straight ahead. The journal must not be flippant but steady, calm and high-toned. . . . Get hold of a band of fine steady writers. . . . Be perfectly unselfish, be steady and work on. We will do great things; do not fear. One thing more. Be the servant of all, and do not try in the least to govern others. That will excite jealousy and destroy everything. . . . Go on. You have worked wonderfully well. We will work it out, my boy, be self-reliant, faithful and patient. Do not antagonise my other friends, live in harmony with all. My eternal love to all.—Ever yours with blessings, VIVEKANANDA.

P. S. Nobody will come to help you, if you put yourself forward as a leader. . . . Kill self first if you want to succeed.

(*127*)

To Mrs. Ole Bull

54, W. 33RD ST., NEW YORK,
7th May, 1895.

DEAR MRS. BULL—. . . I had a newspaper from India with a publication in it of Dr. Barrows' short reply to the thanks sent over from India. Miss Thursby will send it to you. Yesterday I received another letter from India from the president of the Madras Meeting to thank the Americans and to send me an address. . . . This gentleman is the chief citizen of Madras and a Judge of the Supreme Court, a very high position in India.

I am going to have two public lectures more in New York in the upper hall of the Mott's Memorial Building. The first one will be on Monday next, on the Science of Religion. The next, on the Rationale of Yoga. . . .
Ever gratefully your son, VIVEKANANDA.

(*128*)

To Sj. Alasinga Perumal

NEW YORK,
14th May, 1895.

DEAR ALASINGA—. . . . Now I have got a hold on New York, and I hope to get a permanent body of workers, who will carry on the work when I leave the country. Do you see, my boy, all this newspaper blazoning is nothing? I ought to be able to leave a permanent effect behind me when I go; and with the blessings of the Lord it is going to be very soon. . . . *Men* are more valuable than all the wealth of the world.

You need not worry about me. The Lord is always protecting me. My coming to this country and all my labours must not be in vain.

The Lord is merciful and although there are many who try to injure me any way they can, there are many also who will befriend me to the last. Infinite patience, infinite purity, and infinite perseverance are the secret of success in a good cause.—Yours ever with blessings, VIVEKANANDA.

(*129*)

To Swami Saradananda

U. S. A.,
20th May, 1895.

MY DEAR SARAT—. . . . Now I tell you a curious fact. Whenever anyone of you is sick, let him himself or anyone of you visualise him in your mind, and mentally say and strongly imagine that he is all right. That will cure him quickly. You can do it even without his knowledge, and even with thousands of miles between you. Remember it and do not be ill any more. . . .

I cannot understand why Sanyal is so miserable on account of his daughters' marriage. After all, he is going to drag his daughters through the dirty Samsâra which he himself wants to escape! I can have but one opinion of that—condemnation! I hate the very name of marriage, in regard to a boy or girl. Do you mean to say that I have to help in putting someone into bondage, you fool! If my brother Mohin marries, I will throw him off. I am very decided about that. . . .—Yours in love, VIVEKANANDA.

(*130*)

To Mrs. Ole Bull

54, W. 33RD ST., NEW YORK,
May, 1895.

DEAR MRS. BULL—The classes are going on, and the attendance is large. But I shall have to close them this week.

I am going this summer to the Thousand Islands to Miss Dutcher's, one of my students. The different books on Vedanta are now being sent over to me from India. I expect to write a book in English on the Vedanta Philosophy in its three stages when I am at Thousand Islands and I may go to Greenacre later on. Miss Farmer wants me to lecture there this summer.

I am rather busy just now in writing a promised article for the Press Association on Immortality.—Yours, VIVEKANANDA.

(*131*)

To The Same

54, W. 33RD ST., NEW YORK,
May, 1895.

DEAR MRS. BULL—Since writing to you my pupils have come round me with help and the classes will go on nicely now, no doubt. I am so glad of it, because teaching has become a part of my life, as necessary for my life as eating or breathing.—Yours affly., VIVEKANANDA.

P. S. . . . How easily this world can be deluded by humbugs! What a mass of fraud has gathered over the devoted head of poor humanity since the dawn of civilisation!

(*132*)

PERCY, NEW HAMPSHIRE,
7th June, 1895.

DEAR—, I am here at last with Mr. Leggett. This is one of the most beautiful spots I have ever seen. Imagine a lake surrounded with hills covered with a huge forest, with nobody but ourselves. So lovely, so quiet, so restful and you may imagine how glad I am to be here after the bustle of cities.

It gives me a new lease of life to be here. I go into the forest alone and read my Gita and am quite happy. I will leave this place in about ten days and go to the Thousand Island Park. I will meditate by the hour there and be all alone to myself. The very idea is ennobling.—Yours, VIVEKANANDA.

(*133*)

54, W. 33RD ST., NEW YORK,
June, 1895.

DEAR—, I have just arrived home. The trip did me good and I enjoyed the country and the hills, and especially Mr. Leggett's country-house in New York State. . . .

May the Lord bless Landsberg wherever he goes. He is one of the few sincere souls I had the privilege in this life to come across.

All is for good. All conjunctions are for subsequent disjunction. I hope I will be perfectly able to work alone. The less help from men the more from the Lord! Just now I received a letter from an English gentleman in London who had lived in India in the Himalayas with two of my brethren. He asks me to come to London.—Yours, VIVEKANANDA.

(*134*)

To "Kidi"

19, W. 38TH ST., NEW YORK,
22nd June, 1895.

DEAR KIDI—I will write you a whole letter instead of a line. I am glad you are progressing. You are mistaken in thinking that I am not going to return to India; I am coming soon. I am not given to failures, and here I have planted a seed and it is going to become a tree and it must. Only I am afraid it will hurt its growth if I give it up too soon. . . .

Work on, my boy. Rome was not built in a day. I am guided by the Lord, so everything will come all right in the end.

With my love ever and ever to you.—Yours sincerely, VIVEKANANDA.

(*135*)

(*Most probably*)
To Swami Ramakrishnananda

*1895.**

DEAR—, . . . I am quite in agreement with what Sarada is doing, but it is not necessary to preach that Ramakrishna Paramahamsa was an Incarnation, and things of that sort. He came to do good to the world, not to trumpet his own name—you must always remember this. Disciples pay their whole attention to the preservation of their master's name, and throw overboard his teachings, and sectarianism etc., are its result. Alasinga writes of Charu, but I do not recollect him. Write all about him and convey him my thanks. Write in detail about all, I have no time to spare for idle gossip. . . . Try to give up ceremonials. They are not meant for Sannyasins, and one must work only so long as he does not attain to illumination. . . . I have nothing to do with sectarianism, or party-forming and playing the frog-in-the-well, whatever else I may do. . . . It is impossible to preach the catholic ideas of Ramakrishna Paramahamsa and form sects at the same time. . . . Only one kind of work I understand, and that is doing good to others, all else is doing evil. I therefore prostrate myself before the Lord Buddha. . . . I am a Vedantist, Sachchidananda—Existence-Knowledge-Bliss-Absolute—is my God, I scarcely find any other God than the majestic form of my own Self. By the word "Incarnation" are meant those who have attained that Brahmanhood, in other words, the Jivanmuktas—those who have realised this Freedom in this very life. I do not find any speciality in Incarnations: all beings from Brahmâ down to a clump of grass will attain to liberation-in-life in course of time, and our duty lies in helping all to reach that state. This help is called religion—the rest is irreligion. This help is work, the rest is evil-doing—I see nothing else. Other kinds of work, for example, the Vaidika or the Tântrika, may produce results—but resorting to them is simply waste of life—for that purity which is the goal of work is realisable only through doing good to others. Through works such as sacrifices etc., one may get enjoyments, but it is impossible to have the purity of soul. . . Everything exists already in the Self of all beings. He who asserts he is free, shall be free. He who says he is bound, bound he shall remain. To me, the thought of oneself as low and humble is a sin and ignorance. नायमात्मा बलहीनेन लभ्यः—"This Atman is not to be attained by one who is weak." अस्ति ब्रह्म वदसि चेदस्ति भविष्यति नास्ति ब्रह्म वदसि चेन्नास्त्येव भविष्यति—"If you say Brahman *is*, existence will be the result, but if you say Brahman is *not*, non-existent It shall verily become." He who always thinks of himself as weak will never become strong, but he who knows himself to be a lion, "rushes out from the world's meshes, as a lion from its cage"—निर्गच्छति जगज्जालात् पिंजरादिव केशरी। Another point, it was no new truths that Ramakrishna Paramahamsa came to preach, though his advent brought the old truths to light. In other words, he was the embodiment of all the past religious thought of India. His life alone made me understand what the Shâstras really meant, and the whole plan and scope of the old Shastras.

Missionaries and others could not do much against me in this country. Through the Lord's grace the people here like me greatly and are not to be tricked by the opinions of any particular class. They appreciate my ideas in a manner my own countrymen cannot do, and are not selfish. I mean, when it comes to practical work, they will give up jealousy and all those ideas of self-sufficiency. Then all of them agree and act under the direction of a capable man. That is what makes them so great. But then they are a nation of Mammon-worshippers. Money comes before everything. People of our country are very liberal in pecuniary matters, but not so much these people. Every home has a miser. It is almost a religion here. But they fall into the clutches of the priests when they do something bad, and then buy their passage to heaven with money. These things are the same in every country—priestcraft. I can say nothing as to whether I shall go back to India and when. There also I shall have to lead a wandering life as I do here, but here thousands of people listen to and understand my lectures, and these thousands are benefited. But can you say the same thing about India? . . . I am perfectly at one with what Sarada is doing. A thousand thanks to him. . . . In Madras and Bombay I have lots of men who are after my heart. They are learned and understand everything. Moreover, they are kind-hearted and can therefore appreciate the philanthropic spirit. . . . I have printed neither books nor anything of the kind, I simply go on lecturing tours. . . . When I take a retrospective view of my past life, I feel no remorse. From country to country I have travelled teaching something, however little, to people, and in exchange for that have partaken of their slices of bread. If I had found I had done no work, but simply supported myself by imposing upon people, I would have committed suicide to-day. Why do those who think themselves unfit to teach their fellow-beings, wear the teacher's garb and earn their bread by cheating them? Is not that a deadly sin? . . .—Yours etc., VIVEKANANDA.

(*136*)

To Sj. Alasinga Perumal

U. S. A.,
1st July, 1895.

DEAR ALASINGA—Let me tell you, Alasinga, that you have to defend yourselves. Why do you behave like babies? If anybody attacks your religion why cannot you defend it? As for me you need not be afraid, I have more friends than enemies here, and in this country one-third are Christians, and only a small number of the educated care about the missionaries. Again the very fact of the missionaries being against anything makes the educated like it. They are less of a power here now, and are becoming less every day. If their attacks pain you, why do you behave like a petulant child and refer to me? . . . Cowardice is no virtue.

Here I have already got a respectable following. Next year I will organise it on a working basis and then the work will be carried on. And when I am off to India, I have friends who will back me here and help me in India too, so you need not fear. So long as you shriek at the missionary attempts and jump without being able to do anything, I laugh at you—you are little dollies, that is what you are. . . . What can Swami do for old babies!!

I know, my son, I shall have to come and manufacture men out of you. I know that India is only inhabited by women and eunuchs. So do not fret. I will have to get means to work there. I do not put myself in the hands of imbeciles. You need not worry, do what little you can. I have to work alone from the top to the bottom. . . . "This Atman is not to be reached by cowards." You need not be afraid for me. The Lord is with me, you defend yourselves only and show me you can do that and I will be satisfied; don't bother me any more with what any one says about me. I am not waiting to hear any fool's judgment of me. You babies, great results are attained only by great patience, great courage and great attempts. . . . Kidi's mind is taking periodic somersaults, I am afraid. . . .

The brave alone do great things, not the cowards. Know once for all, you faithless ones, that I am in the hands of the Lord. So long as I am pure and His servant, not a hair of my head will be touched. . . . Do something for the nation, then they will help you, then the nation will be with you. Be brave, be brave, man dies but once. My disciples must not be cowards.—Ever yours with love,
VIVEKANANDA.

(137)

To the Maharaja of Khetri

U. S. A.,
9th July, 1895.

. . . About my coming to India, the matter stands thus. I am, as Your Highness well knows, a man of dogged perseverance. I have planted a seed in this country; it is already a plant, and I expect it to be a tree very soon. I have got a few hundred followers. I shall make several Sannyasins and then I go to India, leaving the work to them. The more the Christian priests oppose me, the more I am determined to leave a permanent mark on their country. . . . I have already some friends in London. I am going there by the end of August. . . . This winter anyway has to be spent partly in London, and partly in New York, and then I shall be free to go to India. There will be enough men to carry on the work here after this winter, if the Lord is kind. Each work has to pass through these stages—ridicule, opposition, and then acceptance. Each man who thinks ahead of his time is sure to be misunderstood. So opposition and persecution are welcome, only I have to be steady and pure and must have immense faith in God, and all these will vanish.

(*138*)

To Mr. E. T. Sturdy

19, W. 38TH ST., NEW YORK,
2nd August, 1895.

DEAR FRIEND—. . . . As soon as human beings *perceive* the glory of the Vedanta, all abracadabras fall off of themselves. This has been my uniform experience. Whenever mankind attains a higher vision, the lower vision disappears of itself. Multitude counts for nothing. A few heart-whole, sincere, and energetic men can do more in a year than a mob in a century. If there is heat in one body, then those others that come near it must catch it. This is the law. So success is ours, so long as we keep up the heat, the spirit of truth, sincerity, and love. My own life has been a very chequered one, but I have always found the eternal words verified: "Truth alone triumphs, not untruth. Through truth alone lies the way to God."

May the *Sat* in you be always your infallible guide! May He speedily attain to freedom, and help others to attain it!

(139)

To The Same

NEW YORK.

The work here is going on splendidly. I have been working incessantly at two classes a day since my arrival. To-morrow I go out of town with Mr. Leggett for a week's holiday. Did you know Madame Antoinette Sterling, one of your great singers? She is very much interested in the work.

I have made over all the secular part of the work to a committee and am free from all that botheration. I have no aptitude for organising. It nearly breaks me to pieces.

. . . What about the *Narada Sutra*? There will be a good sale of that book here, I am sure. I have now taken up the Yoga Sutras, and take them up one by one and go through all the commentators along with them. These are all taken down and when completed will form the completest annotated translation of Patanjali in English. Of course it will be rather a big work.

At Trübner's I think there is an edition of कूर्म पुराण *Kurma Puran*. The commentator Vijnana Vikshu is continually quoting from that book. I have never seen the book myself. Will you kindly find time to go and see if in it there are some chapters on Yoga? If so, will you kindly send me a copy? Also of the *Hatha Yoga Pradipika*, *Shiva Samhita* and any other book on Yoga? The originals of course. I will send you the money for them as soon as they arrive. Also a copy of *Sankhya Karika* of Ishwara Krishna by John Davies. Just now your letter reached along with Indian letters. The one man who is ready is ill. The others say that they cannot come over on the spur of the moment. So far it seems unlucky. I am sorry they could not come. What can be done? Things go so slow in India!

Ramanuja's theory is that the bound soul, or Jiva, has its perfections involved, entered into itself. When this perfection again evolves, it becomes free. The Advaitin declares both these to take place only in show; there was neither involution nor evolution. Both processes were Maya, or *apparent* only.

In the first place, the soul is not *essentially a knowing* being. '*Sachchidananda* is only an approximate definition and *Neti Neti* is the essential definition. Schopenhauer caught this idea of willing from the Buddhists. We have it also, in *Vâsanâ* or *Trishnâ*, Pali *tanha*. We also admit that it is the *cause* of all manifestations which are, in their turn, its effects. But, being a cause, it must be a combination of the *Absolute* and *Maya*. Even knowledge, being a compound, cannot be the Absolute itself, but it is the nearest approach to it, and higher than *Vasana*, conscious or unconscious. The Absolute first becomes the mixture of knowledge, then, in the second degree, that of will. If it be said that plants have no consciousness, that they are at best only unconscious wills, the answer is that even this *unconscious plant-will* is a manifestation of the consciousness, not of the plant, but of the cosmos, the Mahat of the Sankhya Philosophy. The Buddhist analysis of everything into will is imperfect, firstly, because will is itself a compound, and secondly, because consciousness or knowledge which is a compound of the first degree, precedes it. *Knowledge is action*. First *action, then reaction*. When the mind perceives, then, as the reaction, it *wills*. The will is in the mind. So it is absurd to say that will is the last analysis. Deussen is playing into the hands of the Darwinists.

But evolution must be brought in accordance with the more exact science of Physics, which can demonstrate that every evolution must be preceded by an involution.

This being so, the evolution of the *Vasana*, or will, must be preceded by the involution of the *Mahat*, or cosmic consciousness.

CONSCIOUSNESS OR MAHAT

Subconscious	Conscious	Superconscious
Unconscious Will	Conscious Will Proper	Superconscious Will

There is no willing without knowing. How can we desire unless we know the object of desire?

The apparent difficulty vanishes as soon as you divide knowledge also into subconscious and conscious. And why not? If will can be so treated, why not its father?

(140)

To Swami Brahmananda

NEW YORK,*
19, WEST 38TH STREET,
1895.

BELOVED RAKHAL—. . . I am now in New York City. This city is hot in summer, exactly like Calcutta. You perspire profusely, and there is not a breath of air. I made a tour in the north for a couple of months. Please answer this letter by return of post to England, for which I shall start before this will have reached you.—Yours affectionately, VIVEKANANDA.

(141)

To Mr. E. T. Sturdy

NEW YORK,
19, WEST 38TH STREET,
9th August, 1895.

. . . It is only just that I should try to give you a

little of my views. I fully believe that there are periodic ferments of religion in human society, and that such a period is now sweeping over the educated world. While each ferment, moreover, appears broken into various little bubbles, these are all eventually similar, showing the cause or causes behind them to be the same. That religious ferment which at present is every day gaining a greater hold over thinking men, has this characteristic, that all the little thought-whirlpools into which it has broken itself declare one single aim—a vision and a search after the Unity of Being. On planes physical, ethical and spiritual, an ever-broadening generalisation—leading up to a concept of Unity Eternal—is in the air; and this being so, all the movements of the time may be taken to represent, knowingly or unknowingly, the noblest philosophy of the unity man ever had—the Advaita-Vedanta.

Again, it has always been observed that as a result of the struggles of the various fragments of thought in a given epoch, one bubble survives. The rest only arise to melt into it, and form a single great wave, which sweeps over society with irresistible force.

In India, America and England (the countries I happen to know about) hundreds of these are struggling at the present moment. In India, dualistic formulæ are already on the wane, the Advaitas alone hold the field in force. In America, many movements are struggling for mastery. All these represent Advaita thought more or less, and that series which is spreading most rapidly, approaches nearer to it than any of the others. Now if anything was ever clear to me, it is that one of these must survive, swallowing up all the rest, to be the power of the future. Which is it to be?

Referring to history, we see that only that fragment which is fit will survive, and what makes fit to survive but *character?* Advaita will be the future religion of thinking humanity. No doubt of that. And of all the sects, they alone shall gain the day, who are able to show most character in their lives—no matter how far they may be.

Let me tell you a little personal experience. When my Master left the body, we were a dozen penniless and unknown young men. Against us were a hundred powerful organisations, struggling hard to nip us in the bud. But Ramakrishna had given us one great gift, the desire, and the lifelong struggle, not to talk alone, but to *live the life.* And to-day all India knows and reverences the Master, and the truths he taught are spreading like wild fire. Ten years ago, I could not get a hundred persons together to celebrate his birthday anniversary. Last year there were fifty thousand.

Neither numbers, nor powers, nor wealth, nor learning, nor eloquence, nor anything else will prevail, but *purity, living the life,* in one word, *anubhuti,* realisation. Let there be but a dozen such lion-souls in each country, lions who have broken their own bonds, who have touched the Infinite, whose whole soul is gone to Brahman, who care neither for wealth, nor power, nor fame, and these will be *enough* to shake the world.

Here lies the secret. Says Patanjali, the father of Yoga: "When a man rejects all the superhuman powers, then he attains to the cloud of virtue." He sees God. He becomes God, and helps others to become the same. This is all I have to preach. Doctrines have been expounded enough. There are books by the million. Oh, for an ounce of practice!

As to societies and organisations, these will come to themselves. Can there be jealousy where there is nothing to be jelaous of? The names of those who will wish to injure us will be legion. But is not that the surest sign of our having the truth? The more I have been opposed, the more my energy has always found expression. I have been driven and worshipped by princes. I have been slandered by priests and laymen alike. But what of it? Bless them all! They are my very Self. And have they not helped me by acting as a spring-board, from which my energy could take higher and higher flights?

. . . I have discovered one great secret—I have nothing to fear from *talkers* of religion. And the great ones who realise—they become enemies to none! Let talkers talk! They know no better! Let them have their fill of name and fame and money and woman. Hold we on to realisation, to being Brahman, to becoming Brahman. Let us hold on to truth unto death, and from life to life! Let us not pay the least attention to what others say, and if, after a lifetime's effort, one, only one, soul can break the fetters of the world and be free, WE HAVE DONE OUR WORK. Hari Om!

. . . One word more. Doubtless I do love India. But every day my sight grows clearer. What is India, or England, or America to us? We are the servants of that God who by the ignorant is called MAN. He who pours water at the root, does he not water the whole tree?

There is but one basis of well-being, social, political or spiritual, to know that I and my brother are *one*. This is true for all countries and all people. And Westerners, let me say, will realise it more quickly than Orientals, who have almost exhausted themselves in formulating the idea and producing a few cases of individual realisation.

Let us work without desire for name or fame or rule over the others. Let us be free from the triple bonds of lust, greed of gain and anger. And the truth is with us!—Ever yours in the Lord, VIVEKANANDA.

(142)

To Mrs. Ole Bull

THOUSAND ISLAND PARK,
August, 1895.

DEAR MRS. BULL—. . . Now here is another letter from Mr. Sturdy. I send it over to you. See how things are being prepared ahead. Don't you think this coupled with Mr. Leggett's invitation as a Divine call? I think so and am following it. I am going by the end of August with Mr. Leggett to Paris and then I go to London.

What little can be done for my brethren and my work is all the help I want from you now. I have done my duty by my people fairly well. Now for the world that gave me this body—the country that gave me the ideas, the humanity which allows me to be one of them!

The older I grow the more I see behind the idea of the Hindus that *man* is the greatest of all beings. So say the Mohammedans too. The angels were asked by Allah to bow down to Adam. Iblis did not and therefore he became Satan. This earth is higher than all heavens; this is the greatest school in the universe; and the Mars or Jupiter people cannot be higher than we, because they cannot communicate with us. The only so-called higher beings are the departed, and these are nothing but men who have taken another body. This is finer, it is true, but still a *man*-body, with hands and feet, and so on. And they live on this earth in another Akasha, without being absolutely invisible. They also think, and have consciousness, and everything else like us. So they also are men, so are the Devas, the angels. But man alone becomes *God*, and they all have to become men again in order to become God. . . .
—Yours, VIVEKANANDA.

(*143*)

To Sj. Alasinga Perumal

U. S. A.,
August, 1895.

By the time this reaches you, dear Alasinga, I shall be in Paris. . . . I have done a good deal of work this year and hope to do a good deal more in the next. Don't bother about the missionaries. It is quite natural that they should cry. Who does not when his bread is dwindling away? The missionary funds have got a big gap the last two years, and it is on the increase. However I wish the missionaries all success. So long as you have love for God and Guru, and faith in truth, nothing can hurt you, my son. But the loss of any of these is dangerous. You have remarked well; my ideas are going to work in the West better than in India. . . . I have done more for India than India ever did for me. I believe in truth, the Lord sends me workers by the scores wherever I go—and they are not like the . . . disciples either—they are ready to give up their lives for their Guru. Truth is my God, the Universe my country. I do not believe in duty. Duty is the curse of the Samsâri, not for the Sannyasin. Duty is a humbug. I am free, my bonds are cut, what care I where this body goes or does not go? You have helped me well right along. The Lord will reward you. I sought praise neither from India nor from America, nor do I seek such bubbles. I have a truth to teach, I, the child of God. And He that gave me the truth will send me fellow-workers from the Earth's bravest and best. You Hindus will see in a few years what the Lord does in the West. You are like the Jews of old—dogs in the manger, neither eat nor give others to eat. You have no religion, your God is the kitchen, your Bible the cooking pots. You are a few brave lads . . . . Hold on, boys, no cowards among my children . . . . Are great things ever done smoothly? Time, patience and indomitable will must show. I could have told you many things that could have made your heart leap, but I will not. I want iron wills and hearts that do not know how to quake. Hold on. The Lord bless you.—Yours ever with blessings, VIVEKANANDA.

(*144*)

To the Same

PARIS,
9th Sept., 1895.

DEAR ALASINGA—. . . I am surprised you take so seriously the missionaries' nonsense. . . . If the people in India want me to keep strictly to my Hindu diet, please tell them to send me a cook and money enough to keep him. This silly *bossism* without a mite of real help makes me laugh. On the other hand, if the missionaries tell you that I have ever broken the two great vows of the Sannyasin—chastity and poverty—tell them that they are *big liars*. Please write to the missionary Hume asking him categorically to write you what misdemeanours he saw in me, or give you the names of his informants, and whether the information was *first-hand or not;* that will settle the question and expose the whole thing.

As for me, mind you, I stand at nobody's dictation. I know my mission in life, and no charivarism about me; I belong as much to India as to the world, no humbug about that. . . . I have helped you all I could. You must now help yourselves. What country has any special claim on me? Am I any nation's slave? Don't talk any more silly nonsense, you faithless atheists.

I have worked hard and sent all the money I got, to Calcutta and Madras, and then after doing all this stand their silly dictation! Are you not ashamed? What do I owe to them? Do I care a fig for their praise or fear their blame? I am a singular man, my son, not even you can understand me yet. Do your work, if you cannot, stop; but do not try to "boss" me with your nonsense. I *see* a greater Power than man, or God, or devil at my back. I require nobody's help. I have been all my life helping others. . . . They cannot raise a few rupees to help the work of the greatest man their country ever produced—Ramakrishna Paramahamsa; and they talk nonsense and want to dictate to the man for whom they did nothing, and who did everything he could for them! Such is the ungrateful world!

Do you mean to say I am born to live and die one of those caste-ridden, superstitious, merciless, hypocritical, atheistic *cowards*, that you find amongst the educated Hindus? I hate cowardice, I will have nothing to do with cowards or political nonsense. I do not believe in any politics. God and truth are the only politics in the world, everything else is trash.

I am going to-morrow to London. . . . —Yours with blessings, VIVEKANANDA.

(*145*)

*1895.**

DEAR BROTHERS—Before this I wrote to you a letter which for want of time was very incomplete. Rakhal and Hari wrote in a letter from Lucknow that Hindu newspapers were praising me, and that they were very glad that twenty thousand people had partaken of food at Sri Ramakrishna's anniversary. I could do much more work, but for the Brahmos and missionaries who have been opposing me unceasingly, and the Hindus of India too did nothing for me. I mean, if the Hindus of Calcutta or

Madras had held a meeting and passed a resolution recognising me as their representative, and thanking the American people for receiving me with kindness, things would have progressed appreciably. But it is over a year, and nothing done. Of course I never relied on the Bengalees, but the Madrasees couldn't do anything either. . . .

There is no hope for our nation. Not one original idea crosses anyone's brains, all fighting over the same old, threadbare rug—that Ramakrishna Paramahamsa was such and such—and cock-and-bull stories—stories having neither head nor tail. My God! Won't you do something to show that you are in any way removed from the common run of men?—Only indulging in madness! . . .To-day you have your bell, to-morrow you add a horn, and follow suit with a chowry the day after; or you introduce a cot to-day, and to-morrow you have its legs silver-mounted, and people help themselves to a rice-porridge, and you spin out two thousand cock-and-bull stories—in short, nothing but external ceremonies. This is called in English Imbecility. Those into whose heads nothing but that sort of silliness enters, are called imbecile. Those whose heads have a tendency to be troubled day and night over such questions as whether the bell should be rung on the right or on the left, whether the sandal-paste mark should be put on the head or anywhere else, whether the light should be waved twice or four times—simply deserve the name of wretches, and it is owing to that sort of notion that we are the outcasts of Fortune, kicked and spurned at, while the people of the West are masters of the whole world. . . . There is an ocean of difference between idleness and renunciation.

If you want any good to come, just throw your ceremonials overboard and worship the Living God, the Man-God—every being that wears a human form—God in His universal as well as individual aspect. The universal aspect of God means this world, and worshipping it means serving it—this indeed is work, not indulging in ceremonials. Neither is it work to cogitate as to whether the rice-plate should be placed in front of the God for ten minutes or for half an hour—that is called lunacy. Millions of rupees have been spent only that the temple-doors at Benares or Brindaban may play at opening and shutting all day long! Now the Lord is having His toilet, now He is taking His meals, now He is busy on something else we know not what. . . . And all this, while the Living God is dying for want of food, for want of education. The banias of Bombay are erecting hospitals for bugs—while they would do nothing for men—even if they die! You have not the brain to understand this simple thing—that it is a plague with our country, and lunatic asylums are rife all over. . . . Let some of you spread like fire, and preach this worship of the universal aspect of Godhead—a thing that was never undertaken before in our country. No quarrelling with people, we must be friends with all. . . .

Spread ideas—go from village to village, from door to door—then only there will be real work. Otherwise, lying complacently on the bed and ringing the bell now and then is a sort of disease, pure and simple. . . . Be independent, learn to form independent judgments.—That such and such a chapter of such and such a Tantra has prescribed a standard length for the handle of a bell—what matters it to me? Through the Lord's Will out of your lips shall come millions of Vedas and Tantras and Puranas. . . . If now you can show this in practice, if you can make three or four hundred thousand disciples in India within a year, then only I may have some hope. . . .

By-the-bye, do you know the boy who had his head shaven and went with Brother Tarak from Bombay to Rameswar? He calls himself a disciple of Ramakrishna Paramahamsa! Let Brother Tarak initiate him. . . . He had never even met Sri Ramakrishna in his life, and yet a disciple!—What impudence! Without an unbroken chain of discipleship— गुरुपरम्परा —nothing can be done, is it a child's play? To have no connection whatsoever and call oneself a disciple! The idiot! If that boy refuses to go on in the right way, turn him out. Nothing, I say, can be done without the chain of discipleship, that is, the power that is transmitted from the Guru to the disciple, and from him to his disciple, and so on. Here he comes and proclaims himself a disciple of Ramakrishna,—is it tomfoolery? Jagmohan told me of somebody calling himself a brother-disciple of mine. I have now a suspicion that it is that boy. To pose as a brother-disciple! He feels humiliated to call himself a disciple, I dare say, and would fain turn a Guru straightway! Turn him out if he does not follow the established procedure.

Talking of the restlessness of Tulsi and Subodh's mind, it all means that they have got no work to do. . . . Go from village to village, do good to humanity and to the world at large. Go to hell yourself to buy salvation for others. There is no Mukti on earth to call my own. Whenever you think of yourself, you are bound to feel restless. What business have you to do with Peace, my boy? You have renounced everything. Come! Now is the turn for you to banish the desire for Peace, and that for Mukti too! Don't worry in the least; heaven or hell, or Bhakti or Mukti—don't care for anything, but go, my boy, and spread the name of the Lord from door to door! It is only by doing good to others that one attains to his own good, and it is by leading others to Bhakti and Mukti that one attains them himself. Take that up, forget your own self for it, be mad over the idea. As Sri Ramakrishna used to love you, as I love you, come, love the world like that. Bring all together. Where is Gunanidhi? You must have him with you. My infinite love to him. Where is Gupta? Let him join if he likes. Call him in my name. Remember these few points:—

1. We are Sannyasins, who have given up *everything* —Bhakti, and Mukti, and enjoyment, and all.

2. To do the highest good to the world, everyone down to the lowest—this is our vow. Welcome Mukti or hell, whichever comes of it.

3. Ramakrishna Paramahamsa came for the good of the world. Call him a man, or God, or an Incarnation, just as you please. Accept him each in your own light.

4. He who will bow before him will be converted into purest gold that very moment. Go with this message from door to door, if you can, my boy, and all your disquietude will be at an end. Never fear—where's the room for fear?—Caring for nothing whatsoever is a part of your life. You have so long spread his name and your character all around, well and good. Now spread them in an organised way. The Lord is with you. Take heart!

Whether I live or die, whether I go back to India or not, you go on spreading love, love that knows no bounds. Put Gupta, too, to this task. But remember one needs weapons to overcome others. सन्निमित्ते वरं त्यागो विनाशे नियते सति —"When death is so certain, it is better to die for a good cause."—Yours affly., VIVEKANANDA.

P. S. Remember my previous letter—we want both men and women. There is no distinction of sex in the soul. It won't do merely to call Sri Ramakrishna an Incarnation, you must manifest power. Where are Gaur Ma, Jogen Ma and Golap Ma? Tell them to spread these ideas. We want thousands of men, and thousands of women, who will spread like wild fire from the Himalayas to Cape Comorin, from the North Pole to the South Pole—all over the world. It is no use indulging in child's play—neither is there time for it. Let those who have come for child's play be off now, while there is time, or they will surely come to grief. We want an organisation. Off with laziness. Spread! Spread! Run like fire to all places.

Do not depend upon me. Whether I live or die, go on spreading, yourselves.—Yours affly., VIVEKANANDA.

(*146*)

To Swami Brahmananda

*1895.**

DEAR RAKHAL—I have now got lots of newspapers etc., and you need not send any more. Let the movement now confine itself to India. . . .

It isn't much use getting up a sensation every day. But avail yourselves of this stir that is rife all over the country, and scatter yourselves in all quarters. In other words, try to start branches at different places. Let it not be an empty sound merely. You must join the Madrasees and start associations etc., at different places. What about the magazine which I heard was going to be started? Why are you nervous about conducting it? . . . . Come! Do something heroic. Brother, what if you do not attain Mukti, what if you suffer damnation a few times? Is the saying untrue:

मनसि वचसि काये पुण्यपीयूषपूर्णा-
स्त्रिभुवनमुपकारश्रेणिभिः प्रीणयन्तः ।
परगुणपरमाणुं पर्वतीकृत्य नित्यं
निजहृदि विकसन्तः सन्ति सन्तः कियन्तः ॥

—"There are some saints who, full of holiness in thought, word and deed, please the whole world by their numerous beneficent acts, and who develop their own hearts by magnifying an atom of virtue in others as if it were as great as a mountain."

What if you don't get Mukti? What childish prattle! Lord! They say, even the venom of a snake loses its power by firmly denying it. Isn't it true? What queer humility is this to say, "I know nothing!" "I am nothing!" This is pseudo-renunciation and mock-modesty, I tell you. Off with such a self-debasing spirit! "If *I* do not know, who on earth does?" What have you been doing so long, if you now plead ignorance? These are the words of an atheist—the humility of a vagabond wretch. We can do everything, and will do everything! He who is fortunate enough will heroically join us, letting the worthless mew like cats from their corner. A saint writes, "Well, you have had enough of blazoning. Now come back home." I would have called him a man if he could build a house and call me. Ten years' experience of such things has made me wiser. I am no more to be duped by words. Let him who has courage in his mind and love in his heart come with me, I want none else. Through Mother's grace, single-handed I am worth a hundred thousand now and will be worth two millions. . . . There is no certainty about my going back to India. I shall have to lead a wandering life there also, as I am doing here. But here one lives in the company of scholars, and there one must live among fools—there is this difference as of the poles. People of this country organise and work, while *our* undertakings all come to dust clashing against laziness—miscalled "renunciation" and jealousy etc. —writes me big letters now and then, half of which I cannot decipher, which is a blessing to me. For a great part of the news is of the following description—that in such and such a place such and such a man was speaking ill of me, and that he, being unable to bear the same, had a quarrel with him, and so forth. Many thanks for his kind defence of me. But what seriously hinders me from listening to what particular people may be saying about me is, स्वल्पश्च कालो बहवश्च विघ्नाः—"Time is short, but the obstacles are many.". . .

An organised society is wanted. Let Sasi look to the household management, Sanyal take charge of money matters and marketing and Sarat act as secretary, that is, carry on correspondence etc. Make a permanent centre—it is no use making random efforts as you are doing now. Do you see my point? I have quite a heap of newspapers, now I want you to do something. If you can build a Math, I shall say you are heroes; otherwise you are nothing. Consult the Madras people when you work. They have a great capacity for work. Celebrate this year's Sri Ramakrishna Festival with such *éclat* as to make it a record. The less the feeding propaganda is, the better. It is enough if you have hand-to-hand distribution of the Prasada. . . .

I am going to write a very short sketch of Sri Ramakrishna's life in English, which I shall send you. Have it printed and translated into Bengali and sell it at the Festival—people do not read books that are distributed free. Fix some nominal price. Have the Festival done with great pomp. . . .

You must have an all-sided intellect to do efficient work. In any towns or villages you may visit, start an association wherever you find a number of people revering Sri Ramakrishna. Have you travelled through so many villages all for nothing? We must slowly absorb the Hari Sabhâs and such other associations. Well, I cannot tell you all—if I could but get another demon like me! The Lord will supply me everything in time. . . . If one has got power, he must manifest it in action. . . . Off with your ideas of Mukti and Bhakti! There is only one way in the world, परोपकाराय हि सतां जीवितं, परार्थे प्राज्ञ उत्सृजेत —" The good live for others alone." " The wise man should sacrifice himself for others." I can secure my own good only by doing your good. There is no other way, none whatsoever. . . . You are God, I am God, and man is God. It is this God manifested through humanity who is doing everything in this world. Is there a different God sitting high up somewhere? To work, therefore!

Bimala has sent me a book written by Sasi (Sanyal)

. . . . From a perusal of that work Bimala has come to know that all the people of this world are impure and that they are by their very nature debarred from having a jot of religion; that only the handful of Brahmins that are in India have the sole right to it, and among these again, Sasi (Sanyal) and Bimala are the sun and moon, so to speak. Bravo! What a powerful religion indeed! In Bengal specially, that sort of a religion is very easy to practise. There is no easier way than that. The whole truth about austerities and spiritual exercises is, in a nutshell, that I am pure and all the rest are impure! A beastly, demoniac, hellish religion this! If the American people are unfit for religion, if it is improper to preach religion here, why then ask their help? . . . . What can remedy such a disease? Well, tell Sasi (Sanyal) to go to Malabar. The Raja there has taken his subjects' land and offered it at the feet of Brahmins. There are big monasteries in every village, where sumptuous dinners are given, supplemented by presents in cash. . . . There is no harm in touching the non-Brahmin classes when it serves one's purpose, and when you have done with it you bathe, for the non-Brahmins are as a class unholy and must never be touched on other occasions! Monks and Sannyasins and Brahmins of a certain type have thrown the country into ruin. Intent all the while on theft and wickedness, these pose as preachers of religion! They will take gifts from the people and at the same time cry, "Don't touch me!" And what great things they have been doing!—"If a potato happens to touch a brinjal, how long will the universe last before it is deluged?" "If they do not apply earth a dozen times to clean their hands, will fourteen generations of ancestors go to hell, or twenty-four?"—For intricate problems like these they have been finding out scientific explanations for the last two thousand years—while one-fourth of the people are starving. A girl of eight is married to a man of thirty and the parents are jubilant over it. And if anyone protests against it, the plea is put forward, " Our religion is being overturned." What sort of a religion have they who want to see their girls becoming mothers before they attain puberty even, and offer scientific explanations for it? Many, again, lay the blame at the door of the Mohammedans. They are to blame, indeed. Just read the Grihya Sutras through and see what is given as the marriageable age of a girl. . . . There it is expressly stated that a girl must be married very young. The entire Grihya Sutras enjoin this. And in the Vedic Ashwamedha sacrifice worse things would be done. All the Brâhmanas mention them, and all the commentators admit them to be true. How can you deny them?

What I mean by mentioning all this is that there were many good things in ancient times, but there were bad things too. The good things are to be retained, but the India that is to be, the future India, must be much greater than ancient India. From the day Sri Ramakrishna was born dates the growth of Modern India and of the Golden Age. And you are the agents to bring about this Golden Age. To work, with this conviction at heart!

Hence, when you call Sri Ramakrishna an Incarnation, and at the same breath plead your ignorance, unhesitatingly I say, " You are false to the backbone!" If Ramakrishna Paramahamsa be true, you also are true. But you must show. . . . In you all there is tremendous power. The atheist has nothing but rubbish in him. Those who are believers are heroes. They will manifest tremendous power. The world will be swept before them. —"Sympathy and help to the poor";—" Man is God, he is Nârâyana ";—" In Atman there is no distinction of male or female, or Brahmin or Kshatriya, and the like "; —" All is Narayana from the Creator down to a clump of grass." The worm is less manifested, the Creator more manifested. Every action that helps a being manifest its divine nature more and more is *good*, every action that retards it is *evil*.

The only way of getting our divine nature manifested is by helping others do the same.

If there is inequality in nature, still there must be equal chance for all—or if greater for some and for some less—the weaker should be given more chance than the strong.

In other words, a Brahmin is not so much in need of education as a Chandâla. If the son of a Brahmin needs one teacher, that of a Chandala needs ten. For, greater help must be given to him whom nature has not endowed with acute intellect from birth. It is a mad man who carries coals to Newcastle. The poor, the downtrodden, the ignorant, let these be your God.

A dreadful slough is in front of you—take care; many fall into it and die. The slough is this, that the present religion of the Hindus is not in the Vedas, nor in the Puranas, nor in Bhakti, nor in Mukti—religion has entered into the cooking-pot. The present religion of the Hindus is neither the path of Knowledge nor that of Reason—it is "Don't-touchism."—"Don't touch me!" "Don't touch me!"—that exhausts its description. See that you do not lose your lives in this dire irreligion of "Don't-touchism." Must the teaching आत्मवत्सर्वभूतेषु—"Looking upon all beings as your own self"—be confined to books alone? How will they grant salvation who cannot feed a hungry mouth with a crumb of bread? How will those who become impure at the mere breath of others, purify others? Don't-touchism is a form of mental disease. Beware! All expansion is life, all contraction is death. All love is expansion, all selfishness is contraction. Love is therefore the only law of life. He who loves lives, he who is selfish is dying. Therefore love for love's sake, because it is the only law of life, just as you breathe to live. This is the secret of selfless love, selfless action and the rest. . . . Try to help Sasi (Sanyal) if you can in any way. He is a very good and pious man, but is of a narrow heart. It does not fall to the lot of all to feel for the misery of others. Good Lord! Of all Incarnations Lord Chaitanya was the greatest, but he was comparatively lacking in Knowledge; in the Ramakrishna Incarnation there is Knowledge, Devotion and Love—infinite Knowledge, infinite Love, infinite Work, infinite Compassion for all beings. You have not yet been able to understand him. श्रुत्वाप्येनं वेद न चैव कश्चित् —"Even hearing about Him, most people do not understand Him." What the whole Hindu race has thought in ages, he *lived* in one life. His life is the living commentary to the Vedas of all nations. People will come to know him by degrees. My old watchword—struggle, struggle up to light! Onward!—Yours in service, VIVEKANANDA.

(*147*)

To Swami Akhandananda

C/o E. T. STURDY, ESQ.,*
HIGH VIEW, ETC.,
1895.

BELOVED AKHANDANANDA—I am glad to go through the contents of your letter. Your idea is grand but our nation is totally lacking in the faculty of organisation. It is this one drawback which produces all sorts of evil. We are altogether averse to making a common cause for anything. The first requisite for organisation is obedience. I do a little bit of work when I feel so disposed, and then let it go to the dogs—this kind of work is of no avail. We must have plodding industry and perseverance. Keep a regular correspondence, I mean, make it a point to write to me every month, or twice a month, what work you are doing, and what has been its outcome. We want here (in England) a Sannyasin well versed in English and Sanskrit. I shall soon go to America again, and he is to work here in my absence. Except Sarat and Sasi—I find no one else for this task. I have sent money to S—and written to him to start at once. I have requested Rajaji that his Bombay agent may help Sarat in embarking. I forgot to write—but if you can take the trouble to do it, please send through Sarat a bag of *mûng*, *gram*, and *arhar dâl*, also a little of the spice called *methi*. Please convey my love to Pandit Narayan Das, Mr. Shankar Lal, Ojhaji, Doctor, and all. Do you think you can get the medicine for Gopi's eyes here? Everywhere you find patent medicines, which are all humbug. Please give my blessings to him and to the other boys. Jajneswar Babu has founded a certain society at Meerut and wants to work conjointly with us. By-the-bye, he has got a certain paper too; send Kali there, and let him start a Meerut centre, if he can, and try to have the paper in Hindi. I shall help a little now and then. I shall send some money when Kali goes to Meerut and reports to me exactly how matters stand. Try to open a centre at Ajmere. . . . Pandit Agnihotri has started some society at Saharanpur. They wrote me a letter. Please keep in correspondence with them. Live on friendly terms with all. Work! Work! Go on opening centres in this way. We have them already in Calcutta and Madras, and it will be excellent if you can start new ones at Meerut and Ajmere. Go on slowly starting centres at different places like that. Here all my letters etc., are to be addressed in C/o E. T. Sturdy, Esq., High View, Caversham, Reading, England, and those for America, C/o Miss Phillips, 19 W. 38th Street, New York. By degrees we must spread the world over. The first thing needed is obedience. You must be ready to plunge into fire—then will work be done. . . . Form societies like that at different villages in Rajputana. There you have a hint.—Yours affectionately, VIVEKANANDA.

(148)

To Mrs. Ole Bull

C/o E. T. STURDY, ESQ.,
HIGH VIEW, CAVERSHAM,
READING, ENG.,
17th Sept., 1895.

DEAR MRS. BULL—Mr. Sturdy and I want to get hold of a few of the best, say, strong and intelligent men in England to form a society and therefore we must proceed slowly. We must take care not to be run over with "fads" from the first. This you will know has been my policy in America too. Mr. Sturdy has been in India living with our Sannyasins in their manner for some time. He is an exceedingly energetic man, educated and well versed in Sanskrit. . . . So far so good. . . . Purity, perseverance and energy—these three I want, and if I get only half a dozen here my work will go on. I have a great chance of such a few.—Yours, VIVEKANANDA.

(149)

To the Same

READING, ENGLAND,
24th Sept., 1895.

DEAR MRS. BULL—. . . I have been helping Mr. Sturdy in studying Sanskrit. . . . Mr. Sturdy wants me to bring over a monk from India from amongst my brethren to help him when I am away in America. I have written to India for one. . . . So far it is all right. I am waiting for the next wave. "Avoid not and seek not—wait for what the Lord sends," is my motto. . . . I am a slow writer, but the heart is full of gratitude.—Yours with best wishes, VIVEKANANDA.

(*150*)

READING, ENGLAND,
4th Oct., 1895.

DEAR—, . . . Purity, patience and perseverance overcome all obstacles. All great things must of necessity be slow. . . . —Yours with love, VIVEKANANDA.

(*151*)

To Swami Brahmananda

C/O E. T. STURDY, ESQ.,*
HIGH VIEW, CAVERSHAM, READING,
4th October, 1895.

MY DEAR RAKHAL—You know that I am now in England. I shall stay here for about a month and go back to America. Next summer I shall again come to England. At present there is not much prospect in England, but the Lord is omnipotent. Let us wait and see. . . .

It is impossible for—to come now. The thing is, the money belongs to Mr. Sturdy, and we must have the kind of man he likes. Mr. Sturdy has taken initiation from me, and is a very enterprising and good man.

In the first place, we want a man who has a thorough mastery of English and Sanskrit. It is true that—will be able to pick up English soon should he come here, but I am as yet unable to bring men here to learn. We want them, first, who will be able to teach. In the second place, I trust those that will not desert me in prosperity and adversity alike. . . . The most trustworthy men are needed, then, after the foundation is laid, let him who will come and make a noise, there is no fear.—gave no proof of wisdom in being carried away by a hubbub and joining the party of those charlatans. Sir, granted that Ramakrishna Paramahamsa was a sham, granted that it has been a very serious mistake, indeed, to take refuge in him, but what is the way out now? What if one life is spent in vain, but shall a *man* eat his own words? Can there be such a thing as having a dozen husbands? Any of you may join any party you like, I have no objection, no, not in the least, but travelling this world over, I find that save and except his circle alone, everywhere else thought and act are at variance. In those that belong to him, I have the utmost love, the utmost confidence. I have no alternative in the matter. Call me one-sided if you will, but there you have my *bona fide* avowal. If but a thorn pricks the foot of one who has surrendered himself to Sri Ramakrishna, it makes my bones ache; all others I love. You will find very few men so unsectarian as I am, but you must excuse me I have that bit of bigotry. . . . If I do not appeal to his name, whose else shall I? It will be time enough to seek for a big Guru in our next birth, but in this, it is that unlearned Brahmin who has bought this body of mine for ever.

I give you a bit of my mind; don't be angry, pray. I am your slave so long as you are his,—step a hair's breadth outside that, and you and I are on a par. All the sects and societies that you see, the whole host of them, inside the country or out, he has already swallowed them all, my brother. मयैवैते निहताः पूर्वमेव निमित्तमात्रं भव सव्यसाचिन् —"These have verily been killed by Myself long ago, be only the instrument, O Arjuna." To-day or to-morrow they will be merged in your own body. O man of little faith! Through his grace ब्रह्माण्डं गोष्पदायते —"The whole universe becomes a hoof-mark of the cow." Be not traitors, that is a sin past atonement. Name, fame, good deeds, यज्जुहोषि, यत्तपस्यसि, यदश्नासि, etc.—"Whatever sacrifices you perform, whatever penances you undergo, whatever you eat," surrender everything to his feet. What on earth do we want? He has given us refuge, what more do we want? Bhakti is verily its own reward—what else is needed? My brother, he who made men of us by feeding and clothing and imparting wisdom and knowledge, who opened the eyes of our self, whom night and day we found the living God—must we be traitors to him!!! And you forget the mercy of such a Lord! The lives of Buddha and Krishna and Jesus are matters of ancient history, and doubts are entertained about their historicity, and you in spite of seeing the greatness of Sri Ramakrishna's life in flesh and blood sometimes lose your head! Fie upon you! I have nothing to say. His likeness is being worshipped in and out of your country, by godless and heartless men, and you are stranded at times on disbelief!! In a breath he will create for himself hundreds of thousands of such as you are. Blessed is your birth, blessed your lineage, and blessed your country that you were allowed to take the dust of his feet. Well, I can't help. He is protecting us, forsooth—I see it before my eyes. Insane that you are, is it through my own strength that beauty like fairies, hundreds of thousands of rupees, lose their attraction and appear as nothing to me? Or is it he who is protecting me? He who has no faith in him and no reverence for Mother will be a downright loser, I tell you plainly.

. . . Haramohan has written about his troubled circumstances, and says he will be dislodged from his home soon. He has asked for some lectures, but I have none at present, but have still some money left in my purse which I shall send him. So he need not be afraid. I could send him at once, but I suspect that the money I last sent miscarried, therefore I postpone sending it. Secondly, I know, besides, of no address to send it to. I see the Madrasees have failed to start the paper. Practical wisdom is altogether wanting in the Hindu nation, I see. Whenever you promise to do any work, you must do it exactly at the appointed time, or people lose their faith in you. Money matters require a speedy reply. . . . If Master Mahashay be willing, tell him to be my Calcutta agent, for I have an implicit faith in him and he understands a good deal of these things, it is not for a childish and noisy rabble to do it. Tell him to fix upon a centre, an address that will not change every hour and to which I shall direct all my Calcutta correspondence. . . . Business is business. . . .—Yours etc., VIVEKANANDA.

(*152*)

To Mrs. Ole Bull

READING,
6th Oct., 1895.

DEAR MRS. BULL—. . . I am translating a little book on Bhakti with Mr. Sturdy with copious commentaries, which is to be published soon. This month I am to give two lectures in London and one in Maidenhead. This will open up the way to some classes and parlour lectures. We do not wish to make any noise but to go quietly. . . . —Yours with best wishes, VIVEKANANDA.

(*153*)

To Sj. Alasinga Perumal

LONDON,
24th Oct., 1895.

DEAR ALASINGA—. . . I have already delivered my first address, and you may see how well it has been received by the notice in the *Standard*. The *Standard* is one of the most influential conservative papers. I am going to be in London for a month, then I go off to America and shall come back again next summer. So far you see the seed is well sown in England. . . .

Take courage and work on. Patience and steady work—this is the only way. Go on, remember patience and purity and courage and steady work. . . . So long as you are pure and true to your principles you will never fail. Mother will never leave you, and all blessings will be yours.—Yours, VIVEKANANDA.

(154)

To Mr. E. T. Sturdy

80, OAKLEY ST., CHELSEA,
31st October, 1895, 5 p.m.

DEAR FRIEND—Just now two young gentlemen, Mr. Silverlock and his friend, left. Miss Müller also came this afternoon and left just when these gentlemen came in.

One is an Engineer and the other is in the grain trade. They have read a good deal of modern philosophy and science and have been much struck by the similarity with the latest conclusions of both with the ancient Hindu Thought. They are very fine, intelligent and educated men. One has given up the Church, the other asked me whether he should or not. Now, two things struck me after this interview. First, we must hurry the book through. We will touch a class thereby who are philosophically religious without the least mystery-mongering. Second, both of them want to know the rituals of my creed!! This opened my eyes. The world in general must have some form. In fact, in the ordinary sense religion is philosophy concretised through rituals and symbols.

It is absolutely necessary to form some ritual and have a Church. That is to say, we must fix on some ritual as fast as we can. If you can come Saturday morning or sooner, we shall go to the Asiatic Society library or you can procure for me a book which is called Hemâdri Kosha, from which we can get what we want, and kindly bring the Upanishads. We will fix something grand, from birth to death of a man. A mere loose system of philosophy gets no hold on mankind.

If we can get it through, before we have finished the classes, and publish it by publicly holding a service or two under it, it will go on. They want to form a congregation, and they want ritual; that is one of the causes why—will never have a hold on Western people.

The Ethical Society has sent me another letter thanking me for the acceptance of its offer. Also a copy of their forms. They want me to bring with me a book from which to read for ten minutes. Will you bring the Gita (translation) and the Buddhist Jâtaka (translation) with you?

I would not do anything in this matter without seeing you first.—Yours with love and blessings, VIVEKANANDA.

(*155*)

To Swami Ramakrishnananda

C/o E. T. STURDY, ESQ.,*
HIGH VIEW, CAVERSHAM,
READING, ENGLAND,
1895.

DEAR SASI—. . . I am in receipt of Rakhal's letter to-day. I am sorry to hear that—has suffered from gravel. Most probably it was due to indigestion. Gopal's debts have been cleared, now ask him to join the monastic order. The worldly-wise instinct is most difficult to root out. . . . Let him come and work in the Math. One is apt to imbibe a lot of mischievous ideas by concerning oneself too long in worldly affairs. If he refuses to take the monastic vow, please tell him to clear out. I don't want amphibious types of men who will be half monks and half householders. . . . Haramohan has coined a *Lord* Ramakrishna Paramahamsa, I see. What does he mean? English Lord, or Duke? Tell Rakhal, let people say whatever they will—"Men (who wrongly criticise) are to be treated as worms!" as Sri Ramakrishna used to say. Let there be no disparity between what you profess and what you do, also eschew the very name of Jesuitism. Was I ever an orthodox, Paurânika Hindu, an adherent of social usages? I do not pose as one. You will not have to say things that will be *pleasant* to any section of people. You must not so much as notice what the—say for or against us. . . . They could not do a penny-worth of service to him whose birth has sanctified their country where the primary laws of health and sanitation are trampled, and yet they would talk big! What matters it, my brother, that such men have got to say! . . . It is for you to go on doing your own work. Why look up to men for approbation, look up to God! I hope Sarat will be able to teach them the Gita and the Upanishads and their commentaries somehow, with the help of the dictionary. Or, is it an empty Vairâgya that you have? The days of such Vairagya are gone! It is not for everyone, my boy, to become Ramakrishna Paramahamsa! I hope Sarat has started by this time. Please send a copy of the Panchadashi, a copy of the Gita (with as many commentaries as possible), a copy each of the Narada and Shandilya Sutras (published from Benares), a translation (good, not worthless) of the Panchadashi, if it is available, translation by Kalivar Vedantavagish of Shankara's commentary. And if there be any translation, Bengali or English (by Srish Basu of Allahabad), of Pânini's Sutras, or the Kâshikâ Vritti, or the Phani Bhâshya, please send a copy of each. . . . Now, just tell your—s to send me a copy of the Vâchaspatya Dictionary, and that will be a good test for those tall-talking people. In England religious movements make very slow progress. These people here are either bigots or atheists. And the former again have only a bit of formal religion. They say, "Patriotism is our religion." That is all.

Send the books to America, C/o Miss Mary Phillips, 19, W. 38th Street, New York, U. S. America. That is my American address. By the end of November I shall go to America. So send my books etc., there. If Sarat has started immediately on your receipt of my letter, then only I may meet him, otherwise not. Business is business, no child's play. Mr. Sturdy will see him in and accommodate him. This time I have come to England just to probe a little. Next summer I shall try to make some stir. The winter after that, I shall go to India. . . . Correspond regularly with those who are interested in us, so as to keep up their interest. Try to open centres in places all over Bengal. . . . This much for the present. In my next I shall give you more details. Mr. Sturdy is a very nice gentleman, a staunch Vedantist, and understands a smattering of Sanskrit. It is with a good deal of labour that you can do a little bit of work in these countries; a sheer uphill task, with cold and rain into the bargain. Moreover, here you must support yourself and do your labour of love. Englishmen won't spend a penny on lectures or things of that sort. If they do come to listen to you, well, thank your stars—as is the case in our country. Besides the common people here do not even know of me now. In addition to all this, they will give you a wide berth if you preach God and such like things to them. They think this must be another clergyman! Well, you just patiently do one thing—set about collecting everything that books, beginning with the Rigveda down to the most insignificant of Purânas and Tantras, have got to say about creation and annihilation of the universe, about race, heaven and hell, the soul, consciousness and intellect, etc., sense-organs, Mukti, transmigration and such like things. No child's play would do, I want real scholarly work. The most important thing is to collect the materials. My love to you all.—Yours affectionately, VIVEKANANDA.

(*156*)

To Swami Akhandananda

LONDON,*
13th Nov., 1895.

MY DEAR AKHANDANANDA—I am very glad to receive your letter. It is excellent work that you are doing. R— is very liberal and open-handed, but there must be no advantage taken over him for that reason. About the raising of funds by Sriman—, well, it is a fair enterprise, but my boy, this is a very queer world, where even the World-Gods Brahmâ and Vishnu find it difficult to evade the clutches of lust and gold. Wherever there is any the least concern with money, there is the chance for misunderstanding. Let therefore nobody undertake such work as raising money on behalf of the Math. . . . Whenever you hear of any householder collecting funds in my or our name on the plea of erecting a Math, or some such thing, the first thing you should do is to distrust him, and never set your hand to it. The more so, as householders of poor means take to various tricks to supply their wants. Therefore, if ever a trusty devotee or a householder with a heart, being of affluent circumstances undertakes such works as the founding of a Math, or if the funds raised be kept in the custody of a trusty householder of wealth—well and good, otherwise never have a hand in it. On the contrary, you must dissuade others from such a thing. You are but a boy and are ignorant of the snare of gold. Opportunities will turn even a staunch moralist into a cheat. This is the way of the world. . . . It is not at all in our nature to do a work conjointly. It is to this that our miserable condition is due. He who knows how to obey, knows how to command. Learn obedience first.

Among these Western nations, with such a high spirit of independence, the spirit of obedience is equally strong. We are all of us self-important—which never produces any work. Great enterprise, boundless courage, tremendous energy and, above all, perfect obedience—these are the only traits that lead to individual and national regeneration. These traits are altogether lacking in us.

Go on with the work as you are doing it, but then you must pay particular attention to study. J— Babu has sent a Hindi magazine, in which Pandit R— of Alwar has published a translation of my Chicago Addresses. Please convey my special indebtedness and thanks to both.

Let me now address myself to you—take particular care to start a centre in Rajputana. It must be in some central place, like Jaipur or Ajmere. Then branches must be established in towns like Alwar and Khetri. You must mix with all, we do not want to quarrel with any. Give my loving embrace to Pandit N—; the man is very energetic, and will be a very practical man in time. Tender my loving regards to Mr. M— and —ji too. A Religious Association or something of the kind has been afoot at Ajmere —what is it? Let me know all about it. M— Babu writes that he and others have written me letters, but I have not received any up till now. . . . About Maths, or centres, or anything of the kind, it is no use starting them in Calcutta; Benares is the place for them. I have many plans like that, but all depends on funds. You will know of them by degrees. You might have noticed from the papers that our movement is steadily gaining ground in England. Every enterprise in this country takes some time to have a go. But once John Bull sets the hand to a thing, he will never let it go. The Americans are quick, but they are somewhat like straw on fire, ready to be extinguished. Do not preach to the public that Ramakrishna Paramahamsa was an Incarnation, and things of that sort. I have some followers at—, look after them.

. . . Infinite power will come unto you—never fear. Be pure, have faith, be obedient.

Teach against the marriage of boys. No scripture ever sanctions it. But for the present say nothing against little girls being married. Directly you stop the marriage of boys, that of girls will stop of itself. Girls surely are not going to marry among themselves! Write to the Secretary, Arya Samaj, Lahore, asking the whereabouts of a Sannyasin named Achyutananda who used to live with them. Make special inquiry of the man. . . . Never fear.—Yours affectionately, VIVEKANANDA.

(*157*)

To Sj. Alasinga Perumal

LONDON,
18th Nov., 1895.

DEAR ALASINGA—. . . In England my work is really splendid. I am astonished myself at it. The English people do not talk much in the newspapers, but they work silently. I am sure of more work in England than in America. Bands and bands come and I have no room for so many; so they squat on the floor, ladies and all. I tell them to imagine that they are under the sky of India, under a spreading banyan, and they like the idea. . . . I shall have to go away next week, and they are so sorry. Some think my work here will be hurt a little if I go away so soon. I do not think so. I do not depend on men or things. The Lord alone I depend upon—and He works through me.

. . . Please everybody without becoming a hypocrite and without being a coward. Hold on to your own ideas with strength and purity, and whatever obstructions may now be in your way, the world is bound to listen to you in the long run.

I have no time even to die, as the Bengalees say. I work, work, work, and earn my own bread and help my country, and this all alone, and then get only criticism from friends and foes for all that! Well, you are but children, I shall have to bear everything. . . . I have sent for a Sannyasin from Calcutta, and shall leave him to work in London. I want one more for America—I want my *own man.* Guru-Bhakti is the foundation of all spiritual development.

. . . I am really tired from incessant work. Any other Hindu would have died if he had to work as hard as I have to. . . . I want to go to India for a long rest.—Ever yours with love and blessings, VIVEKANANDA.

(*158*)

To Swami Brahmananda

C/o E. T. STURDY, ESQ.,*
READING, CAVERSHAM,
ENGLAND,
1895.

DEAR RAKHAL—Glad to receive your letters. There are two defects in the letters which you all write, specially in yours. The first is that very few of the important points I ask are answered. Secondly, there is unusual delay in replying. . . . I have to work day and night, and am always whirling from place to place besides. . . . These are countries where the people are most luxurious, fashionable folk, and nobody would touch a man who has but a speck of dirt on his body. . . . I hoped that somebody would come while I was still here, but as yet nothing has been settled, I see. . . . Business is business, that is, you must do everything promptly, delay and shuffling won't do. By the end of next week I shall go to America, so there is no chance of my meeting him who is coming. . . .

These are countries of gigantic scholars. Is it a fun to make disciples of such people? You are but children and talk like children. Only this much is needed that there should be someone to teach a little Sanskrit, or translate a bit in my absence, that's all. Why not let Girish Babu visit these lands? It is a good idea. It will cost him but 3,000 rupees to visit England and America, and go back. The more people come to these countries, the better. But then it tingles my nerves to look at those who don hats and pose as *Sahibs*!

Black as chimney sweeps, and calling themselves Europeans! Why not wear one's country-dress, as befits gentlemen?—Instead of that, to add to that frightfulness of appearance! Good heavens! . . . Here, as in our country, one has to spend from his own pocket to give lectures, but one can make good the expenses if he lives long enough and makes a reputation. Another thing, my incessant lecturing tours are making my constitution very nervous causing insomnia and other troubles. Over and above that, I have to work single-handed. It is no use depending on my countrymen. No one (in Bengal) has hitherto helped me with a penny, nor has a single soul stepped forward to my assistance. Everybody in this world seeks help, and the more you help him, the more he wants. And if you can do no further, he will call you a cheat. . . . I love—and trust him. . . . He will be free from disease through the Lord's grace. I take all his responsibility. . . . —Yours affectionately, VIVEKANANDA.

(*159*)

LONDON,
21st Nov., 1895.

DEAR—, I sail by the *Britannia* on Wednesday the 27th. My work so far has been very satisfactory here, and I am sure to do splendid work here next summer. . . . —Yours with love, VIVEKANANDA.

(*160*)

228, WEST 39TH ST., NEW YORK,
8th Dec., 1895.

DEAR—, I arrived last Friday after ten days of a very tedious voyage. It was awfully rough and for the first time in my life I was very badly seasick. . . . I have left some strong friends in England who will work in my absence expecting my arrival next summer. My plans are not settled yet about the work here. I have an idea to run to Detroit and Chicago meanwhile, and then come back to New York. The public lecture plan I intend to give up entirely, as I find the best thing for me to do is to step entirely out of the money question—either in public lectures or private classes. In the long run it does harm and sets a bad example.

In England I worked on this principle and refused even the voluntary collections they made. Mr. Sturdy bore the major part of the expenses of lecturing in big halls—the rest, I bore. It worked well. . . . If people want me they will get up lectures. I need not bother myself about these things. If you think after consultation with Mrs. Adams and Miss Locke that it would be practicable for me to come to Chicago for a course of lectures, write to me. Of course the money question should be left entirely out.

My idea is for autonomic, independent groups in different places. Let them work on their own account and do the best they can. As for myself, I do not want to entangle myself in any organisation. . . .—Yours with blessings, VIVEKANANDA.

(*161*)

228, W. 39TH ST., NEW YORK,
10th Dec., 1895.

DEAR—, . . . I have received the Secretary's letter and will be glad to lecture befoie the Harvard Philosophical Club as requested. The only difficulty in the way is: I have begun to write in earnest, as I want to finish some text-books which will be the basis of work when I am gone. I have to hurry through four little books before I go.

This month notices are out for the four Sunday lectures. The lectures for the first week of February in Brooklyn are being arranged by Dr. Janes and others.—Yours with best wishes, VIVEKANANDA.

(*162*)

To Mr. E. T. Sturdy

228, W. 39TH ST., NEW YORK,
16th (?) *Dec., 1895.*

BLESSED AND BELOVED—All your letters reached by one mail to-day. Miss Müller also writes me one. She has read in the *Indian Mirror* that Swami Krishnananda is coming over to England. If that is so, he is the strongest man that I can get.

The classes I had here were six in the week, besides a question class. The general attendance varies between 70 to 120. Besides every Sunday I have a public lecture. The last month my lectures were in a small hall holding about 600. But 900 will come as a rule, 300 standing, and about 300 going off, not finding room. This week therefore I have a bigger hall, with a capacity of holding 1200 people.

There is no admission charged in these lectures, but a collection covers the rent. The newspapers have taken me up this week and altogether I have stirred up New

York considerably this year. If I could have remained here this summer and organised a summer place, the work would be going on sure foundations here. But as I intend to come over in May to England, I will have to leave it unfinished. If, however, Krishnananda comes to England, and you find him strong and able, and if you find the work in London will not be hurt by my absence this summer, I would rather be here this summer.

Again I am afraid my health is breaking down under constant work. I want some rest. We are so unused to these Western methods, especially the time-keeping. I will leave you to decide all these. The *Brahmavadin* is going on here very satisfactorily. I have begun to write articles on Bhakti; also send them a monthly account of the work. Miss Müller wants to come to America. I do not know whether she will or not. Some friends here are publishing my Sunday lectures. I have sent you a few of the first one. I will send you next mail a few of the next two lectures and if you like them I will ask them to send you a number. Can you manage to get a few hundred copies sold in England? That will encourage them in publishing the subsequent ones.

Next month I go to Detroit, then to Boston, and Harvard University. Then I will have a rest, and then I come to England, unless you think that things go on without me and with Krishnananda.—Ever yours with love and blessings, VIVEKANANDA.

(*163*)

To Sj. Alasinga Perumal

228, W. 39TH ST., NEW YORK,
20th Dec., 1895.

DEAR ALASINGA— . . . Have patience and be faithful unto death. Do not fight among yourselves. Be perfectly pure in money dealings. . . . We will do great things yet. . . . So long as you have faith and honesty and devotion everything will prosper.

. . . In translating the Suktas pay particular attention to the Bhâshyakâras and pay no attention whatever to the orientalists. They do not understand a single thing about our Shâstras. It is not given to dry philologists to understand philosophy or religion. . . . For instance, the word आनीदवातम् in Rigveda was translated—" He lived without breathing." Now, here the reference is really to the chief Prâna and अवातम् has the root-meaning for unmoved, that is, without vibration. It describes the state in which the universal cosmic energy or Prana remains before the Kalpa begins; *vide*—the Bhashyakaras. Explain according to our sages and not according to the so-called European scholars. What do they know?

. . . Be bold and fearless and the road will be clear. . . Mind, you have nothing whatsoever to do with the T—s. If you all stand by me and do not lose patience, I assure you we shall do great work yet. The great work will be in England, my boy, by and by. I feel you sometimes get disheartened, and I am afraid you get temptations to play into the hands of the T—s. Mind you, that the Guru-Bhakta will conquer the world—this is the one evidence of history. . . . It is faith that makes a lion of a man. You must always remember how much work I have to do. Sometimes I have to deliver two or three lectures a day—and thus I make my way against all odds—hard work; any weaker man would die.

. . . Hold on with faith and strength; be true, be honest, be pure, and don't quarrel amongst yourselves. Jealousy is the bane of our race.—With love to you and all our friends, VIVEKANANDA.

(*164*)

To Swami Saradananda

228, W. 39TH ST., NEW YORK,
23rd Dec., 1895.

DEAR SARAT—Your letter only made me sad. I see you have lost all enthusiasm. I know all of you, your powers and your limitations. I would not have called you to any task which you are incompetent to do. The only task I would have given you was to teach Elementary Sanskrit, and with the help of dictionaries and other things assist S. in his translations and teachings. I would have moulded you to it. Any one could have done as well—only a little smattering of Sanskrit was absolutely necessary. Well, everything is for the best. If it is the Lord's work the right man for the right place will be forthcoming in the right time. None of you need feel disturbed. As for Sanyal, I don't care who takes money or not, but I have a strong hatred for child-marriage. I have suffered terribly from it and it is the great sin for which our nation has to suffer. As such I would hate myself if I help such a diabolical custom directly or indirectly. I wrote to you pretty plain about it and Sanyal had no right to play a hoax upon me about his "law-suit" and his attempts to become free. I am sorry for his playing tricks on me who have never done him any harm. This is the world. What good you do goes for nothing, but if you stop doing it, then, Lord help you, you are counted as a rogue. Isn't it? Emotional natures like mine are always preyed upon by relatives and friends. This world is merciless. This world is our friend when we are its slaves and no more. This world is broad enough for me. There will always be a corner found for me somewhere. If the people of India do not like me, there will be others who like. I must set my foot to the best of my ability upon this devilish custom of child-marriage. No blame will entail on you. You keep at a safe distance, if you are afraid. I am sorry, very sorry, I cannot have any partnership with such doings as getting husbands for babies. Lord help me, I never had and never will have. Think of the case of—Babu! Did you ever meet a more cowardly or brutal one than that? I can kill the man who gets a husband for a baby. The upshot of the whole thing is—I want bold, daring, adventurous spirits to help me. Else I will work alone. I have a mission to fulfil. I will work it out alone. I do not care who comes or who goes. Sanyal is already done for by Samsâra. Beware, boy! That was all the advice I thought it my duty to give you. Of course you are great folks now—my words will have no value with you. But I hope the time will come when you will see clearer, know better and think other thoughts than you are now doing.

Good-bye! I would not bother you any more, and all blessings go with you all. I am very glad I have been of some service to you sometimes if you think so. At least I am pleased with myself for having tried my best to discharge the duties laid on me by my Guru, and well done or ill, I am glad that I tried. So good-bye. Tell Sanyal that I am not at all angry with him, but I am sorry, very sorry. It is not the money—that counts nothing—but the violation of a principle that pained me, and the trick he played on me. Good-bye to him also, and to you all. One chapter is closed of my life. Let others come in their due order. They will find me ready. You need not disturb yourselves at all about me. I want no help from any human being in any country. So good-bye! May the Lord bless you all for ever and ever!

(*165*)

To Miss S. Farmer

NEW YORK,
29th Dec., 1895.

DEAR SISTER—In this universe where nothing is lost, where we live in the midst of death-in-life, every thought that is thought, in public or in private, in crowded thoroughfare or in the deep recesses of primeval forests, lives. They are continuously trying to become self-embodied, and until they have embodied themselves, they will struggle for expression, and any amount of repression cannot kill them. Nothing can be destroyed—those thoughts that caused evil in the past are also seeking embodiment, to be filtered through repeated expression and, at last, transfigured into perfect good.

As such, there is a mass of thought which is at the present time struggling to get expression. This new thought is telling us to give up our dreams of dualism, of good and evil in essence, and the still wilder dream of suppression. It teaches us that higher direction and not destruction is the law. It teaches us that it is not a world of bad and good, but good and better—and still better. It stops short of nothing but acceptance. It teaches that no situation is hopeless, and as such accepts every form of mental, moral or spiritual thought where it already stands, and without a word of condemnation tells it that so far it has done good, now is the time to do better. What in old times was thought of as the elimination of bad, it teaches as the transfiguration of evil and the doing of better. It above all teaches that the kingdom of heaven is already in existence if we will have it, that perfection is already in man if he will see it.

The Greenacre meetings last summer were so wonderful, simply because you opened yourself fully to that thought which has found in you so competent a medium of expression, and because you took your stand on the highest teaching of this thought that the kingdom of heaven already exists.

You have been consecrated and chosen by the Lord as a channel for converting this thought into life, and every one that helps you in this wonderful work is serving the Lord.

Our Gita teaches that he who serves the servants of the Lord is His highest worshipper. You are a servant of the Lord, and as a disciple of Krishna I will always consider it a privilege and worship to render you any service in the carrying out of your inspired mission wherever I be.—Ever your affectionate brother, VIVEKANANDA.

(*166*)

*1895.**

MY DEAR—, The books that Sanyal sent have arrived. I forgot to mention this. Please inform him about it.

Let me write down something for you all:

1. Know partiality to be the chief cause of all evil. That is to say, if you show towards any one more love than towards somebody else, rest assured, you will be sowing the seeds of future troubles.

2. If anybody comes to you to speak ill of any of his brothers, refuse to listen to him *in toto*. It is a great sin to listen even. In that lies the germ of future troubles.

3. Moreover, bear with everyone's shortcomings. Forgive offences by the million. And if you love all unselfishly, all will by degrees come to love one another. As soon as they fully understand that the interests of one depend upon those of others, everyone of them will give up jealousy. To do something conjointly is not in our very national character. Therefore you must try to inaugurate that spirit with the utmost care, and wait patiently. To

tell you the truth, I do not find among you any distinction of great or small: everyone has the capacity to manifest, in times of need, the highest energy. I see it. Look for instance how Sasi will remain always constant to his spot; his steadfastness is a great foundation-rock. How successfully Kali and Jogen brought about the Town Hall meeting; it was indeed a momentous task! Niranjan has done much work in Ceylon and elsewhere. How extensively has Sarada travelled and sown seeds of gigantic future works! Whenever I think of the wonderful renunciation of Hari, about his steadiness of intellect and forbearance, I get a new access of strength. In Tulsi, Gupta, Baburam, Sarat, to mention a few, in every one of you there is tremendous energy. If you still entertain any doubt as to Sri Ramakrishna's being a jewel-expert, what then is the difference between you and a madman? Behold, hundreds of men and women of this country are beginning to worship our Lord as the greatest of all Avataras! Steady! Every great work is done slowly. . . .

He is at the helm, what fear! You are all of infinite strength—how long does it take you to keep off petty jealousy, or egoistic ideas! The moment such propensity comes, resign yourselves to the Lord! Just make over your body and mind to His work, and all troubles will be at an end for ever.

There will not be room enough, I see, in the house where you are at present living. A commodious building is needed. That is to say, you need not huddle together in one room. If possible, not more than two should live in the same room. There should be a big hall, where the books may be kept.

Every morning there should be a little reading from the scriptures, which Kali, Hari, Tulsi, Sasi and others may superintend by turns. In the evening there should be another class, with a little practice in meditation, and Sankirtanas etc. You may divide the work, and set apart one day for Yoga, a day for Bhakti, another for Jnana, and so forth. It will be excellent if you fix a routine like this, so that outside people also may join in the evening classes. And every Sunday, from ten in the morning up till night, there should be a continuous succession of classes and Sankirtanas etc. That is for the public. If you take the trouble to continue this kind of routine-work for some time, it will gradually make itself easy and smooth. There should be no smoking in that hall, for which another place must be set apart. If you can take the trouble to bring about this state of things by degrees, I shall think a great advance will be made.

What about a certain magazine that Haramohan was trying to publish? If you can manage to start one, it will indeed be nice.—Yours affectionately, VIVEKANANDA.

(*167*)

To Swami Brahmananda

*1895.**

MY DEAR RAKHAL—Just now I got your letter and was glad to go through it. No matter whether there is any work done in India or not, the real work lies here. I do not want anybody to come over now. On my return to India I shall train a few men, and after that there will be no danger for them in the West. Yes, it was of Gunanidhi that I wrote. Give my special love and blessings to Hari Singh and others. Never take part in quarrels and disputes. Who on earth possesses the power to put the Raja of Khetri down? The Divine Mother is at his elbow! I have received Kali's letter too. It will be very good indeed if you can start a centre in Kashmir. Wherever you can, open a centre. . . . Now I have laid the foundations firm here and in England, and nobody has the power to shake them. New York is in a commotion this year. Next year will come the turn of London.

Even big giants will give way, who counts your pigmies! Gird up your loins and set yourselves to work! We must throw the world into convulsions with our triumphal shouts. This is but the beginning, my boy. Do you think there are *men* in our country, it is a Golgotha. There is some chance if you can impart education to the masses. Is there a greater strength than that of knowledge? Can you give them education? Name me the country where rich men ever helped anybody! In all countries it is the middle classes that do all great works. How long will it take to raise the money? Where are the *men*? Are there any in our country? Our countrymen are boys, and we must treat them as such. . . . There are some few religious and philosophical books left—the remnants of the mansion that has been burnt down; take them with you, quick, and come over to this country. . . .

Never fear! The Divine Mother is helping me! This year such work is going to be turned out, that you will be struck dumb to hear of it!

What fear! Whom to fear! Steel your hearts and set yourselves to work!—Yours affectionately, VIVEKANANDA.

P. S.—Sarada is talking of bringing out a Bengali magazine. Help it with all your might. It is not a bad idea. You must not throw cold water on anybody's project. Give up criticism altogether. Help all as long as you find they are doing all right, and in cases where they seem to be going wrong, show them their mistakes gently. It is criticising each other that is at the root of all mischief. That is the chief factor in breaking down organisations. . . .

(*168*)

To Swami Ramakrishnananda

U. S. A.,*
1895.

MY DEAR SASI—Yesterday I received a letter from you

in which there was a smattering of news, but nothing in detail. I am much better now. Through the grace of the Lord I am proof against the severe cold of this year. Oh, the terrible cold! But these people keep all down through scientific knowledge. Every house has its cellar underground, in which there is a big boiler whence steam is made to course day and night through every room. This keeps all the rooms warm, but it has one defect, that while it is summer indoors, it is thirty to forty degrees below zero outside! Most of the rich people of this country make for Europe during the winer, which is comparatively warm.

Now, let me give you some instructions. This letter is meant for you. Please go through these instructions once a day and act up to them. I have got Sarada's letter —he is doing good work but now we want organisation. To him, Brother Tarak and others please give my special love and blessings. The reason why I give you these few instructions is that there is an organising power in you—the Lord has made this known to me—but not yet fully developed. Through His blessings it will soon be. That you never lose your centre of gravity is an evidence of this, but it must be both intensive and extensive.

1. All the Shâstras hold that the threefold misery that there is in this world, is not natural, hence it is removable.

2. In the Buddha Incarnation the Lord says that the root of the Âdhibhautika misery, or misery arising from other terrestrial beings, is the formation of *classes* (Jâti); in other words, every form of class-distinction, whether based on birth, or acquirements, or wealth is at the bottom of this misery. In the Atman there is no distinction of sex, or Varna[1] or Ashrama[2] or anything of the kind, and as

---

[1] The four principal castes, viz., Brahmin, Kshatriya, Vaishya and Shudra.

[2] The four orders of life, viz., Brahmacharya, Gârhasthya, Vânaprastha and Sannyâsa.

mud cannot be washed away by mud, it is likewise impossible to bring about oneness by means of separative ideas.

3. In the Krishna Incarnation He says that the root of all sorts of misery is Avidya (Nescience) and that selfless work purifies the mind. But किं कर्म किमकर्मेति etc.—"Even sages are bewildered to decide what is work and what is no-work." (Gita).

4. Only that kind of work which develops our spirituality is work. Whatever fosters materiality is no-work.

5. Therefore work and no-work must be regulated by a person's aptitude, his country, and his age.

6. Works such as sacrifices were suited to the olden times, but are not for the modern times.

7. From the date that the Ramakrishna Incarnation was born, has sprung the Satya-yuga (Golden Age). . . .

8. In this Incarnation atheistic ideas, . . . will be destroyed by the sword of Jnana (Knowledge), and the whole world will be unified by means of Bhakti (Devotion) and Prema (Divine Love). Moreover, in this Incarnation, *Rajas*, or the desire for name and fame etc., is altogether absent. In other words, blessed is he who acts up to His teachings; whether he accepts Him or not, does not matter.

9. The founders of different sects, in the ancient or modern times, have not been in the wrong. They have done well, but they must do better. Well—better—best.

10. Therefore we must take all up where they are, that is, we must lead them on to higher and higher ideals, without upsetting their own chosen attitude. As to social conditions, those that prevail now are good, but they shall be better—best.

11. There is no chance for the welfare of the world unless the condition of women is improved. It is not possible for a bird to fly on only one wing.

12. Hence, in the Ramakrishna Incarnation, the

acceptance of a woman as the Guru, hence His practising in the woman's garb and attitude[1] hence too His preaching the Motherhood of women, as representations of the Divine Mother.

13. Hence it is that my first endeavour is to start a Math for women. This Math shall be the origin of Gârgis and Maitreyis, and women of even higher attainments than these. . . .

14. No great work can be achieved by humbug. It is through Love, a passion for Truth, and tremendous energy, that all undertakings are accomplished. तत् कुरु पौरुषम्—" Therefore, manifest your manhood."

15. There is no need for quarrel or dispute with anybody. Give your message and leave others to their own thoughts. सत्यमेव जयते नानृतम् —"Truth alone triumphs, not falsehood." तदा किं विवादेन —" Why then fight?"

. . . Combine seriousness with childlike naiveté. Live in harmony with all. Give up all idea of egoism, and entertain no sectarian views. Useless wrangling is a great sin.

. . . From Sarada's letter I came to know that N— Ghosh has compared me with Jesus Christ, and the like. That kind of things may pass muster in our country, but if you send them here in print, there is a chance of my being insulted! I mean, I do not like to hamper anybody's freedom of thought,—am I a missionary? If Kali has not sent those papers to this country, tell him not to do it. Only the Address will do, I do not want the proceedings. Now many respectable ladies and gentlemen of this country hold me in reverence. The missionaries and others of that ilk have tried their utmost to put me down but finding it useless, have now become quiet. Every undertaking must pass through a lot of obstacles. Truth triumphs if only

[1] For some time Sri Ramakrishna dressed himself as a woman and practised Sâdhana conceiving himself as a woman, to get rid of the sex-idea.

one pursues a peaceful course. I have no need to reply to what a Mr. Hudson has spoken against me. In the first place, it is unnecessary, and secondly, I shall be bringing myself down to the level of people of Mr. Hudson's type. Are you mad? Shall I fight from here with one Mr. Hudson? Through the Lord's grace, people who are far above Mr. Hudson in rank listen to me with veneration. Please do not send any more papers. Let all that go on in India, it will do no harm. For the Lord's work at one time there was need for that kind of newspaper blazoning. When that is done, there is no more need for it. . . . It is one of the attendant evils of name and fame that you can't have anything private. . . . Before you begin any undertaking, pray to Sri Ramakrishna and he will show you the right way. We want a big plot of land to begin with, then building and all will come. Slowly our Math is going to raise itself, don't worry about it. . . .

Kali and all others have done good work. Give my love and best wishes to all. Work in unison with the people of Madras, and let someone or other amongst you go there at intervals. Give up for ever the desire for name and fame and power. While I am on earth, Sri Ramakrishna is working through me. So long as you believe in this, there is no danger of any evil for you.

The "Ramakrishna Punthi" (Life of Sri Ramakrishna in Bengali verse) that Akshay has sent is very good, but there is no glorification of the Shakti at the opening, which is a great defect. Tell him to remedy it in the second edition. Always bear this in mind that we are now standing before the gaze of the world, and that people are watching everyone of our actions and utterances. Remember this and work.

. . . Be on the look out for a site for our Math. . . . If it be at some little distance from Calcutta, no harm. Wherever we shall build our Math, there we shall have a stir made. Very glad to learn about Mahim Chakravarty.

The Andes have turned into the holy Gaya, I see! Where is he? Please give him, Sj. Vijay Goswami and our friends my cordial greetings. . . . To beat an opponent one needs sword and buckler, so carefully learn English and Sanskrit. Kali's English is getting nicer every day, while that of Sarada is deteriorating. Tell Sarada to give up the flowery style. It is extremely difficult to write a flowery style in a foreign tongue. Please convey to him a hundred thousand bravos from me! There's a hero indeed. . . . Well done, all of you! Bravo lads! The beginning is excellent. Go on in that way. If the adder of jealousy does not come in, there is no fear! माभैः—"Cheer up!" मद्भक्तानाञ्च ये भक्तास्ते मे भक्ततमा मताः—"Those who serve My devotees are My best devotees." Have all of you a little grave bearing. I am not writing any book on Hinduism at present. But I am jotting down my thoughts. Every religion is an expression, a language to express the same truth, and we must speak to each in his own language. That S— has grasped this, is all right. It will be time enough to look to Hinduism later on. Do you think people in this country would be much attracted if I talk of Hinduism?—The very name of narrowness in ideas will scare them away! The real thing is—*the Religion* taught by Sri Ramakrishna, let the Hindus call it Hinduism—and others call it in their own way. Only you must proceed slowly—शनैः पन्थाः—"One must make journeys slowly." Give my blessings to Dinanath the new recruit. I have very little time to write, always lecture, lecture, lecture. Purity, Patience, Perseverance. . . . You must ask those numerous people who are now paying heed to Sri Ramakrishna's teachings, to help you pecuniarily to a certain extent. How can the Math be maintained unless they help you? You must not be shy of making this plain to all. . . .

There is no gain in my hastening return from this country. In the first place, a little sound made here will resound there a great deal. Then, the people of this country are immensely rich and are bold enough to pay. While the people of our country have neither money nor the least bit of boldness.

You will know everything by degrees. Was Sri Ramakrishna the Saviour of India merely? It is this narrow idea that has brought about India's ruin, and her welfare is an impossibility so long as this is not rooted out. Had I the money I would send each one of you to travel all over the world. No great idea can have a place in the heart unless one steps out of his little corner. It will be verified in time. Every great achievement is done slowly. Such is the Lord's will. . . .

Why didn't any of you write about Daksha and Harish? I shall be glad to know if you watch their whereabouts. That Sanyal is feeling miserable is because his mind is not yet pure like the water of the Ganges. It is not yet selfless, but will be in time. He will have no misery if he can give up the little crookedness and be straightforward. My special loving greetings to Rakhal and Hari. Take great care of them. . . . Never forget that Rakhal was the special object of Sri Ramakrishna's love. Let nothing daunt you, who on earth has the power to snub us so long as the Lord favours us? Even if you are at your last breath, be not afraid. Work on with the intrepidity of a lion but at the same time with the tenderness of a flower. Let this year's Sri Ramakrishna Festival be celebrated in great pomp. Let the feeding be quite ordinary—the Prasâda being distributed off-hand in earthen plates among the assembled. That will do. There should be readings from Sri Ramakrishna's Life. Place books like the Vedas and the Vedanta together and perform Arati before them. . . . Avoid issuing invitation cards of the old style. आमन्त्रये भवन्तं साशीर्वादं भगवतो रामकृष्णस्य बहुमानपुरःसरञ्च—"With Bhagavan Sri Ramakrishna's blessings and our great esteem we have the pleasure to invite you." Write some such line, and then write that to defray the expenses of Sri Ramakrishna's Birthday Festival and those of the maintenance of the Math, you want his assistance. That if he likes, he may kindly send the money to such and such, at such and such address, and so on. Also add a page in English. The term " Lord Ramakrishna " has no meaning. You must give it up. Write " Bhagavan " in English characters, and add a line or two in English:

The Anniversary of Bhagavan Sri Ramakrishna.

Sir, we have great pleasure in inviting you to join us in celebrating the —th anniversary of Bhagavan Ramakrishna Paramahamsa. For the celebration of this great occasion and for the maintenance of the Alambazar Math funds are absolutely necessary. If you think that the cause is worthy of your sympathy, we shall be very grateful to receive your contribution to the great work.

Yours obediently,

(Date) (Place) (Name)

If you get more than enough money, spend only a little of it and keep the surplus as a reserve fund to defray your expenses. On the plea of offering the food to the Lord, do not make everybody wait till he is sick, to have a stale and unsavoury dinner. Have two filters made and use that filtered water for both cooking and drinking purposes. Boil the water before filtering. If you do this, you will never more hear of malaria. Keep a strict eye on everybody's health. If you can give up lying on the floor—in other words, if you can get the money to do it, it will be excellent indeed. Dirty clothes are the chief cause of diseases. . . . About the offering, let me tell you that only a little Pâyasânnam (milk-rice with sugar) will do. He used to love that alone. It is true that the worship-room is a help to many, but it is no use indulging in Râjasika and Tâmasika food. Let the ceremonials give place to a certain extent to a little study of the Gita or the Upanishads or other sacred books. What I mean is this—let there be as little materialism as possible, with the maximum of spirituality. . . . Did Sri Ramakrishna come for this or that particular individual, or for the world at large? If the latter, then you must present him in such a light that the whole world may understand him. *You must not identify yourself with any life of him written by anybody, nor give your sanction to any.* There is no danger so long as they do not come out associated with our name. . . . "Say yea, yea, to all and stick to your own."

. . . A thousand thanks to Mahendra Babu for his kindly helping us. He is a very liberal-hearted man. . . . About Sanyal, he will attain the highest good by doing his bit of work attentively, that is, by simply serving Sri Ramakrishna's children. . . . Brother Tarak is doing very good work. Bravo! Well done! That is what we want. Let me see all of you shoot like so many meteors! What is Ganga doing? Some Zemindars in Rajputana respect him. Tell him to get some money from them as Bhikshâ, then he is a man. . . .

Just now I read Akshay's book. Give him a hundred thousands hearty embraces from me. Through his pen Sri Ramakrishna is manifesting himself. Blessed is Akshy! Let him recite that *Punthi* before all. He must recite it before all in the Festival. If the work be too large, let him read extracts of it. Well, I do not find a single irrelevant word in it. I cannot tell in words the joy I have experienced by reading his book. Try all of you to give the book an extensive sale. Then ask Akshay to go from village to village to preach. Well done Akshay! He is doing his work. Go from village to village and proclaim to all Sri Ramakrishna's teachings, can there be a more blessed lot than this? I tell you, Akshay's book and Akshay himself must electrify the masses. Dear, dear Akshay, I bless you with all my heart, my dear brother. May the Lord sit in your tongue! Go and spread his teachings from door to door. There is no need whatever of your becoming a Sannyasin. . . . Akshay is the future apostle for the masses of Bengal. Take great care of Akshay, his faith and devotion have borne fruit.

Ask Akshay to write these few points in the third section of his book, " The Propagation of the Faith."

1. Whatever the Vedas, the Vedanta and all other Incarnations have done in the past, Sri Ramakrishna lived to practise in the course of a single life.

2. One cannot understand the Vedas, the Vedanta, the Incarnations and such like things without understanding his life. For, he was the explanation.

3. From the very date that he was born, has sprung the Satya-yuga (Golden Age). Henceforth there is an end to all sorts of distinctions, and everyone down to the Chandâla will be sharers in the Divine Love. The distinction between man and woman, between the rich and the poor, the literate and the illiterate, Brahmins and Chandalas—he lived to root out all. And he was the harbinger of Peace—the separation between Hindus and Mohammedans, between Hindus and Christians, all are now things of the past. That fight about distinctions that there was, belonged to another era. In this Satya-yuga the tidal waves of Sri Ramakrishna's Love have unified all.

Tell him to expand these ideas and write them in his own style.

Whoever—man or woman—will worship Sri Ramakrishna, be he or she ever so low, will be then and there converted into the very highest. Another thing, the Motherhood of God is prominent in this Incarnation. He used to dress himself as a woman—he was, as it were, our Mother—and we must likewise look upon all women as the reflections of the Mother. In India there are two great evils. Trampling on the women, and grinding the poor through caste restrictions. He was the Saviour of women, Saviour of the masses, Saviour of all, high and low. And let Akshay introduce his worship in every home—Brahmin or Chandala, man or woman,—everyone has the right to worship him. Whoever will worship him only with devotion, shall be blessed for ever.

Tell him to write in this strain. Never mind for anything—the Lord will be at his side.—Yours affectionately, VIVEKANANDA.

P. S. . . . Ask Sanyal to send me a copy each of the Narada and Shandilya Sutras, and one of the Yoga-vashishtha, that has been translated in Calcutta. I want the English translation of the last, not a Bengali edition. . . .

(169)

To Swami Brahmananda

*1895.**

DEAR RAKHAL—. . . Your suggestion to me to go back to India is no doubt right, but a seed has been sown in this country, and there is the possibility of its being nipped in the bud if I go away all on a sudden. Hence I have to wait some time. Moreover, it will be possible to manage everything nicely from here. Everybody requests me to return to India. It is all right, but don't you see it is not wise to depend upon others. A wise man should stand firm on his own legs and act. Everything will come about slowly. For the present don't forget to be on the look out for a site. We want a big plot—of about ten to twenty thousand rupees—it must be right on the Ganges. Though my capital is small, I am exceedingly bold. Have an eye on securing the land. At present we shall have to work three centres, one in New York, another in Calcutta and a third in Madras. Then, by degrees, as the Lord will arrange. . . . You must keep a strict eye on health; let everything else be subordinated to that. . . .

Brother Tarak is eager for travel. Well, it is good, but these are very expensive countries; a preacher needs here at least a thousand rupees a month. But Brother Tarak has boldness, and it is God who provides everything. Quite true, but he must have to improve his English a little. The thing is, one has to snatch one's bread from the jaws of the missionary scholars. That is, one must prevail over these people by dint of learning, or he will be blown off at a puff. They understand neither Sâdhus nor your Sannyasins, nor the spirit of renunciation. What they do understand is the vastness of learning, the display of eloquence and tremendous activity. Over and above that, the whole country will be searching for flaws, the clergy will day and night try to snub you, through force or guile. You must get rid of these obstructions to preach your doctrines. Through the mercy of the Divine Mother everything is possible. But in my opinion if Brother Tarak goes on starting some societies in the Punjab and Madras, and you become organised, it will be the best thing. It is indeed a great thing to discover a new path, but it is as difficult a task to cleanse that path and make it spacious and nice. If you live for some time in places where I have sown the seeds of our Master's ideals, and succeed in developing the seeds into plants, you will be doing much greater work than I did. What will they who cannot manage some ready-made thing do with regard to things that are yet to come? If you cannot add a little salt to a dish almost done, how am I to believe that you will collect all the ingredients? Let Brother Tarak, as an alternative, start a Himalayan Math at Almora, and have a library there, so that we may spend some of our spare time in a cool place, and practise spiritual exercises. However, I have nothing to say against any particular course which anyone may be led to adopt; on the contrary, God-speed. शिवा वः सन्तु पन्थानः—"May your journey be prosperous." Tell him to wait a bit. What's the good of being in a hurry? You shall all travel the whole world. Courage! Brother Tarak has a great capacity for work within him. Hence I expect much of him. . . . You remember, I suppose, how after Sri Ramakrishna's passing away, all forsook us as so many worthless, ragged boys. Only people like Balaram, Suresh, Master and Chuni Babu were our friends at that hour of need. And we shall never be able to repay our debts to them. . . . Tell Chuni Babu in private that he has nothing to fear, that those who are protected by the Lord must be above fear. I am a puny man, but the glories of the Lord are infinite. मामैः मामैः —discard fear. Let not your faith be shaken. . . . Has danger any power over one whom the Lord has taken into His fold?—Ever yours, VIVEKANANDA.

(*170*)

To Sj. Alasinga Perumal

1895.

DEAR ALASINGA—We have no organisation, nor want to build any. Each one is quite independent to teach, quite free to preach whatever he or she likes.

If you have the spirit within, you will never fail to attract others. The——s' method can never be ours, for the very simple reason that they are an organised sect, we are not.

Individuality is my motto, I have no ambition beyond training individuals up. I know very little: that little I teach without reserve; where I am ignorant I confess it as such, and never am I so glad as when I find people being helped by Theosophists, Christians, Mohammedans or anybody in the world. I am a Sannyasin, as such I consider myself as a servant, not as a master in the world. . . . If people love me they are welcome, if they hate they are also welcome.

Each one will have to save himself, each one to do his

own work. I seek no help, I reject none. Nor have I any right in the world to be helped. Whosoever has helped me or will help, it will be their mercy to me, not my right, and as such I am eternally grateful.

When I became a Sannyasin I consciously took the step, knowing that this body would have to die of starvation. What of that, I am a beggar. My friends are poor, I love the poor, I welcome poverty. I am glad that I sometimes have to starve. I ask help of none. What is the use? Truth will preach itself, it will not die for the want of the helping hands of me! "Making happiness and misery the same, making success and failure the same, fight thou on." (Gita). It is that eternal love, unruffled equanimity under all circumstances, and perfect freedom from jealousy or animosity that will tell. That will tell, nothing else. . . . —Yours, VIVEKANANDA.

(*171*)

To Swami Trigunatitananda

*Jan., 1896.**

DEAR SARADA—. . . Your idea of the paper is very good indeed. Apply yourself to it heart and soul. . . . Never mind for money. . . . There are many to preach Christianity and Mohammedanism—you just go through the preaching of your own country's religion. But then if you can get hold of a Mohammedan who is versed in Arabic, and have old Arabic books translated, it will be a good plan. There is much of Indian history in the Persian language. If you can have the books translated bit by bit, it will be a good regular item. We want quite a number of writers, then there is the difficult task of getting subscribers. The way out is this: You lead a wandering life; wherever you find Bengali language spoken, thrust the paper on whomsoever you can lay your hands on. Enlist them by vehemence!—they would always turn tail the moment they have to spend something. Never mind anything! Push it on! Begin to contribute articles, all of you who can. It won't do merely to sit idle. You have done a heroic deed! Bravo! Those who falter and vacillate will lag behind and you will jump straight on to the top of all! Those that are working for their own salvation will neither have their own nor that of others. Let the commotion that you make be such as to resound to the world's end. There are people who are ready to pick holes in everything, but when it comes to the question of work, not a scent of them can be had! To work!—as far as in you lies! Then I shall go to India and move the whole country. What fear! "Even a snake loses its venom if it is insisted that it has none." These people will go on the negative track till they are actually reduced to nothing! . . .

Gangadhar has done right heroic work! Well done! Kali has joined him in work—thrice well done!! Let one go to Madras, and another to Bombay, let the world shake in its hinges! O the grief! If I could get two or three like me, I could have left the world convulsed. As it is, I have to proceed gently. Move the world to its foundations! Send one to China, another to Japan! What will the poor householders do, with their little bits of life? It is for the Sannyasins, Shiva's demons, to rend the skies with their shouts of हर हर शम्भो—Yours affectionately, VIVEKANANDA.

(*172*)

To Mr. E. T. Sturdy

228, W. 39TH ST., NEW YORK,
16th Jan., 1896.

BLESSED AND BELOVED—Many many thanks for the books. The *Sankhya Karika* is a very good book, and the *Kurma Purana,* though I do not find in it all I expected, has a few verses on Yoga. The words dropped in my last letter were "Yoga Sutra," which I am translating, with notes from various authorities. I want to incorporate the Chapter on *Kurma Purana* in my notes. I have very enthusiastic accounts of your classes from Miss MacLeod. Mr. Galsworthy seems to be very much interested now.

I have begun my Sunday lectures here and also the classes. Both are very enthusiastically received. I make them all free and take up a collection to pay the hall etc. Last Sunday's lecture was very much appreciated and is in the press. I will send you a few copies next week. It was the outline of our work.

As my friends have a stenographer (Goodwin) engaged, all these class lessons and public lectures are taken down. I intend to send you a copy of each. They may suggest you some ideas.

My great want here is a strong man like you, possessing intellect, and ability, and love. In this nation of universal education, all seem to melt down into a mediocrity, and the few able are weighed down by the eternal money-making.

I have a chance of getting a piece of land in the country, and some buildings on it, plenty of trees and a river, to serve as a summer meditation resort. That of course requires a committee to look after it in my absence, also the handling of money and printing and other matters.

I have separated myself entirely from money questions, yet without it the movement cannot go on. So necessarily I have to make over everything executive to a committee, who will look after these things in my absence. Steady work is not in the line of the Americans. The only way they work is in a herd. So let them have it. As to the teaching part, my friends will go over this country from place to place, each one independent, and let them form independent circles. That is the easiest way to spread. Then, when there will be sufficient strength, we will have yearly gatherings to concentrate our energies.

The committee is entirely executive and it is confined to New York alone. . . . —Ever yours with love and blessings, VIVEKANANDA.

(*173*)

23rd January, 1896.

. . . I have been smelling something since last few issues of the *Brahmavadin*. Are you going to join the —s? This time you simply gave yourselves up. Why, you get in a notice of the — lectures in the body of your notes. Any suspicion of my connection with the —s will spoil my work both in America and England and well it may. They are thought by all people of sound mind to be wrong, and true it is that they are held so, and you know it full well. I am afraid you want to overreach me. You think you can get more subscribers in England by advertising C—? Fool that you are.

I do not want to quarrel with the —s, but my position is entirely ignoring them. . . .

Now I would have no traitors, I tell you plainly, I would not be played upon by any rogue. No hypocrisy with me. Hoist your flag and give public notice in your paper that you have given up all connections with me, and join the . . . camp of the —s or cease to have anything whatsoever to do with them. I give you very plain words indeed. I shall have one man only to follow me but he must be true and faithful unto death. I do not care for success or no success. I am tired of this nonsense of preaching all the world over. Did any of C—'s people come to my help when I was in England? Fudge! I must keep my movement *pure* or I will have none.

P. S. Reply sharp your decision. I am very decided on this point. The *Brahmavadin* is for preaching Vedanta and not —. . . . I almost lose my patience when I see these underhand dealings. . . . This is the world—those whom you love best and help most try to cheat you. . . .

(*174*)

To Swami Yogananda

228, W. 39TH ST.,* NEW YORK,
24th Jan., 1896.

DEAR JOGEN—. . . . I am very sorry to hear that your health is not yet all right. Can you go to a very cold climate, where there is plenty of snowfall in the winter, Darjeeling, for instance?—The severity of the cold will set your stomach right, as it has done in my case. And can you give up altogether the habit of using ghee and spices? Butter digests more quickly than ghee. . . .

Three months more and I go to England, to try once more to make some stir; the following winter to India and after that, it depends on the Lord.

Put forth all nerve for the magazine that Sarada is wanting to publish. Ask Sasi to look to it. One thing, neither Kali nor anybody else has any need of coming to England at present. I shall train them first when I go to India, and then they may go wherever they please.

We would do nothing ourselves and would scoff at others who try to do something—this is the bane that has brought about our downfall as a nation. Want of sympathy and lack of energy are at the root of all misery, and you must therefore give these two up. Who but the Lord knows what potentialities there are in particular individuals—let all have opportunities, and leave the rest to the Lord. It is indeed very difficult to have an equal love for all, but without it there is no Mukti.—Yours affectionately, VIVEKANANDA.

(175)

To Mr. E. T. Sturdy

228, W. 39TH ST., NEW YORK,
13th Feb., 1896.

BLESSED AND BELOVED—About the Sannyasi coming over from India, I am sure he will help you in the translation work, also in other work. Later on, when I come, I may send him over to America. To-day another Sannyasi has been added to the list. This time it is a man who is a genuine American and a religious teacher of some standing in the country. He was Dr. Street. He is now Yogananda, as his leaning is all towards Yoga.

I have been sending regular reports to the *Brahmavadin* from here. They will be published soon. It takes such a long time for things to reach India! Things are growing nobly in America. As there was no hocus-pocus from the beginning, the Vedanta is drawing the attention of the highest classes in American society. Sarah Bernhardt, the French actress has been playing "Iziel" here. It is a sort of Frenchified life of Buddha, where a courtesan "Iziel" wants to seduce the Buddha, under the banyan—and the Buddha preaches to her the vanity of the world, whilst she is sitting all the time on Buddha's lap. However all is well that ends well—the courtesan fails. Madame Bernhardt acts the courtesan.

I went to see this Buddha business—and Madame spying me in the audience wanted to have an interview with me. A swell family of my acquaintance arranged the affair. There were besides Madame M. Morrel, the celebrated singer, also the great electrician, Tesla. Madame is a very scholarly lady and has studied up the metaphysics a good deal. M. Morrel was being interested, but Mr. Tesla was charmed to hear about the Vedantic Prâna and Âkâsha and the Kalpas, which according to him are the only theories modern science can entertain. Now both Akasha and Prana again are produced from the cosmic Mahat, the Universal Mind, the Brahma or Ishvara. Mr. Tesla thinks he can demonstrate mathematically that force and matter are reducible to potential energy. I am to go and see him next week, to get this new mathematical demonstration.

In that case, the Vedantic cosmology will be placed on the surest of foundations. I am working a good deal now upon the cosmology and eschatology[1] of the Vedanta. I clearly see their perfect unison with modern science, and the elucidation of the one will be followed by that of the other. I intend to write a book later on in the form of questions and answers.[2] The first chapter will be on Cosmology, showing the harmony between Vedantic theories and modern science.

Brahman = The Absolute
|
Mahat or Ishvara = Primal Creative Energy
|
Prana and Akasha = Force and Matter

The eschatology will be explained from the Advaitic standpoint only. That is to say, the dualist claims that the soul after death passes on to the Solar sphere, thence to the Lunar sphere, thence to the Electric sphere. Thence he is accompanied by a Purusha to Brahmaloka. (Thence, says the Advaitist, he goes to Nirvana).

Now on the Advaitic side, it is held that the soul neither comes nor goes, and that all these spheres or

---

[1] That is, doctrine of the last things—death, judgment, etc.

[2] This plan was never carried out. But in studying the lectures he delivered in London in the year 1896, it is easy to see that his mind was still working on his ideas here announced.

layers of the universe are only so many varying products of Akasha and Prana. That is to say, the lowest or most condensed is the Solar sphere, consisting of the visible universe, in which Prana appears as physical force, and Akasha as sensible matter. The next is called the Lunar sphere, which surrounds the Solar sphere. This is not the moon at all, but the habitation of the gods, that is to say, Prana appears in it as psychic forces, and Akasha as Tanmâtrâs, or fine particles. Beyond this is the Electric sphere, that is to say, a condition in which Prana is almost inseparable from Akasha, and you can hardly tell whether Electricity is force or matter. Next is the Brahmaloka, where there is neither Prana nor Akasha, but both are merged in the mindstuff, the primal energy. And here—there being neither Prana nor Akasha—the Jiva contemplates the whole universe as Samashti, or the sum total of Mahat or mind. This appears as a Purusha, an abstract universal soul, yet not the Absolute, for still there is multiplicity. From this the Jiva finds at last that Unity which is the end. Advaitism says that these are the visions which rise in succession before the Jiva, who himself neither goes nor comes, and that in the same way this present vision has been projected. The projection (Srishti) and dissolution must take place in the same order, only one means going backward, and the other coming out.

Now as each individual can only see his own universe, that universe is created with his bondage and goes away with his liberation, although it remains for others who are in bondage. Now name and form constitute the universe. A wave in the ocean is a wave only in so far as it is bound by name and form. If the wave subsides, it is the ocean, but that name and form have immediately vanished for ever. So that the name and form of wave could never be without the water that was fashioned into the wave by them, yet the name and form themselves were not the wave. They die as soon as ever it returns to water. But other names and forms live in relation to other waves. This name-and-form is called Mâyâ, and the water is Brahman. The wave was nothing but water all the time, yet as a wave it had the name and form. Again this name and form cannot remain for one moment separated from the wave, although the wave as water can remain eternally separate from name and form. But because the name and form can never be separated, they can never be said to exist. Yet they are not zero. This is called Maya.

I want to work all this out carefully, but you will see at a glance that I am on the right track. It will take more study in physiology, on the relations between the higher and lower centres, to fill out the psychology of mind, Chitta and Buddhi, and so on. But I have clear light now, free of all hocus-pocus. I want to give them dry; hard reason, softened in the sweetest syrup of love and made spicy with intense work, and cooked in the kitchen of Yoga, so that even a baby can easily digest it—Yours with blessings and love, VIVEKANANDA.

(*176*)

To Sj. Alasinga Perumal

17th Feb., 1896.

DEAR ALASINGA—. . . . The work is terribly hard and the more it is growing the harder it is becoming. I need a long rest very badly. Yet a great work is before me in England. . . . Have patience, my son—it will grow beyond all your expectations. . . . Every work has got to pass through hundreds of difficulties before succeeding. Those that persevere will see the light sooner or later. . . .

I have succeeded now in rousing the very heart of the American civilisation, New York. But it has been a terrific struggle. . . . I have spent nearly all I had on this New York work and in England. Now things are in such a shape that they will go on.

To put the Hindu ideas into English and then make out of dry Philosophy and intricate Mythology and queer startling Psychology, a religion which shall be easy, simple, popular and at the same time meet the requirements of the highest minds—is a task only those can understand who have attempted it. The abstract Advaita must become living—poetic—in everyday life; out of hopelessly intricate Mythology must come concrete moral forms; and out of bewildering Yogi-ism must come the most scientific and practical Psychology—and all this must be put in a form so that a child may grasp it. That is my life's work. The Lord only knows how far I shall succeed. To work we have the right, not to the fruits thereof. It is hard work, my boy, hard work! To keep one's self steady in the midst of this whirl of Kâma-Kânchana, and hold on to one's own ideals, until disciples are moulded to conceive of the ideas of realisation and perfect renunciation, is indeed difficult work. Thank God, already there is great success. I cannot blame the missionaries and others for not understanding me—they hardly ever saw a man who did not care about women and money. At first they could not believe it; how could they? You must not think that the Western nations have the same ideas of chastity and purity as the Indians. Their equivalents are virtue and courage. . . . People are now flocking to me. Hundreds have become convinced that there are men who can really control their bodily desires; and reverence and respect for these principles are growing. All things come to him who waits. May you be blessed for ever and ever.—Yours, VIVEKANANDA.

(177)

To Mr. E. T. Sturdy

NEW YORK (?),
17th March, 1896.

. . . I pray you again to think about this publishing business. . . . remembering "Ours is the gospel of the oneness of all beings" and all national feelings are but wicked superstitions. Moreover, I am sure that the person who is always ready to give way to others' opinions finds at last that his opinion has triumphed. Yielding always conquers at last.

(178)

To Swami Trigunatitananda

BOSTON,*
22nd March, 1896.

DEAR SARADA—. . . On perusal of your letter on Thibet, I came to lose all regard for your common sense. In the first place, it is nonsense to say that Notovitch's book is genuine. Did you see any original copy, or bring it to India? Secondly, you say you saw in the Kailas Math the portrait of Jesus and the Samaritan Woman. How do you know that it was Jesus's portrait, and not that of a man in the street? Even taking it for granted, how do you know that it was not put up in the said Math by someone who was a Christian? And your opinions on the Thibetans too are unsound; you did not certainly see the heart of Thibet, but only a fringe of the *trade route*. In places like those only the dregs of a nation are to be met. If on seeing the China-bazar and Barabazar quarters of Calcutta, anybody called every Bengali a liar, would that be correct?

. . . What you need is only obedience. . . .—Yours affectionately, VIVEKANANDA.

(*179*)

To Sj. Alasinga Perumal

BOSTON,
23rd March, 1896.

DEAR ALASINGA—. . . One of my new Sannyasins is indeed a woman. . . . The others are men. I am going to make some more in England and take them over to India with me. These "white" faces will have more influence in India than the Hindus—moreover they are vigorous, the Hindus are *dead.* The only hope of India is from the masses. The upper classes are physically and morally dead. . .

My success is due to my popular style—the greatness of a teacher consists in the simplicity of his language.

. . . I am going to England next month. I am afraid I have worked too much; my nerves are almost shattered by this long continued work. I don't want you to sympathise, but only I write this so that you may not expect much from me now. Work on, the best way you can. I have very little hope of being able to do great things now. I am glad, however, that a good deal of literature has been created by taking down stenographic notes of my lectures. Four books are ready. . . . Well, I am satisfied that I have tried my best to do good, and shall have a clear conscience when I retire from work and sit down in a cave.—With love and blessings to all, VIVEKANANDA.

(*180*)

To the Same

U. S. A.,
March, 1896.

DEAR ALASINGA—. . . Push on with the work. I will do all I can. . . . If it pleases the Lord, yellow-garbed

Sannyasins will be common here and in England. Work on, my children.

Mind, so long you have faith in your Guru, nothing will be able to obstruct your way. That translation of the three Bhâshyas will be a great thing in the eyes of the Westerners.

. . . Wait, my child, wait and work on. Patience, patience. . . . I will burst on the public again in good time. . . .—Yours with love, VIVEKANANDA.

(*181*)

To the Same

U. S. A.,
1896.

DEAR ALASINGA—Last week I wrote you about the *Brahmavadin*. I forgot to write about the Bhakti lectures. They ought to be published in a book all together. A few hundreds may be sent to America to Goodyear in New York. Within twenty days I sail for England. I have other big books on Karma, Jnana and Raja Yogas—the Karma is out already, the Raja will be a very big book and is already in the press. The Jnana will have to be published, I think, in England.

A letter you published from K— in the *Brahmavadin* was rather unfortunate. K— is smarting under the blows the ——s have given him and that sort of letter is vulgar, pitching into everybody. It is not in accord with the tone of the *Brahmavadin*. So in future when K——— writes, tone down everything that is an attack upon any sect, however cranky or crude. Nothing which is against any sect, good or bad, should get into the *Brahmavadin*. Of course, we must not show active sympathy with frauds. Again let me remind you that the paper is too technical to find any subscriber here. The average Western neither knows nor cares to know all about jaw-breaking Sanskrit terms and technicalities. The paper is well fitted for India—that is all that I see. Every word of special pleading should be eliminated from the Editorials, and you must always remember that you are addressing the whole world, not India alone, and that the same world is entirely ignorant of what you have got to tell them. Use the translation of every Sanskrit term carefully and make things as easy as possible.

Before this reaches you I will be in England. So address me C/o E. T. Sturdy, Esq., High View, Caversham, Eng.—Yours etc., VIVEKANANDA.

(*182*)

To Mrs. Ole Bull

INDIAN AVE., CHICAGO, ILL.,
6th April, 1896.

DEAR MRS. BULL—Your kind note was duly received. I had beautiful visits with my friends and have already held several classes. I shall have a few more and then start on Thursday.

Everything has been well arranged here, thanks to the kindness of Miss Addams. She is so, so good and kind.

I am suffering from slight fever the last two days; so I can't write a long letter.

My love to all in Boston.—Yours with kind regards, VIVEKANANDA.

(*183*)

125, E. 44TH STREET, NEW YORK,
14th April, 1896.

DEAR—, . . . Here is a curious person who comes to me with a letter from Bombay. He is a practical mechanic and his one idea is to see cutlery and other iron manufactories in this country. . . . I do not know anything about him, but even if he be a rogue I like very much to foster this sort of adventurous spirit among my countrymen. He has money enough to pay his way.

Now, if after testing his genuineness of spirit you feel satisfied, all he wants is to get some opportunities of seeing these manufactories. I hope he is true and that you can manage to help him in this.—Yours with kind regards, VIVEKANANDA.

(*184*)

To Dr. Nanjunda Rao, M.D.

NEW YORK,
14th April, 1896.

DEAR DOCTOR—, I received your note this morning. As I am sailing for England to-morrow, I can only write a few hearty lines. I have every sympathy with your proposed magazine for boys, and will do my best to help it on. You ought to make it independent, following the same lines as the *Brahmavadin*, only making the style and matter much more popular. As for example, there is a great chance, much more than you ever dream of, for those wonderful stories scattered all over the Sanskrit literature, to be rewritten and made popular. That should be the one great feature of your journal. I will write stories, as many as I can, when time permits. Avoid all attempts to make the journal scholarly—the *Brahmavadin* stands for that—and it will slowly make its way all over the world, I am sure. Use the simplest language possible and you will succeed. The main feature should be the teaching of *principles* through stories. Don't make it metaphysical at all. . . . In India the one thing we lack is the power of combination, organisation, the first secret of which is obedience.

. . . Go on bravely. Do not expect success in a day

or a year. Always hold on to the highest. Be steady. Avoid jealousy and selfishness. Be obedient and eternally faithful to the cause of truth, humanity and your country, and you will move the world. Remember, it is the *person*, the life, which is the secret of power—nothing else. Keep this letter and read the last lines whenever you feel worried or jealous. Jealousy is the bane of all slaves. It is the bane of our nation. Avoid that always. All blessings attend you and all success.—Yours affectionately, VIVEKANANDA.

(185)

To Swami Trigunatitananda

NEW YORK,*
14th April, 1896.

DEAR SARADA—Glad to hear everything in your letter. I have got news that Sarat arrived safe. I am in receipt of your letter and the copy of the *Indian Mirror*. Your contribution is good, go on writing regularly. It is very easy to search for faults, but the characteristic of a saint lies in looking for merits—never forget this. . . . You need a little business faculty. . . . Now what you want is organisation—that requires strict obedience and division of labour. I shall write out everything in every particular from England for which I start to-morrow. I am determined to make you decent workers thoroughly organised. . . .

The term "Friend" can be used with all. In the English language you have not that sort of cringing politeness common in Bengali, and such Bengali terms done into English become ridiculous. That Ramakrishna Paramahamsa was God—and all that sort of thing, has no go in countries like this. M.—has a tendency to put that stuff down everybody's throat, but that will make our movement a little sect. You keep separate from such attempts;

at the same time if people worship him as God, no harm. Neither encourage nor discourage. The masses will always have the *person*, the higher ones, the *principle*. We want both. But principles are universal, *not* persons. Therefore stick to the principles he taught, let people think whatever they like of his person. . . . Truce to all quarrels and jealousies and BIGOTRY! These will spoil everything. "The first should be last." . . . मद्भक्तानाञ्च ये भक्तास्ते मे भक्ततमा मताः —"Those who are the devotees of My devotees are My best devotees."—Yours affectionately, VIVEKANANDA.

(*186*)

HIGH VIEW, CAVERSHAM,*
READING,
27th April, 1896.

DEAR—, . . . Let me write something for you all. It is not for gaining personal authority that I do this, but for your good and for fulfilling the purpose for which the Lord came. He gave me the charge of you all, and you shall contribute to the great well-being of the world—though most of you are not yet aware of it—this is the special reason of my writing to you. It will be a great pity if any feeling of jealousy or egotism gain ground amongst you. Is it possible for those to establish cordial relations on earth who cannot cordially live with one another for any length of time? No doubt it is an evil to be bound by laws, but it is necessary at the immature stage to be guided by rules; in other words, as the Master used to say that the sapling must be hedged round, and so on. Secondly, it is quite natural for idle minds to indulge in gossip and faction-mongering and so forth. Hence I jot down the following hints. If you follow them, you will undoubtedly prosper, but if you don't do so, then there is a danger of all our labours coming to naught.

First let me write about the management of the Math:—

1. For the purposes of the Math please hire a commodious house or garden, where everyone may have a small room to himself. There must be a spacious hall where the books may be kept, and a smaller room for meeting the visitors. If possible, there should be another big hall in the house where every day study of the scriptures and religious discourses will be held for the public.

2. Anyone wishing to visit anybody in the Math should see him only and depart, without troubling others.

3. By turns someone should be present in the hall for a few hours every day for the public, so that they may get satisfactory replies to what they come to ask.

4. Everyone must keep to his room and except on special business must not go to others' rooms. Anyone who wishes may go to the Library and read, but it should be strictly forbidden to smoke there or talk with others. The reading should be silent.

5. It shall be wholly forbidden to huddle together in a room and chat the whole day away, with any number of outsiders coming and joining in the hubbub.

6. Only those that are seekers after religion may come and peacefully wait in the Visitors' Hall, and when they have seen the particular persons they want, they should depart. Or, if they have any general question to ask, they should refer to the person in charge of that function for the day, and leave.

7. Tale-bearing, caballing or reporting scandals about others should be altogether eschewed.

8. A small room should serve as the office. The Secretary should live in that room, which should contain paper, ink and other materials for letter-writing. He should keep an account of the income and expenditure. All correspondence should come to him and he should

deliver all letters *unopened* to their addressees. Books and pamphlets should be sent to the Library.

9. There will be a small room for smoking, which should not be indulged in outside this room.

10. He who wants to indulge in invectives or show temper must do so outside the boundaries of the Math. This should not be deviated from even by an inch.

The Governing Body

1. Every year a President should be elected by a majority of votes. The next year, another, and so on.

2. For this year make Rakhal the President and likewise make another the Secretary, and elect a third man for superintending the worship etc., as well as the arrangement of food.

3. The Secretary shall have another function, viz., to keep watch over the general health. Regarding this I have three instructions to give:

(*i*) In every room for each man there shall be a *nair* charpoy and mattress etc. Everyone must keep his room clean.

(*ii*) All arrangements must be made to provide clear and pure water for drinking and cooking purposes, for it is a deadly sin to cook sacramental food in impure or unclean water.

(*iii*) Give everyone two ochre cloaks of the type that you have made for Sarat, and see that clothing is kept clean.

4. Anyone wishing to be a Sannyasin should be admitted as a Brahmacharin first. He should live one year at the Math and one year outside, after which he may be initiated into Sannyasa.

5. Make over charge of the worship to one of these Brahmacharins, and change them now and then.

Departments

There shall be the following departments in the Math: I. *Study*. II. *Propaganda*. III. *Religious Practice*.

I. *Study*.—The object of this department is to provide books and teachers for those who want to study. Every morning and evening the teachers should be ready for them.

II. *Propaganda*.—Within the Math, and abroad. The preachers in the Math should teach the enquirers by reading out scriptures to them and by means of question-classes. The preachers abroad will preach from village to village and try to start Maths like the above in different places.

III. *Religious Practice*.—This department will try to provide those who want to practise with the requisites for this. But it should not be allowed that because one has taken to religious practice he will prevent others from study or preaching. Anyone infringing this rule shall be immediately asked to clear out, and this is imperative.

The preachers at home should give lessons on Devotion, Knowledge, Yoga and Work by turns; for this, the days and hours should be fixed, and the routine hung up at the door of the class-room. That is to say, a seeker after devotion may not present himself on the day fixed for knowledge and feel wounded thereby; and so on.

None of you are fit for the Vâmâchâra form of practice. Therefore this should on no account be practised at the Math. Anyone demurring to this must step out of this Order. This form of practice must never even be mentioned in the Math. Ruin shall seize the wicked man, both here and hereafter, who would introduce vile Vâmâchâra into His fold!

SOME GENERAL REMARKS

1. If any woman comes to have a talk with a Sannyasin, she should do it in the Visitors' Hall. No woman shall be allowed to enter any other room—except the Worship-room.

2. No Sannyasin shall be allowed to reside in the Women's Math. Anyone refusing to obey this rule shall be expelled from the Math. "Better an empty fold than a wicked herd."

3. Men of evil character shall be rigoroulsy kept out. On no pretence shall their shadow even cross the threshold of my room. If anyone amongst you become wicked, turn him out at once, whoever he be. We want no black sheep. The Lord will bring lots of good people.

4. Any woman can come to the class-room (or preaching hall) during class time or preaching hour, but must leave the place directly when that period is over.

5. Never show temper or harbour jealousy, or backbite another in secret. It would be the height of cruelty and hard-heartedness to take note of others' shortcomings instead of rectifying one's own.

6. There should be fixed hours for meals. Everyone must have a seat and a low dining table. He will sit on the former and put his plate on the latter, as is the custom in Rajputana.

THE OFFICE-BEARERS

All the office-bearers you should elect by ballot, as was the mandate of Lord Buddha. That is to say, one should propose that such and such should be the President this year; and all should write on bits of paper "yes" or "no" and put them in a pitcher. If the

" yeas " have a majority, he should be elected President, and so on. Though you should elect office-bearers in this way, yet I suggest that this year Rakhal should be President, Tulsi Secretary and Treasurer, Gupta Librarian, and Sasi, Kali, Hari and Sarada should take charge of the teaching and preaching work by turns, and so on.

It is no doubt a good idea that Sarada has of starting a magazine. But I shall consent to it if only you can work it jointly.

About doctrines and so forth I have to say only this, that if anyone accepts Paramahamsa Deva as Avatara etc., it is all right; if he doesn't do so, it is just the same. The truth about it is that in point of character, Paramahamsa Deva beats all previous record, and as regards teaching, he was more liberal, more original and more progressive than all his predecessors. In other words, the older Teachers were rather one-sided, while the teaching of this new Incarnation or Teacher is that the best point of Yoga, Devotion, Knowledge and Work must be combined now so as to form a new society. . . . The older ones were no doubt good, but this is the new religion of this age—the synthesis of Yoga, Knowledge, Devotion and Work—the propagation of Knowledge and Devotion to all, down to the very lowest, without distinction of age or sex. The previous Incarnations were all right, but they have been synthesised in the person of Ramakrishna. For the ordinary man and the beginner, steady devotion (Nishthâ) to an ideal is of paramount importance. That is to say, teach them that all great Personalities should be duly honoured, but homage should be paid now to Ramakrishna. There can be no vigour without steady devotion. Without it one cannot preach with the intensity of a Mahavira (Hanuman). Besides, the previous ones have become rather old. Now we have a new India, with its new God, new religion and new

Vedas. When, O Lord, shall our land be free from this eternal dwelling upon the past? Well, a little bigotry also is a necessity. But we must harbour no antagonistic feelings towards others.

If you consider it wise to be guided by my ideas and if you follow these rules, then I shall supply you all necessary funds. . . . Moreover, please show this letter to Gaur Ma, Jogen Ma, etc., and through them establish a Women's Math. Let Gaur Ma be the President there for one year, and so on. But none of you shall be allowed to visit the place. They will manage their own affairs. They will not have to work at your dictation. I shall supply all necessary expenses for that work also.

May the Lord guide you in the right direction! Two persons went to see the Lord Jagannath. One of them beheld the Deity, while the other saw some trash that was haunting his mind!

My friends, many have no doubt served the Master, but whenever anyone would be disposed to consider himself an extraordinary personage, he should think that although he has associated with Sri Ramakrishna, he has seen only the trash that was uppermost in his mind! Were it not so, he would manifest the results. The Master himself used to quote, "They would sing and dance in the name of the Lord but come to grief in the end." The root of this degeneration is egotism—to think that one is just as great as any other. Indeed! "He used to love me, too!"—one would plead. Alas, Nick Bottom, would you then be thus translated? Would such a man envy or quarrel with another and degrade himself? Bear in mind that through HIS grace lots of men will be turned out with the nobility of gods—aye, wherever HIS mercy would drop. . . . Obedience is the first duty. Well, just do with alacrity what I ask you to. Let me see how you carry out these few small things. Then gradually great things will come to pass.—Yours, VIVEKANANDA.

P. S. Please read the contents of this letter to all, and let me know whether you consider the suggestions worth carrying out. Please tell Rakhal that he who is the servant of all is their true master. He never becomes a leader in whose love there is a consideration of high or low. He whose love knows no end, and never stops to consider high or low, has the whole world lying at his feet.—V.

(*187*)

63, St. George's Road, London,
May, 1896.

Dear Sister—In London once more. The climate now in England is nice and cool. We have fire in the grate. We have a whole house to ourselves, you know, this time. It is small but convenient, and in London they do not cost so much as in America. Don't you know what I was thinking about your mother? I just wrote her a letter and duly posted it to her, care of Monroe & Co., 7, Rue Scribe, Paris. Some old friends are here, and Miss MacLeod came over from the Continent. She is good as gold, and as kind as ever. We have a nice little family, in the house, with another monk from India. Poor man! —a typical Hindu with nothing of that pluck and go which I have, he is always dreamy and gentle and sweet! That won't do. I will try to put a little activity into him. I have had two classes already—they will go on for four or five months and after that to India I go. But it is to Amerique—there where the heart is. I love the Yankee land. I like to see new things. I do not care a fig to loaf about old ruins and mope a life out about old histories and keep sighing about the ancients. I have too much vigour in my blood for that. In America is the place, the people, the opportunity for everything. I have become horribly radical. I am just going to India to see what I can do in that awful mass of conservative jelly-fish, and start a new thing, entirely new—simple, strong, new and fresh as the first-born baby. The eternal, the infinite, the omnipresent, the omniscient, is a principle, not a person. You, I and everyone are but embodiments of that principle and the more of this infinite principle is embodied in a person, the greater is he, and all in the end will be the perfect embodiment of that and thus all will be one, as they are now essentially. This is all there is of religion, and the practice is through this feeling of oneness that is love. All old fogey forms are mere old superstitions. Now, why struggle to keep them alive? Why give thirsty people ditch water to drink whilst the river of life and truth flows by? This is only human selfishness, nothing else. Life is short—time is flying—that place and people where one's ideas work best should be the country and the people for everyone. Aye for a dozen bold hearts, large, noble and sincere!

I am very well indeed and enjoying life immensely.—Yours ever with love, VIVEKANANDA.

(188)

To Miss Mary Hale

63, ST. GEORGE'S ROAD,
LONDON, S. W.,
30th May, 1896.

DEAR MARY—. . . Day before yesterday I had a fine visit with Prof. Max Müller. He is a saintly man and looks like a young man in spite of his seventy years, and his face is without a wrinkle. I wish I had half his love for India and the Vedanta. At the same time he is a friend of Yoga too and believes in it. Only he has no patience with humbugs.

Above all, his reverence for Ramakrishna Paramahamsa is extreme, and he has written an article on him in the *Nineteenth Century*. He asked me, "What are you doing to make him known to the world?" Ramakrishna has charmed him for years. Is it not good news?. . .

Things are going on here slowly but steadily. I am to begin from next Sunday my public lectures.—Yours ever in grateful affection, VIVEKANANDA.

(*189*)

To the Same

63, ST. GEORGE'S ROAD,
LONDON, S. W.,
30th May, 1896.

DEAR MARY—Your letter reached just now. Of course you were not jealous but all of a sudden were inspired with sympathy for poor India. Well, you need not be frightened. Wrote a letter to mother Church weeks ago, but have not been able to get a line from her yet. I am afraid the whole party have taken orders and entered a Catholic convent—four old maids are enough to drive any mother to a convent. I had a beautiful visit with Prof. Max Müller. He is a saint—a Vedantist through and through. What think you? He has been a devoted admirer of my old Master for years. He has written an article on my Master in the *Nineteenth Century*, which will soon come out. We had long talks on Indian things. I wish I had half his love for India. We are going to start another little magazine here. What about the *Brahmavadin*? Are you pushing it? If four pushful old maids cannot push a journal I am blowed. You will hear from me now and then. I am not a pin to be lost under a bushel. I am having classes here just now. I begin Sunday lectures from next week. The classes are very big and are in the house. We have rented it for the season. Last night I made a dish. It was such a delicious mixture of saffron, lavender, mace, nutmeg, cubebs, cinnamon, cloves, cardamom, cream, limejuice, onions, raisins, almonds, pepper and rice, that I myself could not eat it. There was no asafœtida, though that would have made it smoother to swallow.

Yesterday I went to a marriage *a la mode*. Miss Müller, a rich lady, a friend who has adopted a Hindu boy and to help my work has taken rooms in this house, took us to see it. One of her nieces was married to somebody's nephew I suppose. What tiring nonsense! I am glad you do not marry. Good-bye, love to all. No more time as I am going to lunch with Miss MacLeod.—Yours ever affly., VIVEKANANDA.

(*190*)

63, ST. GEORGE'S ROAD,
LONDON, S. W.,
5th June, 1896.

DEAR—, The Raja-Yoga book is going on splendidly. Saradananda goes to the States soon.

I do not like any one of my blood to become a lawyer, although my father was one. My Master was against it, and I believe that that family is sure to come to grief where there are several lawyers. Our country is full of them; the universities turn them out by the hundreds. What the nation wants is pluck and scientific genius. So I want M—to be an electrician. Even if he fails in life still I will have the satisfaction that he strove to become great and really useful to his country. . . . In *America alone* there is that something in the air which brings out whatever is best in every one. . . . I want him to be daring, bold, and to struggle to cut a new path for himself and his nation. An electrical engineer can make a living in India.

P.S. Goodwin is writing to you this mail with reference to a magazine in America. I think something of the sort is necessary to keep the work together, and shall of course do all that I can to help it on in the line he suggests. . . . I think it very probable that he will come over with Saradananda.—Yours with love, VIVEKANANDA.

(*191*)

To Sister Nivedita

63, ST. GEORGE'S ROAD, LONDON,
7th June, 1896.

DEAR MISS NOBLE—My ideal indeed can be put into a few words and that is: to preach unto mankind their divinity, and how to make it manifest in every movement of life.

This world is in chains of superstition. I pity the oppressed, whether man or woman, and I pity more the oppressors.

One idea that I see clear as daylight is that misery is caused by *ignorance* and nothing else. Who will give the world light? Sacrifice in the past has been the Law, it will be, alas, for ages to come. The earth's bravest and best will have to sacrifice themselves for the good of many, for the welfare of all. Buddhas by the hundred are necessary with eternal love and pity.

Religions of the world have become lifeless mockeries. What the world wants is character. The world is in need of those whose life is one burning love, selfless. That love will make every word tell like thunderbolt.

It is no superstition with you, I am sure, you have the making in you of a world-mover, and others will also come. Bold words and bolder deeds are what we want. Awake, awake, great one! The world is burning with misery. Can you sleep? Let us call and call till the sleeping gods awake, till the god within answers to the call. What more is in life? What greater work? The details come to me as I go. I never make plans. Plans grow and work themselves. I only say, awake, awake!

May all blessings attend you for ever!—Yours affectionately, VIVEKANANDA.

(*192*)

To Swami Ramakrishnananda

LONDON,
63, ST. GEORGE'S ROAD, S. W.,
24th June, 1896.

DEAR SASI—. . . Max Müller wants all the sayings of Sri Ramakrishna classified, that is, all on Karma in one place, on Vairâgya in another place, so on Bhakti, Jnana etc., etc. You must undertake to do this forthwith. . . . We must take care to present only the universal aspect of his teachings. . . .

Sarat starts for America to-morrow. The work here is coming to a head. We have already got funds to start a London Centre. Next month I go to Switzerland to pass a month or two there, then I shall return to London. What will be the good of my going home—this London is the hub of the world. The heart of India is here. How can I leave without laying a sure foundation here? Nonesense! For the present, I shall have Kali here, tell him to be ready. . . .

We want great spirit, tremendous energy and boundless enthusiasm, no womanishness will do. Try to go on exactly as I wrote you to, in my last. We want organisation. Organisation is power, and the secret of that is obedience.—Yours affectionately, VIVEKANANDA.

(*193*)

To the same

HIGH VIEW, CAVERSHAM,
READING,
3rd July, 1896.

DEAR SASI—, Send Kali (Abhedananda) to England as soon as you get this letter. . . . He will have to bring some books for me. I have only got Rigveda Samhitâ. Ask him to bring the Yajurveda, Sâmaveda, Atharva Samhita, as many of the Brâhmanas as he can get, beginning with the Shatapatha, some of the Sutras, and Yâska's Nirukta. . . .

Let there be no delay as in Sarat's case, but let Abhedananda come at once. Sarat has gone to America, as he had no work to do here. That is to say, he came here several months too late, when I was here. . . .—Yours affectionately, VIVEKANANDA.

(*194*)

To Mr. Francis Leggett

63, ST. GEORGE'S ROAD,
LONDON, S. W.,
6th July, 1896.

DEAR FRANKINCENSE—. . . Things are going on with me very well on this side of the Atlantic.

The Sunday lectures were quite successful, so were the classes. The season has ended, and I too am thoroughly exhausted. I am going to make a tour in Switzerland with Miss Müller. The Galsworthys have been very very kind. Joe brought them round splendidly. I simply admire Joe in her tact and quiet way. She is a feminine statesman or woman. She can wield a kingdom. I have seldom seen such strong yet good common sense in a human being. I will return next autumn and take up the work in America.

The night before last I was at a party at Mrs. Martin's about whom you must already know a good deal from Joe.

Well, the work is growing silently yet surely in England. Almost every other man or woman came to me and talked about the work. This British Empire with all its drawbacks is the greatest machine that ever existed for the dissemination of ideas. I mean to put my ideas in the centre of this machine, and they will spread all over the world. Of course, all great work is slow and the difficulties are too many, especially as we Hindus are the conquered race. Yet, that is the very reason why it is bound to work, for spiritual ideals have always come from the downtrodden. Jews overwhelmed the Roman Empire with their spiritual ideals. You will be pleased to know that I am also learning my lessons every day in patience and, above all, in sympathy. I think I am beginning to see the Divine, even inside the high and mighty Anglo-Indians. I think I am slowly approaching to that state when I would be able to love the very "Devil" himself, if there were any.

At twenty years of age I was the most unsympathetic, uncompromising fanatic; I would not walk on the footpath on the theatre side of the streets in Calcutta. At thirty-three, I can live in the same house with prostitutes and never would think of saying a word of reproach to them. Is it degenerate? Or is it that I am broadening out into the Universal Love which is the Lord Himself? Again, I have heard that if one does not see the evil round him, he cannot do good work—he lapses into a sort of fatalism. I do not see that. On the other hand, my power of work is immensely increasing and becoming immensely effective. Some days I get into a sort of ecstasy. I feel that I must bless every one, everything, love and embrace everything, and I do see that evil is a delusion. I am in one of these moods now, dear Francis, and am actually shedding tears of joy at the thought of your and Mrs. Leggett's love and kindness to me. I bless the day I was born. I have had so much of kindness and love here, and that Love Infinite that brought me into being has guarded every one of my actions good or bad (don't be frightened), for what am I, what was I ever, but a tool in His hands? —for whose service I have given up everything, my beloved ones, my joys, my life. He is my playful darling, I am His playfellow. There is neither rhyme nor reason in the Universe! What reason binds Him? He the playful one is playing these tears and laughter over all parts of the play! Great fun, great fun, as Joe says.

It is funny world, and the funniest chap you ever saw is He—the Beloved-Infinite! Fun, is it not? Brotherhood or playmatehood—a school of romping children let out to play in this playground of the world! Isn't it? Whom to praise, whom to blame, it is all His play. They want explanations, but how can you explain Him? He is brainless, nor has He any reason. He is fooling us with little brains and reason, but this time He won't find me napping.

I have learnt a thing or two: Beyond, beyond reason and learning and talking is the feeling, the "Love," the "Beloved." Aye, *Sake* fill up the cup and we will be mad. —Yours ever in madness, VIVEKANANDA.

(*195*)

63, ST. GEORGE'S ROAD,
LONDON, S. W.,
8th July, 1896.

DEAR—, The English peoole are very generous. In three minutes' time the other evening my class raised £150 for the new quarters for next autumn's work. They would have given £500 on the spot if wanted, but we want to go slow, and not rush into expense. There will be many hands here to carry on the work and they understand a bit of renunciation here—the deep English character.—Yours with best wishes, VIVEKANANDA.

(*196*)

To Dr. Nanjunda Rao, M.D.

ENGLAND,
14th July, 1896.

DEAR NANJUNDA RAO—. . . After all, no foreigner will ever write the English language as well as the native Englishman, and the ideas, when put in good English, will spread farther than in Hindu English. Then again it is much more difficult to write a story in a foreign language than an essay. . . .

You must not depend on any *foreign help*. Nations, like individuals, must help themselves. This is real patriotism. If a nation cannot do that, its time has not yet come. It must wait. . . . The new light must spread all over India. With this end you must work. . . .

The lotus is a symbol of regeneration. We are awfully behindhand in art, especially in that of painting. For instance, make a small scene of spring re-awakening in a forest, showing how the leaves and buds are coming again. Slowly go on, there are hundreds of ideas to be put forward. . . .

I am going to Switzerland next Sunday, and shall return to London in the autumn and take up the work again. . . . I want rest very badly, you know.—With all blessings etc., Yours, VIVEKANANDA.

(*197*)

SANS-GRUND, SWITZERLAND,
25th July, 1896.

DEAR—, I want to forget the world entirely at least for the next two months and practise hard. That is my rest. . . . The mountains and snow have a beautifully quieting influence on me, and I am getting better sleep here than for a long time.

My love to all friends.—Yours etc., VIVEKANANDA.

(*198*)

To Mr. E. T. Sturdy

GRAND HOTEL,
VALAI,
SWITZERLAND.

I am reading a little, starving a good deal, and practising a good deal more. The strolls in the woods are simply delicious. We are now situated under three huge glaciers, and the scenery is very beautiful.

By-the-bye, whatever scruples I may have had as to the Swiss-lake origin of the Aryans, have been taken clean off my mind. The Swiss is a Tartar *minus* a pigtail.

(*199*)

To Sj. Lala Badri Sah

C/O E. T. STURDY, ESQ.,
HIGH VIEW, CAVERSHAM,
5th August, 1896.

DEAR SAHJI—Many thanks for your kind greetings.

I have an inquiry to make; if you kindly forward me the information I seek I would be much obliged.

I want to start a Math in Almora or near Almora rather. I have heard that there was a certain Mr. Ramsay who lived in a bungalow near Almora and that he had a garden round his bungalow. Can't it be bought? What is the price? If not to be bought can it be rented?

Do you know of any suitable place near Almora where I can build my monastery with garden etc? I would rather like to have a hill all to myself.

Hoping to get an early reply, I remain with blessings and love to you and all the rest of our friends in Almora.
—VIVEKANANDA.

(*200*)

To Mr. E. T. Sturdy

SWITZERLAND,
5th August, 1896.

A letter came this morning from Prof. Max Müller telling me that the article on Sri Ramakrishna Paramahamsa has been published in the XIX Century August number. Have you read it? He asked my opinion about it. I not having yet seen it, can't write anything to him. If you have it, kindly send it to me. Also the *Brahmavadin*, if any have arrived. Max Müller wants to know about our plans. . . . and again about the magazine. He promises a good deal of help and is ready to write a book on Sri Ramakrishna Paramahamsa.

I think it is better that you should directly correspond with him about the magazine etc. You will see from his letter which I shall send you as soon as I have replied (after reading the XIX Century) that he is very much pleased with our movement, and is ready to help it as much as he can. . . .

P. S. I hope you will consider well the plan for the big magazine. Some money can be raised in America and we can keep the magazine all to ourselves at the same time. I intend to write to America on hearing about the plan you and Prof. Max Müller decide upon. "A great tree is to be taken refuge in, when it has both fruits and shade. If, however, we do not get the fruit who prevents our enjoyment of the shade?" So ought great attempts to be made, is the moral.

(*201*)

To Sj. Alasinga Perumal

SWITZERLAND,
6th August, 1896.

DEAR ALASINGA—. . . . Do not be afraid. Great things are going to be done, my child. Take heart. . .

He (Max Müller) writes me very nice letters, and wants material for a big book on Ramakrishna's life. . . .

Enough of this newspaper blazoning. I am tired of it, anyhow. Let us go our own way and let fools talk. Nothing can resist truth.

I am, as you see, now in Switzerland, and am always on the move. I cannot and must not do anything in the way of writing, nor much reading either. There is a big London work waiting for me from next month. In winter I am going back to India and will try to set things on their feet there.

My love to all. Work on, brave hearts, fail not—no saying nay; work on—the Lord is behind the work. *Mahâshakti* is with you.—Yours with love and blessings,
VIVEKANANDA.

(202)

To the same

SWITZERLAND,
8th August, 1896.

DEAR ALASINGA—. . . Several things are necessary. First, there should be strict integrity, not that I even hint that any of you would digress from it, but Hindus have a peculiar slovenliness in business matters, not being sufficiently methodical and strict in keeping accounts etc.

Secondly, entire devotion to the cause, knowing that your *Salvation* depends upon making the *Brahmavadin* a success. Let this paper be your Ishtadevatâ and then you will see how success comes. I have already sent for Abhedananda from India. . . . Remember that perfect purity and disinterested obedience to the Guru are the secret of all success. . . .

A big foreign circulation of a religious paper is impossible. It must be supported by the Hindus, if they have any sense of virtue or gratitude left to them.

The ideal of the paper, apart from the preaching of Vedanta, should be to make it a magazine of Indian research and scholarship, of course, bearing on religion.

By-the-bye, Mrs. Annie Besant invited me to speak at her Lodge, on Bhakti. I lectured there one night. Col. Olcott was also there. I did it to show my sympathy for all sects. . . . Our countrymen must remember that in things of the Spirit we are the teachers, and no foreigners —but in things of the world we ought to learn from them.

I read Max Müller's article which is a good one, considering that when he wrote it, six months ago, he had no materials except Mazumdar's leaflet. Now he writes me a long and nice letter offering to write a book on Sri Ramakrishna. I have already supplied him with much material, but a good deal more is needed from India.

Work on! Hold on! Be brave! Dare anything and everything!

It is all misery, this Samsâra, don't you see!—Yours with blessings and love, VIVEKANANDA.

(*203*)

To Mr. J. J. Goodwin

SWITZERLAND,
8th August, 1896.

I am now taking rest. I read from different letters a lot about Kripananda. I am sorry for him. There must be something wrong in his head. Let him alone. None of you need bother about him.

As for hurting me, that is not in the power of Gods or devils. So be at rest. It is unswerving love and perfect unselfishness that conquer everything. We Vedantists in every difficulty ought to ask the subjective questions, "Why do I see that?" "Why can I not conquer this with love?"

I am very glad at the reception the Swami has met with, also at the good work he is doing. Great work requires great and persistent effort for a long time. Neither need we trouble ourselves if a few fail. It is in the nature of things that many should fall, that troubles should come, that tremendous difficulties should arise, that selfishness and all the other devils in the human heart should struggle hard, when they are about to be driven out by the fire of spirituality. The road to Good is the roughest and steepest in the universe. It is a wonder that so many succeed, no wonder that so many fall. Character has to be established through a thousand stumbles.

I am much refreshed now. I look out of the window and see the huge glaciers just before me and feel that I am in the Himalayas. I am quite calm. My nerves have regained their accustomed strength; and little vexations like those you write of, do not touch me at all. How shall I be disturbed by this child's play? The whole world is mere child's play—preaching, teaching, and all included. "Know him to be the Sannyasin, who neither hates nor desires." And what is there to be desired in this little mud-puddle of a world, with its ever-recurring misery, disease and death? "He who has given up all deires, he alone is happy."

This rest, eternal, peaceful rest, I am catching a glimpse of now in this beautiful spot. "Having once known that the Atman alone, and nothing else, exists, desiring what, or for whose desire, shall you suffer misery about the body?"

I feel as if I had my share of experience, in what they call "work." I am finished, I am longing now to get out. "Out of thousands, but one strives to attain the Goal. And even of those who struggle hard, but few attain; for the senses are powerful, they drag men down."

"A good world," "a happy world," and "social progress," are all terms equally intelligible with "hot ice" or "dark light." If it were good, it would not be the world. The soul foolishly thinks of manifesting the Infinite in finite matter, Intelligence through gross particles; but at last it finds out its error and tries to escape. This going-back is the beginning of religion, and its method, destruction of self, that is, love. Not love for wife or child or anybody else, but love for everything else except this little self. Never be deluded by the tall talk, of which you will hear so much in America, about "human progress" and such stuff. There is *no progress* without corresponding digression. In one society there is one set of evils, in another, another. So with periods of history. In the Middle Ages, there were more robbers, now more cheats. At one period there is less idea of married life, at another more prostitution. In one, more physical agony, in another, a thousandfold more mental. So with knowledge. Did not gravitation already exist in Nature before it was observed and named? Then what difference does it make to know that it exists? Are you happier than the Red Indians?

The only knowledge that is of any value is to know that all this is humbug. But few, very few, will ever know this. "Know the Atman alone, and give up all other vain words." This is the only knowledge we gain from all this knocking about the universe. This is the only work, to call upon mankind to "Awake, arise, and stop not till the goal is reached." It is renunciation, Tyâga, that is meant by religion, and nothing else.

Ishvara is the sum total of individuals, yet He Himself also is an individual in the same way as the human body is a unit, of which each cell is an individual. Samashti, or the Collective, is God. Vyashti, or the component, is the soul or Jiva. The existence of Ishvara, therefore, depends on that of Jiva, as the body on the cell, and vice versa. Jiva and Ishvara are co-existent beings. As long as the one exists, the other must also. Again, since in all the higher spheres, except on our earth, the amount of good is vastly in excess of the amount of bad, the sum total, or Ishvara, may be said to be All-good, Almighty and Omniscient. These are obvious qualities, and need no argument to prove, from the very fact of totality.

Brahman is beyond both of these, and is not a state. It is the only unit not composed of many units. It is the principle which runs through all, from a cell to God, and without which nothing can exist. Whatever is real, is that principle, or Brahman. When I think "I am Brahman," then I alone exist. It is so also when *you* so think, and so on. Each one is the whole of that principle. . . .

A few days ago, I felt a sudden irresistible desire to write to Kripananda. Perhaps he was unhappy and thinking of me. So I wrote him a warm letter. To-day from the American news, I see why it was so. I sent him flowers gathered near the glaciers. Ask Miss Waldo to send him some money and plenty of love. Love never dies. The love of the father never dies, whatever the children may do or be. He is my child. He has the same or more share in my love and help, now that he is in misery.—Yours with blessings, VIVEKANANDA.

(*204*)

To Mr. E. T. Sturdy

SWITZERLAND,
12th August, 1896.

(A letter about Swami Abhedananda's start and Swami Saradananda's success).

" America is a good training ground to bring out all that is in a man. There is such a sympathy in the air!"

(*205*)

LUCERNE, SWITZERLAND,
23rd August, 1896.

DEAR—, . . . I am very glad to hear that Saradananda and Goodwin are doing good work in the U. S. . . . I have sent for another man from India who will join me next month. I have begun the work, let others work it out. So you see, to set the work going I had to touch money and property, for a time. Now I am sure my part of the work *is* done and I have no more interest in Vedanta or any philosophy in the world or the work itself. I am getting ready to depart to return no more to this hell, this world.

Even its religious utility is beginning to pall me. May Mother gather me soon to Herself never to come back any more!

I do not want to have anything to do with money matters from this time—spend what comes to you just as you like and all blessings follow you.—Yours Sincerely, VIVEKANANDA.

P.S. . . . It was an awful mistake in the Greenacre programme that it was printed that Saradananda was there by the kind permission (leave of absence from England) of Mr. Sturdy. Who is Mr. Sturdy or anybody else to *permit* a Sannyasin?. . . I am no master to any Sannyasin in this world. They do whatever it suits them and if I can help them—that is all my connection with them. I have given up the bondage of iron, the family tie—I am not to take up the golden chain of religious brotherhood. I am free, must always be free. And I wish everyone to be free—free as the air. If New York or Boston or any other place in the U. S. needs Vedanta teachers, they must receive them and keep them and provide for them. As for me I am as good as retired. I have played my part in the world.

(*206*)

LAKE LUCERNE, SWITZERLAND,*
23rd August, 1896.

MY DEAR—, To-day I received a letter from Ramdayal Babu, in which he writes that many public women attend the Sri Ramakrishna Anniversary Festival at Dakshineswar, which makes many less inclined to go there. Moreover, in his opinion, one day should be appointed for men and another for women. My decision on the point is this:—

1. If public women are not allowed to go to such a great place of pilgrimage as Dakshineswar where else shall they go to? It is for the sinful that the Lord manifests Himself specially, not so much for the virtuous.

2. Let distinctions of sex, caste, wealth, learning

and the whole host of them which are so many gateways to hell, be confined to the world alone. If such distinctions persist in holy places of pilgrimage, where then lies the difference between them and hell itself?

3. Ours is a gigantic City of Jagannath, where those who have sinned and those who have not, the saintly and the vicious, men and women and children, irrespective of age, all have equal rights. That for one day at least in the year thousands of men and women get rid of the sense of sin and ideas of distinction and sing and hear the name of the Lord, is in itself a supreme good.

4. If even in a place of pilgrimage people's tendency to evil be not curbed for one day, the fault lies with you, not them. Create such a huge tidal wave of spirituality that whatever people come near will be swept away.

5. Those who, even in a chapel, would think this is a public woman, that man is of a low caste, a third is poor, and yet another belongs to the masses—the less be the number of such people (whom you call gentlemen, that is), the better. Will they who look to the caste, sex or profession of Bhaktas appreciate our Lord? I pray to the Lord that hundreds of public women may come and bow their heads to His feet, it does not matter if not one gentleman comes. Come public women, come drunkards, come thieves and all—His Gate is opened to all. "It is easier for a camel to pass through the eye of a needle than for a rich man to enter the Kingdom of God." Never let such cruel, demoniacal ideas have a place in your mind.

6. But then some social vigilance is needed—how are we to do that? A few men (old men, preferably) should take charge as the warders for the day. They will make circuits round the scene of the festival and in case they find any man or woman engaged in impropriety of speech or conduct, they will at once expel them out of the garden. But so long as they behave like good men and

women, they are Bhaktas and are to be respected—be they men or women, honest citizens or unchaste.

I am at present travelling in Switzerland, and shall soon go to Germany, to see Professor Deussen. I shall return to England from there about the 23rd or 24th September, and the next winter will find me back in my country.

My love to you and all.—Yours etc., VIVEKANANDA.

(207)

To Dr. Nanjunda Rao, M.D.

SWITZERLAND,
26th August, 1896.

DEAR NANJUNDA RAO—I have just now got your letter. I am on the move. I have been doing a great deal of mountain-climbing and glacier-crossing in the Alps. Now I am going to Germany. I have an invitation from Prof. Deussen to visit him at Kiel. From thence I go back to England. Possibly I will return to India this winter.

What I objected to the design for—was not only its tawdriness, but the crowding in of a number of figures without any purpose. A design should be simple, symbolical and condensed. . . .

The work is going on beautifully, I am very glad to say.

. . . I will give you one advice however. All combined efforts in India sink under the weight of one iniquity, we have not yet developed strict business principles. Business is business in the highest sense, and no friendship—or as the Hindu proverb says "eye-shame"—should be there. One should keep the clearest account of everything in his charge—and never, never apply the funds of—to any other use whatsoever—even if one starves the next moment. This is business integrity. Next, energy unfailing. Whatever you do let that be your worship for the time. Let this paper be your God for the time, and you will succeed.

When you have succeeded in this paper, start vernacular ones on the same lines in Tamil, Telugu, Canarese, etc. The Madrasis are good, energetic, and all that, but the land of Shankaracharya has lost the spirit of renunciation, it seems.

My children must plunge into the breach, must renounce the world—then the firm foundation will be laid.

Go on bravely—never mind about designs and other details at present—"With the horse will come the reins." Work on unto death—I am with you, and when I am gone, my spirit will work with you. This life comes and goes—wealth, fame, enjoyments are only of a few days. It is better, far better to die on the field of duty, preaching the truth, than to die like a worldly worm. Advance! —Yours with love and blessings, VIVEKANANDA.

(208)

To a Western disciple

SWITZERLAND,
August, 1896.

Be you holy and above all, sincere and do not for a moment give up your trust in the Lord and you will see the light. Whatever is truth will remain for ever; whatever not, none can preserve. We are helped in being born in a time when everything is quickly searched out. Whatever others think or do, lower not your standard of purity, morality and love of God; above all, beware of all secret organisations. No one who loves God need fear any jugglery. Holiness is the highest and divinest power in earth and in heaven. "Truth alone triumphs, not untruth. Through truth alone is opened the way to God." Do not care for a moment who joins hands with you or not, be sure that you touch the hand of the Lord. That is enough. . . .

I went to the glacier of Monte Rosa yesterday and gathered a few hardy flowers growing almost in the midst of eternal snow. I send you one in this letter hoping that you will attain to a similar spiritual hardihood amidst all the snow and ice of this earthly life. . . .

Your dream was very, very beautiful. In dream our souls read a layer of our mind which we do not read in our waking hours, and however unsubstantial imagination may be, it is behind the imagination that all unknown psychic truths lie. Take heart. We will try to do what we can for the good of humanity—the rest depends upon the Lord. . . .

Well, do not be anxious, do not be in a hurry. Slow, persistent and silent work does everything. The Lord is great. We will succeed, my boy. We must. Blessed be His name ! . . .

Here in America are no Ashramas. Would there was one ! How would I like it and what an amount of good it would do to this country !

(*209*)

To Mr. E. T. Sturdy

KIEL,
10th Sept., 1896.

I have at last seen Prof. Deussen. . . the whole of yesterday was spent very nicely with the Professor, sight-seeing and discussing about the Vedanta.

He is what I should call "a warring Advaitist." No compromise with anything else. "Ishwara" is his bug-bear. He would have none of it if he could. He is very much delighted with the idea of your magazine, and wants to confer with you on these subjects in London, where he is shortly going. . .

(210)

To Miss Harriet Hale

AIRLIE LODGE, RIDGEWAY GARDENS,
WIMBLEDON, ENGLAND,
17th Sept., 1896.

DEAR SISTER—Your very welcome news reached me just now, on my return here from Switzerland. I am very, very happy to learn that at last you have thought it better to change your mind about the felicity of "Old Maids Home." You are perfectly right now—marriage is the truest goal for ninety-nine per cent of the human race, and they will live the happiest life as soon as they have learned and are ready to abide by the eternal lesson—that we are bound to bear and forbear and that life to every one must be a compromise.

Believe me, dear Harriet, perfect life is a contradiction in terms. Therefore we must always expect to find things not up to our highest ideal. Knowing this we are bound to make the best of everything. The best I can do in the circumstances is to quote from one of our books: "May you always enjoy the undivided love of your husband, helping him in attaining all that is desirable in this life, and when you have seen your children's children, and the drama of life is nearing its end, may you help each other in reaching that infinite ocean of Existence, Knowledge and Bliss, at the touch of whose waters all distinctions melt away and we are all one."[1]

From what I know of you, you have the calm power which bears and forbears to a great degree, and therefore I am safe to prophesy that your married life will be very happy.

All blessings attend you and your *fiancé*. . . .

[1] A reminiscence of Kalidasa's Shakuntala, where Kanva gives his benediction to Shakuntala on the eve of her departure to her husband's place.

May you be like Uma, chaste and pure throughout life—may your husband be like Shiva, whose life was in Uma!—Your loving brother, VIVEKANANDA.

(*211*)

C/o E. T. STURDY, ESQ.,*
HIGH VIEW,
CAVERSHAM, READING,
1896.

DEAR—, . . . This City of London is a sea of human heads—ten or fifteen Calcuttas put together. One is apt to be lost in the mazes unless he arranges for somebody to meet him on arrival. . . . However, let Kali start at once. If he be late in starting like Sarat, better let no one come. It won't do to loiter and procrastinate like that. It is a task that requires the height of Rajas (activity). . . . Our whole country is steeped in Tamas, and nothing but that. We want Rajas first, and Sattva will come afterwards—a thing far, far removed.—Yours affectionately, VIVEKANANDA.

(*212*)

To Sj. Alasinga Perumal

14, GREYCOAT GARDENS,
WESTMINSTER, LONDON,
1896.

DEAR ALASINGA—I have returned about three weeks from Switzerland. . . . The work in London is growing apace, the classes are becoming bigger as they go on. . . . In America there is room for twenty preachers on the Vedanta and Yoga. . . . Half the United States can be conquered in ten years, given a number of strong and genuine men. Where are they? You are all boobies over there! Selfish cowards, with your nonsense of lip-patriotism and boasted religious feeling!!! The Madrasis have more of go and steadiness, but every fool is married. . . . It is very good to aspire to be a non-attached householder, but what we want in Madras is not that just now—but non-marriage. . . .

My child, what I want is muscles of iron and nerves of steel, inside which dwells a mind of the same material as that of which the thunderbolt is made. Strength, manhood, *Kshâtra-Virya* and *Brahma-Teja*. Our beautiful, hopeful boys—they have everything, only if they are not slaughtered by the millions at the altar of this brutality they call marriage. O Lord, hear my wails! Madras will then awake when at least one hundred of its very heart's blood, in the form of its educated young men, will stand aside from the world, gird their loins, and be ready to fight the battle of truth, marching on from country to country. One blow struck outside of India is equal to a hundred thousand struck within. Well, all will come if the Lord wills it.

. . . Max Müller is getting very friendly. I am soon going to deliver two lectures at Oxford.

I am busy writing something big on the Vedanta philosophy. I am busy collecting passages from the various Vedas bearing on the Vedanta in its threefold aspect. You can help me by getting some one to collect passages bearing on, first, the Advaitic idea, then, the Vishishtâdvaitic, and the Dvaitic from the Samhitâs, the Brâhmanas, the Upanishads and the Puranas. They should be classified and very legibly written with the name and chapter of the book, in each case. It would be a pity to leave the West, without leaving something of the philosophy in book form.

There was a book published in Mysore in Tamil characters, comprising all the one hundred and eight Upanishads; I saw it in Professor Deussen's library. Is there a reprint of the same in Devanagri? If so, send me a copy. If not, send me the Tamil edition, and also write on a sheet the Tamil letters and compounds, and all juxtaposed with its Nagri equivalents, so that I may learn the Tamil letters.

. . . Mr. Sattyanadhan, whom I met in London the other day, said that there has been a friendly review of my Raja-Yoga book in the *Madras Mail*, the chief Anglo-Indian paper in Madras. The leading physiologist in America, I hear, has been charmed with my speculations. At the same time, there have been some in England, who ridiculed my ideas. Good, my speculations of course are awfully bold, a good deal of them will ever remain meaningless, but there are hints in it which the physiologists had better taken up earlier. Nevertheless, I am quite satisfied with the result. "Let them talk badly of me if they please, but let them talk," is my motto.

. . . Persevere on, my brave lads. We have only just begun. Never despond! Never say, enough!. . . As soon as a man comes over to the West and sees different nations, his eyes open. This way I get strong workers, not by talking, but by practically showing what we have in India and what we have not. I wish at least that a million Hindus had travelled all over the world!—Yours ever with love, VIVEKANANDA.

(*213*)

To the Same

C/o MISS MÜLLER,
AIRLIE LODGE, RIDGEWAY GARDENS,
WIMBLEDON, ENGLAND,
22nd September, 1896.

DEAR ALASINGA—. . . . I had a beautiful time with Prof. Deussen in Germany. Later, he and I came together to London, and we have already become great friends.

. . . There is yet a vast untrodden field, namely—the writing of the lives and works of Tulsi Das, Kabir,

Nanak, and of the saints of Southern India. They should be written in a thorough-going, scholarly style, not in a slipshod, slovenly way.

. . . Work on with all energy.—With love to all, Yours, VIVEKANANDA.

(*214*)

C/o E. T. STURDY, ESQ.,*
HIGH VIEW, CAVERSHAM,
READING, ENGLAND,
1896.

Can anything be done unless everybody exerts himself to his utmost? उद्योगिनं पुरुषसिंहमुपैति लक्ष्मीः etc.—"It is the man of action, the lion-heart, that the Goddess of Wealth resorts to." No need of looking behind, FORWARD! We want infinite energy, infinite zeal, infinite courage and infinite patience, then only will great things be achieved. . . .—Yours affectionately, VIVEKANANDA.

(*215*)

To Miss Josephine MacLeod

C/o MISS MÜLLER,
AIRLIE LODGE, RIDGEWAY GARDENS,
WIMBLEDON, ENGLAND,
7th October, 1896.

Once more in London, dear Joe Joe, and the classes have begun already. Instinctively I looked about for one familiar face which never had a line of discouragement, never changed, but was always helpful, cheerful and strengthening—and in my mind conjured up that face before me, in spite of a few thousand miles of space. For what is space in the realm of spirit? Well, you are gone to your home of rest and peace—for me, ever-increasing mad work—yet I have your blessings with me always, have I not?

My natural tendency is to go into a cave, and be quiet, but a fate behind pushes me forward and I go. Whoever could resist fate?

Why did not Christ say in the Sermon on the Mount, "Blessed are they that are always cheerful and always hopeful for they have already the Kingdom of Heaven?" I am sure He must have said it, He with the sorrows of a whole world in His heart, He who likened the saintly soul with the child—but it was not noted down; of a thousand things they noted down only one, I mean, remembered.

I now live mostly on fruits and nuts; they seem to agree with me well. If ever the old doctor with "land" up somewhere, comes to see you, you may confide to him this secret. I have lost a good deal of my fat, but on days I lecture, I have to go on solid food. How is Hollister? I never saw a sweeter boy. May all blessings ever attend him through life!

I hear your friend Cola is lecturing on Zoroastrian philosophy—surely the stars are not smiling on him. What about your Miss A—? And our Y—? What news about the brotherhood of the Z Z Z's? And our Miss (forgotten!)? I hear that half a ship-load of Hindus and Buddhists and Mohammedans and brotherhoods and what not have entered the U. S. and another cargo of Mahatma-seekers, evangelists, etc., have entered India!! Good. India and the U. S. seem to be the two countries for religious enterprise. Have a care, Joe, this heathen corruption is dreadful. I met Madame S— in the street to-day. She does not come any more to my lectures. Good for her. Too much of philosophy is not good.

Do you remember that lady who used to come to every meeting too late to hear a word, but buttonholed me immediately after and kept me talking till a battle of Waterloo would be raging in my internal economy through hunger? She came, they are all coming and more; that is cheering.

Most of our friends came—one of the Galsworthys, too, the married daughters. Mrs. Galsworthy could not come to-day, it was a very short notice. We have a hall now, a pretty big one holding about two hundred or more. There is a big corner which will be fitted up as a library. I have another man from India now to help me.

I enjoyed Switzerland immensely, also Germany. Prof. Deussen was very kind, we came together to London and had great *fun* here. Prof. Max Müller is very friendly too. In all, the English work is becoming *solid* and respected too, seeing that great scholars are sympathising. Probably I shall go to India this winter with some English friends. So far about my own sweet self.

Now, what about the holy Family? Everything is going on first rate, I am sure. You must have heard of Fox by this time. I am afraid, I rather made him dejected the day before he sailed, by telling him that he could not marry Mabel until he began to earn a good deal of money!! Is Mabel with you now? Give her my love. Also give me your present address.

How is Mother? Francis, same solid sterling gold as ever, I am sure.

Alberta working at her music and languages, and laughing a good deal, and eating a good many apples as usual, by-the-bye?

It is getting late in the night, so good night, Joe. (Is strict etiquette to be followed in New York too?) And Lord bless you ever and ever. . . . —Ever yours with love and blessings, VIVEKANANDA.

P. S. Mr. and Mrs. Sevier in whose house (flat) I am writing now send their kindest regards.

—V.

(*216*)

To Miss S. E. Waldo

AIRLIE LODGE,
RIDGEWAY GARDENS, WIMBLEDON,
8th Oct., 1896.

DEAR—, . . . I had a fine rest in Switzerland and made a great friend of Prof. Paul Deussen. My European work in fact is becoming more satisfactory to me than any other work, and it tells immensely in India. The London classes were resumed; and to-day is the opening lecture. I now have a hall to myself holding 200 or more. . . .

You know of course the steadiness of the English; they are the least jealous of each other of all nations, and that is why they dominate the world. They have solved the secret of obedience without slavish cringing—great freedom with great law-abidingness.

I know very little of the young man R— . . . . You know my settled doctrine. I do not trust any one who has not conquered "lust and gold." You may try him in theoretical subjects, but keep him off from teaching Raja-Yoga—that is a dangerous game except for the regularly trained to play at. Of Saradananda the blessing of the greatest Yogi of modern India is on him—and there is no danger. Why do you not begin to teach? . . . You have a thousand times more philosophy than this boy R—. Send notices to the class and hold regular talks and lectures.

. . . Make a blaze! Make a blaze!—With all love and blessings, VIVEKANANDA.

(*217*)

WIMBLEDON,
8th Oct., 1896.

DEAR—, ... I met in Germany Prof. Deussen. I

was his guest at Kiel and we travelled together to London and had some very pleasant meetings here. . . . Although I am in full sympathy with the various branches of religious and social work, I find that specification of work is absolutely necessary. Our special branch is to preach *Vedanta*. Helping in other work should be subservient to that one ideal. I hope you will inculcate this in the mind of Saradananda very strongly.

Did you read Max Müller's article on Ramakrishna? . . . Things are working very favourably here in England. The work is not only popular but appreciated.—Yours affly., VIVEKANANDA.

(*218*)

To Sj. Alasinga Perumal

C/o E. T. STURDY, ESQ.,
39, VICTORIA STREET, LONDON,
28th October, 1896.

DEAR ALASINGA—, . . . I am not yet sure what month I shall reach India. I will write later about it. The new Swami delivered his maiden speech yesterday at a friendly society's meeting. It was good and I liked it; he has the making of a good speaker in him, I am sure.

. . . You have not yet printed the Karma Yoga. . . . Again, books must be cheap for India to have a large sale; the types must be bigger to satisfy the public. . . . You can very well get out a cheap edition of the Raja Yoga if you like. I have not reserved any copyright on it purposely. You have missed a good opportunity by not getting it out earlier, but we Hindus are so slow that when we have done a work the opportunity has already passed away, and thus we are the losers. Your Bhakti Yoga came out after a year's talk! Did you think the Western people would wait for it till Doomsday? You have lost three-fourths of the sale by this delay. . . . That Haramohan is a fool, slower than you. . . , and his printing is diabolical. There is no use in publishing books that way; it is cheating the public, and should not be done. I shall most probably return to India accompanied by Mr. and Mrs. Sevier, Miss Müller and Mr. Goodwin. Mr. and Mrs. Sevier are probably going to settle in Almora at least for some time, and Goodwin is going to become a Sannyasin. He of course will travel with me. It is he to whom we owe all our books. He took shorthand notes of my lectures, which enabled the books to be published. All these lectures were delivered on the spur of the moment, without the least preparation. Goodwin will have to live with me. He is a strict vegetarian.—With love, Yours etc., VIVEKANANDA.

(*219*)

To Miss Mary Hale

14, GREYCOAT GARDENS,
WESTMINSTER, LONDON,
1st Nov., 1896.

"Gold and silver," my dear Mary, "have I none, but what I have I give to thee freely", and that is the knowledge that the goldness of gold, the silverness of silver, the manhood of man, the womanhood of woman, the reality of everything is the Lord—and that this Lord we are trying to realise from time without beginning in the objective and in the attempt throwing up such "queer" creatures of our fancy as man, woman, child, body, mind, the earth, sun, moon, stars, the world, love, hate, property, wealth, etc.; also ghosts, devils, angels and gods, God, etc.

The fact being that the Lord is in us, we are He, the eternal subject, the real ego, never to be objectified, and that all this objectifying process is mere waste of time and talent. When the soul becomes aware of this it gives up objectifying and falls back more and more upon the subjective. This is the evolution, less and less in the body and more and more in the mind—*man* the highest form, meaning in Sanskrit *manas*, thought—the animal that thinks and not the animal that "senses" only. This is what in theology is called "Renunciation." The formation of society, the institution of marriage, the love for children, our good works, morality and ethics are all different forms of renunciation. All our lives in every society are the subjection of the will, the thirst, the desire. This surrender of the will or the fictitious self—or the desire to jump out of ourselves as it were—the struggle still to objectify the subject— is the one phenomenon in this world of which all societies and social forms are various modes and stages. Love is the easiest and smoothest way towards the self-surrender or subjection of the will, and hatred, the opposite.

People have been cajoled through various stories or superstitions of heavens and hells and Rulers above the sky, towards this one end of self-surrender. The philosopher does the same knowingly without superstition by giving up desires.

An objective heaven or millennium therefore has existence only in the fancy—but a subjective one is already in existence. The musk-deer after vain search for the cause of the scent of the musk, at last will have to find it in himself.

Objective society will always be a mixture of good and evil—objective life will always be followed by its shadow, death, and the longer the life, the longer will also be the shadow. It is only when the sun is on our own head that *there is no shadow*. When God and good and everything else is in us, there is no evil. In objcetive life, however, every bullet has its billet—evil goes with every good as its shadow. Every improvement is coupled with an equal degradation. The reason being that good and evil are not two things but one, the difference being only in manifestation—one of degree, not kind.

Our very lives depend upon the death of others—plants or animals or bacilli! The other great mistake we often make is that good is takes as an ever-increasing item, whilst evil is a fixed quantity. From this it is argued that evil being diminished every day there will come a time when good alone will remain. The fallacy lies in the assumption of a false premise. If good is increasing so is evil. My desires have been much more than the desires of the masses among my race. My joys have been much greater than theirs—but my miseries a million times more intense. The same constitution that makes you feel the least touch of good makes you feel the least of evil too. The same nerves that carry sensations of pleasure carry the sensations of pain too—and the same mind feels both. The progress of the world means more enjoyment and more misery too. This mixture of life and death, good and evil, knowledge and ignorance is what is called Maya—or the universal phenomenon. You may go on for eternity inside this net seeking for happiness—you find much and much evil too. To have good and no evil is childish nonsense.

Two ways are left open—one by giving up all hope to take up the world as it is and bear the pangs and pains in the hope of a crumb of happiness now and then. The other, to give up the search for pleasure, knowing it to be pain in another form and seek for *truth*—and those that dare to try for truth succeed in finding that truth as ever present—present in themselves. Then we also discover how the same truth is manifesting itself both in our relative error and knowledge—we find also that the same truth is bliss which again is manifesting itself as good and evil, and with it also we find real existence which is manifesting itself as both death and life.

Thus we realise that all these phenomena are but the reflections bifurcated or manifolded of the One existence, Truth-bliss-unity—my real Self and the reality of everything else. Then and then only is it possible to do good without evil, for such a soul has known and got the control of the material of which both good and evil are manufactured, and he alone can manifest one or the other as he likes, and we know he manifests only good. This is the Jivanmukti—the living freedom—the goal of the Vedanta as of all other philosophies.

Human society is in turn governed by the four castes :—the priests, the soldiers, the traders and the labourers. Each state has its glories as well as its defects. When the priest (Brahmin) rules, there is a tremendous exclusiveness on hereditary grounds—the persons of the priests and their descendants are hemmed in with all sorts of safeguards—none but they have any knowledge—none but they have the right to impart that knowledge. Its glory is, that at this period is laid the foundation of sciences. The priests cultivate the mind, for through the mind they govern.

The military (Kshatriya) rule is tyrannical and cruel, but they are not exclusive, and during that period arts and social culture attain their height.

The commercial (Vaishya) rule comes next. It is awful in its silent crushing and blood-sucking power. Its advantage is, as the trader himself goes everywhere he is a good disseminator of ideas collected during the two previous states. They are still less exclusive than the military, but culture begins to decay.

Last will come the labourer (Shudra) rule. Its

advantages will be the distribution of physical comforts—its disadvantages, (perhaps) the lowering of culture. There will be a great distribution of ordinary education, but extraordinary geniuses will be less and less.

If it is possible to form a state in which the knowledge of the priest period, the culture of the military, the distributive spirit of the commercial and the ideal of equality of the last can all be kept intact, minus their evils, it will be an ideal state. But is it possible?

Yet the first three have had their day. Now is the time for the last—they must have it—none can resist it. I do not know all the difficulties about the gold or silver standard, (nobody seems to know much as to that), but this much I see that the gold standard has been making the poor poorer, and the rich richer. Bryan was right when he said, "We refuse to be crucified on a cross of gold." The silver standard will give the poor a better chance in this unequal fight. I am a socialist, not because I think it is a perfect system, but half a loaf is better than no bread.

The other systems have been tried and found wanting. Let this one be tried—if for nothing else, for the novelty of the thing. A redistribution of pain and pleasure is better than always the same persons having pains and pleasures. The sum total of good and evil in the world remains ever the same. The yoke will be lifted from shoulder to shoulder by new systems, that is all.

Let every dog have his day in this miserable world, so that after this experience of so-called happiness they may all come to the Lord and give up this vanity of a world and governments and all other botherations.

With love to you all.—Ever your faithful brother,
VIVEKANANDA.

(220)

To Sj. Alasinga Perumal

14, Greycoat Gardens,
Westminster, S.W.,
11th November, 1896.

Dear Alasinga—I shall most probably start on the 16th of December, or may be a day or two later. I go from here to Italy, and after seeing a few places there, join the steamer at Naples. . . .

The first edition of Raja-Yoga is sold out, and a second is in the press. India and America are the biggest buyers. . . .—Yours with love and blessings, Vivekananda.

(221)

Greycoat Gardens,
Westminster, S.W.,
13th November, 1896.

Dear—, . . . I am very soon starting for India, most probably on the 16th of December. As I am very desirous to see India once before I come again to America, and as I have arranged to take several friends from England with me to India, it is impossible for me to go to America on my way, however I might have liked it.

Dr. Janes is doing splendid work indeed. I can hardly express my gratitude for the many kindnesses and the help he has given me and my work. . . . The work is progressing beautifully here.

You will be interested to know that the first edition of Raja-Yoga is sold out, and there is standing order for several hundreds more.—Yours, etc., Vivekananda.

(222)

To Sj. Alasinga Perumal

39, VICTORIA STREET,
LONDON, S.W.,
20th November, 1896.

DEAR ALASINGA—I am leaving England on the 16th of December for Italy, and shall catch the German Lloyd S. S. *Prinz Regent Leopold* at Naples. The steamer is due at Colombo on the 14th of January next. I intend to see a little of Ceylon, and shall then go to Madras.

... Mr. Sevier and his wife are going to start a place near Almora in the Himalayas which I intend to make my Himalayan Centre, as well as a place for Western disciples to live as Brahmacharins and Sannyasins. Goodwin is an unmarried young man who is going to travel and live with me; he is like a Sannyasin.

I am very desirous to reach Calcutta before the birthday festival of Sri Ramakrishna.... My present plan of work is to start two centres, one in Calcutta, and the other in Madras, in which to train up young preachers. I have funds enough to start the one in Calcutta, which being the scene of Sri Ramakrishna's life-work, demands my first attention. As for the Madras one, I expect to get funds in India.

We will begin work with these three centres; and later on, we will get to Bombay and Allahabad. And from these points, if the Lord is pleased, we will invade not only India, but send over bands of preachers to every country in the world. That should be our first duty. Work on with a heart.

... Now we have got one Indian magazine in English fixed. We can start some in the vernaculars also.... Papers of this kind are supported by a little circle of followers.... The Indian papers are to be supported by the Indians. To make a paper equally acceptable to all nationalities, means a staff of writers from all nations, and that means at least a hundred thousand rupees a year.

. . . You must not forget that my interests are *international* and not Indian alone . . .

Miss M. Noble of Wimbledon is a great worker. . . . —With all love and blessings, Yours etc., VIVEKANANDA.

(*223*)

To Sj. Lala Badri Sah

39, VICTORIA STREET,
LONDON, S.W.,
21st November, 1896.

DEAR LALAJI—I reach Madras about the 7th of January; after a few days in the plains I intend to come up to Almora.

I have three English friends with me. Two of them, Mr. and Mrs. Sevier, are going to settle in Almora. They are my disciples you know, and they are going to build the Math for me in the Himalayas. It was for that reason I asked you to look for some suitable site. We want a whole hill, with a view of the snow range all to ourselves. It would of course take time to fix on the site and complete the building. In the meanwhile, will you kindly engage a small bungalow for my friends? The bungalow ought to accommodate three persons. I do not require a large one. A small one would do for the present. My friends will live in this bungalow in Almora and then go about looking for a site and building.

You need not reply to this letter, as before your reply will reach me I shall be on my way to India. I will wire to you from Madras as soon as I reach there.

With love and blessings to you all,—Yours, VIVEKANANDA.

(224)

To Misses Mary and Harriet Hale

39, VICTORIA ST.,
LONDON, S.W.,
28th Nov., 1896.

DEAR SISTERS—. . . I feel impelled to write a few lines to you before my departure for India. The work in London has been a roaring success. The English are not so bright as the Americans, but once you touch their heart, it is yours for ever. Slowly have I gained, and it is strange that in six months' work altogether I would have a steady class of one hundred and twenty persons apart from public lectures. Here every one means work —the practical Englishman. Capt. and Mrs. Sevier and Mr. Goodwin are going to India with me to work and spend their own money on it! There are scores here ready to do the same: men and women of position, ready to give up everything for the idea once they feel convinced! And last though not the least, the help in the shape of money to start my "work" in India has come and more will follow. My ideas about the English have been revolutionised. I now understand why the Lord has blessed them above all other races. They are steady, sincere to the backbone, with great depths of feeling—only with a crust of stoicism on the surface; if that is broken you have your man.

Now I am going to start a centre in Calcutta and another in the Himalayas. The Himalayan one will be an entire hill about 7,000 ft. high—cool in summer, cold in winter. Capt. and Mrs. Sevier will live there, and it will be the centre for European workers, as I do not want to kill them by forcing on them the Indian mode of living and the fiery plains. My plan is to send out numbers of Hindu boys to every civilised country to preach— get men and women from foreign countries to work in India. This would be a good exchange. After having established the centres I go about up and down like the gentleman in the book of Job.

Here I must end to catch the mail. Things are opening for me. I am glad and I know so you are. Now all blessings be yours and all happiness. With eternal love,—VIVEKANANDA.

P.S. What about Dharmapal? What is he doing? Give him my love if you meet him.

(225)

To Mrs. Ole Bull

39, VICTORIA ST., LONDON,
9th Dec., 1896.

DEAR MRS. BULL—It is needless to express my gratitude at your most generous offer.

I don't want to encumber myself with a large amount of money at the first start, but as things progress on I will be very glad to find employment for that sum.

My idea is to start on a very small scale. I do not know anything yet. I will know my bearings when on the spot in India. From India I will write to you more details about my plans and the practical way to realise them.

I start on the 16th and after a few days in Italy take the steamer at Naples.

Kindly convey my love to Mrs. Vaughan and Saradananda and to the rest of my friends there. As for you I have always regarded you as the best friend I have and it will be the same all my life.

With love and blessings,—VIVEKANANDA.

(226)

LONDON,
1896.

[On the eve of the lecture tour of Dr. Barrows in India at the end of 1896, Swamiji in a letter to the *Indian Mirror*, Calcutta, introduced the distinguished visitor to his countrymen and advised them to give him a fitting reception. He wrote among other things as follows:]

Dr. Barrows was the ablest lieutenant Mr. C. Boney could have selected to carry out successfully his great plan of the Congress at the World's Fair, and it is now a matter of history how one of these Congresses scored a unique distinction, under the leadership of Dr. Barrows.

It was the great courage, untiring industry, unruffled patience and never-failing courtesy of Dr. Barrows that made the Parliament a grand success.

India, its people and their thoughts, have been brought more prominently before the world than ever before, by that wonderful gathering at Chicago, and that national benefit we certainly owe to Dr. Barrows more than to any other man at that meeting.

Moreover, he comes to us in the sacred name of religion, in the name of one of the great teachers of mankind, and I am sure, his exposition of the system of the Prophet of Nazareth would be extremely liberal and elevating. The Christ-power this man intends to bring to India, is not that of the intolerant, dominant Superior with heart full of contempt for everything else but its own self, but that of a brother who craves for a brother's place as a co-worker of the various powers, already working in India. Above all, we must remember that gratitude and hospitality are the peculiar characteristics of Indian humanity, and as such, I would beg my countrymen to behave in such a manner, that this stranger from the other side of the globe, may find that in the midst of all our misery, our poverty and degradation, the heart beats as warm as of yore, when the "wealth of Ind" was the proverb of nations, and India was the land of the "Aryas."

(227)

Written to an American lady

LONDON,
13th December, 1896.

DEAR MADAM—We have only to grasp the idea of graduation of morality and everything becomes clear.

Renunciation—non-resistance—non-destructiveness—are the ideals to be attained through less and less worldliness, less and less resistance, less and less destructiveness. Keep the ideal in view and work towards it. None can live in the world without resistance, without destruction, without desire. The world has not come to that state yet when the ideal can be realised in society.

The progress of the world through all its evils is making it fit for the ideals, slowly but surely. The majority will have to go on with this slow growth—the exceptional ones will have to get out to realise the ideal in the present state of things.

Doing the duty of the time is the best way, and if it is done only as a duty it does not make us attached.

Music is the highest art, and to those who understand, is the highest worship.

We must try our best to destroy ignorance and evil. Only we have to learn that evil is destroyed by the growth of good.—Yours affectionately, VIVEKANANDA.

(228)

To Miss Mary Hale

RAMNAD,
30th January, 1897.

MY DEAR MARY—Things are turning out most curiously for me. From Colombo in Ceylon, where I landed, to Ramnad, the nearly southernmost point of the Indian continent where I am just now as the guest of the Raja of Ramnad, my journey has been a huge procession—crowds of people, illuminations, addresses, etc., etc. A monument 40 ft. high is being built on the spot where I landed. The Raja of Ramnad has presented his address to "His Most Holiness" in a huge casket of solid gold beautifully worked. Madras and Calcutta are on the tip-toe of expectation as if the whole nation was rising to honour me. So you see, Mary, I am on the very height of my destiny, yet the mind turns to quietness and peace, to the days we had in Chicago, of rest, of peace and love, and that is why I write just now, and may this find you all in health and peace. I wrote a letter to my people from London to receive Dr. Barrows kindly. They accorded him a big reception, but it was not my fault that he could not make any impression there. The Calcutta people are a hard-headed lot! Now Barrows thinks a world of me, I hear! Such is the world.

With all love to mother, father and you all,—I remain, Yours affectionately, VIVEKANANDA.

(229)

To Swami Brahmananda

MADRAS,
12th February, 1897.

DEAR RAKHAL—I am to start next Sunday. I had to refuse invitations from Poona and other places on account of bad health. I am very much pulled down by hard work and heat.

The T—s and others wanted to intimidate me. Therefore I had to give them a bit of my mind. You know they persecuted me all the time in America because I did not join them. They wanted to begin it here. So I had to clear my position. If that displeases any of my Calcutta friends, "God help them." You need not be afraid, I do not work alone, but He is always with me. What could I do otherwise?—Yours, VIVEKANANDA.

(230)

To Mrs. Ole Bull

ALAMBAZAR MATH, CALCUTTA,
25th Feb., 1897.

DEAR MRS. BULL— S— sends £20 to be placed in the famine-relief in India. But as there is famine in his own home, I thought it best to relieve that at first, as the old proverb says. So it has been employed accordingly.

I have not a moment to die as they say, what with processions and tomtomings and various other methods of reception all over the country; I am almost dead. As soon as the Birthday is over I will fly off to the hills. I received an address from the Cambridge conference as well as one from the Brooklyn Ethical Association. One from the Vedanta Association of New York as mentioned in Dr. Janes's letter has not yet arrived.

Also there is a letter from Dr. Janes suggesting work along the line of your Conference, here in India. It is almost impossible for me to pay any attention to these things. I am so, so tired, I do not know whether I would live even six months more or not, unless I have some rest.

Now I have to start two centres, one in Calcutta, the other in Madras. The Madras people are deeper and more sincere, and, I am sure, will be able to collect funds from Madras itself. The Calcutta people are mostly enthusiastic (I mean the aristocracy) through patriotism and their sympathy would never materialise. On the other hand, the country is full of persons, jealous and pitiless, who would leave no stone unturned to pull my work to pieces.

But as you know well, the more opposition, the more is the demon in me roused. My duty would not be complete, if I die without starting the two places, one for the Sannyasins, the other for the women.

I have already £500 from England, about £500 from Mr. Sturdy and if your money be added to it, I am sure I will be able to start the two. I think, therefore, you ought to send the money as soon as possible. The safest way is to put the money in a bank in America in your and my name jointly, so that either of us may draw it. In case I die before the money is employed you will be able to draw it all and put it to the use I wanted. So that, in case of my death, none of my people would be able to meddle with it. The English money has been put in the bank in the same position in the joint names of Mr. Sturdy and myself.

With love to Saradananda and eternal love and gratitude to yourself,—Yours etc., VIVEKANANDA.

(*231*)

To Sj. Sarat Chandra Chakravarty
TRANSLATION FROM SANSKRIT

DARJEELING,
19th March, 1897.

May you prosper! May this letter conveying blessings and cordial embrace make you happy! Nowadays this fleshy tabernacle of mine is comparatively well.

Meseems, the snow-capped peaks of the Himalayas, the Chief among Mountains, bring even the moribund back to life. And the fatigue of the journey also seems to have somewhat abated. I have already felt that yearning for Freedom—potent enough to put the heart into turmoil—which your letter suggests you are experiencing. It is this yearning that gradually brings on a concentration of the mind on the Eternal Brahman. "There is no other way to go by." May this desire blaze up more and more in you, until all your past Karma and future tendencies are absolutely annihilated. Close upon the heels of that will follow, all on a sudden, the manifestation of Brahman, and with it the destruction of all craving for the sense-world. That this freedom-in-life is approaching for your welfare, is easily to be inferred from the strength of your fervour. Now I pray to that World-teacher, Sri Ramakrishna, the Preacher of the gospel of Universal Synthesis, to manifest himself in the region of your heart, so that, having attained the consummation of your desires, you may with an undaunted heart try your best to deliver others from this dreadful ocean of infatuation. May you be ever possessed of valour! It is the hero alone, not the coward, who has Liberation within his easy reach. Gird up your loins, ye heroes, for before you are your enemies—the dire army of Infatuation. It is undoubtedly true that "all great achievements are fraught with numerous impediments"; still you should exert your utmost for your end. Behold, how men are already in the jaws of the shark of Infatuation! Oh, listen to their piteous heart-rending wails! Advance! Forward! O ye brave souls, to set free those that are in fetters, to lessen the burden of woe of the miserable, and to illumine the abysmal darkness of ignorant hearts! Look, how the Vedanta proclaims by beat of drums, "Be fearless!" May that solemn sound remove the hearts' knot of all denizens of the earth!—Ever your well-wisher, VIVEKANANDA.

(232)

ओं तत् सत्

To Srimati Sarala Ghoshal, B.A., Editor, *Bhârati.*

ROSE BANK,*
THE MAHARAJA OF BURDWAN'S HOUSE,
DARJEELING,
6th April, 1897.

HONOURED MADAM—I feel much obliged for the *Bharati* sent by you, and consider myself fortunate that the cause to which my humble life has been dedicated, has been able to win the approbation of highly talented ladies like you.

In this battle of life, men are rare who encourage the initiator of new thought, not to speak of women who would offer him encouragement; particularly in our unfortunate land. It is therefore that the approbation of an educated Bengali lady is more valuable than the loud applause of all the men of India.

May the Lord grant that many women like you be born in this country, and devote their lives to the betterment of their motherland!

I have something to say in regard to the article you have written about me in the *Bharati*. It is this. It has been for the good of India that religious preaching in the West has been and will be done. It has ever been my conviction that we shall not be able to rise unless the Western people come to our help. In this country no appreciation of merit can yet be found, no financial strength, and what is the most lamentable of all, there is not a bit of practicality.

There are many things to be done, but means are wanting in this country. We have brains, but no hands. We have the doctrine of Vedanta, but we have not the power to reduce it into practice. In our books there is the doctrine of universal equality, but in work we make great distinctions. It was in India that unselfish and disinterested work of the most exalted type was preached, but in practice *we* are awfully cruel, awfully heartless—unable to think of anything besides our own mass-of-flesh bodies.

Yet it is only through the present state of things that it is possible to proceed to work. There is no other way. Every one has the power to judge of good and evil, but he is the hero who undaunted by the waves of Samsâra—which is full of errors, delusions and miseries—with one hand wipes the tears, and with the other, unshaken, shows the path of deliverance. On the one hand there is the conservative society, like a mass of inert matter; on the other, the restless, impatient, fire-darting reformer; the way to good lies between the two. I heard in Japan that it was the belief of the girls of the country that their dolls would be animated if they were loved with the heart. The Japanese girl never breaks her doll. O you of great fortune! I too believe that India will awake again if any one could love with the whole heart, the people of the country—bereft of the grace of affluence, of blasted fortune, their discretion totally lost, downtrodden, ever-starved, quarrelsome and envious. Then only will India awake, when hundreds of large-hearted men and women giving up all desires of enjoying the luxuries of life, will long and exert themselves to their utmost, for the well-being of the millions of their countrymen who are gradually sinking lower and lower in the vortex of destitution and ignorance. I have experienced even in my insignificant life that good motives, sincerity and infinite love can conquer the world. One single soul possessed of these virtues can destroy the dark designs of millions of hypocrites and brutes.

My going over to the West again is yet uncertain; if I go, know that too will be for India. Where is the strength of men in this country? Where is the strength of money? Many men and women of the West are ready to do good to India by serving even the lowest Chandâlas, in the Indian way and through the Indian religion. How many such are there in this country? And financial strength! To meet the expenses of my reception, the people of Calcutta made me deliver a lecture, and sold tickets. I do not blame or censure anybody for this, I only want to show that our well-being is impossible without men and money coming from the West.

Ever grateful and ever praying to the Lord for your welfare,—VIVEKANANDA.

(*233*)

To the Same

DARJEELING,*
C/O M. N. BANERJEE, ESQ.,
24th April, 1897.

DEAR MADAM—. . . In reply to your question about the method of work, the most important thing I have to say is, that the work should be started on a scale which would be commensurate with the results desired. I have heard much of your liberal mind, patriotism and steady perseverance from my friend Miss Müller, and the proof of your erudition is evident. I look upon it as great good fortune that you are desirous to know what little this insignificant life has been able to attempt; I shall state it in this short letter, as far as I can. But first I shall lay before you my mature convictions for your deliberation.

We have been slaves for ever, i.e., it has never been given to the masses in India to express the inner light which is their inheritance. The Occident has been rapidly advancing towards freedom for the last few centuries. In India, it was the king who used to prescribe everything, from Kulinism down to what one should eat and one should not. In Western countries, the people do everything themselves.

The king now has nothing to say to any social matter; on the other hand, the Indian people have not yet even the least faith in themselves, what to say of self-reliance. The faith in one's own self, which is the basis of Vedanta, has not yet been even slightly carried into practice. It is for this reason the Western method—i.e., first of all discussion about the wished-for end, then the carrying it out by the combination of all the forces—is of no avail even now in this country; it is for this reason we appear so greatly conservative under foreign rule. If this be true, then it is a vain attempt to do any great work by means of public discussion. "There is no chance of a headache where there is no head"—where is the public? Besides, we are so devoid of strength that our whole energy is exhausted if we undertake to discuss anything; none is left for work. It is for this reason, I suppose, we observe in Bengal almost always "Much cry but little wool." Secondly, as I have written before, I do not expect anything from the rich people of India. It is best to work among the youth in whom lies our hope—patiently, steadily and without noise.

Now about work. From the day when education and culture etc., began to spread gradually from patricians to plebeians, grew the distinction between the modern civilisation as of Western countries and the ancient civilisation as of India, Egypt, Rome, etc. I see it before my eyes, a nation is advanced in proportion as education and intelligence spread among the masses. The chief cause of India's ruin has been the monopolising of the whole education and intelligence of the land, by dint of pride and royal authority, among a handful of men. If we are to rise again, we shall have to do it in the same way, i.e., by spreading education among the masses. A great fuss has been made for half a century about social reform. Travelling through various places of India these last ten years, I observed the country full of social reform associations. But I did not find one association for them by sucking whose blood the people known as "gentlemen" have become and continued to be gentlemen! How many sepoys were brought by the Musalmans? How many Englishmen are there? Where except in India can be had millions of men who will cut the throats of their own fathers and brothers for six rupees? Sixty millions of Musalmans in seven hundred years of Mohammedan rule, and two millions of Christians in hundred years of Christian rule—what makes it so? Why has originality entirely forsaken the country? Why are our deft-fingered artisans daily becoming extinct, unable to compete with the Europeans? By what power again has the German labourer succeeded in shaking the many-century-grounded firm footing of the English labourer?

Education, education, education alone! Travelling through many cities of Europe and observing in them the comforts and education of even the poor people, there was brought to my mind the state of our own poor people and I used to shed tears. What made the difference? Education was the answer I got. Through education, faith in one's own self, and through faith in one's own self the inherent Brahman is waking up in them, while the Brahman in us is gradually becoming dormant. In New York I used to observe the Irish colonists come—downtrodden, haggard-looking, destitute of all possessions at home, penniless and wooden-headed—with their only belongings, a stick and a bundle of rags hanging at the end of it, fright in their steps, alarm in their eyes. A different spectacle in six months—the man walks upright, his attire is changed. In his eyes and steps there is no more sign of fright. What is the cause? Our Vedanta says that that Irishman was kept surrounded by contempt in his own country—the whole of Nature was telling him with one voice,—"Pat, you have no more hope, you were born a slave and will remain so." Having been thus told from his birth, Pat believed in it and hypnotised himself that he was very low, and the Brahman in him shrank away. While no sooner had he landed in America than the shout went up on all sides—"Pat, you are a man as we are, it is man who has done all, a man like you and me can do everything; have courage!" Pat raised his head and saw that it was so, the Brahman within woke up, Nature herself spoke, as it were, "Arise, awake, etc." (Katha Upa., I. iii. 4).

Likewise the education that our boys receive is very negative. The school-boy learns nothing, but has everything of his own broken down—want of Shraddhâ is the result. The Shraddha which is the key-note of the Vedas and the Vedanta—the Shraddha which emboldened Nachiketa to face Yama and question him, through which Shraddha this world moves—the annihilation of that Shraddha! अज्ञश्चाश्रद्दधानश्च संशयात्मा विनश्यति। —"The ignorant, the man devoid of Shraddha, the doubting self runs to ruin." Therefore are we so near destruction. The remedy now is, the spread of education. First of all, Self-knowledge. I do not mean thereby, matted hair, staff, Kamandalu and mountain caves which the word suggests. What do I mean then? Cannot the knowledge by which is attained even freedom from the bondage of worldly existence, bring ordinary material prosperity? Certainly it can. Freedom, dispassion, renunciation—all these are the very highest ideals, but स्वल्पमप्यस्य धर्मस्य त्रायते महतो भयात्। —"Even a little of this Dharma saves from the great fear (of birth and death)." Dualist, qualified Monist, Monist, Shaiva, Vaishnava, Shâkta, even the Buddhist and the Jain and others—whatever sects have arisen in India are all at one in this respect, that infinite power is latent in this Jivâtman (individualised soul); from the ant to the perfect man there is the same Atman in all, the difference being only in manifestation. "As a farmer breaks the obstacles (to the course of water)" (Patanjali's Yoga Sutra, Kaivalyapâda, 3). That power manifests as soon as it gets the opportunity and the right place and time. From the highest god to the meanest grass, the same power is present in all—whether manifested or not. We shall have to call forth that power by going from door to door.

Secondly, along with this, education has to be imparted. That is easy to say, but how to reduce it into practice? There are thousands of unselfish, kind-hearted men in our country, who have renounced everything. In the same way as they travel about and give religious instructions without any remuneration, so at least half of them can be trained as teachers, or bearers of such education as we need most. For that, we want first of all a centre in the capital of each Presidency, from whence to spread slowly throughout the whole of India. Two centres have recently been started in Madras and Calcutta, there is hope of more soon. Then, the greater part of the education to the poor should be given orally, time is not yet ripe for schools. Gradually in these main centres will be taught agriculture, industry, etc., and workshops will be established for the furtherance of arts. To sell the manufactures of those workshops in Europe and America, associations will be started like those already in existence. It will be necessary to start centres for women exactly like those for men. But you are aware how difficult that is in this country. Again, "The snake which bites must take out its own poison"—and that this is going to be is my firm conviction; the money required for these works would have to come from the West. And for that reason our religion should be preached in Europe and America. Modern science has undermined the basis of religions like Christianity. Over and above that, luxury is about to kill the religious instinct itself. Europe and America are looking towards India with expectant eyes—this is the time for philanthropy, this is the time to occupy the hostile strongholds.

In the West, women rule; all influence and power are theirs. If bold and talented women like yourself, versed in Vedanta, go to England to preach, I am sure that every year hundreds of men and women will become blessed by adopting the religion of the land of Bhârata. The only woman who went over from our country was Româbai; her knowledge of English, Western science and art was limited; still she surprised all. If anyone like you go, England will be stirred, what to speak of America! If an Indian woman in Indian dress preach the religion which fell from the lips of the Rishis of India—I see a prophetic vision—there will rise a great wave which will inundate the whole Western world. Will there be no woman in the land of Maitreyi, Khanâ, Lilâvati, Sâvitri and Ubhayabhârati, who will venture to do this? The Lord knows. England we shall conquer, England we shall possess through the power of spirituality. नान्यः पन्था विद्यतेऽयनाय— "There is no other way of salvation." Can salvation ever come by getting up meetings and societies? Our conquerors must be made Devas by the power of our spirituality. I am a humble mendicant, an itinerant monk; I am helpless and alone; what can I do? You have the power of wealth, intellect and education; will you forgo this opportunity? Conquest of England, Europe and America—this should be our one supreme Mantram at present, in it lies the well-being of the country. Expansion is the sign of life and we must spread over the world with our spiritual ideals. Alas! this frame is poor, moreover, the physique of a Bengali; even under this labour a fatal disease has attacked it, but there is the hope—

उत्पत्स्यतेऽस्ति मम कोऽपि समानधर्मा ।
कालो ह्ययं निरवधिर्विपुला च पृथ्वी ॥ (भवभूतिः)

—"A kindred spirit is or will be born out of the limitless time and populous earth to accomplish the work."

About vegetarian diet I have to say this: first, my Master was a vegetarian; but if he was given meat offered to the Goddess, he used to hold it up to his head. The taking of life is undoubtedly sinful, but so long as vegetable food is not made suitable to the human system, through progress in chemistry, there is no other alternative but meat-eating. So long as man shall have to live a Râjasika (active) life under circumstances like the present, there is no other way except through meat-eating. It is true that the Emperor Ashoka saved the lives of millions of animals by the threat of the sword, but is not the slavery of a thousand years more dreadful than that? Taking the life of a few goats as against the inability to protect the honour of one's own wife and daughter, and to save the morsels for one's children from robbing hands—which of these is more sinful? Rather let those belonging to the upper ten, who do not earn their livelihood by manual labour, not take meat; but the forcing of vegetarianism upon those who have to earn their bread by labouring day and night, is one of the causes of the loss of our national freedom. Japan is an example of what good and nourishing food can do. May All-powerful Vishveshvari inspire your heart!—VIVEKANANDA.

(234)

To Miss Mary Hale

DARJEELING,
28th April, 1897.

DEAR MARY—A few days ago I received your beautiful letter. Yesterday came the card announcing Harriet's marriage. Lord bless the happy pair.

. . . The whole country here rose like one man to receive me. Hundreds of thousands of persons, shouting and cheering at every place, Rajas drawing my carriage, arches all over the streets of the capitals with blazing mottos etc., etc. ! ! ! The whole thing would soon come out in the form of a book, and you will have a copy soon. But unfortunately I was already exhausted by hard work in England and this tremendous exertion in the heat of Southern India prostrated me completely. I had of course to give up the idea of visiting other parts of India and fly up to the nearest hill-station, Darjeeling. Now I feel much better and a month more in Almora would complete the cure. By-the-bye, I have just lost a chance of coming over to Europe. Raja Ajit Singh and several other Rajas start next Saturday for England. Of course, they wanted hard to get me to go over with them. But unfortunately the doctors would not hear of my undertaking any physical or mental labour just now. So with the greatest chagrin I had to give it up, reserving it for a near future. Dr. Barrows has reached America, by this time, I hope. Poor man! He came here to preach the most bigoted Christianity, with the usual result that nobody listened to him. Of course, they received him very kindly. but it was my letter that did it. I could not put brains into him! Moreover, he seems to be a queer sort of man. I hear that he was mad at the national rejoicings over my coming home.

You ought to have sent a brainier man anyway, for the Parliament of Religions has been made a farce of in the Hindu mind by Dr. Barrows. On metaphysical lines no nation on earth can hold a candle to the Hindus; and curiously all the fellows that come over here from Christian land have that one antiquated foolishness of an argument that because the Christians are powerful and rich and the Hindus are not, so Christianity must be better than Hinduism. To which the Hindus very aptly retort that that is the very reason why Hinduism is a religion and Christianity is not; because in this beastly world it is blackguardism and that alone which *prospers*, and virtue always suffers. It seems, however advanced the Western nations are in scientific culture, they are mere babies in metaphysical and spiritual education. Material science can only give worldly prosperity, whilst spiritual science is for eternal life. If there be no eternal life, still the enjoyment of spiritual thoughts as ideals is keener and makes a man happier, whilst the foolery of materialism leads to competition and undue ambition and ultimate death, individual and national.

This Darjeeling is a beautiful spot with a view of the glorious Kanchanjanga (28,146 ft.) now and then when the clouds permit it, and from a near hill-top one can catch a glimpse of Gouri Shanker (29,002 ft.) now and then. Then, the people here too are so picturesque, the Thibetans and Nepalese and above all the beautiful Lepcha women. Do you know one Coulson Turnbull of Chicago? He has been here a few weeks before I reached India. He seems to have had a great liking for me with the result that Hindu people all liked him very much. What about Joe, Mrs. Adams, Sister Josephine and all the rest of our friends? Where are our beloved Mills? Grinding slow but sure? I wanted to send some nuptial presents to Harriet, but with your terrible duties I must reserve it for some near future. Maybe I shall meet them in Europe very soon. I would have been very glad, of course, if you could announce your engagement and I would fulfil my promise by filling up half a dozen papers in one letter. . .

My hair is turning grey in bundles and my face is getting wrinkled up all over; that losing of flesh has given me twenty years of age more. And now I am losing flesh rapidly, because I am made to live upon meat and meat alone, no bread, no rice, no potatoes, not even a lump of sugar in my coffee ! ! I am living with a Brahmin family who all dress in knickerbockers, women excepted of course ! I am also in knickers. I would have given you a surprise if you had seen me bounding from rock to rock like a chamois, or galloping might and main up and down mountain roads.

I am very well here, for life in the plains has become a torture. I cannot put the tip of my nose out into the streets, but there is a curious crowd ! ! Fame is not all milk and honey ! ! I am going to train a big beard, now it is turning grey. It gives a venerable appearance and saves one from American scandal-mongers ! O thou white hair, how much thou canst conceal, all glory unto thee, Hallelujah !

The mail time is nearly up, so I finish. Good dreams, good health, all blessings attend you.

With love to father and mother and you all.—Yours, VIVEKANANDA.

(*235*)

ALAMBAZAR MATH, CALCUTTA,
5th May, 1897.

DEAR—, I have been to Darjeeling for a month to recuperate my shattered health. I am very much better now. The disease disappeared altogether in Darjeeling. I am going to-morrow to Almora, another hill-station, to perfect this improvement.

Things are looking not very hopeful here as I have already written to you—though the whole nation has risen as one man to honour me and people went almost mad over me! The practical part cannot be had in India. Again, the price of the land has gone up very much near Calcutta. My idea at present is to start three centres at three capitals. These would be my normal schools, from thence I want to invade India.

India is already Ramakrishna's whether I live a few years more or not.

I had a very kind letter from Dr. Janes in which he points out my remarks about degraded Buddhism. You also write that D—— is very wroth about it. Mr. D—— is a good man and I love him, but it would be entirely wrong for him to go into fits over things Indian.

I am perfectly convinced that what they call Modern Hinduism with all its ugliness is only stranded Buddhism. Let the Hindu understand this clearly, and then it would be easier for them to reject it without murmur. As for the ancient form which the Buddha preached, I have the greatest respect for it, as well as for His person. And you well know that we Hindus worship Him as an Incarnation. Neither is the Buddhism of Ceylon any good. My visit to Ceylon has entirely disillusioned me, and the only living people there are the Hindus. The Buddhists are all much Europeanised—even Mr. D—— and his father had European names, which they have since changed. The only respect the Buddhists pay to their great tenet of non-killing is by opening "butcher-stalls" in every place! And the priests encourage this. The real Buddhism I once thought of, would yet do *much good*. But I have given up the idea entirely and I clearly see the reason why Buddhism was driven out of India, and we will only be too glad if the Ceylonese carry off the remnant of this religion with its hideous idols and licentious rites.

About the Theosophists, you must remember first that in India Theosophists and Buddhists are nonentities. They publish a few papers and make a lot of splash and try to catch Occidental ears. . . .

I was one man in America and another here. Here the whole nation is looking upon me as their authority—there I was a much reviled preacher. Here Princes draw my carriage, there I would not be admitted to a decent hotel. My utterances here, therefore, must be for the good of the race, my people—however unpleasant they might appear to a few. Acceptance, love, toleration for everything sincere and honest—but never for hypocrisy. The ——s tried to fawn upon and flatter me as I am the authority now in India and therefore it was necessary for me to stop my work giving any sanction to their humbugs, by a few bold, decisive words, and the thing is done. I am very glad. If my health had permitted, I would have cleared India by this time of these upstart humbugs, at least tried my best. . . . Let me tell you that India is already Ramakrishna's, and for a purified Hinduism I have organised my work here a bit.—Yours, VIVEKANANDA.

(236)

To Sister Nivedita

ALAMBAZAR MATH, CALCUTTA,
5th May, 1897.

MY DEAR MISS NOBLE, Your very very kind, loving and encouraging letter gave me more strength than you think of.

There are moments when one feels entirely despondent no doubt—especially when one has worked towards an ideal during a whole life's time and just when there is a bit of hope of seeing it partially accomplished, there comes a tremendous thwarting blow. I do not care for the disease, but that my ideals have not had yet the least opportunity of being worked out. And you know the difficulty is money.

The Hindus are making processions and all that, but they cannot give money. The only help I got in the world was in England, from Miss S., and Mr. S. . . . I thought there that a thousand pounds was sufficient to start at least the principal centre in Calcutta, but my calculation was from the experience of Calcutta ten or twelve years ago. Since then prices have gone up three or four times.

The work has been started anyhow. A rickety old little house has been rented for six or seven shillings where about twenty-four young men are being trained. I had to go to Darjeeling for a month to recover my health, and I am glad to tell you I am very much better,—and would you believe it, without taking any medicine, only by the exercise of mental healing? I am going again to another hill-station to-morrow, as it is very hot in the plains. Your society is still living, I am sure. I will send you a report at least every month of the work done here. The London work is not doing well at all, I hear, and that was the main reason why I would not come to England just now, although some of our Rajas going for the Jubilee tried their best to get me with them, as I would have to work hard again to revive the interest in Vedanta. And that would mean a good deal more trouble physically.

I may come over for a month or so very soon however. Only if I could see my work started here, how gladly and freely would I travel about.

So far about work. Now about you personally. Such love and faith and devotion and appreciation like yours, dear Miss Noble, repays a hundred times over any amount of labour one undergoes in this life. May all blessings be yours. My whole life is at your service, as we may say in our mother tongue.

It never was and never will be anything but very very welcome, any letters from you and other friends in England. Mr. and Mrs. Hammond wrote two very kind and nice letters and Mr. Hammond a beautiful poem in the *Brahmavadin*, although I did not deserve it a bit. I will write to you again from the Himalayas, where thought will be clearer in sight of the snows and the nerves more settled than in this burning plain. Miss Müller is already in Almora. Mr. and Mrs. Sevier go to Simla. They have been in Darjeeling so long. So things come and go, dear friend. Only the Lord is unchangeable and He is Love. May He make your heart His eternal habitation is the constant prayer of—VIVEKANANDA.

(*237*)

ALMORA,
20th May, 1897.

DEAR—, . . . I am glad to learn that the Association in Calcutta is going on nicely. It does not matter if one or two keep out. In time all will join. Have sympathy and good feelings for all. Sweet words carry far. The first thing is to see that new people come. We want ever new members.

Jogen is doing well. As Almora was very hot, I am living in a beautiful garden twenty miles off. It is comparatively cool, but yet hot. I don't find much difference in the heat of this place from that of Calcutta.

. . . To work! In full speed, and with undaunted zeal! Let us once throw the country into convulsions of energy.

Tender my love to all at the Math and give my greetings to the next meeting of the Association, and say that though I am not present in body, yet my soul is there where my Lord's name is sung. यावत्तव कथा राम सञ्चरिष्यति मेदिनीम् etc.—"As far as talk of Thee circulates in the world, O Rama! I am present there!" (Hanumân)—

because, forsooth, the Atman is all-pervading.—Yours affectionately, VIVEKANANDA.

(238)

To Dr. Sasi Bhushan Ghose

ALMORA,
29th May, 1897.

MY DEAR DOCTOR SASI—Your letter and the two bottles containing the medicines were duly received. I have begun from last evening a trial of your medicines. Hope the combination will have a better effect than the one alone.

. . . I began to take a lot of exercise on horseback, both morning and evening. Since that I am very much better indeed. I was so much better the first week of my gymnastics that I have scarcely felt so well since I was a boy and used to have *kusti* exercises. I really began to feel that it was a pleasure to have a body. Every movement made me conscious of strength—every movement of the muscles was pleasurable. That exhilarating feeling has subsided somewhat, yet I feel very strong. In a trial of strength I could make both G. G. and Niranjan go down before me in a minute. In Darjeeling I always felt that I was not the same man. Here I feel that I have no disease whatsoever, but there is one marked change. I never in my life could sleep as soon as I got into bed. I must toss for at least two hours. Only from Madras to Darjeeling (during the first month) I would sleep as soon as my head touched the pillow. That ready disposition to sleep is gone now entirely, and my old tossing habit and feeling hot after the evening meal have come back. I do not feel any heat after the day meal. There being an orchard here, I began to take more fruit than usual as soon as I came. But the only fruit to be got here now is the apricot. I am trying to get more varieties from Naini Tal. There has not been any thirst even though the days are fearfully hot. . . . On the whole my own feeling is one of revival of great strength and cheerfulness, and a feeling of exuberant health, only I am afraid I am getting fat on a too much milk diet. Don't you listen to what Jogen writes? He is a hypochondriac himself and wants to make everybody so. I ate one-sixteenth of a *barphi* (sweetmeat) in Lucknow, and that according to Jogen was what put me out of sorts in Almora! Jogen is expected here in a few days. I am going to take him in hand. By-the-bye, I am very susceptible of malarious influences. The first week's indisposition at Almora might have been caused to a certain extent by my passage through the *terai*. Anyhow I feel very, very strong now. You ought to see me, Doctor, when I sit meditating in front of the beautiful snow-peaks and repeat from the Upanishads,—न तस्य रोगो न जरा न मृत्युः प्राप्तस्य हि योगाग्निमयं शरीरम्—"He has neither disease, nor decay, nor death, for, verily, he has obtained a body full of the fire of Yoga."

I am very glad to learn of the success of the meetings of the Ramakrishna Mission at Calcutta. All blessings attend those that help in the great work. . . . —With all love, Yours in the Lord, VIVEKANANDA.

(239)

To Sj. Pramada Das Mitra

ALMORA,*
30th May, 1897.

DEAR SIR—I hear some unavoidable domestic grief has come upon you. To you, a man of wisdom, what can this misery do? Yet the amenities of friendly intercourse incidental to relative existence in this world require my making mention of it. Those moments of grief, however, very often bring out a better spiritual realisation. As if for a while the clouds withdrew and the sun of Truth shone out. In the case of some, half of the bondage is loosened. Of all bondages the greatest is that of position—the fear of reputation is stronger than the fear of death; and even this bondage appears to relax a little. As if the mind saw for a moment that it was much better to listen to the indwelling Lord than to the opinions of men. But again the clouds close up, and this indeed is Maya.

Though for a long time I had no direct correspondence with you, yet I have often been receiving from others almost all the news about you. Some time ago you kindly sent me to England a copy of a translation of the Gita. The cover only bore a line of your handwriting. The few words in my acknowledgment of this gift, I am told, raised doubts in your mind about my old affection towards you.

Please know these doubts to be groundless. The reason of that laconic acknowledgment is that I was given to see during four or five years only that one line of your handwriting on the cover of an English Gita, from which fact I thought, if you had no leisure to write more, would you have leisure enough to read much? Secondly, I learnt, you were particularly the friend of white-skinned missionaries of the Hindu religion and the roguish black natives were repelling! There was apprehension on this score. Thirdly, I am a Mlechchha, Shudra and so forth, I eat anything and everything and with anybody and everybody—and that in public both abroad and here. In my views, besides, much perversion has supervened—one attributeless absolute Brahman, I see, I fairly understand, and I see in some particular individuals the special manifestations of that Brahman; if those individuals are called by the name of God, I can well follow—otherwise the mind does not feel inclined towards intellectual theorisings such as the postulated creator and the like.

Such a God I have seen in my life and his commands I live to follow. The Smritis and the Puranas are productions of men of limited intelligence and are full of fallacies, errors, the feelings of class and malice. Only parts of them breathing broadness of spirit and love are acceptable, the rest is to be rejected. The Upanishads and the Gita are the true scriptures—Rama, Krishna, Buddha, Chaitanya, Nanaka, Kabir and so on are the true Avataras; for they had their hearts broad as the sky; —and above all, Ramakrishna. Ramanuja, Shankara, etc., seem to have been mere Pundits with much narrowness of heart. Where is that love, that weeping heart at the sorrow of others? Dry pedantry of the Pundit—and the feeling of only oneself getting to salvation hurry-scurry! But is that going to be possible, sir? Was it ever likely or will it ever be so? Can anything be attained with any shred of "I" left anyhow?

Another great discrepancy: the conviction is daily gaining on my mind that the idea of caste is the greatest dividing factor and the root of Maya—all caste either on the principle of birth or of merit is bondage. Some friends advise, "True, lay all that at heart, but outside, in the world of relative experience, distinctions like caste must needs be maintained." . . . The idea of oneness at heart (with a craven importance of effort, that is to say), and outside, the hell-dance of demons—oppression and persecution—aye, the dealer of death to the poor, but if the pariah be wealthy enough, "Oh, he is the protector of religion!"

Over and above, I come to see from my studies that the disciplines of religion are not for the Shudra; if he exercises any discrimination about food or about going out to foreign lands, it is all useless in his case, only so much labour lost. I am a Shudra, a Mlechchha, so I have nothing to do with all that botheration. To me what would Mlechchha's food matter or pariah's? It is in the books written by priests that madnesses like that of caste are to be found, and not in books revealed from God. Let the priests enjoy the fruits of their ancestors' achievement, while I follow the word of God, for my good lies there.

Another truth I have realised is that altruistic service only is religion, the rest such as ceremonial observances is madness—even it is wrong to hanker after one's own salvation. Liberation is only for him who gives up everything for others, whereas others who tax their brains day and night harping on "my salvation," "my salvation," wander about with their true well-being ruined both present and prospective, and this I have seen many a time with my own eyes. Reflecting on all these sundry matters I had no heart for writing a letter to you. If notwithstanding all these discrepancies you find your attachment for me intact, I shall feel it to be a very happy issue indeed.[1]—Yours etc., VIVEKANANDA.

(240)

ALMORA,
1st June, 1897.

DEAR MR.—, The objection you show about the Vedas would be valid if the word Vedas meant Samhitâs. The word Vedas includes the three parts, the Samhitas, the Brâhmanas and the Upanishads according to the universally received opinion in India. Of these, the first two portions, as being the ceremonial parts, have been nearly put out of sight; the Upanishads have alone been taken up by all our philosophers and founders of sects.

[1] This is the last letter written to Babu Pramada Das Mitra. It is a bold challenge to the old love and spiritual fellowship of the two master minds of that age, and as such Swamiji states his own case in it in all its extreme trend and tendency so as to demand of his correspondent a sincere depth of love and of the power to harmonise.

The idea that the Samhitas are the only Vedas is very recent and has been started by the late Swami Dayananda. This opinion has not got any hold on the orthodox population.

The reason of this opinion was that Swami Dayananda thought he could find a consistent theory of the whole, based on a new interpretation of the Samhitas, but the difficulties remained the same, only they fell back on the Brahmanas. And in spite of the theories of interpretation and interpolation a good deal still remains.

Now if it is possible to build a consistent religion on the Samhitas, it is a thousand times more sure that a very consistent and harmonious faith can be based upon the Upanishads, and moreover, here one has not to go against the already received national opinion. Here all the Acharyas of the past would side with you, and you have a vast scope for new progress.

The Gita no doubt has already become the Bible of Hinduism, and it fully deserves to be so, but the personality of Krishna has become so covered with haze, that it is impossible to-day to draw any life-giving inspiration from that *life*. Moreover, the present age requires new modes of thought and new life. Hoping this will help you in thinking along these lines—I am yours with blessings,—VIVEKANANDA.

(*241*)

TRANSLATION FROM SANSKRIT

To Swami Suddhananda

ALMORA,
1st June, 1897.

DEAR SUDDHANANDA—Glad to know from your letter that all are doing well there, and to go through the news in detail. I too am in better health, the rest you will know from Dr. Sasi Bhushan. Let the teaching go on for the present in the method revised by Brahmananda, and if any changes are needed in future have them done. And it should never be lost sight of that this must be done with the consent of all.

I am now living in a garden belonging to a merchant, situated a little to the north of Almora. Before me are the snow-peaks of the Himalayas looking, in the reflection of the sun, like a mass of silver, a delight to the heart. By taking free air, regular diet, and plenty of exercise, I have grown strong and healthy in body. But I hear that Yogananda is very ill. I am inviting him to come here. But then he fears the mountain air and water. I wrote to him to-day, saying, "Stay in this garden for some days, and if you find your illness shows no improvement, you may go to Calcutta." He will do as he pleases.

At Almora, every evening Achyutananda gathers the people together and reads to them the Gita and other Shâstras. Many residents of the town, as also soldiers from the cantonment come there daily. I learn also that he is appreciated by all.

The Bengali interpretation that you have done of the Shloka यावानर्थः etc.,[1] does not seem to me to be right.

The interpretation in question is this: "When (the land) is flooded with water, what is the use of drinking water?"

If the law of nature be such that when a land is flooded with water, drinking it is useless, that through certain air passages or through any other recondite ways people's thirst may be allayed, then only can this novel interpretation be relevant, otherwise not.

It is Shankara whom you should follow.

Or, you may do it in this way:—

[1] यावानर्थ उदपाने सर्वतः संप्लुतोदके ।
तावान्सर्वेषु वेदेषु ब्राह्मणस्य विजानतः ॥
—Gita, II. 46.

As, even when whole tracts are flooded with water, small pools are also of great use to the thirsty, (that is to say, just a little water suffices him, and he says, as it were, "Let the vast sheet of water be, even a little of water will satisfy my object.")—of identical use are the whole Vedas to a learned Brahmin. As even when the land is over-flooded, one's concern lies in drinking the water and no more, so in all the Vedas illumination alone is the concern.

Here is another interpretation which hits better the meaning the author wishes to convey:

Even when the land is overflooded, it is only that water which is drinkable and salutary, that people seek for, and no other kind. There are various kinds of water, which differ in quality and properties—even though the land be flooded over—according to the differences in property of their substratum, the soil. Likewise a skilful Brahmin, too, will, for the quenching of the worldly thirst, choose from that sea of words known as the Vedas, which is flooded over with diverse courses of knowledge, that which alone will be of potence to lead to liberation. And it is the knowledge of the Brahman which will do this.

With blessings and good wishes,—Yours, VIVEKANANDA.

(*242*)

ALMORA,
3rd June, 1897.

DEAR—, . . . As for myself I am quite content. I have roused a good many of our people and that was all I wanted. Let things have their course and Karma its sway. I have no bonds here below. I have seen life and it is all self—life is for self, love is for self, honour for self, everything for self. I look back and scarcely find any action I have done for self—even my wicked deeds were not for self. So I am content; not that I feel I have done anything specially good or great, but the world is so little, life so mean a thing, existence so, so servile—that I wonder and smile that human beings, rational souls, should be running after this self—so mean and detestable a prize.

This is the truth. We are caught in a trap, and the sooner one gets out the better for one. I have seen the truth—let the body float up or down, who cares?

It is a beautiful mountain park I am living in now. On the north, extending almost all along the horizon, is peak after peak of the snow-clad Himalayas—forests abounding. It is not cold here, neither very warm; the evenings and mornings are simply delicious. I should be here this summer and when the rains set in, like to go down to the plains to work.

I was born for the life of a scholar—retired, quiet, poring over my books. But the Mother dispenses otherwise—yet the tendency is there.—Yours etc., VIVEKANANDA.

(*243*)

To Swami Brahmananda

ALMORA,
14th June, 1897.

DEAR RAKHAL—I am wholly in sympathy with the subject-matter of the letter of Charu that you have sent me.

In the proposed Address to the Queen-Empress the following points should be noted:

1. That it must be free from exaggeration, in other words, statements to the effect that she is God's regent and so forth, which are so common to us, natives.

2. That all religions having been protected during her reign we have been able fearlessly to preach our Vedantic doctrines both in India and England.

3. Her kindness towards the Indian poor—as for

instance, her inspiring the English to unique acts of charity by contributing herself to the cause of famine relief.

4. Prayer for her long life and for the continual growth of happiness and prosperity among the people of her dominions.

Have this written in correct English and send it to me at Almora, and I shall sign it and send it to Simla. Let me know to whom it should be addressed, at Simla.—Yours affectionately, VIVEKANANDA.

P. S.—Let Suddhananda preserve a copy of the weekly letters that he writes to me from the Math.—V.

(244)

To Swami Akhandananda

ALMORA,*
15th June, 1897.

MY DEAR AKHANDANANDA—I am getting detailed reports of you and getting more and more delighted. It is that sort of work which can conquer the world. What do differences of sect and opinion matter? Bravo! Accept a hundred thousand embraces and blessings from me. Work, work, work—I care for nothing else. Work, work, work, even unto death! Those that are weak must make themselves great workers, great heroes—never mind for money, it will drop from the heavens. Let them whose gifts you will accept, give in their own name if they like, no harm. Whose name, and what is it worth? Who cares for name? Off with it! If in the attempt to carry morsels of food to starving mouths, name and possession and all be doomed even— अहो भाग्यमहो भाग्यम् —thrice blessed art thou! It is the heart, the heart, that conquers, not the brain. Books and learning, Yoga and meditation and illumination—all are but dust compared with love. It is love that gives you the supernatural powers, love that gives you Bhakti, love that gives illumination, and love, again, that leads to emancipation. This indeed is worship, worship of the Lord in the human tabernacle, नेदं यदिदमुपासते —"not this that people worship."[1] This is but the beginning, and unless we spread over the whole of India, nay, the whole earth, in that way, where lies the greatness of our Lord!

Let people see whether or not the touch of our Lord's feet confers divinity on man! It is this that is called liberation-in-life—when the last trace of egoism and selfishness is gone. Well done! Glory to the Lord! Gradually try to spread. If you can, go to Calcutta, and raise a fund with the help of another band of boys; set one or two of them to work at some place, and begin somewhere else. Spread in that way, and go on inspecting them. You will see that the work will gradually become permanent, and spread of religion and education will follow as a matter of course. I have given particular instructions to them in Calcutta. Do that kind of work, and I shall carry you on my shoulders—bravo! You will see that by degrees every district will become a centre—and that a permanent one. I am soon going down to the plains. I am a fighter and shall die in the battle-field. Does it behove me to sit up here like a zenana lady?—Yours with all love, VIVEKANANDA.

(245)

To Sister Nivedita

ALMORA,
20th June, 1897.

MY DEAR MISS NOBLE—. . . Let me tell you plainly. Every word you write I value, and every letter is welcome a hundred times. Write whenever you have a mind, and opportunity, and whatever you like, knowing that nothing will be misinterpreted, nothing unappreciated. I have not

[1] Things other than God.

had any news of the work for so long. Can you tell me anything? I do not expect any help from India, in spite of all the jubilating over me. They are so poor!

But I have started work in the fashion in which I myself was trained—that is to say, under the trees, and keeping body and soul together anyhow. The plan has also changed a little. I have sent some of my boys to work in the Famine districts. It has acted like a miracle. I find, as I always thought, that it is through the *heart*, and that alone, that the world can be reached. The present plan is, therefore, to train up numbers of young men (from the highest classes, not the lowest. For the latter I shall have to wait a little), and the first attack will be made by sending a number of them over a district. When these sappers and miners of religion have cleared the way, there will then be time enough to put in theory and philosophy.

A number of boys are already in training, but the recent earthquake has destroyed the poor shelter we had to work in, which was only rented, anyway. Never mind. The work must be done without shelter, and under difficulties. . . . As yet it is shaven heads, rags and casual meals. This must change, however, and will, for are we not working for it, head and heart? . . .

It is true in one way that the people here have so little to give up—yet renunciation is in our blood. One of my boys in training has been an executive engineer, in charge of a district. That means a very big position here. He gave it up like straw!. . . With all love, yours in the Truth, VIVEKANANDA.

(*246*)

To Swami Brahmananda

ALMORA,*
20th June, 1897.

DEAR RAKHAL—Glad to learn that you are better in

health than before. Well, it is seldom that Brother Jogen reports the bare truths, so do not at all be anxious to hear them. I am all right now, with plenty of muscular strength, and no thirst. . . . The liver, too, acts well. I am not certain as to what effects Sasi's medicine had. So I have stopped using it. I am having plenty of mangoes. I am getting exceptionally adept in riding, and do not feel the least pain or exhaustion even after a run of twenty or thirty miles at a stretch. Milk I have altogether stopped for fear of corpulence.

Yesterday I came to Almora, and shall not go any more to the garden. Henceforth I am to have three meals a day in the English fashion, as Miss Müller's guest. . . .

Suddhananda writes to say that they are going on with Ruddock's Practice of Medicine or something of that sort. What nonsense do you mean by having such things taught in the class? A set of common apparatus for physics and another for chemistry, an ordinary telescope and a microscope—all these can be had for Rupees 150 to 200. Sasi Babu may give a lecture on practical chemistry once a week, and Hariprasanna on physics etc. *And buy all the good scientific books that you can have in Bengali, and have them read.*—Yours affectionately, VIVEKANANDA.

(247)

To Swami Akhandananda

ALMORA,*
30th June, 1897.

MY DEAR AKHANDANANDA—According to your instructions I write a letter to Mr. Levinge, the District Magistrate. Besides, you will write a big letter to the *Indian Mirror*, describing in detail his method of work (having got the same revised by Dr. Sasi), and send a copy of it to the gentleman named above. Our fools only search for people's shortcomings. Let them see some virtues too.

I am leaving this place next Monday. . . .

What do you talk of the difficulty in getting orphans? Better ask for four or five men from the Math, if you like; you can find some orphans in two days, if you seek from village to village.

Of course we must have a permanent centre. And can anything be done in this country unless the—help? Do not mix in politics etc., nor have any connection with them. At the same time you need not have any quarrel with anybody. You must put your body, mind and all you have to some one work. Here I gave a lecture to a European audience in English, and another to the Indian residents in Hindi. This is my maiden speech in Hindi, but everyone liked it for all that. Of course the Westerners, as is their wont, were in raptures over it, as coming from a "nigger"! "Oh, how wonderful!" and that sort of thing. Next Saturday there will be another lecture for the Europeans. A big Association has been set on foot here—let us wait and see how far it works in future. The object of the Association is to impart education and religion.

Monday next, trip to Bareilly, then to Saharanpur, next to Umballa, thence, most probably, to Mussoorie with Captain Sevier, and as soon as it is a little cool, return to the plains and journey to Rajputana etc. Go on working at top-speed. Never fear! I, too, have become very idle, I see. The body must go, no mistake about that. Why then let it go in idleness? "It is better to wear out than rust out." Don't be anxious; even when I die, my very bones will work miracles. We must spread over the whole of India in ten years, short of this it is no good. To work, like an athlete!—Victory to the Guru! Money and all will come of themselves, we want men, not money. It is man that makes everything, what can money do?—Men we want, the more you get, the better. . . . Here, for instance, was M— who brought together a lot of money, but there was no man, and what good did he achieve? —Yours affectionately, VIVEKANANDA.

(*248*)

TRANSLATION FROM SANSKRIT

To Sj. Sarat Chandra Chakravarty

ALMORA,
3rd July, 1897.

Constant salutation be to Sri Ramakrishna, the Free, the Ishvara, the Shiva form, by whose power we and the whole world are blessed.

Mayest thou live long, O Saratchandra,—

Those writers of Shâstra who do not tend towards work say that all-powerful destiny prevails, but others who are workers consider the will of man as superior. Knowing that the quarrel between those who believe in the human will as the remover of misery, and others who rely on destiny is due to indiscrimination—try to ascend the highest peak of knowledge.

It has been said that adversity is the touchstone of true knowledge, and this may be said a hundred times with regard to the truth: "Thou art That." This truly diagnoses the Vairâgya (dispassion) disease. Blessed is the life of one who has developed this symptom. In spite of your dislike I repeat the old saying, "Wait for a short time." You are tired with rowing; rest on your oars. The momentum will take the boat to the other side. This has been said in the Gita passage (IV. 38), "In good time, having reached perfection in Yoga, one realises that oneself in one's own heart"; and in the Upanishad, "Immortality can be attained neither by riches nor by progeny, but by renunciation alone" (Kaivalya, 2). Here, by the word renunciation, Vairagya is referred to. It may be of two kinds, with or without purpose. If the latter, then none but worm-eaten brains will try for it. But if the other is referred to, then renunciation would mean the withdrawal of the mind from other things and concentrating it on God or on Atman. The Lord of all cannot be any particular individual. He must be the sum total. One possessing Vairagya does not understand by Atman the individual ego but the All-pervading Lord, residing as the Self and internal Ruler in all. He is perceivable by all as the sum total. This being so, as Jiva and Ishvara are in essence the same, serving the Jivas and loving God must mean one and the same thing. Here is a peculiarity: When you serve a Jiva with the idea that he is a Jiva, it is Dayâ (compassion) and not Prema (love); but when you serve him with the idea that he is the Self, that is Prema. That the Atman is the one objective of love is known from Shruti, Smriti and direct perception. Bhagavan Chaitanya was right therefore, when he said: "Love to God and compassion to the Jiva." This conclusion of the Bhagavan, intimating differentiation between Jiva and Ishvara was right, as he was a dualist. But for us, Advaitists, this notion of Jiva as distinct from God is the cause of bondage. Our principle should be, therefore, love, and not compassion. The application of the word compassion even to Jiva seems to me to be rash and vain. For us, it is not to pity but to serve. Ours is not the feeling of compassion but of love, and the feeling of Self in all.

O Sharman, may thine for thy good be Vairagya,—the feeling of which is love, which unifies all inequalities, cures the disease of Samsâra, removes the threefold misery inevitable in this phenomenal world, reveals the true nature of all things, destroys the darkness of Maya, and which brings out the Selfhood of everything from Brahmâ to the blade of grass! This is the constant prayer of VIVEKANANDA, ever bound to thee in love.

(249)

To Sister Nivedita

ALMORA,
4th July, 1897.

MY DEAR MISS NOBLE—I am being played upon curiously by both good and evil influences from London these times here . . . . on the other hand your letters are full of life and sunshine, and bring strength and hope to my spirits, and they sadly want these now. God knows.

Although I am still in the Himalayas, and shall be here for at least a month more, I started the work in Calcutta before I came, and they write progress every week.

Just now I am very busy with the famine, and except for training a number of young men for future work, have not been able to put more energy into the teaching work. The "feeding work" is absorbing all my energy and means. Although we can work only on a very small scale as yet, the effect is marvellous. For the first time since the days of Buddha, Brahmin boys are found nursing by the bed-side of cholera-stricken pariahs.

In India, lectures and teaching cannot do any good. What we want is Dynamic Religion. And that, "God willing," as the Mohammedans say, I am determined to show. . . . I entirely agree with the prospectus of your Society, and you may take for granted my agreement with everything you will do in the future. I have entire faith in your ability and sympathy. I already owe you an immense debt and you are laying me every day under infinite obligations. My only consolation is that it is for the good of others. Else I do not deserve in the least the wonderful kindness shown to me by the Wimbledon friends. You good, steady, genuine English people, may the Lord always bless you. I appreciate you every day more and more from a distance. Kindly convey my love everlasting to—and all the rest of our friends there. With all love, yours ever in the Truth, VIVEKANANDA.

(250)

To Miss Mary Hale

ALMORA,
9th July, 1897.

DEAR SISTER—I am very sorry to read between the lines the desponding tone of your letter, and I understand the cause; thank you for your warning, I understand your motive perfectly. I had arranged to go with Ajit Singh to England but, the doctors not allowing, it fell through. I shall be so happy to learn that Harriet has met him. He will be only too glad to meet any of you.

I had also a lot of cuttings from different American papers fearfully criticising my utterances about American women and furnishing me with the strange news that I had been outcasted! As if I had any caste to lose, being a Sannyasin!

Not only no caste has been lost, but it has considerably shattered the opposition to sea-voyage—my going to the West. If I should have to be outcasted, I shall have to be done so with half the ruling princes of India and almost all of educated India. On the other hand, a leading Raja of the caste to which I belonged before my entering the order got up a banquet in my honour, at which were most of the *big bugs* of that caste. The Sannyasins, on the other hand, may not dine with any one in India as it would be beneath the dignity of gods to dine with mere mortals. They are regarded as Nârâyanas while the others are mere men. And dear Mary, these feet have been washed and wiped and worshipped by the descendants of kings, and there has been a progress through the country which none ever commanded in India.

It will suffice to say that the police were necessary to keep order if I ventured out into the street! That is outcasting indeed! Of course that took the starch out of the missionaries, and who are they here? Nobodies. We are in blissful ignorance of their existence all the time. I had in a lecture said something about the missionaries and the origin of that species except the English church gentlemen, and in that connection had to refer to the very churchy women of America and their power of inventing scandals. This the missionaries are parading as an attack on American women *en masse* to undo my work there, as they well know that anything said against themselves will rather please the U. S. people. My dear Mary, supposing I had said all sorts of fearful things against the "Yanks"—would that be paying off a millionth part of what they say of our *mothers* and *sisters*? "Neptune's waters" would be perfectly useless to wash off the hatred the Christian "Yanks" of both sexes bear to us, "heathens of India"—and what harm have we done them? Let the "Yanks" learn to be patient under criticism and then criticise others. It is a well-known psychological fact that those who are ever ready to abuse others cannot bear the slightest touch of criticism from others. Then again, what do I owe them? Except your family, Mrs. Bull, the Leggetts and a few other kind persons, who else has been kind to me? Who came forward to help me work out my ideas? I had to work till I am at death's door and had to spend nearly the whole of that in America, so that the Americans may learn to be broader and more spiritual. In England I worked only six months. There was not a breath of scandal save one and that was the working of an American woman, which greatly relieved my English friends—not only no attacks, but many of the best English church clergymen became my firm friends, and without asking I got much help for my work and I am sure to get much more. There is a society watching my work and getting help for it and four respectable persons followed me to India to help my work, and dozens were ready, and the next time I go, hundreds will be.

Dear, dear Mary, do not be afraid for me. . . . The world is big, very big and there must be some place for me even if the "Yankees" rage. Anyhow, I am quite satisfied with my work. I never planned anything. I have taken things as they came. Only one idea was burning in my brain—to start the machine for elevating the Indian masses, and that I have succeeded in doing to a certain extent. It would have made your heart glad to see how my boys are working in the midst of famine and disease and misery—nursing by the mat-bed of the cholera-stricken Pariah and feeding the starving Chandâla, and the Lord sends help to me and to them all. "What are men?" He is with me, the Beloved, He was when I was in America, in England, when I was roaming about unknown from place to place in India. What do I care about what they talk—the babies, they do not know any better. What? I, who have realised the spirit and the vanity of all earthly nonsense, to be swerved from my path by babies' prattle? Do I look like that?

I had to talk a lot about myself because I owed that to you. I feel my task is done—at most three or four years more of life is left. I have lost all wish for my salvation. I never wanted earthly enjoyments. I must see my machine in strong working order, and then knowing sure that I have put in a lever for the good of humanity, in India at least, which no power can drive back, I will sleep, without caring what will be next; and may I be born again and again, and suffer thousands of miseries, so that I may worship the only God that exists, the only God I believe in, the sum total of all souls—and above all, my God the wicked, my God the miserable, my God the poor of all races, of all species, is the special object of my worship.

" He who is in you and is outside of you, who works through every hand, who walks through every foot, whose body you are, Him worship, and break all other idols."

" He who is the high and the low, the saint and the sinner, the god and the worm, Him worship, the visible, the knowable, the real, the omnipresent, break all other idols.

" In whom there is neither past life nor future birth, nor death nor going nor coming, in whom we always have been and always will be one, Him worship, break all other idols.

" Aye, fools, neglecting the living Gods and His infinite reflection with which the world is full, and running after imaginary shadows, Him worship, the only visible, and break all other idols."

My time is short. I have got to unbreast whatever I have to say, without caring if it smarts some or irritates others. Therefore, my dear Mary, do not be frightened at whatever drops from my lips, for the power behind me is not Vivekananda but He the Lord, and He knows best. If I have to please the world, that will be injuring the world; the voice of the majority is wrong, seeing that they govern and yet there is the sad state of the world. Every new thought must create opposition—in the civilised a polite sneer, in the vulgar savage howls and filthy scandals.

Even these earthworms must stand erect, even children must see light. The Americans are drunk with new wine. A hundred waves of prosperity have come and gone over my country. We have learned the lesson which no child can yet understand. It is vanity. This hideous world is Maya. Renounce and be happy. Give up the idea of sex and possessions. There is no other bond. Marriage and sex and money are the only living devils. All earthly love proceeds from the body. No sex, no

possessions; as these fall off, the eyes open to spiritual vision. The soul regains its own infinite power. . . .
—Yours ever affly., VIVEKANANDA.

(251)

To Swami Brahmananda

ALMORA,
9th July, 1897.

MY DEAR RAKHAL—To-day I sent back the proofs of the Objects of our Association that you sent me, corrected. The rules and regulations portion (which the members of our Association had read) is full of mistakes. Correct it very carefully and reprint it, or people will laugh.

. . . The kind of work that is going on at Berhampore is exceedingly nice. It is those works that will triumph—can doctrines and dogmas touch the heart? Work, work—live the life—what do doctrines and opinions count? Philosophy and Yoga and penance—the worship-room—your sunned rice or vegetable offerings—all these constitute the religion of one man or one country; doing good to others is the one great, universal religion. Men and women, young and old, down to the Pariah, nay, the very animal—all can grasp this religion. Can a merely negative religion be of any avail? The stone is never unchaste, the cow never tells a lie, nor do trees commit theft or robbery, but what does it matter? Granted that you do not steal, nor tell a lie, nor lead an unchaste life, but meditate four hours a day, and religiously ring the bell for twice as many hours—yet, what matters it after all? That work, little as it is, that you have done, has brought Berhampore to your feet for ever—now people will do whatever you wish them to. Now you will no longer have to argue to the people that "Ramakrishna *is* God." Without it what will mere lecture do?—Do fair words butter any parsnips? If you could do like that in ten districts, all the ten would become yours to have and hold. Therefore, like the intelligent boy that you are, lay your greatest stress, for the present, on that work department, and try heart and soul to augment the utility of that alone. Organise a number of boys to go from door to door, let them fetch, in the manner of the Alakhia Sadhus, whatever they can get—money, or worn out clothes, or rice and eatables or anything. Then distribute them. That is work, work indeed. After that people will have faith, and will then do what they are told.

Whatever is left over after defraying the expenses of the Calcutta meeting, remit for famine relief, or help with it the countless poor that live in the slums of Calcutta:—let Memorial Halls and things of that kind go to the dogs. The Lord will do what He thinks best. I am at present in excellent health. . . .

Why are you not collecting materials?—I shall go down and start the paper myself. Kindness and love can buy you the whole world; lectures and books and philosophy—all stand lower than these.

Please write to Sasi to open a work department like this for the service of the poor.

. . . Curtail the expenses of worship to a rupee or two per mensem. The children of the Lord are dying of starvation. . . . Worship with water and *tulasi* leaves alone, and let the allowance for His Bhoga (food offerings) be spent in offering food to the Living God who dwells in persons of the poor—then will His grace descend on everything. Jogen felt unwell here; so to-day he started for Calcutta. I shall again go to Dewaldhar to-morrow. Please accept my love and tender it to all.—Affectionately yours, VIVEKANANDA.

(252)

To Swami Suddhananda

ALMORA,
11th July, 1897.

MY DEAR SUDDHANANDA—I was very glad to receive your last report. I have very little criticism to make except that you ought to write a bit more legibly.

I am quite satisfied with the work done as yet, but it must be pushed forward. I have not learnt as yet of the suggestion I made before as to getting a set of chemical and physical apparatus and starting classes in elementary and experimental chemistry and physics, especially in physiology.

What about the other suggestion of buying sets of all the scientific books that have been translated into Bengali?

It now seems to me that there must at least be three Mohants (heads) elected at a time—one to direct the business part, one the experimental, the other the intellectual part.

The difficulty is to get the director of education. Brahmananda and Turiyananda may well fill the other two. Of visitors I am sorry to learn that you are only getting Babus from Calcutta. They are no good. What we want are brave young men, who will work; not tom-fools.

Ask Brahmananda to write to both Abhedananda and Saradananda to send weekly reports to the Math without fail, also to send Bengali articles and notes for the would-be paper. Is G. C. Ghose getting up things for the paper? Work on with a will and be ready.

Akhandananda is working wonderfully at Mahula, but the system is not good. It seems they are frittering away their energies in one little village and that to only doling out rice. I do not hear that any preaching has been done along with this helping. All the wealth of the world cannot help one little Indian village if the people are not taught to help themselves. Our work should be mainly *educational*, both moral and intellectual. I have not learnt anything about it—only so many *beggars are helped*! Ask Brahmananda to open centres in different *districts* so as to cover the largest space, with our small means.

And then, so far it seems to have been ineffectual, for they have not succeeded in rousing the people of the place to start societies to educate the people, so that they may learn to be self-reliant, frugal and not given to marrying, and thus save themselves from future famine. Charity opens the heart, but work on through that wedge.

The easiest way is to take a hut—make it into a temple of Guru Maharaj. Let the poor come there to be helped, also to worship. Let there be Kathâ (Puranic recitals) morning and evening there—through that you may teach all you want to teach the people. By degrees the people will be interested. They will keep up the temple themselves; maybe the hut-temple will evolve into a great institution in a few years. Let those that go to relief-work first select a central spot in each district and start such a hut-temple, from which all our little work is to proceed.

Even the greatest fool can accomplish a task if it be after his heart. But the intelligent man is he who can convert every work into one that suits his taste. No work is petty. Everything in this world is like a banyan-seed, which, though appearing tiny as a mustard-seed, has yet the gigantic banyan tree latent within it. He indeed is intelligent who notices this and succeeds in making all work truly great.[1]

[1] This paragraph only is translated from Bengali.

Moreover they have to see that cheats do not get the food of the deserving. India is full of lazy rogues, and curious, they never die of hunger, they always get something. Ask Brahmananda to write this to everyone in relief-work—they must not be allowed to spend money to no good. We want the greatest possible good work permanent from the least outlay.

Now you see you must try to think out original ideas —else, as soon as I die, the whole thing will tumble to pieces. For example, you hold a meeting to consider, "How we can reap the best permanent results out of the small means at our disposal." Let all have notice a few days before and let each suggest something and discuss all the suggestions, criticising them, and then send me a report.

Lastly, you must remember I expect more from my children than from my brethren. I want each one of my children to be a hundred times greater than I could ever be. Everyone of you *must be a giant—must*, that is my word. Obedience, readiness, and love for the cause —if you have these three, nothing can hold you back.— With love and blessings, VIVEKANANDA.

(253)

To Sister Nivedita

ALMORA,
23rd July, 1897.

MY DEAR MISS NOBLE—Excuse these few lines. I shall write more fully as soon as I reach some place, I am on my way from the hills to the plains.

I do not understand what you mean by frankness without familiarity—I for one will give anything to get rid of the last lingering bit of Oriental formality in me and speak out like a child of nature. Oh, to live even for a day in the full light of freedom, to breathe the free air of simplicity! Is not that the highest purity?

In this world we work through fear of others, we talk through fear, we think through fear, alas! we are born in a land of enemies. Who is there who has been able to get rid of this feeling of fear, as if everyone is a spy set specially to watch him? And woe unto the man who pushes himself forward! Will it ever be a land of friends? Who knows? We can only try.

The work has already begun and at present famine-relief is the thing next to hand. Several centres have been opened and the work goes on; famine-relief, preaching and a little teaching. As yet of course it is very very insignificant, the boys in training are being taken out as opportunity is offering itself. The sphere of action at present is Madras and Calcutta. Mr. Goodwin is working in Madras. Also one has gone to Colombo. From the next week a monthly report of the whole work will be forwarded to you if it has not already reached you. I am away from the centre of work, so things go a little slow, you see, but the work is satisfactory on the whole.

You can do more work for us from England than by coming here. Lord bless you for your great self-sacrifice for the poor Indians.

I entirely agree with you that the work in England will look up when I am there. But all the same it is not proper to leave India before the machine is moving at some rate, and I am sure that there are many to guide it in my absence. That will be done in a few months, "God willing," as the Mussalmans say. One of my best workers is now in England, the Rājā of Khetri. I expect him soon in India and he will be of great service to me no doubt. With everlasting love and blessings from VIVEKANANDA.

(254)

To Swami Akhandananda

ALMORA,*
24th July, 1897.

MY DEAR AKHANDANANDA—I am very glad to receive your letter and go through all the contents. Your wishes about the orphanage are very good, and Sri Maharaj will not fail to fulfil them at an early date. Try your best to found a permanent centre. . . . Never worry about money. To-morrow I shall leave Almora for the plains, and wherever there will be made some stir, I shall open a subscription list for famine—set your mind easy on that score. When in every district there will be a Math on the model of our Math in Calcutta, then will my heart's desire be fulfilled. Let not the work of preaching, too, be at a standstill, and greater even than preaching, is the work of imparting education. By means of lectures and the like, the village people must be taught religion, history and such other subjects—specially, history. To help our educational work there is a Society in England, which, as I find from reports, is doing excellent work. In time we shall get help of this kind from everywhere, don't be frightened. They only do work who think that help *will* come, directly they are on the field of work.

All strength is in you, have faith in it. It will not go unmanifested. Accept my heartiest love and blessings, and convey them to the Brahmacharin. Write now and then fiery letters to the Math so that all may take heart and work. Victory to the Guru!—Yours affectionately, VIVEKANANDA.

(255)

To Sister Nivedita

ALMORA,
29th July, 1897.

MY DEAR MISS NOBLE—A letter from Mr. Sturdy reached me yesterday, informing me that you are determined to come to India and see things with your own eyes. I replied to that yesterday, but what I learnt from Miss Müller about your plans makes this further note necessary, and it is better that it should be direct.

Let me tell you frankly that I am now convinced that you have a great future in the work for India. What was wanted was not a man but a woman; a real lioness, to work for the Indians, women specially.

India cannot yet produce great women, she must borrow them from other nations. Your education, sincerity, purity, immense love, determination and above all, the Celtic blood make you just the woman wanted.

Yet the difficulties are many. You cannot form any idea of the misery, the superstition, and the slavery that are here. You will be in the midst of a mass of half-naked men and women with quaint ideas of caste and isolation, shunning the white skin through fear or hatred and hated by them intensely. On the other hand, you will be looked upon by the white as a crank and every one of your movements will be watched with suspicion.

Then the climate is fearfully hot; our winter in most places being like your summer, and in the south it is always blazing.

Not one European comfort is to be had in places out of the cities. If in spite of all this you dare venture into the work, you are welcome, a hundred times welcome. As for me, I am nobody here as elsewhere, but what little influence I have, shall be devoted to your service.

You must think well before you plunge in, and after work, if you fail in this or get disgusted, on my part I promise you *I will stand by you unto death* whether you work for India or not, whether you give up Vedanta or remain in it. "The tusks of the elephant come out but never go back";—so are the words of a man never retracted. I promise you that. Again I must give you a bit of warning. You must stand on your own feet and not be under the wings of Miss Müller or anybody else. She is a good lady in her own way, but unfortunately it got into her head, when she was a girl, that she was a born leader and that no other qualifications were necessary to move the world but money! This idea is coming on the surface again and again in spite of herself and you will find it impossible to pull on with her in a few days. She now intends to take a house in Calcutta for herself and yourself and other European or American friends who may come.

It is very kind and good of her, but her Lady Abbess plan will never be carried out for two reasons—her violent temper and overbearing conduct, and her awfully vacillating mind. Friendship with many is best at a distance and everything goes well with the person who stands on his own feet.

Mrs. Sevier is a jewel of a lady, so good, so kind. The Seviers are the *only* English people who do not hate the *natives*, Sturdy not excepted. Mr. and Mrs. Sevier are the only persons who *did not come* to patronise us but they have no fixed plans yet. When you come, you may get them to work with you and that will be really helpful to them and to you. But after all it is absolutely necessary to stand on one's own feet.

I learn from America two friends of mine, Mrs. Bull of Boston and Miss MacLeod, are coming on a visit to India this autumn. Miss MacLeod you already know in London, that Paris-dressed young American lady; Mrs. Bull is about fifty and has been a kind friend to me in America.

I may suggest that your joining the party may while away the tedium of the journey, as they also are coming by way of Europe.

I am glad to receive a note at last from Mr. Sturdy after long. But it was so stiff and cold. It seems he is disappointed at the collapse of the London work.

With everlasting love,—Yours ever in the Lord, VIVEKANANDA.

(256)

To Mrs. Ole Bull

THE MATH, BELUR,
19th August, 1897.

DEAR MRS. BULL,—. . . My health is indifferent and although I have some rest I do not think I shall be able to regain my usual vigour till winter next. I had a letter from Joe saying that you are both coming to India. I, of course, shall be very glad to see you in India, only you ought to know from the first that India is the dirtiest and unhealthiest hole in the world, with scarcely any European comforts except in the big capitals.

I learn from England that Mr. Sturdy is sending Abhedananda to New York. It seems that the English work is impossible without me. Only a magazine will be started and worked by Mr. Sturdy. I had arranged to come to England this season, but I was foolishly prevented by the doctors. In India the work is going on.

I do not think any European or American will be of any service here just now, and it will be hard for any Westerner to bear the climate. Mrs. Annie Besant with her exceptional powers works only among the Theosophists and thus she submits to all the indignities of isolation which a Mlechchha is made to undergo here. Even Goodwin smarts now and then and has to be called to order. He is doing good work as he is a man and can mix with the people. Women have no place in men's society here, and she can do good only among her own sex in India. The English friends that came over to India have not been of any help as yet and do not know whether they will be of any in the future. With all these, if anybody wants to try she is welcome.

If Saradananda wants to come he may and I am sure he will be of very good service to me just now in organising the work, now that my health is broken. There is a young English woman, Miss Margaret Noble very eager to come to India to learn the state of things, so that she may do some work when she is back home. I have written her to accompany you in case you come via London. The great difficulty is that you can never understand the situation here from a distance. The two types are so entirely different in all things that it is not possible to form any idea from America or England.

You ought to think that you are starting for the interior of Africa and if you meet anything better that will be unexpected. . . . Ever yours etc., VIVEKANANDA.

(257)

To Srimati Indumati Mitra

*1897.**

DEAR MOTHER—Please be not anxious because I could not write to you and could not go to Belgaon. I was suffering very much from illness and it was impossible for me to go then. Now, thanks to my travels in the Himalayas, I have greatly regained my health. I shall soon resume work. In two weeks I am going to the Punjab, and just after delivering a lecture or two at Lahore and

Amritsar, I shall start via Karachi for Gujrat, Cutch, etc. I shall surely see you at Karachi.

This Kashmir is a veritable heaven on earth. Nowhere else in the world is such a country as this. Mountains and rivers, trees and plants, men and women, beasts and birds—all vie with one another for excellence. I feel a pang at heart not to have visited it so long. Please write to me in detail how you are doing, mentally and physically, and accept my special blessings. I am constantly having your welfare at heart, know this for certain. —Yours sincerely, VIVEKANANDA.

(*258*)

To Swami Brahmananda

SRINAGAR, KASHMIR,
30th September, 1897.

DEAR RAKHAL—I received your affectionate letter and also the letter from the Math. I am leaving for the Punjab in two or three days. I have received the foreign mail. The following are my answers to Miss Noble's questions in her letter:

1. Nearly all the branches have been started, but the movement is only just the beginning.

2. Most of the monks are educated. Those that are not, are also having secular education. But above all, to do good, perfect unselfishness is absolutely necessary. To ensure that, more attention is given to spiritual exercises than to anything else.

3. Secular educators: We get mostly those who have already educated themselves. What is needed, is training them into our method and building up of character. The training is to make them obedient and fearless;

and the method is to help the poor physically first and then work up to higher regions of mentality.

Arts and Industries: This part of the programme alone cannot be begun for want of funds. The simplest method to be worked upon at present is to induce Indians to use their own produce and get markets for Indian art-wares etc., in other countries. This should be done by persons who are not only not middlemen themselves, but will devote the entire proceeds of this branch to the benefit of the workmen.

4. Wandering from place to place will be necessary till "people come to education." The religious character of the wandering monks will carry with it a much greater weight than otherwise.

5. All castes are open to our influence. So long the highest only have been worked upon. But since the work department is in full operation in different famine-centres, we are influencing the lower classes more and more.

6. Nearly all the Hindus approve our work, only they are not used to practical co-operation in such works.

7. Yes, from the very start we are making no distinction in our charities or other good works between the different religions of India.

Reply to Miss Noble according to these hints.—VIVEKANANDA.

(259)

To Sister Nivedita

SRINAGAR, KASHMIR,
1st October, 1897.

Some people do the best work when *led.* Not every one is *born to lead.* The best leader, however, is one who "leads like the baby." The baby, though apparently depending on every one, is the king of the household. At least, to my thinking, that is the secret. . . . Many feel, but only a few can express. It is the power of expressing one's love and appreciation and sympathy for others, that enables one person to succeed better in spreading the idea than others. . . .

I shall not try to describe Kashmir to you. Suffice it to say, I never felt sorry to leave any country except this Paradise on earth; and I am trying my best, if I can, to influence the Raja in starting a centre. So much to do here, and the material so hopeful! . . . .

The great difficulty is this: I see persons giving me almost the whole of their love. But I must not give any one the whole of mine in return, for that day the work would be ruined. Yet there are some who will look for such a return, not having the breadth of the impersonal view. It is absolutely necessary to the work that I should have the enthusiastic love of as many as possible, while I myself remain entirely impersonal. Otherwise jealousy and quarrels would break up everything. A leader must be impersonal. I am sure you understand this. I do not mean that one should be a brute, making use of the devotion of others for his own ends, and laughing in his sleeve meanwhile. What I mean is what I am, intensely personal in my love, but having the power to pluck out my own heart with my own hand, if it becomes necessary, "for the good of many, for the welfare of many," as Buddha said. Madness of love, and yet in it no bondage. Matter changed into spirit by the force of love. Nay, that is the gist of our Vedanta. There is but One, seen by the ignorant as matter, by the wise as God. And the history of civilisation is the progressive reading of spirit into matter. The ignorant see the person in the non-person. The sage sees the non-person in the person. Through pain and pleasure, joy and sorrow, this is the one lesson we are learning. . . . Yours ever with love and truth, VIVEKANANDA.

(260)

To Swami Brahmananda

*10th October, 1897.**

Dear Rakhal—Reached Murree from Kashmir in the evening of the day before yesterday. Everybody had an enjoyable time of it, only Krishnalal and Gupta suffered now and then from fever, which, however, was but slight. This Address is to be sent to the Raja of Khetri. Have it printed in gilt etc. The Raja is expected at Bombay about the 21st or 22nd of October. None of us is staying at Bombay at present—if there be any, send him a copy so that he may present the same to the Raja even on board the ship, or somewhere in the city of Bombay. Send the superior copy to Khetri. Have this passed in a meeting, and if any change is needed, no harm. Then sign it, all of you, only leaving a blank for my name, and I shall sign it on going to Khetri. Let no pains be spared in this. . . .

. . . Captain Sevier says he is very anxious for a site. He wishes to have a spot near Mussoorie or in some other central place, as soon as possible. . . . The thing is that we do not want a place which is too cold, at the same time it must not be too hot. Dehra Dun is unbearable in summer, but pleasant in winter; Mussoorie itself is, I dare say, not the right place for many in winter. Above or below it, that is, in British or Gharwal territory, some land is sure to be found. At the same time there must be a supply of water at the place throughout the year, for drinking purposes and for everyday use. My plan is this: With only Achyutananda and Gupta I go from Murree to Rawalpindi, thence to Jammu, thence to Lahore, and from Lahore straight to Karachi. . . . Give my hearty love and blessings to Sasi Babu. I see that Master Mahashay has buckled to work after such a long time. Give him my special love and greetings. To see him, with his feminine retiringness, stirred to work, my courage has gone up by leaps and bounds. I am writing to him to-morrow even. Victory to the Lord!—To work! To work!—Yours affectionately, VIVEKANANDA.

(*261*)

MURREE,*
10th October, 1897.

DEAR—, I am sorry to learn from your letter that you are not doing well. If you can make an unpopular man popular, there I call you a clever fellow. There is no prospect of work there in the future; it would have been better had you gone rather to Dacca, or some other place. However, it is a good thing that the work will close in November. If you get very badly off in health, you should better come away. There is much field for work in the Central Provinces, and even without famine there is no lack of poverty-stricken people in our country. Wherever it is, if you can choose a site with an eye to prospect, you are sure to turn out good work. However, be not sorry. What one does has no destruction—no, never. Who knows, at that very place the future may reap golden results.

I shall very soon begin my work in the plains. I have now no need of travelling over the mountains.

Keep watch over your health.—Yours affectionately, VIVEKANANDA.

(*262*)

To Swami Akhandananda

MURREE,*
10th October, 1897.

MY DEAR AKHANDANANDA—I am very glad to receive your letter. You need not make a big plan for the present, but do only what is possible under existing circumstances. Gradually the way will open to you. We must certainly have the orphanage, no hesitating in that. We must not leave the girls in the lurch, either. But then we must have a lady superintendent for an orphanage of girls. I believe Mother — will be a very good hand for that. Or, engage for this task some aged widow of the village, who has no issue. And there must be separate places for the boys and girls. Captain Sevier is ready to send you money to help in this. Nedou's Hotel, Lahore — that is his address. If you write to him, write the words, "To wait arrival," on the letter. I am soon going to Rawalpindi, to-morrow, or the day after; then I visit Lahore and other places via Jammu, and return to Rajputana via Karachi etc.

I am doing well.—Yours, VIVEKANANDA.

P. S. You must admit Mohammedan boys too, but never tamper with their religion. The only thing you will have to do is to make separate arrangements for their food etc., and teach them so that they may be moral, manly, and devoted to doing good to others. This indeed is religion.

Shelve your intricate philosophical speculations for the present.—V.

In our country we at present need manhood and kindness. स ईशः अनिर्वचनीयप्रेमस्वरूपः—"The Lord is the Essence of unutterable Love." But instead of saying प्रकाश्यते क्वापि पात्रे —"He is manifested in special objects," we should say, स प्रत्यक्ष एव सर्वेषां प्रेमरूपः—"He is ever manifest as Love in all beings." What other God—the creation of your mind—are you then going to worship? Let the Vedas, the Koran, the Puranas, and all scriptural lumber rest now for some time—let there be worship of the visible God of Love and Kindness in the country. All idea of separation is bondage, that of non-differentiation is Mukti. Let not the words of people dead-drunk with worldliness terrify you. अभीरभीः —"Be fearless!" Not men, but worms! Admit boys of all religions—Hindu, Mohammedan, Christian or anything, but begin rather gently—I mean, see that they get their food and drink a little separately, and teach them only the universal side of religion.—V.

Be mad over this, and strike others with this madness! This life has no other end. Preach His name, let His teachings penetrate the world to the very bone. Never forget. Repeat this Mantram in your heart of hearts unceasingly, as you go the round of your daily duties.—Yours, V.

(263)

To "Master Mahashay"

C/o LALA HANSRAJ,
RAWALPINDI,
Oct., 1897.

DEAR M—, *C'est bon, mon ami*—now you are doing just the thing. Come out, man! No sleeping all life; time is flying. Bravo! That is the way.

Many thanks for your publication—only I am afraid it will not pay its way in a pamphlet form. . . . Never mind, pay or no pay—let it see the blaze of daylight. You will have many blessings on you and many more curses—but that is always the way of the world!

This is the time.—Yours in the Lord, VIVEKANANDA.

(264)

To Sister Nivedita

JUMMOO,
3rd Nov., 1897.

. . . Too much sentiment hurts work. "Hard as steel and soft as a flower" is the motto.

I shall soon write to Sturdy. He is right to tell you

that in case of trouble I will stand by you. You will have the whole of it, if I find a piece of bread in India—you may rest assured of that. I am going to write to Sturdy from Lahore, for which I start to-morrow. I have been here for 15 days to get some land in Kashmir from the Maharaja. I intend to go to Kashmir again next summer if I am here, and start some work there.

With everlasting love,—Yours, VIVEKANANDA.[1]

(265)

To Srimati Indumati Mitra

LAHORE,*
15th November, 1897.

DEAR MOTHER—It is a matter of deep regret that in spite of my earnest wishes I do not find it feasible to go to Karachi this time and see you. First, because Captain and Mrs. Sevier, who have come from England and are travelling with me for the last nine months nearly, are very anxious to buy some land at Dehra Dun and start an orphanage there. It is their special request that I should go and open the work. This makes it unavoidable to go to Dehra Dun.

Secondly, owing to my kidney troubles I cannot count upon a long life. Even now it is one of my desires to start a Math in Calcutta, towards which as yet I could do nothing. Moreover, the people of my country have withheld the little help that they used to give to our Math of late. They have got a notion that I have brought plenty of money from England!! Over and above that, it is impossible to celebrate Sri Ramakrishna's Festival this year, for the proprietors of Rasmani's garden would not let me go there as I am returned from the West!! Hence my

[1] This was the last letter received by Sister Nivedita in England.

first duty lies in seeing the few friends we have in Rajputana and trying my best to have a centre in Calcutta. For these reasons I have been very sorry to postpone my tour to Sindh for the present. I shall try my best to go there via Rajputana and Kathiawar. Please do not be sorry. Never for a day do I forget you all. But duty must be done first. It will ease me of my anxiety when a Math is established in Calcutta. Then I can hope that the work at which I struggled all my life through all sorts of privation and suffering will not die out after I cease to live in this body. I start for Dehra Dun this very day. After a week's stay there, to Rajputana, thence to Kathiawar, and so on.

With blessings,—Yours sincerely, VIVEKANANDA

(*266*)

To the Same

DEHRA DUN,*
24th November, 1897.

DEAR MOTHER—I have duly received your letter and that of dear Haripada. Of course you have ample reason to feel sorry, but you see, I couldn't help it. And what took me here also became a fiasco; neither could I go to Sindh. It is the Lord's will. . . . You must have suffered much inconvenience, in taking leave of absence, coming to Hyderabad, and so forth, all for nothing. All is the Lord's will. Any least trouble undergone, is bound to produce its excellent results. Friday next I shall leave this place, and have a mind to go via Saharanpur to Rajputana direct. I am doing well now, and trust you too are in health and peace of mind. . . . .

With best love and blessings,—Yours sincerely, VIVEKANANDA.

(267)

To Master Mahashay

DEHRA DUN,
24th November, 1897.

MY DEAR M—, Many many thanks for your second leaflet.[1] It is indeed wonderful. The move is quite original, and never was the life of a great Teacher brought before the public untarnished by the writer's mind, as you are doing. The language also is beyond all praise, so fresh, so pointed and withal so plain and easy.

I cannot express in adequate terms how I have enjoyed them. I am really in a transport when I read them. Strange, isn't it? Our Teacher and Lord was so original, and each one of us will have to be original or nothing. I now understand why none of us attempted his life before. It has been reserved for you, this great work. He is with you evidently.—With all love and Namaskâr, VIVEKANANDA.

P. S. The Socratic dialogues are Plato all over; you are entirely hidden. Moreover, the dramatic part is infinitely beautiful. Everybody likes it, here and in the West.

(268)

To Swami Shivananda

JEYPORE,
27th December, 1897.

MY DEAR SHIVANANDA, Mr. Setlur of Girgaon, Bombay, whom you know very well from Madras, writes to me to send somebody to Africa to look after the religious needs of the Indian emigrants in Africa. He will of course send the man and bear all expenses.

[1] The Leaves, etc.

The work will not be very congenial at present, I am afraid, but it is really the work for a perfect man. You know the emigrants are not liked at all by the white people there. To look after the Indians, at the same time with a cool-headedness not to create more strife—is the work there. No immediate result can be expected, but in the long run it will prove a more beneficial work for India than any yet attempted. I wish you try your luck in this. If so, please write to Setlur about your willingness and asking more information, mentioning this letter, and god-speed to you. I am not very well, but am going to Calcutta in a few days and will be all right.—Yours in the Lord, VIVEKANANDA.

(269)

To Srimati Mrinalini Bose

DEOGHAR, VAIDYANATH,
3rd January, 1898.

DEAR MOTHER—Some very important questions have been raised in your letter. It is not possible to answer them fully in a short note, still I reply to them as briefly as possible.

(1) Rishi, Muni or God—none has power to force an institution on society. When the needs of the times press hard on it, society adopts certain customs for self-preservation. Rishis have only recorded those customs. As a man often resorts even to such means as are good for immediate self-protection but which are very injurious in the future, similarly, society also not infrequently saves itself for the time being, but these immediate means which contributed to its preservation turn out to be terrible in the long run.

For example take the prohibition of widow-marriage in our country. Don't think that Rishis or wicked men introduced the law pertaining to it. Notwithstanding the desire of men to keep women completely under their control, they never could succeed in introducing those laws without betaking themselves to the aid of a social necessity of the time. Of this custom two points should be specially observed:

(a) Widow-marriage takes place among the lower classes.

(b) Among the higher classes the number of women is greater than that of men.

Now, if it be the rule to marry every girl, it is difficult enough to get one husband apiece; then how to get, by and by, two or three for each? Therefore has society put one party under disadvantage, i.e., it does not let her have a second husband, who has had one; if it did, one maid would have to go without a husband. On the other hand, widow-marriage obtains in communities having a greater number of men than women, as in their case the objection stated above does not exist. It is becoming more and more difficult in the West too, for unmarried girls to get husbands.

Similar is the case with the caste system, and other social customs.

So, if it be necessary to change any social custom, the *necessity* underlying it should be found out first of all, and by altering it the custom will die of itself. Otherwise no good will be done by condemnation or praise.

(2) Now the question is, is it for the good of the public at large that social rules are framed, or society is formed? Many reply to this in the affirmative; some again may hold that it is not so. Some men, being comparatively powerful, slowly bring all others under their control and by stratagem, force or adroitness gain their own objects. If this be true, what can be the meaning of the statement, that there is danger in giving liberty to the ignorant? What, again, is the meaning of liberty?

Liberty does not certainly mean the absence of

obstacles in the path of misappropriation of wealth etc., by you and me, but it is our natural right to be allowed to use our own body, intelligence or wealth according to our will, without doing any harm to others; and all the members of a society ought to have the same opportunity for obtaining wealth, education or knowledge. The second question is, those who say that if the ignorant and the poor be given liberty, i.e., full right to their body, wealth, etc., and if their children have the same opportunity to better their condition and acquire knowledge as that of the rich and the highly situated, they would be perverse —do they say this for the good of the society, or blinded by their selfishness? In England, too, I have heard, "Who will serve us, if the lower classes get education?"

For the luxury of a handful of the rich, let millions of men and women remain submerged in the hell of want and abysmal depth of ignorance, for if they get wealth and education, society will be upset!

Who is society? The millions, or you, I and a few others of the upper classes?

Again, even if the latter be true, what ground is there for our vanity that we lead others? Are we omniscient? उद्धरेदात्मनात्मानम् —"Raise self by self." Let each work out one's own salvation. It is freedom in every way, i.e., advance towards Mukti is the worthiest gain of man. To advance oneself towards freedom, physical, mental and spiritual, and help others to do so is the supreme prize of man. Those social rules which stand in the way of unfoldment of this freedom are injurious, and steps should be taken to destroy them speedily. Those institutions should be encouraged by which men advance in the path of freedom.

That, in this life, we feel a deep love at first sight, towards a particular person, who may not be endowed with extraordinary qualities, is explained by the thinkers of our country as due to the associations of a past incarnation.

Your question regarding the will is very interesting: it is the subject to know. The essence of all religions is the annihilation of desire, along with which comes, therefore, of a certainty, the annihilation of the will, for desire is only the name of a particular mode of will. Why, again, is this Jagat? Or why are these manifestations of the will? Some religions hold that the evil will should be destroyed and not the good. The denial of desire here would be compensated by enjoyments hereafter. This reply does not of course satisfy the wise. The Buddhists, on the other hand, say that desire is the cause of misery, its annihilation is quite desirable. But like killing a man in the effort to kill the musquito on his cheek, they have gone to the length of annihilating their own selves in their efforts to destroy misery according to the Buddhist doctrine.

The fact is, what we call will is the inferior modification of something higher. Desirelessness means the disappearance of the inferior modification in the form of will and the appearance of that superior state. That state is beyond the range of mind and intellect. But though the look of the gold mohur is quite different from that of the rupee and the pice, yet as we know for certain that the gold mohur is greater than either, so, that highest state, Mukti, or Nirvâna, call it what you like, though out of the reach of mind and intellect, is greater than will and all other powers. It is no power, but power is its modification, therefore it is higher. Now you will see that the result of the proper exercise of the will, first with motive for object, and then without motive, is that the will-power will attain a much higher state.

In the preliminary state, the form of the Guru is to be meditated upon by the disciple. Gradually it is to be merged in the Ishtam. By Ishtam is meant the object of love and devotion. . . .

It is very difficult to superimpose divinity on man, but one is sure to succeed by repeated efforts. God is in every man, whether man knows it or not; your loving devotion is bound to call up the divinity in him.—Ever your well-wisher, VIVEKANANDA.

(270)

ALMORA,
20th May, 1898.

DEAR—, . . . Duty has no end and the world is extremely selfish.

Be of good cheer. "Never a worker of good came to grief." . . . —Ever yours etc., VIVEKANANDA.

(271)

To Mohammed Sarfaraz Husain

ALMORA,
10th June, 1898.

MY DEAR FRIEND—I appreciate your letter very much and am extremely happy to learn that the Lord is silently preparing wonderful things for our motherland.

Whether we call it Vedantism or any *ism*, the truth is that Advaitism is the last word of religion and thought and the only position from which one can look upon all religions and sects with love. We believe it is the religion of the future enlightened humanity. The Hindus may get the credit of arriving at it earlier than other races, they being an older race than either the Hebrew or the Arab; yet practical Advaitism, which looks upon and behaves to all mankind as one's own soul, is yet to be developed among the Hindus universally.

On the other hand our experience is that if ever the followers of any religion approach to this equality in an appreciable degree in the plane of practical work-a-day life—it may be quite unconscious generally of the deeper meaning and the underlying principle of such conduct, which the Hindus as a rule so clearly perceive—it is those of Islam and Islam alone.

Therefore we are firmly persuaded that without the help of practical Islam, theories of Vedantism, however fine and wonderful they may be, are entirely valueless to the vast mass of mankind. We want to lead mankind to the place where there is neither the Vedas nor the Bible, nor the Koran; yet this has to be done by harmonising the Vedas, the Bible and the Koran. Mankind ought to be taught that religions are but the varied expressions of THE RELIGION, which is Oneness, so that each may choose the path that suits him best.

For our own motherland a junction of the two great systems, Hinduism and Islam—Vedanta brain and Islam body—is the only hope.

I see in my mind's eye the future perfect India rising out of this chaos and strife, glorious and invincible, with Vedanta brain and Islam body.

Ever praying that the Lord may make of you a great instrument for the help of mankind, and especially of our poor, poor motherland.—Yours with love, VIVEKANANDA.

(*272*)

KASHMIR,

25th Aug., 1898.

DEAR—, It is a lazy life I am leading for the last two months, floating leisurely in a boat, which is also my home, up and down the beautiful Jhelum, through the most gorgeous scenery God's world can afford, in nature's own park, where the earth, air, land, grass, plants, trees, mountains, snows and the human form, all express on the outside at least the beauty of the Lord;—with almost no possessions, scarcely a pen or an inkstand even, snatching up a meal whenever or wherever convenient, the very ideal of a Rip Van Winkle! . . .

Do not work yourself out. It is no use; always remember, "Duty is the midday sun whose fierce rays are burning the very vitals of humanity." It is necessary for a time as a discipline; beyond that, it is a morbid dream. Things go on all right whether we lend them a helping hand or not. We in delusion only break ourselves. There is a false sentiment which goes the extreme of unselfishness, "only to injure others by its submission to every evil." We have no right to make others selfish by our unselfishness; have we? . . . —Yours etc., VIVEKANANDA.

(*273*)

THE MATH, BELUR,
15th Dec., 1898.

DEAR—, . . . The Mother is our guide and whatever happens or will happen is under Her ordination. . . . Yours etc., VIVEKANANDA.

(*274*)

To Mrs. Ole Bull

BAIDYANATH, DEOGHAR,
29th Dec., 1898.

MY DEAR DHIRA MATA—, You know already my inability to accompany you. I cannot gather strength enough to accompany you. The cold in the lungs continues, and that is just what makes me unfit for travel. On the whole I hope to improve here.

I find my cousin has been all these years cultivating her mind with a will, and she knows all that the Bengali literature can give her and that is a good deal, especially of metaphysics. She has already learnt to sign her name in English and the Roman alphabet. It is now real brain work to teach her, and therefore I have desisted. I am trying simply to idle away my time and force myself to take rest.

Ere this I had only love for you, but recent developments prove that you are appointed by the Mother to watch over my life, hence, faith has been added to love! As regards me and my work I hold henceforth that you are inspired and will gladly shake off all responsibilities from my shoulder and abide by what the Mother ordains through you.

Hoping soon to join you in Europe or America.—I remain, ever your loving son, VIVEKANANDA.

(275)

THE MATH, BELUR,
11th April, 1899.

DEAR—, . . . Two years of physical suffering have taken away twenty years off my life. Well, but the soul changeth not, does it? It is there, the same madcap Atman, mad upon one idea, intent and intense. . . . —Yours etc., VIVEKANANDA.

(276)

To Srimati Sarala Ghoshal, B.A.

BELUR MATH,*
16th April, 1899.

DEAR MADAM—Very glad to receive your kind note. If by the sacrifice of some specially cherished object of either myself or my brother-disciples many pure and genuinely patriotic souls come forward to help our cause, rest assured, we will not hesitate in the least to make that sacrifice, nor shed a tear-drop—you will see this verified in action. But up till now I have seen nobody coming forward to assist in this way. Only some have wished to put their own hobby in place of ours—that is all. If it really help our country, or humanity—not to speak of giving up Guru-worship—believe me, we are prepared to commit any dire iniquity and suffer the eternal damnation of the Christians. But my hairs have turned grey since I began the study of man. This world is a most trying place, and it is long since I have taken to wandering with the lantern of the Grecian Philosopher in hand. A popular song my Master often used to sing comes to my mind:

" He who's a man after one's heart
Betrays himself by his very looks.
Rare indeed is such a one!
He's a man of aesthetic perceptions
Who treads a path contrary to others."

This much from my side. Please know that not one word of it is exaggerated—which you will find to be actually the case.

But then I have some doubts about those patriotic souls who can join with us if only we give up the worship of the Guru. Well, if, as they pose, they are indeed panting and strugging so much—almost to the point of dissolution from their body—to serve the country, how can the single accident of Guru-worship stop everything?

(277)

To Mr. E. T. Sturdy

PORT SAID,
14th July, 1899.

MY DEAR STURDY—I got your letter all right just now. I have one from M. Nobel of Paris too. Miss Noble has several from America.

M. Nobel writes to me to defer my visit to him at

Paris to some other date, from London, as he will have to be away for a long time. As you know sure I shall not have many friends staying now in London, and Miss MacLeod is so desirous I should come. A stay in England under these circumstances is not advisable. Moreover, I do not have much life left. At least I must go on with that supposition. I mean if anything has to be done in America, it is high time we bring our scattered influence in America to a head—if not organise regularly. Then I shall be free to return to England in a few months and work with a will till I return to India.

I think you are absolutely wanted to gather up, as it were, the American work. If you can, therefore, you ought to come over with me. Turiyananda is with me. Saradananda's brother is going to Boston. . . . In case you cannot come to America, I ought to go, ought I not?

(*278*)

RIDGELY,
2nd September, 1899.

DEAR—, . . . Life is a series of fights and disillusionments. . . . The secret of life is not enjoyment but education through experience. But, alas, we are called off the moment we begin really to learn. That seems to many a potent argument for a future existence. . . . Everywhere it is better to have a whirlwind come over the work. That clears the atmosphere and gives us a true insight into the nature of things. It is begun anew, but on adamantine foundations. . . . —Yours with best wishes, VIVEKANANDA.

(*279*)

To Mr. E. T. Sturdy

RIDGELY MANOR,
14th Sept., 1899.

MY DEAR STURDY—I have simply been taking rest at

the Leggetts' and doing nothing. Abhedananda is here. He has been working hard.

He goes in a day or two to resume his work in different places for a month. After that he comes to New York to work.

I am trying to do something in the line you suggested, but don't know how far an account of the Hindus will be appreciated by the Western public when it comes from a Hindu. . . .

Mrs. Jonson is of opinion that no spiritual person ought to be ill. It also seems to her now that my smoking is sinful etc., etc. That was Miss Müller's reason for leaving me, my illness. They may be perfectly right, for aught I know—and you too—but I am what I am. In India, the same defects plus eating with Europeans, have been taken exception to, by many. I was driven out of a private temple by the owners for eating with Europeans. I wish I were malleable enough to be moulded into whatever one desired, but unfortunately I never saw a man who could satisfy every one. Nor can any one who has to go to different places possibly satisfy all.

When I first came to America, they ill-treated me if I had not trousers on. Next I was forced to wear cuffs and collars, else they would not touch me etc., etc. They thought me awfully funny if I did not eat what they offered etc., etc. . . .

In India the moment I landed they made me shave my head, and wear "Kaupin," with the result that I got diabetes etc. Saradananda never gave up his underwear —this saved his life, with just a touch of rheumatism and much comment from our people.

Of course, it is my Karma and I am glad that it is so. For, though it smarts for the time, it is another great experience of life, which will be useful, either in this or in the next. . . .

As for me, I am always in the midst of ebbs and

flows. I knew it always and preached always that every bit of pleasure will bring its quota of pain, if not with compound interest. I have a good deal of love given to me by the world; I deserve a good deal of hatred therefore. I am glad it is so— as it proves my theory of "Every wave having its corresponding dip" on my own person.

As for me, I stick to my nature and principle—once a friend, always a friend—also the true Indian principle of looking subjectively for the cause of the objective.

I am sure that the fault is mine, and mine only, for every wave of dislike and hatred that I get. It could not be otherwise. Thanking you and Mrs. Jonson for thus calling me once more to the internal,

I remain as ever with love and blessings,—
VIVEKANANDA.

(*280*)

RIDGELY,
September, 1899.

DEAR—, . . . Mother knows best, that is all about me. . . . —Yours etc., VIVEKANANDA.

(*281*)

RIDGELY,
1st November, 1899.

DEAR—, . . . It seems there is a gloom over your mind. Never mind, nothing is to last for ever. Anyhow life is not eternal. I am so, so thankful for it. Suffering is the lot of the world's best and bravest—yet, for aeons yet—till things are righted, if possible, here—at least it is a discipline which breaks the dream. In my sane moments I rejoice for my sufferings. Some one must suffer here;—I am glad it is I, amongst others of nature's sacrifices.—Yours etc., VIVEKANANDA.

(282)

NEW YORK,
15th November, 1899.

DEAR—, . . . On the whole I don't think there is any cause for anxiety about my body. This sort of nervous body is just the instrument to play great music at times and at times to moan in darkness.—Yours etc., VIVEKANANDA.

(283)

To Sister Nivedita

LOS ANGELES,
6th December, 1899.

DEAR MARGO—Your sixth has arrived, but with it yet no change in my fortune. Would change be any good, you think? Some people are made that way, to love being miserable. If I did not break my heart over people I was born amongst, I would do it for somebody else. I am sure of that. This is the way of some, I am coming to see it. We are all after happiness, true, but that some are only happy in being unhappy—queer, is it not? There is no harm in it either, except that happiness and unhappiness are both infectious. Ingersoll said once that if he were God, he would make health catching, instead of disease, little dreaming that health is quite as catching as disease, if not more! That is the only danger. No harm in the world in my being happy, in being miserable, but others must not catch it. This is the great tact. No sooner a prophet feels miserable for the state of man than he sours his face, beats his breast and calls upon everyone to drink tartaric acid, munch charcoal, sit upon a dung-heap covered with ashes and speak only in groans and tears!—I find they all have been wanting. Yes, they have. If you are really ready to take the world's burden, take it by all means. But do not let us hear your groans and curses. Do not frighten us with your sufferings, so that we come to feel we were better off with our own burdens. The man who really takes the burden, blesses the world and goes his own way. He has not a word of condemnation, a word of criticism, not because there was no evil but that he has taken it on his own shoulders, willingly, voluntarily. It is the Saviour who should "go his way rejoicing," and not the saved.

This is the only light I have caught this morning. This is enough if it has come to live with me and permeate my life.

Come ye that are heavily laden and lay all your burden on me and then do whatever you like and be happy and forget that I ever existed.—Ever with love, Your father, VIVEKANANDA.

(284)

To Mrs. Ole Bull

12th December, 1899.

MY DEAR MRS. BULL—You are perfectly right; I am brutal, very indeed. But about the tenderness etc., that is my fault. I wish I had less, much less, of that—that is my weakness—and alas! all my sufferings have come from that. Well, the municipality is trying to tax us out—good, that is my fault as I did not make the Math public property by a deed of trust. I am very sorry I use harsh language to my boys, but they also know, I love them more than anybody else on earth. I may have had Divine help—true, but oh, the pound of blood every bit of Divine help has been to me!! I would be gladder and a better man without that. The present looks very gloomy indeed, but I am a fighter and must die fighting—not give way—that is why I get crazy at the boys. I don't ask them to fight, but ask them not to hinder my fight.

I don't grudge my fate. But oh, now I want a man, one of my boys, to stand by me and fight against all odds! Don't you vex yourself; if anything is to be done in India my presence is necessary, and I am much better in health, possibly the sea will make me better. Anyway I did not do anything this time in America except bother my friends. Possibly Joe will help me out with the passage, and I have some money with Mr. Leggett. I have hopes of collecting some money in India yet. I did not see any of my friends in different parts of India. I have hope of collecting the fifteen thousand that will make up the fifty thousand and a deed of trust will bring down the municipal taxes. If I cannot collect that—it is better to struggle and die for it than vegetate here in America. My mistakes have been great, but everyone of them was from too much love. How I hate *love*! Would I never had any! Bhakti! Indeed! I wish I could be an Advaitist, calm and heartless. Well, this life is done. I will try in the next. I am sorry, especially now, that I have done more injury to my friends than there have been blessings to them. The peace, the quiet I am seeking, I never found.

I went years ago to the Himalayas, never to come back; and my sister committed suicide, the news reached me there, and that weak heart flung me off from that prospect of peace!! It is the weak heart that has driven me out of India to seek some help for those I love, and here I am! Peace have I sought, but the heart, that seat of Bhakti, would not allow me to find it. Struggle and torture, torture and struggle! Well, be it then, since it is my fate, and the quicker it is over, the better. They say I am impulsive but look at the circumstances!!! I am sorry I have been the cause of pain to you, to you above all, who love me so much, who have been so, so kind. But it is done—was a fact. I am now going to cut the knot or die in the attempt.—Ever your son, VIVEKANANDA.

P. S. As Mother wants it, so let it be. I am going to beg of Joe a passage via San Francisco to India. If she gives it I start immediately via Japan. It would take a month. In India, I think, I can raise some money to keep things straight or on a better footing—at least to leave things where I get them all muddled. The end is getting very dark and very much muddled; well, I expected it so. Don't think I give in a moment. Lord bless you;—if the Lord has made me His hack to work and die on the streets, let Him have it. I am more cheerful just now after your letter than I was for years—*Wah Guru ki fateh*! Victory unto the Guru!! Yes, let the world come, the hells come, the gods come, let Mother come. I fight and do not give in. Ravana got his release in three births by fighting the Lord Himself! It is glorious to fight Mother.

All blessings on you and yours. You have done for me more, much more, than I deserved ever.

Love to Christine and Turiyananda.—VIVEKANANDA.

(*285*)

To Sister Nivedita

LOS ANGELES,
421, 21ST. STREET,
23rd Dec., 1899.

MY DEAR MARGO—Yes, I am really getting well under the manipulations of magnetic healing! At any rate I am all right. There was never anything serious with my organs—it was nerves and dyspepsia.

Now I walk miles every day, at any time—before or after meals. I am perfectly well—and am going to remain so, I am sure.

The wheel is turning up, Mother is working it up. She cannot let me go before Her work is done—and that is the secret. . . .

See, how England is working up. After this blood-letting people will then have time of thinking better and higher things than war, war, war. That is our opportunity. We run in quick, get hold of them by the dozens, and then set the Indian work in full swing. . . . —VIVEKANANDA.

(*286*)

LOS ANGELES, CALIFORNIA,
24th January, 1900

DEAR—, I am afraid that the rest and peace I seek for will never come. But Mother does good to others through me, at least some to my native land, and it is easier to be reconciled to one's fate as a sacrifice. We are all sacrifices—each in his own way. The great worship is going on—no one can see its meaning except that it is a great sacrifice. Those that are willing, escape a lot of pain. Those who resist are broken into submission and suffer more. I am now determined to be a willing one.—Yours etc., VIVEKANANDA.

(*287*)

To Sister Nivedita

C/O MISS MEAD,
447, DOUGLAS BUILDING,
LOS ANGELES, CALIFORNIA,
15th Feb., 1900.

MY DEAR NIVEDITA—Yours of the — reached me to-day at Pasadena. I see Joe has missed you at Chicago —although I have not heard anything from them yet from New York.

There was a bundle of English newspapers from England with a line on the envelope expressing good wishes for me and signed. F. H. M. Nothing important was in those, however. I would have written a letter to —, but I do not know the address; then I was afraid to frighten her. . . .

I get news from Mrs. Sevier that Niranjan is seriously ill in Calcutta. I do not know if he has passed away. Well—but I am strong now. Stronger than ever.

I was mentally getting a sort of ironing over my heart. I am getting nearer a Sannyasin's life now. . . . Going to San Francisco next week and hope to do better there.

. . . I am glad you got the stories; rewrite them if you think so—get them published if you find anybody to do it and take the proceeds, if any, for your work. . . .

Well—money will come for your school, never fear—it has got to come; if it does not come, who cares. One road is quite as good as the other. Mother knows best. I don't know whether I am very soon going to the East. If I have an opportunity, of course I will go to India.

The international scheme is a good one, and by all means join it, and be the medium of getting some Indian women's clubs to join it through you, which is better. . . .

Things shall look up for us, never mind. As soon as the war is finished we go to England and try to do a big work there. What do you think? Shall I write to Mother Superior? If so, send her whereabouts. Has she written to you? . . .

Sturdies and. Shakies will all come round—hold on.

You are learning your lessons—that is all I want. So am I; the moment we are fit, money and men must flow towards us. Between my nerves and your emotion we may make a mess of everything just now. So Mother is curing my nerves and drilling you into level-headedness—and then we go. This time good is coming in chunks, I am sure. We will make the foundations of the old land shake this time.

. . . I am getting cool as a cucumber—let anything come, I am ready—the next move—any blow shall tell—

not one miss—such is the next chapter.—With all love, VIVEKANANDA.

(288)

To Swami Akhandananda

CALIFORNIA,*
21st February, 1900.

MY DEAR AKHANDANANDA—I am very glad to receive your letter and go through the details of news. Learning and wisdom are superfluities, the surface glitter merely, but it is the heart that is the seat of all power. It is not in the brain but in the heart that the Atman, possessed of knowledge, power and activity, has Its seat. शतं चैका च हृदयस्य नाड्यः —"The nerves of the heart are a hundred and one", etc. The chief nerve-centre near the heart, called the sympathetic ganglia, is where the Atman has Its citadel. The more heart you will be able to manifest, the greater will be the victory you achieve. It is only a few that understand the language of the brain, but everyone, from the Creator down to a clump of grass, understands the language that comes from the heart. But then, in our country, it is a case of rousing men that are, as it were, dead. It will take time, but if you have *infinite* patience and perseverance, success is bound to come. No mistake in that.

How are the English officials to blame? Is the family, of whose unnatural cruelty you have written, an isolated one in India? Or, are there plenty of such? It is the same story all the country over. But then, it is not as a result of pure wickedness that the selfishness commonly met with in our country has come. This bestial selfishness is the outcome of centuries of failure and repression. It is not real selfishness, but deep-rooted despair. It will be cured at the first inkling of success. It is only this that the English officials are noticing all round, so how can they have faith at the very outset? But tell me, do they not sympathise with any real work that they meet with? . . .

In these days of dire famine, flood, disease and pestilence, tell me where your Congressmen are! Will it do merely to say, "Hand the government of the country over to us"? And who is there to listen to them? If a man does work, has he to open his mouth to ask for anything? If there be two thousand people like you working in several districts, won't it be the turn of the English themselves to consult you in matters of political moment? स्वकार्यमुद्धरेत्प्राज्ञः— "The wise man should achieve his object." . . . A— was not allowed to open a centre, but what of that? Has not Kishengarh allowed it?—Let him work on without ever opening his lips, there is no use of either telling anything to anybody, or quarrelling with any. Whoever will assist in this work of the Divine Mother of the universe, will have Her grace, and whoever will oppose it will not only be—अकारणाविष्कृतवैरदारुणः— "raising a deadly enemy for nothing", but also laying the axe to his own prospects. शनैः पन्थाः etc.— all in good time. Many a little makes a mickle. When a great work is being done, when the foundations are laid or a road constructed, when superhuman energy is needed—it is one or two extraordinary men who silently and noiselessly work through a world of obstacles and difficulties. When thousands of people are benefited, there is a great hue and cry, and the whole country is loud in notes of praise. But, then the machine has already been set agoing, and even a boy can work it, or a fool add to it some impetus. Grasp this, that that benefit done to a village or two, that orphanage with its twenty orphans, those ten or twenty workers—that all these are enough, that they form the nucleus, never to be destroyed. From these, hundreds of thousands of people will be benefited in time. Now we want half-a-dozen lions, then excellent work will be turned out by even hundreds of jackals.

If orphan girls happen to come to your hands for shelter, you must take them up above all else. Otherwise, Christian missionaries will take them, poor things, away! What matters it that you have no particular arrangements for them? Through the Divine Mother's will, they will be provided for. When you get a horse, never you worry about the whip. . . . Get together whomsoever you can lay your hands on, no picking and choosing now—everything will be set right in course of time. In every attempt there are many obstacles to cope with, but gradually the path becomes smooth.

Convey to the European officer many thanks from me. Work on fearlessly—there is a hero! Bravo! Thrice well done! The starting of a centre at Bhagalpur that you have written about is no doubt a good idea—enlightening the school-boys and such like things. But our mission is for the destitute, the poor, and the illiterate peasantry and labouring classes, and if after everything has been done for them first, there is spare time, then only for the gentry. Those peasants and labouring people will be won over by love. Afterwards it will be they who will collect small sums and start missions at their own villages, and gradually, among those very men teachers will spring.

Teach some boys and girls of the peasant classes the rudiments of learning and infuse a number of ideas into their brains. Afterwards the peasants of each village will collect funds and have one of these in their village. उद्धरेदात्मनात्मानम्— "One must raise oneself by one's own exertions"—this holds good in all spheres. We help them to help themselves. That they are supplying you with your daily bread, is a real bit of work done. The moment they will come to understand their own condition, and feel the necessity of help and improvement, know that your work is taking effect and is in the right direction.

While the little good that the moneyed classes will, out of pity, do to the poor, does not last, and ultimately it does nothing but harm to both parties. The peasant and labouring classes are in a moribund condition, so what is needed is that the moneyed people will only help them to regain their vitality, and nothing more. Then leave the peasants and labourers to look to their own problem to grapple with and solve it. But then you must take care not to set up class-strife between the poor peasants, the labouring people and wealthy classes. Make it a point not to abuse the moneyed classes —स्वकार्यमुद्धरेत्प्राज्ञः— "the wise man should achieve his own object".

Victory to the Guru! Victory to the Mother of the Universe! What fear! Opportunity, remedy and its application—will present themselves. I do not care about the results, well or ill. I shall be happy if only you do this much of work. Wordy warfares, texts and scriptures, doctrines and dogmas—all these I am coming to loathe as poison in this my advanced age. Know this for certain that he who will work will be the crown on my head. Useless bandying of words and making noise is taking away our time, is consuming our life-energy, without pushing the cause of humanitarianism a step farther. माभैः —"Away with fear!" Bravo! There is a hero indeed! May the blessed Guru be enthroned in your heart, and the Divine Mother guide your hands!—Yours affectionately, VIVEKANANDA.

(*291*)

To Mrs. Ole Bull

SAN FRANCISCO,
4th March, 1900.

DEAR DHIRA MATA—, I don't want to work. I want to be quiet, and rest. I know the time and the place, but the fate or Karma, I think, drives me on—work, work.

We are like cattle driven to the slaughter-house—hastily nibbling a bite of grass on the road-side as they are driven along under the whip. And all this is our work, our fear—fear, the beginning of misery, of disease, etc. By being so fearful to hurt we hurt more. By trying so much to avoid evil we fall into its jaws.

What a mass of namby-pamby nonsense we create 'round ourselves!! It does us no good, it leads us on to the very thing we try to avoid—misery. . . .

Oh, to become fearless, to be daring, to be careless of everything! . . . —Yours etc., VIVEKANANDA.

(*290*)

SAN FRANCISCO,
25th March, 1900.

DEAR—, I am much better and am growing very strong. I feel sometimes that freedom is near at hand and the tortures of the last two years have been great lessons in many ways. Disease and misfortune come to do us good in the long run, although at the time we feel that we are submerged for ever.

I am the infinite blue sky; the clouds may gather over me but I am the same infinite blue.

I am trying to get a taste of that peace which I know is my nature and every one's nature. These tin-pots of bones and foolish dreams of happiness and misery—what are they?

My dreams are breaking, Om Tat Sat!—Yours, VIVEKANANDA.

(*291*)

To Sister Nivedita

1779, TURK STREET,
SAN FRANCISCO,
28th March, 1900.

MY DEAR MARGO—I am so glad at your good fortune. Things have got to come round if we are steady. I am sure you will get all the money you require here or in England.

I am working hard—and the harder I work the better I feel. This ill health has done me a great good, sure. I am really understanding what non-attachment means. And I hope very soon to be perfectly non-attached.

We put all our energies to concentrate and get attached to one thing, but the other part, though equally difficult, we seldom pay any attention to—the faculty of detaching ourselves at a moment's notice from anything.

Both attachment and detachment perfectly developed make a man great and happy.

I am so glad at Mrs. Leggett's gift. She is working up, wait. She has a great part to play in Ramakrishna's work, whether she knows it or not.

I enjoyed your account of Prof. Geddes and Joe has a funny account of a clairvoyant. Things are just now beginning to turn. . . .

This letter, I think, will reach you at Chicago. . . .

I had a nice letter from Max Geysic, the young Swiss who is a great friend of Miss Soutter. Miss Soutter also sends her love and they ask to know the time when I come over to England. Many people are enquiring, they say.

Things have got to come round—the seed must die underground to come up as the tree. The last two years were the underground rotting. I never had a struggle in the jaws of death but it meant a tremendous upheaval of the whole life. One such brought me to Ramakrishna, another sent me to the U. S., this has been the greatest of all. It is gone—I am so calm that it astonishes me sometimes!! I work every day morning and evening, eat anything any hour—and go to bed at 12 P.M. in the night—but such fine sleep!! I never had such power of sleeping before!!—Yours with all love and blessings, VIVEKANANDA.

(292)

CHICAGO,
6th April, 1900.

DEAR—, . . . The mind is omnipresent and can be heard and felt anywhere. . . . —Yours etc., VIVEKANANDA.

(293)

To an American friend

SAN FRANCISCO,
7th April, 1900.

But I am more calm and quiet now than I ever was. I am on my own feet, working hard and with pleasure. To work I have the right. Mother knows the rest.

You see, I shall have to stay here longer than I intended, and work. But don't be disturbed. I shall work out all my problems. I am on my own feet now, and I begin to see the light. Success would have led me astray, and I would have lost sight of the truth that I am a Sannyasin. That is why Mother is giving me this experience.

My boat is nearing the calm harbour from which it is never more to be driven out. Glory, glory unto Mother! I have no wish, no ambition now. Blessed be Mother! I am the servant of Ramakrishna. I am merely a machine. I know nothing else. Nor do I want to know. Glory, glory unto Sri Guru!

(294)

To an American friend

ALAMEDA, CALIFORNIA,
12th April, 1900.

Mother is becoming propitious once more. Things are looking up. They must.

Work always brings evil with it. I have paid for the accumulated evil with bad health. I am glad. My mind is all the better for it. There is a mellowness and a calmness in life now, which was never there before. I am learning now how to be attached as well as detached, and mentally becoming my own master. . . .

Mother is doing Her own work; I do not worry much now. Moths like me die by the thousand every instant, Her work goes on all the same. Glory unto Mother! . . . Alone and drifting about in the will-current of the Mother, has been my whole life. The moment I have tried to break this, that moment I have been hurt. Her will be done! . . .

I am happy, at peace with myself, and more of the Sannyasin than I ever was before. The love for my own kith and kin is growing less every day, and that for Mother increasing. Memories of long nights of vigil with Sri Ramakrishna under the Dakshineswar Banyan are waking up once more. And work? What is work? Whose work? Whom shall I work for?

I am free. I am Mother's child. She works, She plays. Why should I plan? What should I plan? Things came and went, just as She liked, without my planning. We are Her automata. She is the wire-puller.

(295)

To Miss Josephine MacLeod

ALAMEDA, CALIFORNIA,
18th April, 1900.

MY DEAR JOE—Just now I received yours and Mrs. Bull's welcome letter. I direct this to London. I am so glad Mrs. Leggett is on the sure way to recovery.

I am so sorry Mr. Leggett resigned the presidentship.

Well, I keep quiet for fear of making further trouble.

You know my methods are extremely harsh and once roused I may rattle—too much for his peace of mind.

I wrote to him only to tell him that his notions about Mrs. Bull are entirely wrong.

Work is always difficult; pray for me, Joe, that my work may stop for ever, and my whole soul be absorbed in Mother. Her works She knows.

You must be glad to be in London once more—the old friends—give them all my love and gratitude.

I am well, very well mentally. I feel the rest of the soul more than that of the body. The battles are lost and won. I have bundled my things and am waiting for the great deliverer.

"Shiva, O Shiva, carry my boat to the other shore."

After all, Joe, I am only the boy who used to listen with rapt wonderment to the wonderful words of Ramakrishna under the Banyan at Dakshineswar. That is my true nature; works and activities, doing good and so forth are all superimpositions. Now I again hear his voice; the same old voice thrilling my soul. Bonds are breaking—love dying, work becoming tasteless—the glamour is off life. Now only the voice of the Master calling.—" I come Lord, I come."—" Let the dead bury the dead, follow thou Me." " I come, my beloved Lord, I come."

Yes, I come. Nirvâna is before me. I feel it at times, the same infinite ocean of peace, without a ripple, a breath.

I am glad I was born, glad I suffered so, glad I did make big blunders, glad to enter peace. I leave none bound, I take no bonds. Whether this body will fall and release me or I enter into freedom in the body, the old man is gone, gone for ever, never to come back again!

The guide, the Guru, the leader, the teacher, has passed away; the boy, the student, the servant, is left behind.

You understand why I do not want to meddle with.—

Who am I to meddle with any, Joe? I have long given up my place as a leader—I have no right to raise my voice. Since the beginning of this year I have not dictated anything in India. You know that. Many thanks for what you and Mrs Bull have been to me in the past. All blessings follow you ever. The sweetest moments of my life have been when I was drifting; I am drifting again—with the bright warm sun ahead and masses of vegetation around—and in the heat everything is so still, so calm—and I am drifting, languidly—in the warm heart of the river. I dare not make a splash with my hands or feet—for fear of breaking the wonderful stillness, stillness that makes you feel sure it is an illusion!

Behind my work was ambition, behind my love was personality, behind my purity was fear, behind my guidance the thirst of power. Now they are vanishing and I drift. I come. Mother, I come, in thy warm bosom, floating wheresoever thou takest me, in the voiceless, in the strange, in the wonderland, I come—a spectator, no more an actor.

Oh, it is so calm! My thoughts seem to come from a great, great distance in the interior of my own heart. They seem like faint, distant whispers, and peace is upon everything, sweet, sweet peace—like that one feels for a few moments just before falling into sleep, when things are seen and felt like shadows—without fear, without love, without emotion.—Peace that one feels alone, surrounded with statues and pictures.—I come, Lord, I come.

The world *is*, but not beautiful nor ugly, but as sensations without exciting any emotion. Oh, Joe, the blessedness of it! Everything is good and beautiful; for things are all losing their relative proportions to me—my body among the first. Om That Existence!

I hope great things to come to you all in London and Paris. Fresh joy — fresh benefits to mind and body.

With love as ever to you and Mrs. Bull, —Yours faithfully, VIVEKANANDA.

(*296*)

SAN FRANCISCO,
24th May, 1900.

(*In answer to a few questions put by Sister Nivedita, Swamiji jotted down the following replies.*)

Q. I cannot remember what parts Prithvi Rai and Chand disguised themselves to play, when they determined to attend the Svayamvara at Kanauj.

A. Both went as minstrels.

Q. Also did Prithvi Rai determine to marry Samyuktâ partly because she was the daughter of his rival and partly for the fame of her great beauty? Did he then send a woman-servant to obtain the post of her maid? And did this old nurse set herself to make the princess fall in love with Prithvi Rai?

A. They had fallen in love with each other, hearing deeds and beauty and seeing portraits. Falling in love through portraits is an old Indian game.

Q. How did Krishna come to be brought up amongst the shepherds?

A. His father had to fly with the baby to save it from the Tyrant Kamsa, who ordered all the babes (male) from that year to be killed, as he was afraid one of them would be Krishna and dethrone him (through prophecy). He kept Krishna's father and mother in prison (they were his cousins) for fear of that prophecy.

Q. How did this part of his life terminate?

A. He came with his brother Baladeva and Nanda, his foster-father, invited by the Tyrant to a festival.

(The Tyrant had plotted his destruction.) He killed the Tyrant and instead of taking the throne placed the nearest heir on it. Himself he never took any fruit of action.

Q. Can you give me any dramatic incident of this period?

A. This period is full of miracles. He as a baby was once naughty and the cowherd-mother tried to tie him with her churning string, and found she could not bind him with all the strings she had. Then her eyes opened and she saw that she was going to bind him who had the whole universe in his body. She began to pray and tremble. Immediately the Lord touched her with his Maya and she saw only the child.

Brahmâ, the chief of gods, disbelieving that the Lord had become a cowherd, stole one day all the cows and cowherd boys and put them to sleep in a cave. When he came back, he found the same boys and cows round Krishna. Again he stole the new lot and hid them away. He came back and saw there the same again. Then his eyes opened and began to see numerous worlds and heavens and Brahmas by the thousands, one greater than the preceding, in the body of the Lord.

He danced on the Serpent Kâliya who had been poisoning the water of the Yamuna, and held up the Mount Govardhana in defiance of Indra whose worship he had forbidden and who in revenge wanted to kill all the people of Vraja by deluge of rain. They were all sheltered by Krishna under the hill Govardhana which he upheld with a finger on their head.

He from his childhood was against Snake-worship and Indra-worship. Indra-worship is a Vedic ritual. Throughout the Gita he is not favourable to Vedic ritual.

This is the period of his love to Gopis. He was fifteen years of age.

(297)

To Sister Nivedita

SAN FRANCISCO,
26th May, 1900.

All blessings on you. Don't despond in the least. *Sri wah Guru! Sri wah Guru!* You come of the blood of a Kshatriya. Our yellow garb is the robe of death on the field of battle. Death for the cause is our goal, not success. *Sri wah Guru!!!* . . .

Black and thick are the folds of sinister fate. But I am the Master. I raise my hand, and lo, they vanish! All this is nonsense and fear. I am the Fear of fear, the Terror of terror. I am the fearless, secondless One. I am the Ruler of destiny, the Wiper-out of fact. *Sri wah Guru!* Steady, child, don't be bought by gold or anything else, and we win!

(298)

NEW YORK,
20th June, 1900.

DEAR—, . . . Well, Mother seems to be kind again and the wheel is slowly rising up. . . —Yours etc., VIVEKANANDA.

(299)

NEW YORK,
2nd July, 1900.

DEAR—, . . . Mother knows, as I always say. Pray to Mother. It is hard work to be a leader—one must crush all one's own self under the feet of the community. . . .—Yours etc., VIVEKANANDA.

(300)

To Sister Christine

PARIS,
17th August, 1900.

If things go ill or well,—
If joy redounding shows her face,
Or seas of sorrow swell,—
'Tis but a dream, a play,
A play where each has part,
Each one to weep or laugh as may;
Each one his robe to don;
Its scenes, alternative shine and rain.
Thou dream, O blessed dream!
Spread near and far thy veil of haze,
Tone down the lines so sharp,
Make smooth what roughness seems.
No magic but in thee!
Thy touch makes deserts bloom to life,
Harsh thunder blessed song,
Fell death the sweet release.

(301)

To Sister Nivedita

6, PLACE DES ETATS UNIS,
PARIS,
25th Aug., 1900.

DEAR NIVEDITA—Your letter reached just now. Many thanks for the kind expressions. . . .

Now I am free, as I have kept no power or authority or position for me in the work. I also have resigned the Presidentship of the Ramakrishna Mission.

The Math etc., belong now to the immediate disciples of Ramakrishna except myself. The Presidentship is now Brahmananda's—next it will fall on Premananda etc., in turn.

I am so glad a whole load is off me, now I am happy. . . .

I no longer represent anybody, nor am I responsible to anybody. As to my friends I had a morbid sense of obligation. I have thought well and find I owe nothing to anybody—if anything, I have given my best energies, unto death almost, and received only hectoring and mischief-making and botheration. . . .

Your letter indicates that I am jealous of your new friends. You must know once for all I am born without jealousy, without avarice, without the desire to rule—whatever other vices I am born with.

I never directed you before; now, after I am nobody in the work, I have no direction whatever. I only know this much, so long as you serve "Mother" with a whole heart, She will be your guide.

I never had any jealousy about what friends you made. I never criticised my brethren for mixing up in anything. Only I do believe the Western people have the peculiarity of trying to force upon others whatever seems good to them, forgetting that what is good for you may not be good for others. As such I am afraid you would try to force upon others whatever turn your mind might take in contact with new friends. That was the only reason I sometimes tried to stop any particular influence and nothing else.

You are free, have your own choice, your own work. . . .

Friends or foes, they are all instruments in Her hands to help us work out our own Karma, through pleasure or pain. As such " Mother " bless them all.

With all love and blessings,—Yours truly, VIVEKANANDA.

(302)

PARIS,
28th August, 1900.

DEAR—, Such is life—grind, grind; and yet what else are we to do? Grind, grind! Something will come—some way will be opened. If it does not, as it probably never will—then, then—what then? All our efforts are only to stave off—for a season—the great climax—death! Oh, what would the world do without you, Death! Thou great healer!

The world as it is, is not real, is not eternal, thank the Lord! How can the future be any better? That must be the effect of this one—at least like this, if not worse!

Dreams, oh, dreams! Dream on! Dream, the magic of dream, is the cause of this life, it is also the remedy. Dream, dream, only dream! Kill dream by dream!

I am trying to learn French, talking to — here. Some are very appreciative already. Talk to all the world—of the eternal riddle, the eternal spool of fate—whose thread-end no one finds and everyone seems to find, at least to his own satisfaction, at least for a time—to fool himself a moment, is it?

Well, now great things are to be done—who cares for great things? Why not do small things as well? One is as good as the other. The greatness of little things, that is what the Gita teaches, bless the old book!! . . .

I had not much time to think of the body. So it must be well. Nothing is ever well here. We forget them at times, and that is being well and doing well. . . .

We play our parts here—good or bad. When the dream is finished, and we have left the stage, we shall have a hearty laugh at all this—of this only I am sure.
—Yours etc., VIVEKANANDA.

(303)

To Swami Turiyananda

Da Forest P. O.,*
Santa Clara Co.,
6, Place des Etats Unis,
Paris, France,
1st September, 1900.

My Dear Hari—I learnt everything from your letter. Earlier I had an inkling of some trouble between the full-fledged Vedantist and the Home of Truth—some one wrote that. Such things do occur; wisdom consists in carrying on the work by cleverly keeping all in good humour.

For some time now I have been living *incognito*. I shall stay with the French to pick up their language. I am somewhat freed from worries, that is to say, I have signed the Trust Deed etc., and sent them to Calcutta. I have not reserved any right or ownership for myself. You now possess everything, and will manage all work by the Master's grace.

I have no longer any desire to kill myself by touring. For the present I feel like settling down somewhere and spending my time among books etc. I have somewhat mastered the French language; but if I stay among them for a month or two, I shall have proficiency in carrying on conversations well. If one can master this language and German sufficiently, one can virtually become well acquainted with European learning. The people of this France are mere intellectualists, run after worldly things, and firmly believe God and souls to be superstitions; they are extremely loath to talk on such subjects. This is a truly materialistic country! Let me see what the Lord does. But this country is at the head of Western culture, and Paris is the capital of that culture.

Brother, free me from all work connected with preaching. I am now aloof from all that, you manage it yourselves. It is my firm conviction that Mother will get works done through a hundredfold more than through me.

Many days ago I received a letter from Kali. He must have reached New York by now. Miss Waldo sends news now and then.

I keep sometimes well and sometimes bad. Of late I am again having that massage treatment by Mrs. Waldon, who says, "You have already recovered!" This much I see—whatever the flatulence, I feel no difficulty in moving, walking, or even climbing. In the morning I take vigorous exercise, and then have a dip in cold water.

Yesterday I went to see the house of the gentleman with whom I shall stay. He is a poor scholar, has his room filled with books, and lives in a flat on the fifth floor. And as there are no lifts in this country like America, one has to climb up and down. But it is no longer trying to me.

There is a beautiful public park round the house. The gentleman cannot speak English; that is a further reason for my going. I shall have to speak French perforce. It is all Mother's will. She knows best what she wants to have done. She never speaks out, " only keeps mum." But this much I notice that for a month or so I have been having intense meditation and repetition of the Lord's name.

Please convey my love to Miss Boocke, Miss Bell, Mrs. Aspinel, Miss Beckham, Mr. George, Dr. Logan, and other friends and accept it yourself. My love to all in Los Angeles also.—Yours, VIVEKANANDA.

(*304*)

To the Same

6, PLACE DES ETATS UNIS.*

MY DEAR TURIYANANDA—Just now received your letter. Through Mother's will all work will go on; don't be afraid. I shall soon leave for some other place.

Perhaps I shall be on a tour of Constantinople and other places for some time. Mother knows what will come next. I have received a letter from Mrs. Wilmot. From this, too, it appears that she is very enthusiastic. Sit firm and free from worries. Everything will be all right. If hearing of the *nâda*, etc. does any one harm he can get rid of it if he gives up meditation for a time and takes to fish and meat. If the body does not become progressively weak, there is no cause for alarm. Practice should be slow.

I shall leave this place before your reply comes. So do not send the reply to this letter here. I have received all the papers of Sarada, and wrote to him lots a few weeks ago. I have a mind to send more later on.

There is no knowing where my next stop will be. This much I can say that I am trying to be free from care.

I received a letter from Kali, too, to-day. I shall send him a reply to-morrow. The body is somehow rolling on. Work makes it ill, and rest keeps it well—that is all. Mother knows. Nivedita has gone to England. She and Mrs. Bull are collecting funds. She has a mind to run a school at Kishengarh with the girls she got there. Let her do what she can. I do not intervene any more in any matter—that is all.

My love to you. But I have nothing more to advise as regards work.—Yours in service, VIVEKANANDA.

(305)

To Miss Alberta Sturgis

PERROS GUIRCE,
BRETAGNE,
22nd September, 1900.

To———

The Mother's heart, the hero's will,
The softest flowers' sweetest feel;

The charm and force that ever sway
The altar-fire's flaming play;
The strength that leads, in love obeys,
Far-reaching dreams and patient ways!
Eternal Faith in Self, in all,
The light divine in great, in small;
All these and more than I could see,
To-day may "Mother" grant to thee!

Ever yours with love and blessings,
VIVEKANANDA.

(*306*)

To Miss Josephine MacLeod

THE MATH, BELUR,
11th Dec., 1900.

DEAR JOE—I arrived night before last. Alas! my hurrying was of no use.

Poor Captain Sevier passed away, a few days ago—thus two great Englishmen gave up their lives for us—us the Hindus. This is martyrdom if anything is. Mrs. Sevier, I have written to just now, to know her decision.

I am well, things are well here—every way. Excuse this haste. I will write longer ere long.—Ever yours in truth, VIVEKANANDA.

(*307*)

THE MATH, BELUR, HOWRAH,
19th Dec., 1900.

DEAR—, Just a voice across the continents to say, how do you do? Are you not surprised? Verily I am a bird of passage. Gay and busy Paris, grim old Constantinople, sparkling little Athens, and pyramidal Cairo, are left behind, and here I am writing in my room on the Ganges, in the Math. It is so quiet and still! The broad river is dancing in the bright sunshine, only now and then an occasional cargo boat breaking the silence with the splashing of the oars. It is the cold season here, but the middle of the day is warm and bright every day. But it is the winter of Southern California. Everything is green and gold and the grass is like velvet, yet the air is cold and crisp and delightful.—Yours etc., VIVEKANANDA.

(*308*)

To Srimati Mrinalini Basu

DEOGHAR, VAIDYANATH,*
C/o BABU PRIYANATH MUKHERJI,
23rd Dec., 1900.

DEAR MOTHER—I am very glad to receive your letter. What you have understood is right. स ईशोऽनिर्वचनीयप्रेमस्वरूपः —"The Lord is identical with unspeakable love." That this characteristic of God mentioned by Narada is manifest and admitted on all hands is the firm conviction of my life. The aggregate of many individuals is called Samashti (the whole), and each individual is called Vyashti (a part). You, and I—each is Vyashti, society is Samashti. You, I, an animal, a bird, a worm, an insect, a tree, a creeper, the earth, a planet, a star—each is Vyashti, while this universe is Samashti, which is called Virât, Hiranyagarbha, or Ishvara in Vedanta, and Brahmâ, Vishnu, Devi, etc., in the Puranas. Whether or not Vyashti has individual freedom, and if it has, what should be its measure, whether or not Vyashti should completely sacrifice its own will, its own happiness for Samashti—are the perennial problems before every society. Society everywhere is busy finding the solution of these problems. These, like big waves, are agitating modern Western society. The doctrine which demands the sacrifice of individual freedom to social supremacy is called socialism, while that which advocates the cause of the individual is called individualism.

Our motherland is a glowing example of the results and consequences of the eternal subjection of the individual to society and forced self-sacrifice by dint of institution and discipline. In this country men are born according to Shâstric injunctions, they eat and drink by prescribed rules throughout life, they go through marriage and kindred functions in the same way; in short, they even die according to Shastric injunctions. This hard discipline, with the exception of one great good point, is fraught with evil. The good point is that men can do one or two things well, with very little effort, having practised them every day through generations. The delicious rice and curry which a cook of this country prepares with the aid of three lumps of earth and a few sticks can be had nowhere else. With the simple mechanism of an antediluvian loom, worth one rupee, and the feet put in a pit, it is possible to make kincobs worth twenty rupees a yard, in this country alone. A torn mat, an earthen lamp, and that fed by castor oil, —with the aid of materials such as these, wonderful *savants* are produced in this country alone. An all-forbearing attachment to an ugly and deformed wife, and a lifelong devotion to a worthless and villainous husband, are possible in this country alone. Thus far the bright side.

But all these things are done by people guided like lifeless machines;—there is no mental activity, no unfoldment of the heart, no vibration of life, no flux of hope; there is no strong stimulation of the will, no experience of keen pleasure, nor the contact of intense sorrow; there is no stir of inventive genius, no desire for novelty, no appreciation of new things. Clouds never pass away from this mind, the radiant picture of the morning sun never charms this heart. It never even occurs to the mind if there is any better state than this; where it does, it cannot convince; in the event of conviction, effort is lacking; and even where there is effort, lack of enthusiasm kills it out.

If living by rule alone ensures excellence, if it be virtue strictly to follow the rules and customs handed down through generations, say, then, who is more virtuous than a tree, who is a greater devotee, a holier saint than a railway train? Who has ever seen a piece of stone transgress a natural law? Who has ever known cattle to commit sin?

The huge steamer, the mighty railway engine—they are non-intelligent, they move, turn and run, but they are without intelligence. And yonder tiny worm which moved away from the railway line to save its life, why is it intelligent? There is no manifestation of will in the machine, the machine never wishes to transgress law; the worm wants to oppose law, rises against law whether it succeeds or not, therefore it is intelligent. Greater is the happiness, higher is the Jiva, in proportion as this will is more successfully manifest. The will of God is perfectly fruitful, therefore He is the highest.

What is education? Is it book-learning? No. Is it diverse knowledge? Not even that. The training by which the current and expression of will are brought under control and become fruitful, is called education. Now consider, is that education, as a result of which the will being continuously choked by force through generations, is now well-nigh killed out; under whose sway—why mention new ideas—even the old ones are disappearing one by one—is that education which is slowly making man a machine? It is more blessed, in my opinion, even to go wrong impelled by one's free will and intelligence than to be good as an automaton. Again, can that be called society which is formed by an aggregate of men who are like lumps of clay, like lifeless machines, like heaped up pebbles? How can such society fare well? Were good possible, then instead of being slaves for hundreds of years we would have been the greatest nation on earth, and this soil of India, instead of being a mine of stupidity, would have been the eternal fountain-head of learning.

Is not self-sacrifice, then, a virtue? Is it not the most virtuous deed to sacrifice the happiness of one, the welfare of one, for the sake of the many? Exactly, but as the Bengali adage goes, "Can beauty be manufactured by rubbing and scrubbing? Can love be generated by effort and compulsion?" What glory is there in the renunciation of an eternal beggar? What virtue is there in the sense-control of one devoid of sense-power? What again is the self-sacrifice of one devoid of idea, devoid of heart, devoid of high ambition and devoid of the conception of what constitutes society? What expression of devotedness to a husband is there by forcing a widow to commit Sati? Why make people do virtuous deeds by teaching superstitions? I say, liberate, undo the shackles of people as much as you can. Can dirt be washed by dirt? Can bondage be removed by bondage? Where is the instance? When you would be able to sacrifice all desire for happiness for the sake of society, then you would be the Buddha, then you would be free; that is far off. Again, do you think the way to it lies through oppression? "Oh, what example of self-denial are our widows! Oh, how sweet is child-marriage! Is another such custom possible? Can there be anything but love between husband and wife in such a marriage?"—such is the whine going round nowadays. But as to the men, the masters of the situation, there is no need of self-denial for them! Is there a virtue higher than serving others? But the same does not apply to Brahmins—you others do it! The truth is, that in this country parents and relatives can ruthlessly sacrifice the best interests of their children and others, for their own selfish ends, to save themselves by a compromise to society, and the teaching of generations rendering the mind callous, has made it perfectly easy. He, the brave alone can deny self. The coward, afraid of the lash, with one hand wipes his eyes and gives with the other. What avail such gifts? It is a far cry to love universal. The young plant should be hedged in and taken care of. One can hope to gradually attain to universal love, if one can learn to love one object unselfishly. If devotion to one particular Ishtadeva is attained, devotion to the universal Virat is gradually possible.

Therefore, when one has been able to deny self for an individual, one should talk of self-sacrifice for the sake of society, not before. It is action with desire that leads to action without desire. Is the renunciation of desire possible, if desire did not exist in the beginning? And what could it mean? Can light have any meaning if there is no darkness?

Worship with desire, with attachment, comes first. Commence with the worship of the little, then the greater will come of itself.

Mother, be not anxious. It is against the big tree that the great wind strikes. "Poking a fire makes it burn better"; "A snake struck on the head raises its hood"; and so on. When there comes affliction in the heart, when the storm of sorrow blows all around, and it seems light will be seen no more, when hope and courage are almost gone, it is then, in the midst of this great spiritual tempest, that the light of Brahman within, gleams. Brought up in the lap of luxury, lying on a bed of roses and never shedding a tear, who has ever become great, who has ever unfolded the Brahman within? Why do you fear to weep? Weep! Weeping clears the eyes and bring about intuition. Then the vision of diversity—man, animal, tree—slowly melting away, makes room for the infinite realisation of Brahman everywhere and in everything. Then,—

समं पश्यन् हि सर्वत्र समवस्थितमीश्वरम्।
न हिनस्त्यात्मनात्मानं ततो याति परां गतिम्॥

"Verily, seeing the same God equally existent everywhere, he does not injure the self by the self, and so goes to the Supreme Goal."—Ever your well-wisher, VIVEKANANDA.

(310)

To Miss Josephine MacLeod

THE MATH, BELUR, HOWRAH,
26th Dec., 1900.

DEAR JOE—This mail brought your letter including that of Mother and Alberta. What the learned friend of Alberta says about Russia is about the same I think myself. Only there is one difficulty of thought—is it possible for the Hindu race to be Russianised?

Dear Mr. Sevier passed away before I could arrive. He was cremated on the banks of the river that flows by his Ashrama *à la* Hindu, covered with garlands, the Brahmins carrying the body and boys chanting the Vedas.

The cause has already two martyrs. It makes me love dear old England and its heroic breed. The Mother is watering the plant of future India with the best blood of England. Glory unto Her!

Dear Mrs. Sevier is calm. A letter she wrote me to Paris comes back this mail. I am going up to-morrow to pay her a visit. Lord bless her, dear brave soul!

I am calm and strong. Occasion never found me low yet; Mother will not make me now depressed.

It is very pleasant here, now the winter is on. The Himalayas will be still more beautiful with the uncovered snows.

The young man who started from New York, Mr. Johnston, has taken the vow of a Brahmacharin and is at Mayavati.

Send the money to Saradananda in the Math, as I will be away in the hills.

They have worked all right as far as they could; I am

glad and feel myself quite a fool on account of my nervous chagrin.

They are as good and as faithful as ever, and they are in good health. Write all this to Mrs. Bull, and tell her she was always right and I was wrong, and I beg a hundred thousand pardons of her.

Oceans of love for her and for M—.

I look behind and after
And find that all is right,
In my deepest sorrows
There is a soul of light.

All love to M—, Mrs. C—, to dear Jules Bois, and to you, dear Joe, Pranams.—VIVEKANANDA.

(*311*)

To Mr. E. T. Sturdy

AT MAYAVATI,
HIMALAYAS,
15th Jan., 1901.

MY DEAR STURDY—I learn from Saradananda (that) you have sent over Rs. 1,529-5-5 to the Math, being the money that was in hand for work in England. I am sure it will be rightly used.

Capt. Sevier passed away about three months ago. They have made a fine place here in the mountains and Mrs. Sevier means to keep it up. I am on a visit to her and I may possibly come over to England with her.

I wrote you a letter from Paris. I am afraid you did not get it.

So sorry to learn the passing away of Mrs. Sturdy. She has been a very good wife and good mother and it is not ordinarily one meets with such in this life.

This life is full of shocks, but the effects pass away, anyhow that is the hope.

It is not because of your free expression of opinion in

your last letter to me that I stopped writing. I only let the wave pass, as is my wont. Letters would only have made a wave of a little bubble.

Kindly tender my regards and love to Mrs. Johnson and other friends if you meet them.

And I am ever yours in the Truth,—VIVEKANANDA.

(*312*)

THE MATH,
15th May, 1901.

DEAR S——, Your letter from—— is qüite exciting. I have just returned from my tour through East Bengal and Assam. As usual I am quite tired and broken down.

If some real good comes out of a visit to H. H. of—— I am ready to come over, otherwise I don't want to undergo the expense and exertion of the long journey. Think it well over and make enquiries, and write me if you still think it would be best for the Cause for me to come to see H. H. . . . —Yours with love and blessings, VIVEKANANDA.

(*313*)

THE MATH, BELUR,
6th July, 1901.

Things come to me by fits---to-day I am in a fit of writing. The first thing to do is, therefore, to pen a few lines to you. I am known to be nervous, I worry much; but it seems, dear Christine, you are not far behind in that trick. One of our poets says: "Even the mountains will fly, the fire will be cold, yet the heart of the great will never change." I am small, very, but I know you are great, and my faith is always in your true heart. *I worry about everything except you.* I have dedicated you to the *Mother*. She is your shield, your guide. No harm can reach you--nothing hold you down a minute, I know it.—Ever yours in the Lord, VIVEKANANDA.

(*314*)

THE MATH, BELUR,
7th Sept., 1901.

DEAR—, We all work by fits, that is to say, in this cause. I try to keep down the spring, but something or other happens and the spring goes whirr, and there you are—thinking, remembering, scribbling, scrawling and all that!

Well, about the rains—they have come down now in right earnest and it is a deluge, pouring, pouring, pouring night and day. The river is rising, flooding the banks; the ponds and tanks have overflown. I have just now returned from lending a hand in cutting a deep drain to take off the water from the Math grounds. The rain-water stands at places some feet high. My huge stork is full of glee and so are the ducks and geese. My tame antelope fled from the Math and gave us some days of anxiety in finding him out. One of my ducks unfortunately died yesterday. She had been gasping for breath more than a week. One of my waggish old monks says, "Sir, it is no use living in this Kali-yuga when ducks catch cold from damp and rain and frogs sneeze!"

One of the geese had her plumes falling off. Knowing no other method I left her some minutes in a tub of water mixed with mild carbolic, so that it might either kill or heal—and she is all right now.—Yours etc., VIVEKANANDA.

(*315*)

BELUR,
8th October, 1901.

DEAR—, . . . I am bobbing up and down in the current of life—to-day it is rather down. . . . —Yours etc., VIVEKANANDA.

(*316*)

To Swami Swarupananda

GOPAL LAL VILLA,
BENARES CANTONMENT,
9th February, 1902.

MY DEAR SWARUP— . . . In answer to Charu's letter, tell him to study the Brahma-Sutras himself. What does he mean by the Brahma-Sutras containing references to Buddhism? He means the Bhâshyas, of course, or rather ought to mean, and Shankara was only the last Bhâshyakâra. There are references, though in Buddhistic literature, to Vedanta, and the Mahâyâna school of Buddhism is even Advaitistic. Why does Amara Singha, a Buddhist, give as one of the names of Buddha—Advayavâdi? Charu writes, the word Brahman does not occur in the Upanishads! *Quelle bêtise*!

I hold the Mahayana to be the older of the two schools of Buddhism.

The theory of Maya is as old as the Rik Samhitâ. The Shvetâshvatara Upanishad contains the word "Maya" which is developed out of Prakriti. I hold that Upanishad to be at least older than Buddhism.

I have had much light of late about Buddhism, and I am ready to prove—(1) that Shiva-worship, in various forms, antedated the Buddhists, that the Buddhists tried to get hold of the sacred places of the Shaivas but, failing in that, made new places in the precincts just as you find now at Bodh-Gaya and Sarnath (Benares).

(2) The story in the Agni Purana about Gayâsura does not refer to Buddha at all—as Dr. Rajendralal will have it—but simply to a pre-existing story.

(3) That Buddha went to live on Gayashirsha mountain proves the pre-existence of the place.

(4) Gaya was a place of ancestor-worship already,

and the footprint-worship the Buddhists copied from the Hindus.

(5) About Benares, even the oldest records go to prove it as the great place of Shiva-worship; etc. etc.

Many are the new facts I have gathered in Bodh-Gaya and from Buddhist literature. Tell Charu to read for himself, and not be swayed by foolish opinions.

I am rather well here, in Benares, and if I go on improving in this way it will be a great gain.

A total revolution has occurred in my mind about the relation of Buddhism and Neo-Hinduism. I may not live to work out the glimpses, but I shall leave the lines of work indicated, and you and your brethren will have to work it out.—Yours with all blessings and love, VIVEKANANDA.

(317)

To Sister Nivedita

BENARES,
12th February, 1902.

May all powers come unto you! May Mother Herself be your hands and mind! It is immense power—irresistible—that I pray for you, and, if possible, along with it infinite peace. . . .

If there was any truth in Sri Ramakrishna, may He take you into His leading, even as He did me, nay, a thousand times more!

(318)

To Mrs. Ole Bull

THE MATH, BELUR,
14th June, 1902.

DEAR——, . . . In my opinion, a race must first cultivate a great respect for motherhood, through the sanctification and inviolability of marriage, before it can attain to the ideal of perfect chastity. The Roman Catholics and the Hindus, holding marriage sacred and inviolate, have produced great chaste men and women of immense power. To the Arab, marriage is a contract or a forceful possession, to be dissolved at will, and we do not find there the development of the idea of the virgin or the Brahmacharin. Modern Buddhism—having fallen among races who had not yet come up to the evolution of marriage—has made a travesty of monasticism. So until there is developed in Japan a great and sacred ideal about marriage (apart from mutual attraction and love), I do not see how there can be great monks and nuns. As you have come to see that the glory of life is chastity, so my eyes also have been opened to the necessity of this great sanctification for the vast majority, in order that a few lifelong chaste powers may be produced.

I wanted to write many things, but the flesh is weak . . . . "Whosoever worships Me, for whatsoever desire, I meet him with that." . . . —VIVEKANANDA.

Notes on Persons mentioned in the Letters

ABHEDANANDA, SWAMI: a disciple of Sri Ramakrishna. His pre-monastic name was Kali.

ACHYUTANANDA SARASWATI: same as Gunanidhi. Swamiji calls him "brother-disciple" (p. 17) by courtesy it seems.

AJIT SINGH: the Maharaja of Khetri and a disciple of Swami Vivekananda.

AKHANDANANDA, SWAMI: a disciple of Sri Ramakrishna. His pre-monastic name was Gangadhar (Ganga). He was the President of the Ramakrishna Math and Mission (1934-1937).

AKSHAY KUMAR GHOSE: a Bengali youngman who afterwards became a well-known attorney of Calcutta.

AKSHAY: Sj. Akshay Kumar Sen, a disciple of Sri Ramakrishna, and the author of the Bengali book—*Ramakrishna Punthi* (life of Sri Ramakrishna in verse).

ALASINGA PERUMAL: a devoted follower of Swami Vivekananda. He was one of the enthusiastic group of young disciples of Madras who raised subscriptions and helped Swami Vivekananda with passage money to go to America. The letters written to him by Swami Vivekananda will indicate how deep was his devotion to the Swami.

ALBERTA: Miss Alberta Sturgis: afterwards the Countess of Sandwich. She was the daughter of Mrs. Leggett.

ATUL BABU: Atul Chandra Ghose, a Vakil of Calcutta High Court and a brother of Girish Chandra Ghose.

BABURAM: see Swami Premananda.

BALAJI: D. R. Balaji Rao (Triplicane, Madras) who afterwards became the Secretary to the Indian Bank, Madras.

BALARAM BOSE: a very favourite disciple of Sri Ramakrishna.

BARROWS, DR.: Rev. J. H. Barrows, Chairman of the General Committee of the Parliament of Religions, Chicago.

BHATTACHARYA: Manmatha Nath Bhattacharya, assistant to the Accountant General, Madras. Swami Vivekananda was his guest in Madras during his wandering life.

BHAVANATH: a disciple of Sri Ramakrishna.

BIMALA: son-in-law of Sj. Kalikrishna Tagore.

BRAHMANANDA, SWAMI: one of the foremost disciples of Sri Ramakrishna. First President of the Ramakrishna Math and Mission (1899—1922). His pre-monastic name was Rakhal.

BULL (MRS.): Mrs. Ole Bull—wife of the celebrated violinist and Norwegian nationalist. She became a disciple of Swami Vivekananda. Sometimes the Swami would address her as "mother." She gave much financial help to Swamiji in establishing the monastery at Belur.

CHARU: Charu Chandra Bose, a Pali scholar. He translated the *Dhammapada* into Bengali.

CHRISTINE, SISTER: Miss Greenstidel of Detroit, a disciple of Swami Vivekananda. Her love for India was next only to her devotion to the Guru. She was a radiant spiritual soul whose parallel is rare. Swami Vivekananda bestowed unreserved blessings on her.

CHUNI: Sj. Chunilal Bose, a disciple of Sri Ramakrishna.

DAKSHA: Swami Jnanananda, a disciple of Swami Vivekananda.

DASU: Dasarathi Sanyal, a Vakil of Calcutta High Court, and a College friend of Swami Vivekananda.

DHARMAPAL: (afterwards) Anagarika Dharmapal, founder of the Mahabodhi Society in Calcutta.

DHIRA MATA: same as Mrs. Ole Bull.

DINANATH: afterwards Swami Sachchidananda, a disciple of Swami Saradananda.

DIWANJI SAHEB: *see* Haridas Viharidas Desai.

DOCTOR: *see* Dr. Nanjunda Rao.

DUTCHER, MISS: a disciple of Swami Vivekananda. It was she who was the hostess of Swami Vivekananda at the Thousand Island Park, U. S. A.

FAKIR: Private tutor to Ram, son of Balaram Bose. His real name was Yajneswar Bhattacharya. His picture appears in the Cossipore garden Mahasamadhi group (centre).

FARMER: Miss S. Farmer, an American devotee of Swami Vivekananda. At the time Miss Farmer met Swamiji, she had an organisation of which she was the Head. Swamiji spent some time there.

FRANKINCENSE: *see* Leggett.

GANGADHAR (also GANGA): *see* Swami Akhandananda.

GAUR MA: a lady-disciple of Sri Ramakrishna.

G. C. GHOSE: the great actor-dramatist of Bengal and a staunch devotee of Sri Ramakrishna.

GEDDES: Professor Patrick Geddes of Edinburgh University.

G. G.: G. G. Narasimhachariar (of Bangalore).

GIRISH BABU: same as G. C. Ghose.

GOLAP MA: a lady-disciple of Sri Ramakrishna.

GOODWIN: J. J. Goodwin, an English disciple of Swami Vivekananda. It was Goodwin who mostly took down the notes of Swami Vivekananda's lectures. His was a life of complete self-effacement to the Guru. He was with the Swami in America and England and accompanied him to India, where he died. On his death, the Swami wrote: "The debt of gratitude I owe him can never be repaid, and those who think they have been helped by any thought of mine, ought to know that almost every word of it was published through the untiring and most unselfish exertions of Mr. Goodwin. In him I have lost a friend true as steel, a disciple of never-failing devotion, a worker who knew not what tiring was, and the world is less rich by one of those few who are born, as it were, to live only for others."

GOODYEAR: Mr. and Mrs. Walter Goodyear of New York. They helped the Vedanta work in America.

GOPAL: Gopal Junior, a disciple of Sri Ramakrishna.

GOVINDA SAHAY: a resident of Alwar and a disciple of Swami Vivekananda.

GUERNSEY (MRS.): of New York, a disciple of Swami Vivekananda. For a time (in 1894) he stayed with Guernsey family and held classes and conversaziones.

GUNANIDHI: same as Achyutananda.

GUPTA: Sarat Chandra Gupta: afterwards Swami Sadananda—a disciple of Swami Vivekananda.

HALE (MR. and MRS.): George W., disciples of Swami Vivekananda. When the Swami found himself stranded and in a helpless condition in Chicago on the day before the session of the Parliament of Religions, Mrs. George W. Hale accidentally saw him. She took him to her house, gave him the warmest hospitality and made necessary arrangements for his attending the Parliament. Afterwards the Swami often spoke of the loving kindness of the whole family.

HAMLIN: Miss Hamlin was a devotee of Swami Vivekananda. She very much helped to organise the classes of Swamiji in New York City, but did not stay very long.

HAMMOND: Mr. and Mrs. Eric Hammond of England. They were both devoted admirers of Swami Vivekananda.

HARAMOHAN (MITRA): a devotee of Sri Ramakrishna and an enthusiastic admirer of Swami Vivekananda.

HARI: *see* Swami Turiyananda.

HARIDAS VIHARIDAS DESAI (addressed as Diwanji Saheb, sometimes as Haridas Bhai): Dewan of Junagad State, West India.

HARIPADA MITRA: a forest officer of Belgaum. Swami Vivekananda became his guest and stayed with him for a few days during his wandering life. Though an atheist, he became so impressed with the Swami that he, along with his wife, became his disciple.

HARIPRASANNA: afterwards Swami Vijnanananda. He was the President of the Ramakrishna Math and Mission (1937—1938).

HARISH: Harish Chandra Mustafi, a disciple of Sri Ramakrishna.

HARI SINGH: Thakur Hari Singh Ladhkani, at one time the Commander-in-Chief of the Jaipur State.

HARRIET HALE: a daughter of Mr. George W. Hale.

INDU: a grand-daughter of Balaram Bose.

INDUMATI MITRA: wife of Haripada Mitra and a disciple of Swami Vivekananda.

INGERSOLL: Mr. Robert Ingersoll, a famous writer and lecturer of America. He was a great agnostic.

JAGMOHAN: Munshi Jagmohan Lal, the Private Secretary to the Maharaja of Khetri.

JANES: Dr. Lewis G. Janes, who was long President of the Brooklyn Ethical Association. He was an eminent scholar and lecturer of science, ethics, and religion and a great friend of the Vedanta movement in America.

JOE: *see* Miss MacLeod.

JOGEN: *see* Swami Yogananda.

JONSON: Mrs. Aston Jonson. She was one of the supporters of the Vedanta movement in England.

JULES BOIS: a famous philosopher, journalist and writer of France. Swami Vivekananda was his guest for a period in Paris.

KALI: *see* Swami Abhedananda.

KALIKRISHNA BABU: Sj. Kalikrishna Tagore of Calcutta.

KIDI: Singaravelu Mudaliar, Assistant Professor of Science in the Christian College, Madras. He was an atheist but afterwards became an ardent disciple of Swami Vivekananda. The Swami loved him very much and called him "Kidi."

KRIPANANDA, SWAMI: *see* Sanyal.

KRIPANANDA, SWAMI: of America. *see* Landsberg.

KRISHNALAL: afterwards Swami Dhirananda, a disciple of Swami Vivekananda.

KRISHNAMAYI: daughter of Balaram Bose.

KRISHNANANDA, SWAMI: a famous lecturer and champion of Hinduism. He was born in Bengal and his pre-monastic name was Krishnaprasanna Sen. He wrote a very nice commentary on the Gita in Bengali.

LALAJI: same as Sahji.

LANDSBERG: Herr Leon Landsberg. By birth a Russian Jew, he was employed on the staff of a prominent New York paper. He became a monastic disciple of Swami Vivekananda with the name of Swami Kripananda.

LEGGETT: Mr. and Mrs. Francis H. Leggett, well-known society family of New York, became disciples of Swami Vivekananda and helped him in various ways. Sometimes the Master used to address Mr. Francis Leggett in the endearing term of "Frankincense."

LOGAN: Dr. M. H. Logan, a disciple of Swami Vivekananda, and President of the Vedanta Society in San Francisco.

M. (also MASTER MAHASHAY): Mahendra Nath Gupta, a disciple of Sri Ramakrishna and author of *The Gospel of Sri Ramakrishna*. Sometimes mentioned as Mahendra Babu.

MACLEOD: Miss Josephine MacLeod of New York, one of the foremost American disciples of Swami Vivekananda. She helped Swami Vivekananda and his work in very many ways. She is full of "Swamiji" and fortunately is still living. Her enthusiasm for the cause of Swamiji is unbounded. To Miss MacLeod he was Guru and friend in one. Sometimes she would be addressed as "Joe" by Swamiji.

MAHENDRA BABU: *see* M.

MAHIM CHAKRAVARTY: Mahima Charan Chakravarty, mentioned in *Sri Ramakrishna Kathamrita* and *Leelaprasanga*.

MANI IYER: same as Subrahmanya Iyer.

MARGO: same as Sister Nivedita.

MARY: Miss Mary Hale, daughter of Mr. George W. Hale.

MOHAMMED SARFARAZ HUSAIN: a Mohammedan gentleman of Naini Tal, who wished to retire and serve humanity.

MOHIN: Mahendra Nath Dutta, younger brother of Swami Vivekananda.

MOTHER CHURCH: Swami Vivekananda styled Mrs. George W. Hale " Mother Church " and Mr. Hale " Father Pope." *see* Hale.

MRINALINI BOSE: a distant relative and a disciple of Swami Vivekananda.

MÜLLER: Miss Henrietta Müller, an English disciple of Swami Vivekananda.

NANJUNDA RAO (DR.): of Madras. A disciple of Swami Vivekananda.

NARASIMHACHARIAR (Rao Bahadur R.): He was the Director of Archaeological Survey, the Government of Mysore.

NIRANJAN: *see* Swami Niranjanananda.

NIRANJANANANDA, SWAMI: a disciple of Sri Ramakrishna. His pre-monastic name was Niranjan.

NIRMALANANDA, SWAMI: a disciple of Swami Vivekananda. His pre-monastic name was Tulsi.

NIVEDITA, SISTER: (Miss Margaret E. Noble) an English disciple of Swami Vivekananda. She completely identified herself with the mission of her Guru and the cause of India. Swami Vivekananda gave her the new name Nivedita—meaning dedicated, which was so appropriate with her life and activities.

NOBLE: Miss Margaret E. Noble. *see Nivedita.*

PAVHARI BABA: the famous saint of Ghazipur.

PRAMADA DAS MITRA: an inhabitant of Benares. For his profound erudition and piety, Swami Vivekananda had the highest regard.

PREMANANDA, SWAMI: a disciple of Sri Ramakrishna. His pre-monastic name was Baburam.

PYARI BABU: Raja Pyari Mohan Mukherjee, C.S.I., who presided over the meeting organised by the citizens of Calcutta, to congratulate Swami Vivekananda on his success at the Parliament of Religions.

RAKHAL: *see* Swami Brahmananda.

RAM: son of Balaram Bose.

RAMABAI: a Brahmin widow of Maharashtra who embraced Christianity and became a devout follower of Jesus. She was in America when Swami Vivekananda went there.

RAMAKRISHNANANDA, SWAMI: a disciple of Sri Ramakrishna. His pre-monastic name was Sasi.

RAMDAYAL: Sj. Ramdayal Chakravarty of Antpur, a devotee of Sri Ramakrishna. He belonged to the priest-family of Sj. Balaram Bose, and was an employee of Messrs. Hoare, Miller & Co., Calcutta.

RAMLAL: a nephew of Sri Ramakrishna.

SAHJI: Lala Badri Sah of Almora.

SANYAL: Vaikuntha Nath Sanyal, a disciple of Sri Ramakrishna.

SARA: Mrs. Sara C. Bull—same as Mrs. Ole Bull.

SARADA: *see* Swami Trigunatitananda.

SARADANANDA, SWAMI: a disciple of Sri Ramakrishna. First Secretary of the Ramakrishna Math and Mission, holding the office from 1899 till his passing away in 1927.

SARALA GHOSHAL: afterwards known as Sarala Devi Chaudhurani, a niece of Rabindra Nath Tagore.

SARAT: *see* Swami Saradananda.

SARAT CHANDRA CHAKRAVARTY: a disciple of Swami Vivekananda. It is to him that the reading public owe the famous Bengali book—*Swami Sishya Samvada*, afterwards translated into English as *Talks with Swami Vivekananda.*

SASI: *see* Swami Ramakrishnananda.

SASI (SANYAL): an orthodox Brahmin with bigoted views. He had a good following.

SASIBHUSHAN: Dr. Sasibhushan Ghosh. He came into contact with Sri Ramakrishna and afterwards wrote a biography of Sri Ramakrishna in Bengali.

SEVIER: Mr. and Mrs. J. H. Sevier, English disciples of Swami Vivekananda who dedicated their lives to the cause of Vedanta. They came to India and established the Advaita Ashrama at Mayavati, Almora, where they settled down.

SHANKARLAL, PANDIT: an inhabitant of Khetri and a great devotee of Swami Vivekananda.

SHIVANANDA, SWAMI: a disciple of Sri Ramakrishna. President of the Ramakrishna Math and Mission (1922—1934). His pre-monastic name was Tarak.

STURDY: Mr. E. T. Sturdy, an English devotee of Swami Vivekananda. He gave immense help to the Vedanta work of Swamiji in England. In his early days he came to India and underwent severe asceticism in the hill-station of Almora, U. P.

SUBODH: *see* Swami Subodhananda.

SUBODHANANDA, SWAMI: a disciple of Sri Ramakrishna. His pre-monastic name was Subodh.

SUBRAHMANYA IYER: Justice Sir S. Subrahmanya Iyer.

SUDDHANANDA, SWAMI: a disciple of Swami Vivekananda. Latterly he became the Secretary, and afterwards President, of the Ramakrishna Math and Mission (1938).

SURESH: Sj. Surendra Nath Mitra, a disciple of Sri Ramakrishna, who would call him Suresh.

SWARUP: Swami Swarupananda, a disciple of Swami Vivekananda. He was the first President of the Advaita Ashrama, Mayavati.

TESLA: Mr. Nicolas Tesla, a distinguished electrician of America.

THURSBY: Miss Emma Thursby, the famous singer. She was a devoted worker in the cause of Vedanta movement in America.

TRIGUNATITANANDA, SWAMI: a disciple of Sri Ramakrishna. His pre-monastic name was Sarada.

TULSI: *see* Swami Nirmalananda.

TULSI BABU: Tulsiram Ghose, elder brother of Swami Premananda. He was a close devotee of Sri Ramakrishna.

TURIYANANDA, SWAMI: a disciple of Sri Ramakrishna. His pre-monastic name was Hari.

VEHEMIA CHAND: a citizen of Limbdi.

VIJAY GOSWAMI: Vijay Krishna Goswami, a noted religious leader of Bengal and a contemporary of Swami Vivekananda.

WALDO: Miss S. E. Waldo, of Brooklyn. She was an ardent disciple of Swami Vivekananda. It was she who took down notes of conversations of Swamiji at Thousand Island Park, which afterwards were published as *Inspired Talks*. All lovers of Swami Vivekananda are greatly indebted to her for these immortal words.

YAJNESWAR: *see* Fakir.

YOGANANDA, SWAMI: a disciple of Sri Ramakrishna. His pre-monastic name was Jogen.

INDEX

ERRATUM

The Letter on page 465 should be numbered 309 *instead of 310*, and so on for the Letters that follow.